D0934544

Dante, Petrarch, Boccaccio

Studies in the Italian Trecento
In Honor of Charles S. Singleton

medieval & renaissance texts & studies

VOLUME 22

Charles Southward Singleton

Dante, Petrarch, Boccaccio

Studies in the Italian Trecento
In Honor of Charles S. Singleton

EDITED BY

Aldo S. Bernardo and Anthony L. Pellegrini

medieval & renaissance texts & studies
Binghamton, New York
1983

Library of Congress Cataloging in Publication Data
Main entry under title:

Dante, Petrarch, Boccaccio.

   (Medieval & Renaissance texts & studies ; 22)
   Bibliography: p. xxiii–xxviii
   1. Italian literature—To 1400—History and criticism—
Addresses, essays, lectures. 2. Dante Alighieri, 1265–1321—
Criticism and interpretation—Addresses, essays, lectures.
3. Petrarca, Francesco, 1304–1374—Criticism and
interpretation—Addresses, essays, lectures. 4. Singleton, Charles
Southward, 1909-   . II. Bernardo, Aldo S. III. Pellegrini,
Anthony L., 1921-   . IV. Series.
PQ4065.D36   1983   850'.9'001   83–717
ISBN 0–86698–061–X

Printed in the United States of America

Preface

W ITH THIS VOLUME two former students of Charles S. Singleton pay modest but affectionate tribute to his genius for
rendering unforgettable the experience of that monumental
work of the human spirit that is Dante's *Commedia*. Indeed the volume
is a token of the esteem felt by many other students, friends, and admirers
of this extraordinary American scholar and his work.

Faced with an excess of eager contributors, the editors decided to limit
the scope of the volume to the Italian *Trecento* and specifically to original
studies that afforded special insights into some significant aspect of the
period. The resulting essays have proven most interesting, for while those
selected are not restricted to Dante, they all seem to celebrate in one way
or another the critical approach so carefully developed by Singleton in his
reading of Dante. As one reader of the typescript observed, the studies
form a truly varied Analytic—not Mystic—Processional celebrating
Singleton's exegetical subtlety, depth, and persistence in a way that makes
of him an exemplary standard-bearer or trailblazer of complementary and
even divergent modes. If we view each of the studies as way-stations, we
can see most if not all of them bearing some imprint of Singleton's exegetical methodology.

Two of the essays deal with earlier exegetes: Vallone on Jacopo della
Lana, and Raimondi on Castelvetro. Durling's essay involves the most

famous and most devoted of such exegetes, Boccaccio, not only as theorist of the act of interpretation but also as actual interpreter of Dante.

The approach of Freccero and Shapiro to formal elements in the prosody of Dante and Petrarch, as well as Ferrante's analysis of "divine" words and images in the *Paradiso*, are reminiscent of Singleton's deep interest in such linguistic and stylistic devices. Cassell turns to another interpretative tool held in high regard by Singleton—iconography. The elements of the *Comedy* and of the *Decameron* studied by Kirkham, Chiarenza, and Kaske are in the best Singletonian tradition, while the concern with modes of interpreting medieval texts displayed in the essays by Petrocchi, Hollander, and Sturm-Maddox reflect Singleton's method of close reading of texts in their historical-cultural context. Finally, Bergin's translation of and commentary on a primary *Metrica* of Petrarch brings us close to the moment of historical shift in modes of allegory, not only in Petrarch's use of Virgil in his verse text but also in his celebration of the supreme value of poetry in both the classical and Christian tradition as symbolized by his coronation on the Roman Capitoline.

The editors wish to express their special gratitude to Reta Bernardo for the many hours spent in editing the notes, retyping texts, and chasing down important bits of overlooked information. Hers was a true labor of love. Our special thanks also go to the director of the Medieval & Renaissance Texts & Studies program, Mario A. Di Cesare, who designed the book and whose interest and dedication helped prevent further delays in publishing this volume dedicated to one whom the late Nobel laureate, Eugenio Montale, called "the greatest living *dantista* of his day."

The Editors

Tabula Gratulatoria

John Ahern
Alfred F. Alberico
John J. Alfieri
Judson Boyce Allen
David Ambrose
Ashley Crandell Amos
Rose T. Antosiewicz
Grazia Avitabile
Gianni Azzi
Constance Anne Barbantini
Joseph A. Barber
Teodolinda Barolini
John Barth
Mrs. Stephen Basarab
Chandler Beall
Thomas G. Bergin
Aldo & Reta Bernardo
Gian-Paolo Biasin
Giuseppe Billanovich
Morton W. Bloomfield
Dennis J. Bottino

Irma Brandeis
Wilmon Brewer
Eugene Brown
Kevin Brownlee
Douglas Bush †
Huntington Cairns
Frank G. Carrino
Anthony K. Cassell
Salvatore & Pierina Castiglione
Elena Bianchini Catelli
Giovanni Cecchetti
James T. Chiampi
Fredi Chiappelli
Marguerite Chiarenza
Dorothy Clotelle Clarke
Diskin Clay
Alice M. Colby-Hall
Isabel Pope Conant
Giles Constable
Gustavo & Natalia Costa
Charles T. Davis

Celestino De Iuliis

Joseph F. De Simone

Dante Della Terza

Mario A. & Lee Di Cesare

Andrea di Tommaso

John B. Dillon

Daniel J. Donno

Benedetto Fabrizi

Joan M. Ferrante

Merle Fifield

Francis M. Gambacorta

J. D. Gauthier, S.J.

Ernest Germano

Antonio Alfredo Giarraputo

Felix Gilbert

Sister Cyrille Gill

Stephen Gilman

Morris Gitlitz

Richard A. Goldthwaite

John E. Grant

Robert A. Hall

Colin Hardie

Edward Harvey

Elizabeth R. Hatcher

Emmanuel Hatzantonis

Ronald Herzman

Irene Hijmans-Tromp

Donald L. Hoffman

Julia Bolton Holloway

Lloyd H. Howard

Nicolae Iliescu

Jeremy Ingalls

Donato Internoscia

Rachel Jacoff

Carlo Jahn-Rusconi

Walter Kaiser

Carol V. Kaske

Richard J. A. Kerr

Pearl Kibre

Victoria E. Kirkham

Christopher Kleinhenz

Philip Koch

Benjamin G. Kohl

Paul Oskar Kristeller

Marion & Paul G. Kuntz

Gerhart B. Ladner

Frederic C. Lane

Rensselaer W. Lee

Bernard S. Levy

Mrs. Raimundo Lida

Richard & Catherine Macksey

Frederick & Matillda Mascioli

Antonio C. Mastrobuono

J. Chesley Mathews

Francesco Mazzoni

William H. McClain

Antonio L. Mezzacappa

Ellen Mickiewicz

Rigo Mignani

Anthony J. Morandi

L. A. Murillo

F. Musarra

Richard G. Newton

Conrad Nobili

Edward P. Nolan

Paul R. Olson

Kenneth E. Owen

Anthony J. Pansini

Anthony L. Pellegrini

Nicolas J. Perella

Armando & Franca Petrucci

Matilde & Luisa Pfeiffer

Angelina R. Pietrangeli

Nino Pirrotta

J. G. A. Pocock

Alexander Pogo

John C. Pope
Susan Potters
James W. Poultney
Paul L. Priest
Olga Ragusa
Joseph Reino
Mary T. Reynolds
Philip H. Rhinelander
Elias Rivers & Georgina Sabat
Albert S. Roe
Rinaldina Russell
Eduardo Saccone
A. William Salomone
Peter Sammartino
Daniel Sargent
S. Eugene Scalia
J. A. Scott
Jean Seznec
Anne Shaver
John T. Shawcross
R. A. Shoaf
Nancy G. Siraisi
Janet Levarie Smarr
Nathaniel B. Smith
Philip J. Spartano

Charles Speroni
Arnold Stein
William A. Stephany
Sara Sturm-Maddox
Pasquale G. Tatò
Owsei Temkin
E. Katharine Tilton
William J. & Lita Tognotti
Joseph Tusiani
Willi A. Uschald
Huling E. Ussery
Aldo Vallone
Massimo Verdicchio
Anthony J. Vetrano
Anthony Viscusi
James B. Wadsworth
Bruce W. Wardropper
Dr. & Mrs. Gilmore Warner
James A. Weisheipl, O.P.
Elizabeth B. Welles
Bonnie Wheeler
Alice S. Wilson
Chauncey Wood
Ambrosina Lydia Francesca Woodruff
Ruth E. Young

SUNY Binghamton Fellows of CEMERS
Dickinson College English Department
Istituto Italiano di Cultura
Istituto Nazionale di Studi sul Rinascimento
The Johns Hopkins University Department of History
Manhattan College Dante Seminar
Nazareth College of Rochester Casa Italiana
The Newberry Library
Società Dantesca Italiana
Trinity College, Hartford
Victoria University Library, Toronto

Contents

Preface   VII

Tabula Gratulatoria   IX

Introduction   XVII

The Publications of Charles S. Singleton   XXIII

The Significance of *terza rima*
JOHN FRECCERO   3

Tassonomie dantesche
EZIO RAIMONDI   19

Pier della Vigna: History and Iconology
ANTHONY K. CASSELL   31

Purgatorio XIX: Dante's Siren/Harpy
ROBERT HOLLANDER   77

The Seven *Status Ecclesiae* in *Purgatorio* XXXII–XXXIII
ROBERT KASKE   89

Words and Images in Dante's *Paradiso: Reflections of the Divine*
JOAN FERRANTE   115

Time and Eternity in the Myths of *Paradiso* XVII
MARGUERITE M. CHIARENZA   133

Jacopo della Lana, interprete di Dante
ALDO VALLONE   151

An Annotated Translation of Petrarch's *Epistola metrica* II.10
THOMAS G. BERGIN   183

The Adynaton in Petrarch's Sestinas
MARIANNE SHAPIRO   231

La pianta più gradita in cielo: Petrarch's Laurel and Jove
SARA STURM-MADDOX   255

Boccaccio on Interpretation: Guido's Escape (*Decameron* VI.9)
ROBERT DURLING   273

"Chiuso parlare" in Boccaccio's *Teseida*
VICTORIA KIRKHAM   305

Metodi di lettura degli scritti ascetici trecenteschi
GIORGIO PETROCCHI   353

Dante, Petrarch, Boccaccio

Studies in the Italian Trecento
In Honor of Charles S. Singleton

Introduction

Charles S. Singleton and *Dante Redivivus*

ANYONE WHO TAKES A DANTE COURSE under Charles Singleton learns to *see* how a poem *happens*. Not only does the course leave echoes that linger indefinitely, but it communicates a sense of what it feels like to unravel the mysteries that inform a work of art.

Singleton's explanation for this is that in teaching Dante he manages to convey to the student the manner in which a poem *happens*. His course reflects his conviction that the mark of a great work of literature is that it virtually comes alive, as does great music, each time it is properly experienced. He found himself almost abandoning his doctoral studies at Berkeley when he discovered that the *Canti carnascialeschi* on which he was writing his dissertation were not coming alive for him. He has since believed that when a poem or a work of literature fails to *come alive* or to *happen*, there must be a flaw either in the reader or in the work.

His formula for restoring life to a work is to consider not only *text* but *context* as well. This does not mean simply a consideration of the historical and cultural environment of the text, but careful control of all possible contextual factors. He defines the process as "the *control* of the *experience* of the text by *controlling* what we admit into our reading from the area of *context*, on a principle of relevance, tested within the work itself." If, therefore, we have the sensibility for poetry and the control needed for the proper application of all that is meant by "*context*," works such as the *Vita nuova* and the *Divine Comedy* can indeed *happen* for us over and over again.

Such has been Singleton's approach to Dante since at least the late 1940's when he gave his first course at Harvard, on the *Vita nuova*. As he asserts in the Foreword of his *Essay on the 'Vita nuova'*, that early work of Dante lacks the power of the *Divine Comedy* because "It will not come all the way to meet us." We must therefore make a special effort to get back to its own day if it is to come alive for us. This process has unfortunately become quite burdensome ever since the second half of the sixteenth century when a new vision of the world made subsequent generations incapable of seeing the world as it was viewed in Dante's day. What Singleton calls "the public context" of the work had undergone a radical change. As a result, "the balance of forces which the artist had created between the inside of his work and the outside" was disturbed, and the tension so vital to the work of art was lost. What was inner and "private" had no longer anything to play against since the new "public dimension" was so different. In Dante's time, "that dimension in its broadest extension was simply the belief that there is nothing which so much matters in this world as the salvation of the soul—and that through Christ only is true salvation possible." It is by fully realizing the implications of such a "dimension" that the reader of the *Vita nuova* will understand, for example, why the analogy of Beatrice with Christ was not seen as a sacrilege in Dante's day, but very decidedly was so viewed a few years after the Council of Trent.

It follows that one who desires fully to understand a work such as the *Vita nuova* must consider "matters that seem to lie outside the work and beyond it." And only by testing the relevance of such matters within the work itself can such a reader restore in some degree a sense of the true form of the work of art and arrive at an intepretation that causes the work to live again. What is ultimately involved is the adjusting of "fixed" texts to their original contexts. In the case of Dante and the Middle Ages generally, the key contextual element for Singleton and his followers is *salus* or Christian salvation (just as it is Christian charity, for example, for D. W. Robertson and his followers).

Two criticisms occasionally levelled at Singleton's approach to Dante, that it is too heavily theological and allegorical and that it tends to be mystical, are hardly justifiable. Both charges are the result of a superficial reading of Singleton's work. They ignore the essential nature of Dante's work and its context, along with the principle of relevance as defined by Singleton. If there is a mysticism involved, it is the "mystique" of the scholar with implicit faith in the powers of criticism to penetrate and define the vital ingredients of Dante's incomparable artistry.

To understand the development of Singleton's approach, it is well to recall that his career began with two specific interests, Lorenzo's Florence and the art of the *Decameron*. It was not until 1941 that he first turned to Dante with a short study in *Italica* on " 'Dante' in the *Divine Comedy*," only to return once again to further study of Boccaccio and his masterpiece. His study on "*Vita nuova* XVII: Love's Obscure Words," which appeared in the *Romanic Review* in 1945, marked his decisive turn to Dante. Since that time he has devoted himself primarily to the challenge of making Dante's masterpiece *happen* for the modern reader.

From his earliest forays into the mystery of the power and beauty of Dante's poetry, Singleton has acknowledged that direct confrontation, getting involved, coming to grips with the text, getting inside the text itself, as it were, constitute the principal thrust of his approach. In the case of the *Comedy*, his primary concern has always remained its *poetry* rather than its ideas, allegories, or spiritual meanings for their own sake. To understand the degree to which this has been so, one must first learn Singleton's use of the medieval idiom. Assuming that Dante's poetic inspiration did indeed rest upon religious and spiritual convictions of his time, Singleton has always felt that these cannot be overlooked in analyzing the artistic power and intensity of Dante's great poem. Once versed in the theology and philosophy that influenced Dante, the critic must undertake to discover in the text the magic whereby Dante's genius transformed such convictions into a poem whose basic structure was modelled analogically on God's creation with all its complex and fathomless beauty.

This conception of a poet undertaking to imitate God's creation lies at the heart of the misunderstandings that have arisen concerning Singleton's approach. Had Dante sought to imitate the painting techniques of a Cimabue or a Giotto, modern critics would have applauded the scholarly assessment of such imitation. But because Singleton sought to prove that Dante deliberately composed the *Comedy* in imitation of the Master Craftsman, such applause has at times been witheld in the name of modern theories of aesthetics.

Singleton's approach to the *Comedy* is actually quite simple. Starting with the premise that the educated medieval reader would have had little difficulty in seeing the analogy between Dante's way of writing and the two "books" of the Christian God, the Book of the Universe and Holy Scripture, he proceeds to examine the principal ingredients constituting such similarity. An example of this may be seen particularly in his study entitled, "The Poet's Number at the Center." First, however, he posits two points to be kept constantly in mind. The first is that the medieval mind considered the two divine "books" as primary guides offered by God to man for his salvation. The second is the absolute need of remaining at all times in touch with the entire structure of the *Comedy* and its medieval foundations.

In examining, in *Dante Studies 1*, the primary structural elements of the *Comedy*—allegory, symbolism, and analogy—Singleton shows how, by analogy, a human poem can participate in a divine poem and be made in its image. In so doing, he concludes, "a poem does what all created things do in a Christian universe, a poem participates in true existence, in Being." This is the sense in which, for Singleton, the *Comedy* can truly happen or come alive. But in order to experience this, one must understand the extent to which Dante's allegory is explicit in the theology of his day. As he writes in *Dante Studies 2*, "We have only to learn to recognize it there in the theology when we meet it. And when we become able to do this, then at once we find ourselves confronted with an embarrassment of riches. Instead of one good text to cite in evidence of a given point or pattern there are at least twenty." Only then may we "finally be persuaded that the poet constructed his allegory on points of doctrine firmly established and widely current in his time."

In sum, then, the basic principles underlying Singleton's approach to the *Comedy* are (a) a firm grasp and appreciation of how the doctrine of salvation through Christ permeated medieval life and thought, (b) a recognition of Dante's conscious imitation of God's two "books," and (c) the need for understanding the poem as a whole. In such fashion does Singleton restore to the *Comedy* not only its Christian allegorical and symbolic structure, but also the manner in which such a structure contributes to a resolution of the mystery underlying the poem. It is that vital mystery that provides the ground of being and of beauty often totally overlooked by the school of "aesthetic" criticism which limits itself to those parts of the poem that can be read without reference to the transcendental, not to mention the contextual, whole.

Perhaps understandably, Singleton's approach to Dante was at first and

for some time quite slow in gaining adherents, but with the recent publication of his key studies in Italian translation, with the Bollingen six–volume
edition of his translation and commentary, and with the reprinting of his
major studies by Princeton (including a paper-back version of the Bollingen edition in three volumes), the last decade has witnessed a decided movement toward wider acceptance of his critical approach. Interestingly,
Singleton's most consistent admirers have been creative writers of note,
starting with T. S. Eliot and continuing more recently with Montale and
Nabokov. In an interview, Montale referred to Singleton as "il maggior
dantista vivente;" while Nabokov in a review assessing the Bollingen edition of Singleton's translation and commentary remarked: "What triumphant joy it is to see the honest light of literality take over again after
ages of meretricious paraphrase!" As for the acknowledgement of his critical
approach by Italian scholars, the process has taken much longer than in
America, no doubt in large part because of the language and stylistic barrier. This difficulty may now be on its way to resolution with the recent
publication in first-rate Italian versions of all of Singleton's most significant
critical essays on Dante. Moreover, about a decade ago, a uniquely accurate understanding and appreciation of Singleton's approach to Dante
was already evinced by Angelo Jacomuzzi in his survey of a twenty-year
period of Dante criticism, "La Divina Commedia: figura, allegoria, visione,"
which appeared in Rivista di storia e letteratura religiosa (1970) and was subsequently reprinted in his volume, Il palinsesto della retorica e altri saggi danteschi
(1972). By 1979, in a long and perceptive review of the Italian edition
of Singleton's books and studies, Domenico De Robertis noted that "the
very 'structure' [of Dante's poem] which for so long, and well before Croce's
essay, was being contrasted to the 'poetry' as its negation, now appears
[in Singleton's studies] not simply as the substance from which the poetry
springs, but as the poetry itself, the mode of being of the entire poem,
the form of its imagination." One year later, in a special number of the
Yearbook of Italian Studies largely dedicated to Singleton, Dante Della Terza,
in speaking of "the web of intuitions which constitute the supporting
ground for the Singletonian way of reading Dante," and of "the refreshing
sensation of newness" imparted by the Italian edition of his studies, observes
how "Intellectual and theological background—the poem's structure—
and the foreground represented by the pilgrim's journey interact to create
the great poetic invention that we have learned to call 'Divine' Comedy."
Except for a nine-year interlude (1948–57) at Harvard, Singleton has

taught at The John Hopkins University since 1939. His career at the Hopkins was crowned by his being awarded in 1979 the Milton Stover Eisenhower Medal for Distinguished Service. His outstanding contribution to scholarship on Italian literature in this country was similarly recognized by a Gold Medal Award bestowed upon him on the steps of the U.S. Capitol by the organizers of the World Petrarch Congress in 1974. Italy too has paid special tribute to him for his achievements in the study of Dante and Boccaccio. In 1961 at an elaborate ceremony in the Palazzo Vecchio, Florence made him the third and last recipient of its Gold Medal for Dante Studies. The honor had previously fallen to T. S. Eliot and to André Pézard, and has gone to no one else since. In 1963 he was awarded in Pisa the Premio Internazionale Forte dei Marmi-Galileo by the Italian Rotary for his contribution to the history of Italian literature. And in 1975 the municipality of Certaldo conferred upon him its Honorary Citizenship for his distinctive contribution to Boccaccian studies. Such honors, it can be assumed, will continue, as attested by the two honorary degrees conferred upon him in 1981 by Princeton and SUNY-Binghamton. The achievement and importance of Charles Singleton can perhaps be epitomized in the opening words of citation accompanying his award of the Milton Stover Eisenhower Medal:

> Humanist in a Renaissance mold, celebrated translator, editor and interpreter of the living monuments of Italian literature, educator of vision and dedication . . . you have been honored by your peers throughout the world. Your influence has extended wherever the enduring literature of Italy, wherever the learning of the Middle Ages and the Renaissance is cherished.

A. S. B.

The Publications of
Charles S. Singleton

(The arrangement is chronological within groups—books, articles, and reviews.)

Books

[*The Literature of Pageantry in Florence during the Renaissance.* Berkeley, California, 1936. 5 + 401 leaves. Doctoral dissertation, Romance Literature, University of California, Berkeley, August 1936.]

(Editor) *Canti carnascialeschi del Rinascimento.* Bari: Laterza, 1936. (Scrittori d'Italia.)

(Editor) *Nuovi canti carnascialeschi del Rinascimento, con un'appendice; tavola generale dei canti carnascialeschi editi e inediti.* Modena: Società Tipografica Modenese, 1940. (Istituto di Filologia Romanza della R. Università di Roma. Studi e testi.)

An Essay on the "Vita Nuova." Cambridge, Massachusetts: Harvard University Press, 1949. Soft-cover edition, 1958; and an identical British edition, 1958, by Oxford University Press.

Dante Studies 1. "Commedia": Elements of Structure. Cambridge, Massachusetts: Harvard University Press, 1954.

(Editor) Boccaccio, Giovanni, *Il Decameron.* Bari: Laterza, 1955. 2 v. (Scrittori d'Italia.)

Dante Studies 2. Journey to Beatrice. Cambridge, Massachusetts: Harvard University Press, 1958. Reprinted in 1967.

(Translator) Castiglione, Baldassare. *The Book of the Courtier.* A new translation . . . Illustrative material edited by Edgar de N. Mayhew. Garden City, New York: Doubleday, 1959. (Anchor Books.)

Studi su Dante. I. *Introduzione alla Divina Commedia.* Premessa di Giulio
   Vallese e nuova Prefazione dell'Autore. Naples: G. Scalabrini Editore,
   1961. Italian version of the original American edition, *Dante Studies
   1. "Commedia": Elements of Structure* (1954).
(Editor) Toynbee, Paget. *Dante Alighieri: His Life and Works.* Edited with
   an introduction, notes, and bibliography . . . New York: Harper and
   Row, 1965. (Harper Torchbooks: The Academy Library.)
Dante Studies 2. Journey to Beatrice. Cambridge, Massachusetts: Harvard
   University Press, 1967. Reprint of the original 1958 edition.
(Editor) *Art, Science, and History in the Renaissance.* Baltimore: The Johns
   Hopkins Press, 1967. (The Johns Hopkins Humanities Seminars.)
Saggio sulla "Vita Nuova." Bologna: Il Mulino, 1968. (Saggi, 79.) Italian
   version, by Gaetano Prampolini, of the original American edition, *An
   Essay on the Vita Nuova* (1949).
Viaggio a Beatrice. Bologna: Il Mulino, 1968.(Saggi, 67.) Italian version,
   by Gaetano Prampolini, of the original American edition, *Dante Studies
   2. Journey to Beatrice* (1958).
(Editor) Toynbee, Paget. *A Dictionary of Proper Names and Notable Matters
   in the Works of Dante.* [New Edition] revised . . . Oxford: Clarendon
   Press, 1968.
(Joint author and editor) Brieger, Peter, Millard Meiss, and Charles S.
   Singleton. *Illuminated Manuscripts of the Divine Comedy.* Bollingen Series,
   LXXXI. Princeton, New Jersey: Princeton University Press, 1969. 2 v.
   Contains his essay, "The Irreducible Vision," pp. 1–29, in Vol. I.
The Irreducible Vision. Princeton, New Jersey: Princeton University Press,
   1969. A separate printing of the essay in *Illuminated Manuscripts of the
   Divine Comedy* (1969).
(Editor) *Interpretation: Theory and Practice.* Baltimore: The Johns Hopkins
   Press, 1969. (The Johns Hopkins Humanities Seminars.)
(Translator and commentator) Dante. *The Divine Comedy.* Translated, with
   a commentary . . . . Bollingen Series, LXXX. Princeton, New Jersey:
   Princeton University Press, 1970–75. 3 v. in 6. I. *Inferno* (1970)—1.
   Italian text and prose translation; 2. Commentary. II. *Purgatorio* (1973)
   . . . III. *Paradiso* (1975) . . . .
(Editor) Dante. *La Divina Commedia.* Edited and annotated by C. H. Grand-
   gent; revised by Charles S. Singleton. Cambridge, Massachusetts: Har-
   vard University Press, 1972.
(Editor) Boccaccio, Giovanni. *Decameron.* Edizione diplomatico-interpre-

tativa dell'autografo Hamilton 90, a cura di . . . . Baltimore: The Johns Hopkins University Press, 1974.

(Editor) Grandgent, Charles H. *Companion to the Divine Comedy.* Commentary by C. H. Grandgent as edited by Charles S. Singleton. Cambridge, Massachusetts: Harvard University Press, 1975.

An Essay on the "Vita Nuova." Baltimore and London: The Johns Hopkins University Press, 1977. Reprint of the original edition of 1949 (Harvard University Press).

Dante's "Commedia": Elements of Structure. Baltimore and London: The Johns Hopkins University Press, 1977. Reprint of the original edition of 1954 (Harvard University Press), *Dante Studies 1. Commedia: Elements of Structure.*

Journey to Beatrice. Baltimore and London: The Johns Hopkins University Press, 1977. Reprint of the original edition of 1958 (Harvard University Press), *Dante Studies 2. Journey to Beatrice.*

La poesia della Divina Commedia. Bologna: Società Editrice Il Mulino, 1978. (Collezione di testi e di studi: Linguistica e critica letteraria.) Gathers together, in Italian, previously published essays—*Dante Studies* 1 and 2, respectively, *"Commedia": Elements of Structure* (1954) and *Journey to Beatrice* (1958), which already appeared in Italian (1961 and 1968 resp.), and four essays not published in Italian before: "The Poet's Number at the Center" (1965), "The Vistas in Retrospect" (1965), "In Exitu Israel de Aegypto" (1960), and "The Irreducible Vision" (1969). (N.B. *Dante Studies 1* . . . comes here in a new translation, by Gaetano Prampolini.)

Saggio sulla "Vita Nuova." Bologna: Il Mulino, 1979. (Saggi, 79.) Further printing of the original Italian edition (1968), to accompany his *La Poesia della Divina Commedia* (1978) as its ideal preface.

(Translator and commentator) Dante. *The Divine Comedy.* Translated, with a commentary . . . . Bollingen Series, LXXX. Princeton, New Jersey: Princeton University Press, 1980–82. 3 v. Reprint as the first "Princeton / Bollingen Paperback" printing, combining the two parts (translation and commentary) of each volume in one and preserving the pagination of the original edition. I. *Inferno* (1980); II. *Purgatorio* (1982); III. *Paradiso* (1982).

(Editor and commentator) Boccaccio, Giovanni. *The Decameron.* Translated by John Payne; revised, and with a commentary, by Charles S. Singleton. Berkeley and Los Angeles: University of California Press, 1983. 3v.

Articles

"A Note on the Improvement of Reading." *Italica*, xv (1938), 66–69.

"Some More Sixteenth-Century Italian Songs." *Italica*, xv (1938), 175–78.

" 'Dante' in the *Divine Comedy*." *Italica*, xviii (1941), 109–16.

"On *Meaning* in the *Decameron*." *Italica*, xxi (1944), 117–24.

"*Vita Nuova* xii: Love's Obscure Words." *Romanic Review*, xxxvi (1945), 89–102.

"The Use of Latin in the *Vita Nuova*." *Modern Language Notes*, lxi (1946), 108–12.

Several articles (on Verga, Francesco Chiesa, and other Italian authors). *Columbia Dictionary of Modern Literature*, edited by Horatio Smith (New York: Columbia University Press, 1947).

" 'Sulla fiumana ove 'l mar non ha vanto' (*Inferno* ii, 108)." *Romanic Review*, xxxix (1948), 269–77.

" 'La Porta del piacere.' " *Modern Language Notes*, lxiii (1948), 339–42.

"Dante and Myth." *Journal of the History of Ideas*, x (1949), 482–502. Reprinted in his *Dante Studies 1* (1954), pp. 61–83, as "The Substance of Things Seen."

"Dante's Allegory." *Speculum* xxv (1950), 78–86. Reprinted in his *Dante Studies 1*, pp. 84–98, as an appendix: "The Two Kinds of Allegory."

"Dante's Comedy: The Pattern at the Center." *Romanic Review*, xlii (1951), 169–77. Reprinted in his *Dante Studies 1*, pp. 45–60; and in Italian as "*Vita Nuova e Divina Commedia*: lo schema al centro," in *Le Parole e le idee*, ii (1960), 111–22.

"The Other Journey." *Kenyon Review*, xiv (1952), 189–206. Reprinted in his *Dante Studies 1*, pp. 1–17, as "Allegory."

"End of a Poem." *Hudson Review*, vi (1953), 529–39.

"The Perspective of Art" [on Machiavelli]. *Kenyon Review*, xv (1953), 169–89.

"Justice in Eden." *68th–72nd Annual Reports of the Dante Society* (1954), 3–33. Reprinted in his *Dante Studies 2*, pp. 72–85; and in Italian as "La giustizia nel Paradiso terrestre," in *Delta*, N. S., No. 7–8 (1955), 1–25.

"Italian Literature: Three Masters, Three Epochs." *World Literature*, by Joseph Remenyi [and others], (Pittsburgh: University of Pittsburgh

Press, 1956), pp. 154–69. On Dante's *Comedy*, Boccaccio's *Decameron*, and Leopardi's *Infinito*.

"Virgil Recognizes Beatrice." *74th Annual Report of the Dante Society* (1956), 29–38.

"The Goal at the Summit." *Delta*, N. S., No. 11–12 (1957), 61–76. Reprinted from his *Dante Studies 2*, pp. 101–21.

"The Irreducible Dove." *Comparative Literature*, IX (1957), 129–35.

"Stars Over Eden." *75th Annual Report of the Dante Society* (1957), 1–18.

"In Exitu Israel de Aegypto." *78th Annual Report of the Dante Society* (1960), 1–24. Reprinted in John Freccero, ed., *Dante: A Collection of Critical Essays* (Englewood Cliffs, N.J.: Prentice-Hall, 1965), pp. 102–21, and, in Italian, in his *La poesia della Divina Commedia* (Bologna: Il Mulino, 1978), pp. 495–520.

"*Inferno* X: Guido's Disdain." *Modern Language Notes*, LXXVII (1962), 49–65.

"The Uses of the *Decameron*." *Modern Language Notes*, LXXIX (1964), 71–76. Review-article on Aldo Scaglione, *Nature and Love in the Late Middle Ages* (Berkeley: University of California Press, 1963).

"*Inferno* XIX: O Simon Mago!" *Modern Language Notes*, LXXX (1965), 92–99.

"The Poet's Number at the Center." *Modern Language Notes*, LXXX (1965), 1–10. Reprinted, in Italian, in his *La poesia della Divina Commedia* (Bologna: Il Mulino, 1978), pp. 451–62.

"The Vistas in Retrospect." *Atti del Congresso Internazionale di Studi Danteschi* . . . (20–27 aprile 1965), Vol. I (Firenze: Sansoni, 1965), pp. 279–304. Reprinted in *Modern Language Notes*, LXXXI (1966), 55–80, and in Italian in his *La poesia della Divina Commedia* (Bologna: Il Mulino, 1978), pp. 463–94.

"Sull'intervento di G. Padoan." *Atti del Congresso Internazionale di Studi Danteschi* . . . (20–27 aprile 1965), Vol. II (Firenze: Sansoni, 1966), p. 75. (On the two kinds of allegory, concluded with a reading from the appendix of his *Studi su Dante*. I. Introduzione alla Divina Commedia (Napoli: Scalabrini, 1961), Italian version of *Dante Studies 1. Commedia: Elements of Structure* (1954).

"Campi semantici dei canti XII dell'*Inferno* e XIII del *Purgatorio*." *Miscellanea di studi danteschi*, a cura dell'Istituto di Letteratura Italiana (Università degli Studi, Genova; Genova: Bozzi, 1966), pp. 11–22.

"Dante's Allegory." *American Critical Essays on the Divine Comedy*, edited by Robert J. Clements (New York: New York University Press, 1967), pp. 91–103. Reprinted from *Dante studies 1. "Commedia": Elements of Structure* (1954), pp. 84–98.

"Dante: Within Courtly Love and Beyond." *The Meaning of Courtly Love;* Papers of the First Annual Conference of the Center for Medieval and Early Renaissance Studies, State University of New York at Binghamton, March 17–18, 1967; edited by F. X. Newman (Albany: State University of New York Press, 1968), pp. 43–54.

Reviews

Rimatori del 'Dolce stil novo', a cura di Luigi Di Benedetto (Bari: Laterza, 1939). *Modern Language Notes*, LV (1940), 626–28.

Gordon R. Silber, *The Influence of Dante and Petrarch on Certain of Boccaccio's Lyrics* (Menasha, Wisconsin: George Banta Publishing Co., 1940). *Italica*, XVII (1940), 118–22.

Angelina La Piana, *Dante's American Pilgrimage: A Historical Survey of Dante Studies in the United States, 1800–1944.* (New Haven, Connecticut: Yale University Press, 1948). *Modern Language Notes*, LXIV (1949), 198–99.

Leonardo Olschki, *The Myth of Felt* (Berkeley, California: University of California Press, 1949). *Italica*, XXVII (1950), 187–88.

Dante. *The Comedy of Dante Alighieri the Florentine,* I: Hell, trans. by Dorothy L. Sayers (New York: Penguin Books, 1949). *Speculum*, XXV (1950), 394–95.

James E. Shaw, *Guido Cavalcanti's Theory of Love . . .* (Toronto: University of Toronto Press, 1949). *Speculum*, XXV (1950), 144–48.

Nancy Lenkeith, *Dante and the Legend of Rome* (London: The Warburg Institute, 1952). *Speculum*, XXIX (1954), 127–31.

Dorothy L. Sayers, *Introductory Papers on Dante* (New York: Harper; London: Methuen, 1954). *Kenyon Review*, XVII (1955), 656–61.

Joseph A. Mazzeo, *Structure and Thought in the "Paradiso"* (Ithaca, New York: Cornell University Press, 1958). *Romanic Review*, L (1959), 55–59.

A. L. P.

Dante, Petrarch, Boccaccio

Studies in the Italian Trecento
In Honor of Charles S. Singleton

The Significance of Terza Rima

JOHN FRECCERO

T HE PERENNIAL PROBLEM IN LITERARY INTERPRETATION is the problem of the relationship of form to content, or of poetics to thematics. In recent years, there can be little doubt that formalism
has occupied our attention, both in linguistics and in criticism, with Rus-
sian formalism, American New Criticism and the formalism of the French
Structuralists. The proper concern of poetics, according to Roman Jakobson, for example, is metalinguistic: not with the message itself, but rather
with the message's awareness of itself as message. The most creative and
interesting critical developments of the past few decades have been
characterized by a concern for poetics, in Jakobson's sense, at least in the
study of modern literature.

The single exception I can think of to this dominance of formal studies
is in the field of medieval literature. Here the most significant contribu-
tions have involved taking content, particularly theology, very seriously.
Perhaps Leo Spitzer was the precursor of this tendency, with his insistence
on the importance of historical semantics for examining the coherence of
the works he studied. In our own day, literary students, particularly in
English, have found in the Bible and in the exegetical tradition a repository
of semantic values and symbolic associations that seem essential for the
coherence and meaning of medieval works. They have shown convincingly that it is impossible any longer to treat those works in the same

way that we treat contemporary secular texts, written in our own cultural context.

In the field of Dante studies, it is the unique and permanent contribution of Charles Singleton to have brought poetics and thematics together in the interpretation of the poem. By refusing to accept the traditional dichotomy of poetry and belief, an older version of the opposition I have been describing, he demonstrated the relevance of theology not only to the literary archeologist, but also to the literary critic. His formal criticism represents a dramatic departure from the tradition of the *lectura dantis*, for it deals with the unity and coherence of the entire poem, rather than with single cantos or lyric passages. At the same time, that view of the whole necessarily involves accepting theology as part of that coherence. In this essay, I should like to extend his assertion of the relationship of theology to poetry in Dante's poem by offering one example where they are, quite literally, indistinguishable. I have deliberately chosen a title that brings together both meaning and form in a way that may sound simplistic but that I hope will prove nonetheless exact.

To say that poetry and theology are indistinguishable at a certain point in the poem is not to say that they should be indistinguishable in our analysis. As obvious as this remark sounds, there is still a great deal of critical confusion about the difference between what Dante believed and what we believe. Nowhere is this clearer than in discussions of Dante's allegory or "figural typology." Sometimes the word "allegory" is used to describe what *Dante* thought he was doing: writing a poem patterned on the Bible, for which a divine privilege was claimed in the Middle Ages. Because "allegory" is also a general literary term, however, others speak of it as though it were a formal characteristic of the poem, comparable to other examples of literary allegory. Erich Auerbach's otherwise masterly essay, "Figura,"[1] illustrates the confusion by first celebrating the mimetic power of Dante's representation, which is presumably a literary judgment, and then claiming to have found "the solid historical grounding" for this judgment in the theory of figural representation. It is as if the earlier critical perception required the medieval theory of *figura* in order to be validated or, conversely, as if the theological theory were somehow established by the power of Dante's poetry. The fact remains that any modern reader would accept Auerbach's literary judgment, but no modern reader could possibly accept the theory in which it is presumably grounded. This confusion, pervasive in Dante studies, can be resolved only by showing *how* a medieval conception of theological allegory can be reconciled to a formal pattern and so be made accessible to any reader, without theological presuppositions. In my effort to show how theological meaning and poetic form are, in at least one instance, inseparable, I shall also have something to say concerning the *form* of theological allegory.

To begin with an abstract form is to proceed in a manner that is the reverse of what one might expect of a cultural historian. The coherence of Dante's poem is often taken to be a reflection of the coherence of his faith, which we take as the primary cultural reality, but the formula might well be reversed, by suggesting that the apparent coherence of Dante's belief is at least in part a projection of the coherence of his poem. The reversal is not meant to be cynically de-constructive; there are good historical grounds for maintaining a certain reversibility of terms. In a culture which called its central principle "the Word," a certain homology between the order of things and the order of words is strongly implied. This is another way of stating what Kenneth Burke has referred to in another context as the "logological" principle. If theology is words about God, wherein linguistic analogies are used to describe a transcendent divinity, then "logology" is the reduction of theological principles back into the realm of words.[2] What ensures the possibility of the reversal is the central tenet of Christianity, the doctrine of the Word, according to which language and reality are structured analogously. We need not privilege either pole: thematics (that is, theology) and poetics might conceivably be joined in such a way as to offend neither historical understanding nor contemporary skepticism, for in either case, we are discussing a coherence that is primarily linguistic. The traditional problem of poetry and belief would then be shifted onto a philosophical plane. Does the order of language reflect the order of reality or is "transcendent reality" simply a projection of language? What we had always taken to be a problem of Dante criticism turns out to be the central epistemological problem of all interpretation.

The formal aspect of the poem that I have chosen to discuss is Dante's rhyme scheme, *terza rima*. Its significance has rarely been questioned because it has seemed too obviously to represent the Trinity. While this may be true, it tells us very little. For one thing, virtually everything represents God in this poem; the abstraction is so remote as to be meaningless. For another, and perhaps more importantly, a verse scheme is necessarily temporal, or at least a spatial representation of time. It is not self–evident that a temporal scheme could serve to represent a timeless deity.

Dante derived his rhyme scheme especially for the *Divine Comedy*. It is very simply expressed: ABA, BCB, CDC, etc. Some critics believe it to have been adapted from previously existing verse forms, sirvente, sestina or sonnet, but most of their discussions are clearly attempts to deduce influence from metric analogies. In any case, the *terzina* is characterized by a basically triadic structure, like the sirvente, and by a forward *entrelacement*, like both the sirvente and the sestina. Unlike the sestina, however, the rules for closure are not inherent in the form: the *terzina* as a metric pattern could theoretically go on forever and must be arbitrarily ended.

It is this open-endedness that has moved some theorists to object that pure *terza rima* does not exist, since it would have to violate its own rules in order to begin or end. So it is with Dante's *terzina*, which has a dyadic beginning and end. In each canto, it begins and ends with what are sometimes called *rime rilevate*. The rhyme A in the scheme ABA, BCB, CDC . . . appears only twice, rather than three times, while at the end, the last rhyme, Z, also appears only twice: XYX, YZY, Z (fig. 1). A and Z (or Alpha and Omega, to hint at a more accurate theological analogy) are *rime rilevate*, arbitary beginnings and endings for an otherwise

Fig. 1.

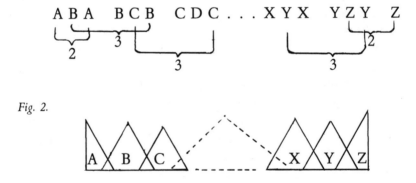

Fig. 2.

autonomous and infinite forward movement, whose progress is also recapitulation. So *terza rima* may be characterized as a movement that begins and ends arbitrarily. This heterogeneity of the form would seem to be incompatible with the idea that it might represent the Trinity (fig. 2).

Not only was Dante's rhyme form unique, but his organization of tercets into *canti* was also a formal innovation, transforming the arbitrary element of versification into a higher formal exigency. Since his verses are hendecasyllables, each of his *terzine* consists of 33 syllables. So too, each of his *cantiche* consists of 33 *canti*, if we except the first canto as prologue to the rest. We have then a formal structure which suggests a certain homology between the versification and the formal divisions of the poem. The 33 syllables of a *terzina* are mirrored in the 33 *canti* of a *cantica* and the three *cantiche* thus represent a kind of cosmic tercet, an encyclopedic representation of the number three.

We are familiar with this kind of numerology from Dante himself who, in the *Vita Nuova*, refers to the mystic power of the number three and its square, nine. Here, however, I should like to stress not the static value of divisions by the number three, but rather the reconciliation of motion that *terza rima* implies: a forward motion, closed off with a recapitulation that gives to the motion its beginning and end. Any complete appearance of a rhyme, . . . BA BCB . . . , incorporates at the same time a recall to the past and a promise of the future that seem to meet in the *now* of the central rhyme (fig. 3).

The formal pattern of interlocking rhymes arbitrarily closed off in a way that is symmetrical with its beginning becomes more significant when we reflect for a moment on its thematic counterpart, the forward motion of the pilgrim toward a goal which is, at the same time, the narrative's logical point of departure. Readers have for centuries noted innumerable correspondences between the three *cantiche*, constituting retrospective recalls over the course of the poem, the most familiar of which, perhaps, is the recurrence of the word *stelle* at the end of each of them. So far as I know, however, Singleton's essay on the "Vistas in Retrospect" is the only full treatment of the subject at both the lexical and thematic levels.[3] Singleton brilliantly illustrates the manner in which the theme proceeds by a gradual

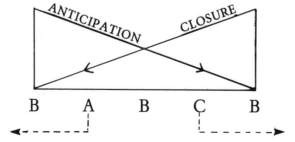

Fig. 3.

unfolding that is recaptured en route in a series of retrospectives that range from the minute (the retrospective gloss on the word *ruina*, for example) to the cosmic (as in the backward glance of the pilgrim from the Gemini in the starry heaven). The final recapitulation is at the same time the logical justification for the poem's beginning, the transformation of the pilgrim into the author, whose story we have just finished reading. When Singleton paradoxically suggests that the story must be read from the ending, as well as from the beginning, he confirms the analogy we have drawn between the movement of the verse and the movement of the theme.

Perhaps the most astonishing parallel between the theme and the formal pattern is established by the dramatic action of the poem, the pilgrim's path. The geometric representation of forward motion which is at the same time recapitulatory is the spiral. Whatever thematic importance we wish to attach to the spiral path in Dante's story (and I have said elswhere what I take that importance to be),[4] it happens to be a geometric synthesis of the contradictory theses that are presented temporally by the verse pattern and thematically by the story line. From a purely geometric standpoint, the first two *cantiche* are replicas of each other, with the cavity of Hell inversely symmetrical with the Mount of Purgatory, while the representation of Paradise recapitulates both of those shapes with the celestial rose mirroring the God–head and the surrounding angels "come clivo in acqua . . . si specchia" (*Par.* xxx.109–110). The geometric complexities of the spiral theme are spatial analogues of the temporal paradox of *terza rima*, forward motion which recapitulates the beginning in the end.

We have seen that both the verse pattern and the theme proceed by a forward motion which is at the same time recapitulatory. I should now like to suggest that this movement also can serve as the spatial representation of narrative logic, particularly autobiography. The paradoxical logic of all such narratives is that beginning and end must logically coincide, in order for the author and his *persona* to be the same. This exigency, analogous to what Kenneth Burke in another context refers to as "the Divine tautology,"[5] takes the form, "I am I, but I was not always so." The whole of temporal sequence in such a narrative, then, is generated by some form of negation introduced into the principle of identity and then refined away. Logically, autobiograhy is a sequential narrative that moves toward its own origin. If that statement seems paradoxical, it is no more so than the premise of all autobiography—that one can judge one's own life as though that life were concluded. The ending of such a story implies its beginning, for the *persona's* experience must be concluded before the author's voice (and hence the story) can come into existence. The paradox of continuity/discontinuity in the formal representation of *terza rima* is matched by the paradox of continuity/discontinuity involved in the logic of autobiographical narrative: I am I, but I was not always so.

Thus far, we have traced a pattern in three conceptual orders: the formal, the thematic, and the logical. *Terza rima*, Dante's theme, and the logic of autobiographical narrative all may be represented as forward motion that moves toward its own beginning, or as a form of advance and recovery, leading toward a final recapitulation. All that is required in order to move from the realm of poetics to the realm of theology in this context is to assert that the pattern we have been describing has a *necessary* rather than arbitrary justification. Thus far we have been dealing with a formal characteristic of the poem that is discernible to any reader; the theological leap requires only that we ascribe this pattern, not simply to the poem, but to metaphysical reality. Notice, however, that our description of the pattern in either case remains the same. Doubtless Dante believed that his verse pattern reflected some transcendent reality, while a contemporary skeptic might claim that the verse pattern is constitutive of that imagined reality. Since we are dealing with a linguistic coherence, however, we need not decide that issue.

Let us turn now to the "theologizing" of this formal pattern. I shall begin with the theological counterpart of the logical structure of autobiography, because it is so clear. The narrative structure we have been describing, like the verse pattern, privileges the *ending*, the moment of closure and makes it coincide with the beginning. This logical reversal is theologically the movement of *conversion*, of death and resurrection. The Christian theme of conversion satisfies the contrary exigencies of autobiography by introducing a radical discontinuity into the sequence of a life thanks to which one can tell one's life story as though it were true, definitive, and concluded. Death in life is closure in the story, but it is thanks to a spiritual resurrection that the story can be told. It was Augustine who set the pattern for this Christian thematization of narrative structure in his *Confessions*, although it might equally well be said that it was the Christian theme that gave rise to the narrative. The logic of definitive autobiography demands conversion, just as conversion, death, and resurrection imply the continuity/discontinuity of the autobiographic form. In this case, the formal pattern and the theology of conversion are identical.

The analogy between this Augustinian pattern and Dante's story is evident in the gap that separates pilgrim and poet. It is further reinforced by about twenty-three addresses to the reader, each of which suggests a progressive movement toward a goal that is the poem's beginning: the pilgrim's story leads to the establishment of the author's status as storyteller, so that the story of the *Divine Comedy* is in part the story of how the story came to be written. The addresses to the reader create a chronological illusion, leading us to understand the evolution of the pilgrim as preceding the telling of the story. In fact, however, the experience of the pilgrim and the telling of the story are one and the same: pilgrim and author are *dialectically* related by the action of the story, for the narrative voice is created by the action of the protagonist in the very act of interrupting it. It is only at the poem's ending that the retrospective illusion is completed, when pilgrim and poet become one. If we were to represent that dialectic in logical form, we would have to describe it as a movement forward in time that is simultaneously a recapitulation. That Dante thinks of this movement as a series of conversions can scarcely be doubted. The ending of the *Inferno* is marked by a literal conversion, a turning upside-down of the pilgrim and his guide, providing a continuity and discontinuity in spatial terms as well as in spiritual terms. The second part of the journey also ends in a *conversion*, with the theological motifs of sanctifying grace whose presence has been convincingly demonstrated by Singleton. Finally, in the transition between nature and supernature, the whole of the universe is turned to mirror the image of God surrounded by his angels.

The theology of conversion perfectly illustrates the tautological argument of autobiography: "I am I, but it was not always so." Here again, I must make reference to Singleton's work on the *Purgatorio*, where he explores the attempts in the Middle Ages to describe conversion, death, and resurrection, in Aristotelian terms, as a movement toward form.[6] Logically, conversion implies a destruction of a previous form and the creation of a new form. Like the process of autobiography, conversion begins with *two* subjects: the sinner who *is* and the saint who *will be*, like the pilgrim who *is* and the author who will be. The evolution of the sinner is toward destruction, the evolution of the saint is toward regeneration. Logically, the movement is two-fold, chronologically it is one, for the first step toward salvation is the first away from sin. Like the dialectics of the poem, wherein pilgrim and narrator are created at the same time, conversion is a *dialectic* of death and resurrection. We may observe in passing that this theological paradox is illustrated in the poem by the symmetry and asymmetry of Hell and Purgatory. The center of the universe is no space-occupying place in the coordinates of moral theology, but simply the logical zero-point of a moral dialectic that leads from mountain-top to mountain-top, from the Prologue scene to the ending of the *Purgatorio*. When the pilgrim says "Io non mori' e non rimasi vivo" (*Inf.* XXXIV.25), he indicates a purely logical point that marks the destruction of an anterior form and the beginning of the generation of a new form, sanctifying grace. From the standpoint of theology, the two processes take place together.

We have discussed the theology of autobiographic structure. It remains for us now to discuss the theology of the movement represented in the formal pattern of both the verse and the pilgrim's path. *Conversion* is the technical term used by theologians to describe the transformation of the Old Testament into the New. That transformation is precisely in the form we have been describing, forward motion toward recapitulation. This movement is the essence of the Christian theory of history referred to by the early Greek fathers of the Church as ἀνακεφαλαίωσις, or *recapitulation*. Irenaeus is the church father most often associated with the theory, which is defined by a modern theologian in words which might equally well describe *terza rima:*

> It means not just flowing backward to the beginning, but movement forward in time as the integration of the beginning in the end, and this is the significance of the movement forward itself, insofar as it is at once in time and above time.[7]

The word itself, ἀνακεφαλαίωσις, comes from Ephesians 1:10, where Christ is described as "the fullness of time." We are told that the eternal plan of the Father was realized by the Son: "and this His good pleasure He purposed in Him, to be dispensed in the fullness of time: to *re-establish* [recapitulate] all things in Christ, both those in the heavens and those on earth."[8] Thus, Christ *is* the recapitulation, the fulfillment of the promise and the return to the beginning, as is said in the Gospel of John: "In the beginning was the Word."

This theory of history is the foundation of Biblical Allegory, God's way of writing narrative, with things rather than signs. It is what Dante called the Allegory of Theologians. According to it, Christ, as the fullness of time, recapitulates all of the preceding history and gives to it its moment of closure. The New Testament must be understood as the fulfillment of the Old, which is to say, its ending. Thus history is the movement of time away from the Word and back to the Word, with all of the persons and events having their own autonomy, yet functioning prefiguratively as signs of their own truth: "di lor vero umbriferi prefazii" (*Par.* xxx.78). The moment of reversal was referred to as the *conversio* of the Old Testament into the New. Christian history or Biblical allegory (they are one and the same) move in the same way as *terza rima* (fig. 4).

Dante gives us only one clue as to the significance of his verse form. The forward movement of *terza rima* is interrupted in the *Paradiso*, where the name of Christ, *Cristo*, appears in rhyme only with itself. It must not be imagined that this is merely pietistic reticence—the name of God, the Holy Spirit and of Mary all appear in rhyme at some point or other in the text. Even if it were, however, we should have to ask why rhyme would be inappropriate for the name of Christ. The answer must be that rhyme *is* the movement of temporality and Christ transcends time. The *now* of the Christ event is underscored even in the tenses of verbs in the *Paradiso* with latinisms "ciò che . . . fatto avea prima, e poi era fatturo" (vi.82–83), said of the eagle, or again, Ripheus and Trajan, who lived in faith, "quel d'i passuri, e quel d'i passi piedi" (xx.105). The three-fold appearance of "Cristo" in the tercet points unmistakably to a recapitulation of past, present, and future in His transcendence. Finally, the name

Fig. 4.

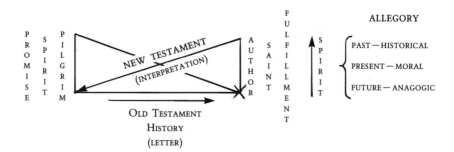

of Christ rhymes with itself twelve times in the *Paradiso*, as if to underscore the zodiacal all-inclusiveness of the fullness of time.

The appearance of the name of Christ three times in a tercet suggests a further elaboration of Biblical allegory which may be worth mentioning here. I have said that Old Testament time should be regarded as the unfolding of time toward its fullness, the New Testament, which is in a sense a recapitulation of all that went before. This structure is the basis of what is usually called figural typology or, to use the language of St. Paul, of the difference between the Letter and the Spirit. The Spirit is the end-term, the moment of closure, the New Testament that gives meaning to the Old. Yet this moment was transcendent—it is the New *and External* Testament, which means that it has three hypostases in time: past, present and future. From this consideration, born in the tradition, no doubt, when it became clear that the fullness of time was not in fact the end of the world, there arose a further elaboration of Christian allegory—the so-called four-fold theory, which should be understood as one plus three: the literal, fulfilled by the Christ-event in history (allegory in the past), the Christ-event in the individual soul (allegory in the present or tropological sense) and finally, the Second Coming (allegory in the future or anagogic sense). In the interstices between the first coming and the second, there is the founding of the Church and the work of the Redemption of individual souls, but history properly speaking is concluded with the first coming (fig. 5).

With reference to the time after the Crucifixion, the word *recapitulatio* has a history in the Latin West. As originally used in the Greek church, it suggested above all universal restoration, a theory that survives in Latin exegesis in the idea of Christ as the New Adam. In the West, with the

Fig. 5.

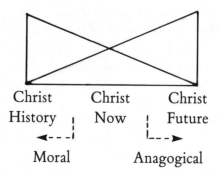

Donatist Tychonius, it comes to have a more specialized meaning, as one
of the seven rules for the interpretation of Scripture. A recapitulation is
made when a Biblical writer speaks simultaneously of both the type and
the anti-type, the promise and the fulfillment.[9] It was in this form that
the term was passed on to the Latin West, through the extensive paraphrase
made of Tychonius' remarks by Augustine in the *De doctrina christiana*.
Like the story of the *Divine Comedy*, Christian history is a forward motion toward an end-term which is the beginning: "In the beginning was
the word . . . and the word was made flesh."

We have examined a formal pattern in Dante's work and have explored
theological parallels, ancient and medieval thematizations of that pattern.
I do not by any means wish to suggest that these theological motifs are
"solid historical grounding" for Dante's poetics, as does Auerbach in his
search for an historical valorization of his critical judgement. On the contrary, I should like to suggest quite the reverse: the theological principles
that seem to underlie Dante's formal pattern are themselves in turn derived from literary principles. The Christian theory of recapitulation is
derived from linguistic categories. If one wished to trace the origins of the
use of the word ἀνακεφαλαιώσις, it would surely be in the realm of rhetoric. Both the orator Lysias and Aristotle use the word to mean a verbal
summary, or the summation of a statement: "rerum congregatio et repe-
titio," to use the definition of Quintilian.[10] It would seem that the theory
of history derives from the attempt to superimpose linguistic closure on
the realm of temporality, transforming entropy, what Augustine would
call fallen time, into formal discourse, the time redeemed. If it is possible
to see in Dante's literary form a reflection of his theological beliefs, then it
is equally possible to see in that theology the projection of literary forms.

Of all of the Fathers of the Church, Augustine, orator and Bishop,
was most aware of the analogy between the realm of words and the
Theology of the Word. His discussion of the rule of recapitulation in the
De doctrina christiana moves from an understanding of the term as a literary
device to its application to Biblical exegesis. There is no conflict in his
mind between literary interpretation and salvation history; on the contrary, poetry was for him the emblem of intelligibility in the cosmos. Just
as meter gave a pattern and a regularity to the otherwise open-ended flow
of our words, so God's providential intent gave meaning to the flow of
time. History itself might be said to be God's poem, saved from both
the timeless eternity of the Platonists and the death of the fall by the Word,

through whom the time was redeemed. In such a plan, human lives are the syllables, ordered to one another according to the meter of Providence, and death is no more than the syntactic silence necessary for meaning to emerge.[11]

One passage from the *Confessions* might well serve as a recapitulation of all that I have said. It is so suggestive for understanding the homologies in Dante's poem that Dante might well have had it in mind. It occurs as an illustration of the nature of time:

> Suppose that I am going to recite a song (*canticum*) that I know. Before I begin, my faculty of expectation is engaged by the whole of it. But once I have begun, as much of the song as I have removed from the province of expectation and relegated to the past now engages my memory, and the scope of the action which I am performing is divided between the two faculties of memory and expectation, the one looking back to the part which I have already recited, the other looking forward to the part which I have still to recite. But my faculty of attention is present all the while, and through it passes what was the future in the process of becoming the past. As the process continues, the province of memory is extended in proportion as that of expectation is reduced, until the whole of my expectation is absorbed. This happens when I have finished my recitation and it has all passed into the province of memory.[12]

This discussion of the nature of time conforms exactly to the movement of *terza rima*. If we think of the second of the triple rhyme as the *now* of recitation, it is equally divided between the memory of repetition and the anticipation of the third and last rhyme of the series (fig. 6).

Fig. 6.

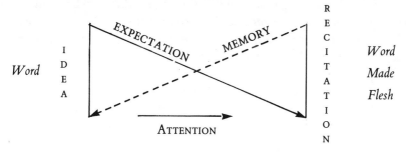

Augustine refers to the *canticum* as known by heart, which is another way of referring to its tautological character. The ending is the beginning, for recitation is the performance, or unfolding, of a text previously known in its entirety. As in the act of speech, we move from the intentionality of the speaker to the performance of the speech, syllable by syllable, until it is completely sounded in time. The silence that follows the speech exactly corresponds to the silence that preceded it. Time, in such a context, is impressed, like syntax, into the service of significance.

This, of course, is the central metaphor of Christian history. God's Word, pre-existing for all time, is recited by all of history until, in the fullness of time, it is made flesh. The human spirit, which repeats this action with its three faculties of memory, attention, and expectation (or, to use later Augustinian terminology, memory, intelligence, and will) reflects, in this respect, the Trinity of Father, Son, and Holy Spirit. It is in the *now* of the Word, the Logos, that the present moment becomes all-encompassing.

Augustine's passage on the nature of time goes on to express the series of homologies, of ever-increasing dimension, from the syllabic to the autobiographical to the eschatological:

> What is true of the whole song is also true of all its parts and of each syllable. It is true of any longer action in which I may be engaged and of which the recitation of the song may be only a small part. It is true of a man's whole life, of which all his actions are parts. It is true of the whole history of mankind, of which each man's life is a part.

Whether the grounding of Dante's poem is in the formal, syllabic structure of its cantos or in the *canticum* of the universe, its rhyme scheme remains the same. It begins and ends in duality, for there can be no memory in the first instant nor any further expectation at the last. Like the Hegelian dialectic,[13] its modern analogue, *terza rima* represents a model for the synthesis of time and meaning into history.

Notes

1. "Figura," in *Scenes from the Drama of European Literature* (New York: Meridian, 1959).

2. *The Rhetoric of Religion: Studies in Logology* (Berkeley: University of California Press, 1970), pp. 1–7.

3. "The Vistas in Retrospect," in *Atti del Congresso internazionale di studi danteschi 20–27 Aprile 1965* (Florence: Sansoni, 1965), pp. 279–303.

4. "Dante's Pilgrim in a Gyre," *PMLA*, LXXVI, 4 (1961).

5. Freccero, p. 183.

6. *Dante Studies 2: Journey to Beatrice* (Cambridge, Mass.: Harvard University Press, 1958), pp. 57ff.

7. Hans Urs von Balthasar, *A Theology of History* (New York: Sheed and Ward, 1963), p.59.

8. For the doctrine, see E. Scharl, *Recapitulatio mundi*, Freiburger Theologische Studien, LX (Freiburg im Breisgau: Herder u. Co., 1941).

9. St. Augustine, *On Christian Doctrine* III.30, trans. D. W. Robertson (New York: Liberal Arts Press, 1958), p. 104 and the notes on Tychonius *ad loc*. I am grateful to my friend Robert Kaske for calling this passage to my attention.

10. See Scharl, p. 6–7.

11. *Confessions* IV.10, trans. R. S. Pine-Coffin (London: Penguin, 1961), p. 80.

12. Ibid., XI.28; p. 278. I have changed the word "psalm" to "song," which I believe to be more accurate.

13. The analogy between the theory of history of Ephesians and Hegel's dialectic is implicit in the title used by the theologian A. Lindemann, *Die Aufhebung der Zeit* (Gütersloh: Gütersloher Verlagshaus, 1975).

Tassonomie dantesche

EZIO RAIMONDI

ERNST ROBERT CURTIUS, in un paragrafo dantesco del suo *Europäische Literatur und lateinisches Mittelalter*, lamentava l'assenza di studi intorno al raggruppamento e alla classificazione dei personaggi nella *Commedia*, per quanto questa sintagmatica, a volerla chiamare con un termine di oggi, restasse il presupposto di ogni analisi del poema. L'esegesi critica, egli suggeriva, doveva dunque portare la sua attenzione sull'inventario enciclopedico del "personale" dantesco ed esplorarne analiticamente l'architettura interna, tanto più in quanto da una simile indagine tecnico-artistica dipendeva poi la possibilità di riconoscere non solo in che modo il poeta avesse strutturato il suo museo di eroi e anti-eroi ma ancora se l'operazione comportasse diverse fasi stilistiche. A giudizio del Curtius, dopo una prima serie di abili sondaggi, la straordinaria novità della regìa dantesca nello sfruttare il tesoro onomastico della cultura classica e di quella medievale nasceva dall'irruzione della storia, dall'ansia appassionata del presente, dalla violenza univoca di un destino che conferiva un senso omogeneo e drammaticamente personale alla *summa* delle figure e degli esempi nel loro stesso articolarsi narrativo. La storia si congiungeva con ciò che era fuori del tempo per formare un'unica realtà, in funzione di un io penitente identificato con la coscienza offesa di tutti gli uomini.[1]

Proprio nel senso auspicato dal Curtius, ma partendo da altre premesse di cultura, ancora lontane dallo storicismo della filologia romantica, un tentativo d'analisi del principio secondo cui si organizza una "serie" o un blocco di personaggi danteschi si può già ritrovare nella *Sposizione* del Castelvetro: e giova allora prenderne conoscenza sia per la forte personalità del critico, a cui il Vico non negava la lode di "acutissimo", sia per il procedimento di cui si vale la sua lettura, che in fondo costituisce un esempio quanto mai lucido di strutturalismo aristotelico. L'occasione per l'appunto è offerta al Castelvetro dai canti di Malebolge, nelle ultime pagine del suo commento, allorché "l'artificio del poeta" sta dinanzi al lettore in tutti i suoi effetti e se ne può quindi ricostruire la formula generativa risalendo dal particolare al generale, quasi fosse una veduta d'insieme in grado finalmente di cogliere i rapporti, le costanti architettoniche di uno spettacolo. L'interesse del critico si appunta perciò non sulla individualità delle persone o sulla loro valenza connotativa, come vorrebbe un Curtius, ma sulla distribuzione della loro immagine nello spazio del racconto, sulla tipologia dei gesti e dei comportamenti, sulla grammatica delle posizioni che si determinano a volta a volta nei confronti di Dante personaggio. Il testo intanto si traduce in una sorta di luogo teatrale e richiede in chi legge l'occhio d'un osservatore o di uno scenografo, tanto più pronto a visualizzare una mimesi narrativa, "guardando la favola", quanto più gli riesce di rintracciarne l'ordine combinatorio, la sintassi dei predicati e le sue invarianti rispetto alla molteplicità dei soggetti. Il metodo che gli occorre poi è quello della logica aristotelica secondo i modi che il Castelvetro coniuga nella sua interpretazione della *Poetica*, con una tendenza evidentissima verso una forma di pensiero spaziale abbastanza simile all'orientamento visivo della nuova scuola ramista.

E difatti anche il critico dantesco adotta nel suo esercizio la tecnica della "distinzione", vale a dire della dicotomia riproposta a gradi successivi in modo da ordinare tutti i termini di un insieme. Così, in rapporto alla topografia e all'alto conseguente del vedere i "dannati" dell'ottavo cerchio "ora d'in su la ripa più alta e d'in su il ponte, ed ora d'in su il colmo del ponte, ed ora nelle bolge stesse, ed ora d'in su la ripa più bassa", la prima distinzione che s'istituisce riguarda il movimento poiché "alcuni vanno intorno" e "alcuni stanno fermi".[2] Essa conduce subito alla ripartizione, tanto in un gruppo come nell'altro, di "cinque maniere", con una simmetria, si potrebbe dire, imperfetta: "Vanno intorno i ruffiani e gli ingannatori delle donne nella prima bolgia; vanno intorno gli indovini ed i negromanti nella quarta bolgia; vanno intorno gl'ipocriti nella sesta bolgia; vanno intorno gli astuti nell'ottava bolgia; vanno intorno gli scismatici e gli scandalosi nella nona bolgia. Stanno fermi i lusinghieri nella seconda bolgia; stanno fermi i simoniaci nella terza bolgia; stanno fermi i barattieri nella quinta bolgia; stanno fermi i ladri nella settima bolgia; stanno fermi i falsari nella decima bolgia".

Se poi, continuando, si esamina il sottoinsieme caratterizzato dal movimento, si scoprono al suo interno due nuove disgiunzioni. L'una deriva dal fatto che alcuni dei peccatori procedono "tutti insieme col volto volto verso il ponte dalla mano destra" di Dante e altri "vanno intorno" parte rivolti verso il ponte "dalla sinistra" parte con lo sguardo verso il ponte "dalla destra". Gli indovini e i negromanti, gli ipocriti, gli astuti, gli scismatici e gli scandalosi guardano a destra, mentre la sinistra orienta i ruffiani e la destra interessa di nuovo gli ingannatori. La seconda "distinzione" si determina invece considerando la possibilità di vedere i peccatori "nel volto", come accade per i ruffiani e gli ingannatori delle donne, per gli indovini e i negromanti, per gli scismatici e gli scandalosi, oppure l'esserne privati, e questo è il caso degli ipocriti e degli astuti, i quali a propria volta si suddividono in altre due categorie secondo che si possa parlare o non parlare con loro "di lontano". Quanto al sottoinsieme vuoto di movimento, la dicotomia che la attraversa somma di fatto le azioni del "vedere" e del "parlare di lontano": dalla parte positiva del processo ottico-acustico si dispongono i lusinghieri, i barattieri e i falsari, e a quella negativa si aggregano i simoniaci e i ladri.

A questo punto diventa necessario per il nostro critico l'ausilio grafico di una "figura", la quale non è altro che uno schema riassuntivo di tipo diagrammatico, perché "meglio s'apprenda" il sistema di relazioni disgiuntive che si sono venute disegnando. Ma per ora conviene lasciarlo da parte e seguire piuttosto il ragionamento che si sviluppa dopo, non appena il discorso ritorna alle funzioni dello spazio, definite dal parametro dell'altezza. Esse sono la "ripa più alta", il "ponte", la "ripa più bassa", il "fondo della bolgia", e condizionando sempre il campo ottico e verbale del pellegrino dantesco di fronte ai peccatori, fissano un nuovo reticolato di rapporti. Scrive il Castelvetro nel suo stile didascalico, fermo e preciso, quasi da catalogo tecnico:

1. 1. Dalla ripa più alta della prima bolgia si veggono i ruffiani. II.
1. Dal ponte della prima gli 'ngannatori delle donne. 2. Dal ponte della seconda i lusinghieri. 3. Dal ponte della quarta gli 'ndovini ed i negromanti. 4. Dal ponte della quinta i barattieri. 5. Dal ponte

dell'ottava gli astuti. 6. Dal ponte della nona gli scismatici e gli scandalosi. 7. Dal ponte della decima i falsari. III. 1. Dalla ripa più bassa della quinta i barattieri. 2. Dalla ripa più bassa della decima i falsari. IV. 1. Nel fondo della terza i simoniaci. 2. Nel fondo della sesta gl'ipocriti. 3. Nel fondo della settima i ladri. V. 1. Dalla ripa più alta e dal ponte della prima bolgia i ruffiani e gli 'ngannatori delle donne. VI. 1. Dal ponte e dalla ripa più bassa della quinta i barattieri. 2. Dal ponte e dalla ripa più bassa della decima i falsari.

Tratteggiata la mappa funzionale di Malebolge e correlata con la doppia costante della direzione verso destra o sinistra e dell'incontro a faccia a faccia, si può finalmente affrontare la dinamica narrativa della "favola" e misurarne la coerenza una volta che vi si inserisce il movimento di Dante personaggio con le necessità strutturali delle sue parti dialogiche. Alla lucerna del suo razionalismo aristotelico, puntiglioso e implacabile, il Castelvetro definisce "sconvenevolezza", anomalia, deviazioni, smagliatura, tutto ciò che non risulta motivato all'interno del modello che ha costruito; e tuttavia, proprio mentre segnala gli esiti abnormi e incongrui, rende anche conto di un processo inventivo nel suo margine di arbitrio, di gioco a sorpresa, di tattica contingente. Si direbbe anzi che il metodo critico del Castelvetro abbia bisogno del negativo per qualificare gli aspetti più interessanti di un testo. Così, per l'appunto, nel racconto dantesco la norma del salire "in su il colmo del ponte" e del guardare i dannati "in faccia rivolta verso il ponte a destra" viene a cadere nel caso dei ruffiani che hanno il viso "verso il ponte a sinistra", ed ecco perché il protagonista "si fa porre giù da Gerione in su la ripa più alta della prima bolgia, lontano alquanto dal ponte" in modo da poterli vedere "in faccia" prima di giungere a quest'ultimo. Ma l'espediente produce di riflesso due "sconvenevolezze": l'una in quanto Gerione depone i pellegrini "in luogo dove non gli doveva porre, cioè lontano dal ponte", mentre sarebbe stato ragionevole lasciarli "a piè del ponte, sapendo egli la cagione per la quale andavano per lo 'nferno, e quale via era buona per loro"; e l'altra legata al fatto che i peccatori vengono scorti e apostrofati "dalla ripa più alta della prima bolgia" senza che si spieghi come mai, contrariamente a quanto accade nelle altre bolge, dove non è possibile "vedere i puniti della ripa più alta", essi possano "prestare più agio di veduta e di favella" che altrove. Allo stesso modo, siccome gli ipocriti nascondono il proprio volto col cappuccio e non si può discorrere con loro a una certa distanza, si capovolge la situazione facendo sì che non vi sia "ponte sopra la sesta bolgia" in seguito al terremoto per la passione di Cristo e che Dante e Virgilio siano costretti a "lasciarsi cadere giù dalla ripa più alta infino al fondo della bolgia", vicino ai peccatori, per paura dei demonî e della loro ira. L'aggiustatura è possibile solo a prezzo di altre incongruenze, dal momento che resta inesplicabile perché sia andato in rovina proprio il ponte della sesta bolgia, inoltre non si comprende un mutamento nei diavoli così maligno dopo che tutto l'escludeva, e infine bisogna che Virgilio assuma un "corpo saldo" in contraddizione con l'"ombra" che gli viene attribuita nel *Purgatorio*.

Senonché, rileva subito il critico citando la *Poetica* di Aristotele, si tratta di contraddizioni o dissonanze "tolerabili" giacché "servono alla constituzione della favola" e sono quindi indispensabili all'ordito del racconto, che verrebbe compromesso se si cercasse di sopprimerle.[3] La loro motivazione è data dall'impossibilità di "levare via" la sequenza "non ragionevole" senza "distruggere la favola" al livello della forma del contenuto. Tale principio però vale assai meno allorché si esaminano le discordanze negli incontri con i peccatori "fermi", i quali, quando se ne vuole avere "poca sperienza" sono ritratti "d'in su l'arco del ponte", ma per una conoscenza "più piena" si offrono alla vista e alla parola del viandante mentre egli entra nel loro campo semantico dopo averli adocchiati "d'in su l'arco del ponte" o "andando lungo la ripa più bassa" o "scendendo nel fondo della bolgia". Viceversa i "lusinghieri attuffati nello sterco" vengono visti "d'in su il ponte" in quanto il pellegrino non può "scendere al fondo" per via del liquame e le "ripe" risultano tali da impedire lo sguardo, non avendo lo scrittore trovato, al pensiero del Castelvetro, una "cagione opportuna per la quale potesse andare lungo la ripa più bassa" a causa del "terzo ponte" unito col secondo. A sua volta la ragione per cui si possono osservare i barattieri "d'in su l'arco del ponte ed ancora andando lungo la ripa più bassa" sta nella "rottura del ponte sesto", che costringe Dante a camminare "lungo la ripa" alla ricerca di un altro passaggio. E la stessa cosa si ripete per i falsari, nella bolgia decima, poiché il movimento "lungo la ripa" deve portare a scoprire "la via che conduce al pozzo de' giganti", di nuovo contro la legge della "verisimilitudine", rispetto alla quale non sembra affatto conveniente la trovata messa in atto dal narratore.

Se si ragiona sulla base del verosimile, punto d'approdo e di verifica di ogni modello narrativo, appare anomala anche la discesa del pellegrino "co' suoi piedi" "nel fondo" della settima bolgia "per le pietre che si sporgevano in fuori dalla ripa e per poco facevano scala", con l'effetto di rendere impossibile la visuale dal "ponte" al contrario di quella da tutti gli altri. Altrettanto illogico, nota il Castelvetro, è che la "ripa più bassa" consenta a chi vi s'inoltra di procedere a piedi e nello stesso tempo neghi ai suoi occhi di mirare i ladri nella bolgia. Ma che dire allora di quanto succede nella terza bolgia, dove il personaggio di Dante non può calarsi da solo ma viene portato da Virgilio senza che vi sia un motivo specifico per differenziare l'evento da quello del tutto simile della settima, e dove la variante implica per giunta che la guida sia dotata anch'essa di un corpo, riproponendo così l'incongruenza della discesa. Infatti, se Virgilio può muoversi con il peso del compagno verso il "foro" di papa Nicolò terzo, non si vede perché non possa farlo anche lo stesso Dante, libero com'è da ogni carico.

In definitiva l'attenzione del critico si concentra tutta sulle trasgressioni del sistema e sulle loro conseguenze a catena. Eppure non vi è dubbio, quanto più esse divengono palesi tanto più si entra nell' "artificio" dello scrittore, che nella fattispecie è "l'artificio usato intorno a' luoghi", e se ne svelano le astuzie segrete, i ricuperi interni, le mistificazioni e le manovre per aggirare la norma del verosimile quando essa viene a porsi in conflitto con le ragioni inventive o espressive del racconto. Come insegnava il commentatore aristotelico, nella "particella quarta" della "parte quarta" della *Poetica* a cui rinvia anche l'esegeta dantesco, ogni volta che la "favola" è costruita di elementi "non ragionevoli" e questi non fungono da cardine necessario della sua armatura generativa "bisogna fare sparire la sconvenevolezza con la conditura della vaghezza de' sentimenti e della favella", cioè "coprirle col mantello d'altri beni" con un'arte che ha il suo esempio più alto in Omero.[4] E anche per Malebolge il Castelvetro sottoscrive tacitamente la stessa conclusione.

Ora che si è percorso l'intero tracciato del discorso critico intorno all' "artificio" dell'episodio dantesco, diventa più facile e quasi naturale retrocedere alla "figura" con cui il lettore della *Sposizione* aveva riassunto, al modo di una sintesi visiva, il suo capitolo di rilievi e di categorie binarie. In un procedimento come quello del Castelvetro, che si fonda sulle "distinzioni" e sul loro snodarsi a livelli successivi entro la forma del contenuto, il ragionamento comporta una serie di formule fisse, quasi di unità classematiche, usate come cifre di un calcolo dove si registrano presenza e assenza, positivo e negativo; e perciò il modo migliore per presentarne i risultati, per metterli a frutto in un'analisi successiva con un massimo di evidenza e di ordine, è quello di una tabella schematica sincronizzando nell'immagine della pagina il quadro di relazioni che si sono scoperte a

poco a poco. Ecco allora la "figura" antropologica di Malebolge, che non
sarà inutile, a questo punto, avere sotto gli occhi:

Dannati o puniti nelle bolge

Alcuni vanno intorno		*Alcuni stanno fermi*	
	Ruffiani ed ingannatori delle donne		Lusinghieri
	Indovini e negromanti		Simoniaci
	Ipocriti		Barattieri
	Astuti		Ladri
	Scismatici		Falsari

Degli andanti intorno

Alcuni voltano il volto a destra verso il ponte		*Alcuni parte verso il ponte a sinistra e parte a destra*	
	Indovini		Ruffiani
	Ipocriti		ed ingannatori
	Astuti		di donne
	Scismatici		

Degli andanti intorno

Alcuni si possono vedere		*Alcuni non si possono vedere*	
	Ruffiani ed ingannatori di donne		Ipocriti
	Indovini e negromanti		Astuti
	Scismatici e scandalosi		

Degli andanti intorno che non si possono vedere

Con alcuni si può favellare di lontano		*Con alcuni non si può favellare di lontano*	
	Astuti		Ipocriti

Di coloro che stanno fermi

Alcuni si possono vedere di lontano e si può favellare con loro		*Alcuni non si possono vedere di lontano, né si può favellare con loro*	
	Lusinghieri		Simoniaci
	Barattieri		Ladri
	Falsari		

Il commento dantesco non prospetta altri esempi di visualizzazione argomentativa a "gioghi", il termine risale allo stesso Castelvetro: quello che s'è appena visto resta l'unico, anche se sintomatico. Ma basta riprendere in mano la *Poetica* per accertare attraverso la sua frequenza d'uso che il processo diagrammatico gioca una parte importante nel metodo analitico del Castelvetro, il quale è quanto mai consapevole della sua funzione, come indicano le didascalie che introducono sempre le "figure". La frase d'apertura del grafico dantesco, che vuole "far vedere tutta la distinzione come in figura accioché meglio s'apprenda", si moltiplica nelle pagine della *Poetica* con la costanza di un formulario, dal tipo "E accioché si comprenda meglio la predetta distinzione, la proporremo come in figura dinanzi agli occhi", "Ma accioché si comprenda meglio quello che è stato detto e quasi si sottoponga al senso dell'occhio, si figurerà nella 'nfrascritta forma", "Ora acciochè le cose di sopra dette si possano meglio comprendere e riporre nella memoria, le raccoglieremo in poche parole e proporremo come in figura", "La quale, accioché più chiaramente si comprenda, mostrerò come in figura"; a quelli "E chiaramente ciò si può vedere nella 'nfrascritta figura", "Ma prima facciamo vedere in brievi e manifeste parole le divisioni di sopra poste", "veggiamo come in figura le cose dette infino a qui", "Ora dimostriamo i capi delle cose ragionate da noi in questa materia del riso in figura", "Ora le cose dette, per le 'nfrascritte cinque differenze possonsi quasi sottoporre agli occhi della fronte", "la qual cosa si può ancora più manifestamente vedere per la 'nfrascritta figura", "Adunque mostreremo come in figura le sopradette sei differenzie di vocali", "Le quali composizioni riescono diciotto, come si può vedere chiaramente per gli 'nfrascritti accompagnamenti", "Solamente faremo vedere come in figura di sei carrette i sei trapassamenti, così", "Ma accioché pienamente e distintamente si conosca la cosa star così, le porrò per ordine seperate e accompagnate".[5]

In tutti questi casi lo schema che viene a disegnarsi è sempre a elenco dicotomico e ramificato, con "brievi e manifeste parole". Solo in due circostanze si ricorre a un diagramma di altro genere, una volta per "assomigliare non senza debita proporzione ciascuna diceria e ciascuna tragedia ad una grata che abbia per la lunghezza le parti di qualità che discorrano per tutta lei come verghe e per lo traverso le parti di quantità che non comprendano se non certo spazio prescritto come altre verghe", e una seconda per descrivere, a proposito del dramma di Fedra, come "la cagione, l'operazione e la passione generano e sieno generate l'una dall'altra", raffigurandone il movimento e lo spettro in un "cerchio o rota". Ma più

ancora della griglia e del suo sistema di coordinate, che pure è di grande
interesse, richiederebbe forse un'analisi a parte l'anatomia del personaggio
tragico perché essa si integra, con un'eleganza grafica che di solito non
è concessa alla parola del Castelvetro, in una prospettiva strutturale di carattere dinamico, modellata intelligentemente sul campo di forze che si
muovono e s'affrontano nello spazio scenico.[6]

Di fatto, a giudicare dalle stesse dichiarazioni del critico, il metodo delle
"figure" viene incontro a un'esigenza pedagogica di economia e di chiarezza,
di "ordine" razionale e di "disposizione" efficace per "riporre nella memoria"
un materiale diviso o distinto con "regolata via d'insegnamento": e in questo
il Castelvetro sembra vicinissimo a Pierre de la Ramée, al suo programma
di una dialettica moderna nella quale l'astrazione scientifica viene mediata
da una componente visiva come *dispositio* geometrica dei concetti, come
inventario di elementi che si possono manovrare e riaggregare secondo
leggi appropriate. L'altro punto di forza del metodo ramista è poi un'arte
topologica della memoria, a quanto risulta dalle indagini informatissime
e sapienti della Yates, di Paolo Rossi e di Walter J. Ong. Quest'ultimo,
a cui si devono gli studi più suggestivi sul ramismo e sul suo significato
nella storia della cultura, ha anche sottilmente chiarito come non si possa
intendere l'affermarsi della logica ramista senza una nuova sensibilità
"diagrammatica" promossa e amplificata dall'uso della stampa e dai modelli
spaziali che essa impone. Nella pratica del ramismo la fortuna di cui godono
gli schemi e i diagrammi didascalici è dovuta al fatto che l'operazione mentale
viene iscritta in uno spazio che è un insieme di "luoghi" e i termini del
linguaggio si riducono a segmenti permutabili, a strutture che si possono
rappresentare nella pagina, e divengono così segni di un universo silen-
zioso dove il suono perde la sua aura magica a mano a mano che il discorso si fa chiaro e distinto. Alla geometrizzazione della logica, sempre per
seguire l'itinerario dell'Ong, si accompagna un'attitudine percettiva d'ordine strutturale che traduce ogni processo della mente in un reticolo di
dicotomie grafiche, con un incremento notevolissimo dell'immaginazione
ottica e del suo modo analitico di distinguere il rapporto delle forme col-
locandole sempre in un ambito preciso che le contenga e le ordini. Così
l'uomo del ramismo è anche l'uomo di Gutenberg: il senso che prevale
in lui è la vista, l'occhio che contempla e misura un'estensione spaziale.[7]

Se anche il Castelvetro, il quale non per nulla cita Rodolfo Agricola,
condivide l'impulso intellettuale che si esprime nella cultura ramista e vi
ritrova forse un'altra conferma del suo razionalismo ascetico di cristiano

riformato, non stupisce affatto che proprio nella *Poetica* si legga un paragrafo quasi canonico sull' "occhio della fronte" e su quello della "mente", che sembra dare ragione, con la forza di una testimonianza interna, alla tesi riflessa dell'Ong. È il punto, alla "particella quinta" della "parte quarta", in cui l'interprete aristotelico conclude che "conviene il tutto dell'animale sia compreso dall'occhio in uno sguardo e 'l tutto della favola sia compreso dalla memoria in un tempo, se se ne dee trarre compiuto diletto". Subito dopo, integrando Aristotele, egli soggiunge:

> l'occhio della fronte e l'occhio della mente paiono essere dotati in certo modo d'una medesima potenza e in congiugnere e mettere insieme le cose divise e seperate e di più farne una, e in dividere e seperare l'unità delle cose e la congiunzione e d'una farne più. Come l'occhio corporale, se altri d'in su un colle rimira uno essercito posto in un piano, cioè tante cose divise che sono in uno essercito e seperate, uomini, cavalli, padiglioni, tende, lance, spade, usberghi, elmi e che no?, congiugne e mette insieme, e di tutte le predette cose fa una sola e la riguarda e la comprende in una sola veduta. E dall'altra parte, pogniamo, d'una donna, che è cosa sola e una, fa più parti e divisioni, seperando ancora dal tutto un picciolo neo o alcuni pelucci, li quali solamente vede in uno sguardo, non adocchiando alcuna dell'altre parti. E l'occhio della mente vede e considera come una cosa sola la spezie dell'uomo o del cavallo o d'altro animale, che si riempie d'infiniti uomini o cavalli o altri animali, e divide e sepera con la considerazione le cose che sono une e inseperabili per natura e le vede come se fossero più, sì come s'imagina la sustanza nuda senza gli accidenti o gli accidenti senza la sustanza.[8]

Nessuno avrebbe potuto illustrare meglio la natura dell'astrazione visiva e la logica analitico-sintetica immanente alla costituzione del diagramma, per cui la "figura" funziona come una scena tanto per l'occhio della fronte quanto per quello dell'intelletto: una scena non dissimile da una tavola anatomica, dove, ancora secondo le parole della *Poetica*, "molti, non potendo senza noia guardare le membra umane secate per imparare a medicare, le considerano dipinte con diletto e ne traggono utili insegnamenti" in virtù della "somiglianza con la cosa rassomigliata".[9] E in più appare ora evidente che l'immagine del guardare un esercito "d'in su un colle" nell'unità delle sue forme molteplici delinea in anticipo, sul piano per l'appunto di un modello, l'operazione che compie il lettore dell'*Inferno* dantesco allorché divide e ricombina, sino ai "pelucci", gli elementi narrativi e topologici di Malebolge. D'altro canto, se si torna alla *Sposizione*, vi s'incontra di nuovo il riferimento all'occhio esterno e interno dell'osservatore, ma solo per censurare il *vidi* del poeta al principio del canto XXVIII: "altri potrebbe opporre a Dante così: più potente è l'occhio della mente che non è l'occhio della fronte e più vede quello che questo: come dunque, se Dante vide quelle diversità di fedite con gli occhi della fronte, sì come egli afferma, 'che io ora vidi,' non si potrebbono ancora vedere con gli occhi della mente e comprendere assai più agevolmente?" L'occhio mentale non è altro, in fondo, che l'acume dell'intelletto e dell'immaginazione, da cui dipende il "trovare e riconoscere le similitudini e le dissimilitudini in cose diverse".[10]

Si è già notato che il negativo rende sempre lo sguardo critico del Castelvetro più penetrante, e anche qui la sua domanda definisce *e contrario* il carattere plastico e concreto della visione dantesca, l'unica degna, per la *Poetica*, del "particolareggiare" omerico. Ma la dichiarazione della superiorità dell'occhio intellettuale su quello sensibile, la potenza del vedere con l'"immaginazione" di un "ingegno acuto", ha soprattutto un significato per il critico che scrive, per il lettore "filosofante".[11] In essa sembra racchiusa la sua ambizione, la sua utopia: l'utopia di una critica che vuole essere l'occhio speculativo puntato su un testo per "separare e congiungere" le cose a cui ha dato forma e parola l'occhio della fronte, lo sguardo del poeta attraverso il quale si rinnova lo spettacolo dell'universo.

Note

1. Cfr. E. R. Curtius, *Europäische Literatur und lateinisches Mittelalter* (Bern: H. Francke AG Verlag, 1948), p. 368 sgg.

2. Cfr. *Sposizione di Lodovico Castelvetro a* xxix *canti dell'Inferno dantesco* ora per la prima volta data in luce da Giovanni Franciosi (Modena: Tipi della Società tipografica, 1886), p. 403 sgg.

3. Cfr. appunto la *Poetica d'Aristotele vulgarizzata et sposta per Lodovico Castelvetro* (Basilea, 1576), p. 566 o 571, dove si può ritrovare la formula "constituzione della favola" usata anche nel commento dantesco.

4. Cfr. *Poetica d'Aristotele*, p. 571.

5. Ibid., pp. 523, 287, 202, 349, 175, 272, 230, 98, 421, 49, 415, 440, 28, 46.

6. Ibid., pp. 258 e 231.

7. Cfr. W. J. Ong, S.J., *Ramus: Method, and the Decay of Dialogue* (Cambridge, Massachusetts: Harvard University Press, 1958).

8. Cfr. *Poetica d'Aristotele*, p. 167.

9. Ibid., p. 71. Anche il Castelvetro, se si deve stare a queste riflessioni che approfondiscono il senso e il metodo della "figura", dovrebbe prendere posto in quella "storia dei diagrammi e degli schemi" che vagheggia un critico d'intelligente e moderna sensibilità come John Hollander (cfr. il suo *Vision and Resonance: Two Senses of Poetic Form* [New York: Oxford University Press, 1975], p. 226).

10. Cfr. *Sposizione*, p. 373. Quanto al "riconoscere le similitudini in cose diverse", che è poi, aristotelicamente, la ragione stessa del metaforeggiare e del pensiero analogico, si deve sempre avere presente l'esegesi filosofica di G. Della Volpe, *Poetica del Cinquecento* (Bari: Laterza, 1954).

11. Anche il poeta, del resto, secondo il Castelvetro, "in componendo la favola e in vestendola di favella, non se la fa rappresentare in atto o tutta o parte, ma se la propone davanti con l'immaginazione come se la vedesse rappresentare in atto" (*Poetica d'Aristotele*, p. 369).

Pier della Vigna's Metamorphosis: Iconography and History

ANTHONY K. CASSELL

A CURIOUS MYOPIA HAS LED CRITICS examining Dante's episode of the suicides in *Inferno* XIII and XIV to concentrate on the surface value of the episode, on the literal significance of the verses while blinding them to the profound moral and spiritual questions.[1] Historians and literary critics generally divide into two camps concerning Pier della Vigna. The former, though giving lip service to the greatness of the *Commedia*, usually see Dante as only a rather poor, somewhat biased secondary source for the facts of Piero's guilt and death. While *letterati* take Piero's words in the poem at face value and declare his tragic innocence, historians examine contemporary documents and declare his ignominious guilt.[2] There is, critics must accept, ample historic evidence of the Notary's criminality, not of *lèse majesté*, but of corruption in office, perversion of justice, and self-enrichment at the expense of the innocent and the state. In addition, a close examination of the poem's major images and a new analysis of the iconography of the cantos will show that the Poet, far from exculpating his personage, considers him guilty, not only of suicide, but indeed of other crimes which led, in the view of an orthodox Christian, typically, dogmatically, and almost inexorably to it.

Though the greater number of Dante scholars now distinguishes between "Dante Poet" and "Dante Wayfarer," critics examining these cantos, almost without exception, have ignored this useful separation. They accept the narrow view of Dante *personaggio,* sympathizing without reflection with Piero's protestation of innocence and with the sense of loss and despair he suffers through eternity. In so doing, they put aside the objective judgment of Dante *poeta* as a reflection of Divine Justice, ignoring that this very judgment condemned Piero to the circle of the violent, amidst the horror and repugnance of a trackless waste, a poisonous wood populated with filthy Harpies, resounding with moans and cries of despair and pain. The romantic elevation of Pier della Vigna to the status of great-souled hero is unacceptable in the context of the poem as a whole and such a reading is impossible in the Poet's own severe concept of Christian justice. In the following pages we will demonstrate that Dante was aware that Pier della Vigna's violence toward himself was historically the culmination of an inveterate rapacity and violence against others. Clearly, Piero's self-righteous view of himself as "giusto" cannot be shared by God nor, ultimately, by the Poet. No clearer discrepancy between the views of the damned and the divine perspective could be cited than the manner in which Piero praises Frederick II, "che fu d'onor sì degno" ("who was so worthy of honor"), and the reality of the place which the Emperor holds in Hell among the burning heretics. Indeed, in the Poet's view the suicides are lower than the animals. Their souls are turned to stocks, sentient but knotted, warped, sterile and poisonous; the wild boar of the Tuscan Maremma do not inhabit "sì aspri sterpi né sì folti" ("thickets so rough or dense"). Piero has lost his human form through lack of Christian virtue and ethics, through shame and despair. The rhetorical brilliance of the episode, particularly Piero's self-serving *apologia,* must not lead us away from the moral lesson. In setting forth the state of this character after death, the Poet presents not some anachronistic facsimile of a Greek heroic tragedy but a vibrant Gothic exemplum for the guidance of his readers' souls: Hell is the fearful place of God's wrath where mercy and pity have no place. We must delve beyond the surface of the poem to the moral, allegorical and anagogical levels by a close examination of the biblical, patristic, historical, pictorial and iconographic foundations of the episode's imagery. In so doing we shall not only clarify the *contrapasso,* the divine retaliation for which the Poet expects us to see the sufficient reason, but also, perhaps find satisfying solutions to other, secondary *cruces.*

In reading this most Christian of poems, our horror of Hell is intensified when we view the punished as inverse images of the Persons of the Trinity Whom they rejected. Francesca whirls like a dove, a lustful counterpart of the loving symbol of the Holy Spirit; the heretics waist-up in their "arche" reflect the dead Christ, the Man of Sorrows in His Tomb; Caiaphas is crucified like Christ among the Hypocrites; the tongues of flame which "steal away" the counsellors of fraud are likewise a pentecostal simulacrum of the Third Person of the Trinity; the Giants in their "pozzo" ("pit" or "well") mirror the God who says of Himself, "They have laid me in the lower pit, in the dark places, and in the shadow of death" (Psalm 87:7 [Douay]); Satan's triune form dripping tears and bloody foam is a clear, intentionally banal, parody.

Man is made in the image of God, and this image extends to eternity, though in Hell ghastly changes are wrought upon the creatures in torment.[3] The suicides who wickedly tore asunder the image of their Maker also reflect a similarly perverted Christological pattern. Their infernal existence as trees apes Christ as symbolized by the Tree of the Cross in Christian art,[4] and such images as those in the Easter Hymn to which Dante ironically refers in the first line of *Inferno* xxxiv, "Vexilla regis prodeunt inferni" ("abroad the regal banners of Hell do fly.")[5] In *Inferno* xiii.107-8 we are told that after Christ's Last Coming as Judge, the bodies of the suicides too will hang upon trees as once did the Redeemer's. As once bled the wounds of Christ, the branch of Jesse's Tree, so bleed the wounds of the branches of the damned. We immediately perceive the just and terrifying irony of the punishment. The Poet implicitly invites us to contrast Piero's proud and selfish act of suicide to escape earthly shame and calumny with Christ's willing suffering of similar torture and mockery for the remission of mankind's sin and His submission to death for man's eternal life. The words of the second suicide, the anonymous Florentine, well reflect the profound, cold egoism of the damned:

> che colpa ho io de la tua vita rea?

> (*Inf.* xiii.135: What blame have I for your sinful life?)

These sinners did not lay down their lives for the love of another, but for their own earthly reputation and pride. As in life they contemned God's mercy, so they contemn it in death. The state of their souls in the afterlife is an eternal manifestation of their selfish iniquity.[6] In the symbolism of Christianity which nourished the Poet, the soul's metamorphosis into a thornbush alludes inevitably to the Crown of Thorns and to the Passion. We must see Dante's image in its obvious and blatant reversal: a Man crowned with thorns inverted as a thornbush crowned with a human body.

Piero's barren metamorphosis contrasts ironically with his surname, "della Vigna" or "de Vinea" ("vineyard" or "vine"). Indeed, the binary image of the vine and the thorn forms an important unifying factor in the metaphors and symbols of the episode (though modern commentators have ignored this aspect as, perhaps, too primitive or naive). During Piero's life his family name offered a fertile field for puns of adulation, and after his death it became the source of many a frivolous tale in the chroniclers.[7] Flatterers vied in superlatives comparing the powerful minister to Joseph and even to the Messiah reincarnate. Gushing their paeans they described him as the "vine" which refreshed the state. His friend Nicola della Rocca indulged himself and the Notary with "O blessed root which hath brought forth such a fruitful branch, O blessed vine [*felix vinea*] who hath produced such precious wine!" and later "O blessed vine, who refreshest Capua with the abundance of your delicious fruit . . . from whose stock the branches differ not!"[8] The Poet's stress upon the barrenness of the forest of thorn trees at the opening of *Inferno* XIII thus grows more terrible in the context of the whole and more gruesome in the context of the laudatory word play which Piero enjoyed while alive.

There are still deeper resonances to the double image of the vine and the thorn. On various premises, Christian literature and art most commonly related the *arbor crucis* to the vine. In many passages of the Old Testament, such as Micheas 4:4, Zacharias 3:10 and Psalm 80:9 (Vulgate), the vine figured the promise of redemption, and in late medieval depictions of the Tree of the Cross, Christ is depicted hanging upon a vine.[9] The sinner's metamorphosis into a sterile stock ironically reverses and eschatalogically fulfills Jesus' words in John 15:1–8 (Douay):

> I am the true vine: and my Father is the husbandman. Every branch in me that beareth not fruit, he will take away . . . I am the vine: you are the branches. He that abideth in me, and I in him, the same beareth much fruit. . . . In this is my Father glorified: that you bring forth very much fruit and become my disciples.

St. Augustine (cited later by St. Thomas in the *Catena aurea*) glossed this passage explaining Christ's own separation from the damned using the very metaphor of the vine and thorn:

But when he says, "I am the true Vine," he discriminates Himself from that vine to which it is said, "How art thou turned into bitterness, O strange vine!" (Jerem. 2:21). For how should that be the true vine, which, when one "looked that it should bring forth grapes" (Isaias 5:4–6), bore thorns?[10]

Further, Dante's poetic inversion of the damned as the barren "plants" of Hell is a parody and an intellectual pun on theological vocabulary. St. Bernard uses the same metaphor boldly in his *Sermons on the Song of Songs*, XXIII.4, as he asks, "Who can question that a good man is, as it were, *a plant of God*?"[11] Particularly, the same terminology is traditionally used of the newly baptized entering the "Vineyard" of the Church. The image of the Christian "planted" as Christ is biblical and is thus common in the Fathers. According to dogma, by the sacrament of baptism, every Christian is joined in the Vine of Christ, in His Passion, and in His Death, both by participation and in similitude. St. Cyril of Jerusalem explains to his catechumens how the soul is "planted" in imitation of the Saviour's death and how the righteous shall rise like Him in resurrection:

> But so that we may learn . . . what Christ . . . endured for us and our salvation . . . and that we are partakers in His sufferings, Paul insists: "If we have been planted together with Him in the likeness of His death [*conplantati facti sumus similitudine mortis eius*], we shall be so in the likeness of His resurrection also" (Romans 6:5). And he is right in saying this; for now that the true Vine has been planted, we also at Baptism have been grafted into His death by participation. Consider this idea most attentively, following the words of the Apostle. He did not say: "If we have been grafted into his death," but "into the likeness of His death." For Christ actually died, His soul was really separated from His body.[12]

Never to experience the reality of the resurrection of their flesh, the suicides are literally "planted" as trees in an image of Christ's sufferings; by their pain and bleeding they inversely "participate" in His Passion as punishment.

Dante will use the words "vigna" and "pruno" for Christ's Church in the *Paradiso* (XII.86; XVIII.132). In the last case (*Paradiso* XXIV.111) Dante echoes Isaias 5:4–6 as he mourns the decay of the Church, "la buona pianta che fu già vite e ora è fatta pruno" ("the good plant which was once a vine and is now become a thorn"). Here in the *Inferno*, instead of a vineyard tended by the Saints, he creates an image of an uncultivated trackless wilderness, of a "della Vigna" wasted by Harpies, Black Hounds and the profligate. The Poet concentrates ironically on the lifeless sterility of the "pruno" which della Vigna has become (*Inferno* XIII.4–6). Even in the opening lines of the episode, the Poet employs a negative vocabulary of spines and barren branches, calculatedly evocative of sin and damnation. As St. Gregory the Great defines: "In truth a spine is all kinds of sinfulness."[13] The pseudo-Rabanus Maurus' *Allegoriae in Sacram Scripturam* glosses "spines" as:

> *Pride of the heart*, as in the Psalms [31:4, Douay]: "whilst the thorn is fastened," that is, "whilst pride is humbled in me." By "thorns" the malice of the heart, as in Isaias [34:13, Douay]: "Thorns shall grow up in his houses," that is, malice will grow in his thoughts.

It also glosses "branches" as " '*Base men*' as in Job [15:30, Douay] 'The flame shall dry up his branches' because eternal damnation will lay waste base men" (my italics).[14] In Dante's inversion, the soul of "Petrus de Vinea" is planted randomly in Hell as the infernal counterpart of the cursed vine of whom it is indeed said in the Vulgate version of Jeremias 2:21.: "Ego autem plantavi te vineam electam omne semen verum, quomodo ergo conversa es mihi *in pravum vinea aliena*?" ("Yet I planted thee a chosen vine, wholly a good seed; how art thou turned unto me into one degenerate, o strange vine?")

Piero's description of his soul's fall to the depths and its metamorphosis evokes other Christological patterns. The manner in which the soul-seeds sprout randomly into many untidy shoots to form the tangled mass upon which nest foul hybrid birds (XIII.10, 97–102) parodies also the genealogy of Christ conceived as the biblical Tree of Jesse upon which rests the Holy Spirit: "And there shall come forth a rod out of the root of Jesse: and a flower shall rise up out of his root. *And the spirit of the Lord shall rest upon him*: the spirit of wisdom and of understanding, the spirit of counsel and of fortitude, the spirit of knowledge and of godliness. And he shall be filled with the spirit of the fear of the Lord" (Isaias 11:1–3) (my italics). The image of the sinners' bodies hanging from the thorn trees makes an even closer analogy with this image (*Inferno* XIII.106–8). Dante's description of harpies nesting in the "piante silvestre" and feeding on them also parodies late medieval (twelfth- to fourteenth-century) artistic depictions of Jesse's Tree, its boughs laden with the images of the Virgin, Christ, the Patriarchs and the Prophets, and surmounted by the single dove of the Holy Ghost or by seven doves representing the Gifts of the Holy Spirit (fig. 1).[15]

Occasionally a pelican feeding its nest of young with blood from its own breast replaces the dove or doves.[16] The Poet's Harpies ("quivi le brutte Arpie lor nidi fanno") in their rapacious feeding reverse the selfless sacrifice of Christ whose bird-symbols they recall. After the end of the tenth century, often a single artistic representation would combine the Tree of Jesse with the Tree of the Cross (fig. 2). Both motifs represented the *salutifera arbor*, the Tree of Salvation; as the Tree of Jesse figured the first step towards redemption, so the Tree of the Cross was its fulfillment.[17] In reversing both these images of salvation into an image of damnation, Dante makes effective use of the Christian tradition of employing the same symbols *in bono* and *in malo*.[18] It is particularly fitting, as will later become apparent, that the figure of Christ as the Rod of Jesse is also the figure of Christ as Judge (Isaias, 11:3–5).

Let us now, however, turn briefly to the historical facts about Pier della Vigna and to their intimate relation to other poetic and iconographic images. The case of the Protonotary was a *cause célèbre*: Dante has no need even to mention his name. Piero had been born in Capua towards the end of the twelfth century to an impoverished but well-respected family.[19] His father, Angelo, at least in later life, was a judge, and Piero himself studied both canon and civil law in Bologna. The family's circumstances allowed Piero no help in his education, but a stipend granted by the University or by the Commune of Bologna conceded him at least subsistence. From later demonstrations of talent in Italian rhyme and Latin prose, we can be sure that he also studied *ars dictaminis*. Upon Piero's elegantly written request, Archbishop Berardo of Palermo, an intimate associate of the Emperor, introduced the future minister to Frederick, probably in 1221. Piero's extraordinary gifts in linguistic style and his knowledge of the law were immediate grounds for an appointment to the imperial chancery.[20] He developed a close friendship with the Emperor, with whom he shared cultural, philosophical, artistic and social interests. Piero's climb through the ranks of the imperial civil service was swift. From 1225 until 1247, officially Piero filled only the position of High Court judge, "judex magnae

Fig. 1
Tree of Jesse. *Miniature from the Ingeburg Psalter, ca. 1210, Paris.*
MS 9 (1965), f. 14ᵛ, Chantilly, Musée Condé. Photo: Giraudon.

Fig. 2
Tree of Jesse and the Tree of the Cross. Speculum humanae salvationis,
area of Lake Constance, ca. 1340–1350. Kremsmünster Stiftbibliothek.

curiae"[21]; but from 1238 to 1247 his real post was that of "familiaris," or privy counsellor to the King, since Piero had ceased to function in his office of judge of the court of appeal in 1234.[22] The most significant imperial documents bear Piero's stylistic imprint; of his fashioning is the charter founding the University of Naples in 1224.[23] The most important effect of his tenure in Frederick's service, however, was the imperial constitution promulgated at Melfi in 1231, the *Liber Augustalis*, whose formulation was probably, at least in great part, the work of Piero's own hand.[24] His close association with the Emperor and his primacy among the notaries of the chancery allowed him to hold sway over imperial decisions and privileges granted from about 1239 to 1246. Through him passed all the Emperor's private correspondence and by him were drawn up the edicts and manifestos of the Emperor's virulent quarrel with the Papacy. In May 1247, after the death of his peer and colleague Taddeo da Sessa, Piero was at last given the official title of his full administrative authority, "imperialis aulae protonotarius et regni Siciliae logotheta" ("Protonotary of the Imperial Court and Logothete of the Kingdom of Sicily").[25] Though never styled chancellor, he became, in effect, the head of the imperial chancery, the Emperor's spokesman in all matters legal, diplomatic, social and political, and the director of the Empire's finances. He formed the sole link between the Emperor and the people for petitions and pleas. In the royal palace in Naples, a wall fresco, now no longer extant, was painted to depict him in this role.[26]

Piero's professional success was coupled with extraordinary personal gain. Some estimates place his fortune at 900,000 Neapolitan ducats and others at 10,000 pounds in gold *Augustales*.[27] Such sums do not include, among other landed properties, his large palace in Naples, his vast gardens outside the city, and his conglomerate of estates near Capua. It is evident, as most historians have seen, that his position presented great temptations for self-aggrandisement at the expense of the public coffers, temptations made even greater by the fact that the monarch allowed him to act upon his own initiative in many matters. The contemporary astrologer, Guido Bonatti (punished by Dante as a diviner in *Inferno* xx.118, and an excellent first-hand source) avers that Piero often subverted the Emperor's orders.[28] Suddenly, in February of 1249, under circumstances which remain unclear, and which indeed seem to have been intentionally shrouded in mystery by the Crown, Piero fell from grace. He was arrested in Cremona, his eyes were put out, and he was led from town to town to be mocked by the populace until the death sentence was to be executed. In May of the same year, however (accounts differ concerning precise location and method), Piero cheated his prince, and, in depair, dashed his own skull against a stone wall or column in San Miniato.[29]

As we would expect, the fall and death of the Logothete brought with it a flood of unfounded speculation. Various chronicles and commentaries on the *Commedia* present conflicting versions. Contemporaries erroneously linked an earlier poisoning attempt on the Emperor's life to the later ruin of the King's minister. Rumors told that Pier della Vigna had conspired with Frederick's personal physician in a plot with the Pope.[30] Matthew Paris, an otherwise well-respected and informed chronicler, relates that Piero was involved in a poisoning attempt with his *own* physician to murder the King.[31] Fra Salimbene di Adamo, of the Minorite Order which the Pope used so widely to disseminate propaganda and scandal against Frederick II, feigned belief in the innocence of Pier della Vigna: the disloyal Emperor Frederick, in order to ruin Piero with a charge of treason and seize his property, used the calumny that the Logothete had secretly treated with the Pope at the Council of Lyons without imperial witnesses. Historians have shown Salimbene to be totally without credence, for Pier della Vigna did not attend the Council of Lyons.[32] The *Historia anonymi remensis* (ca. 1260) tells a different tale: the Emperor had had Piero's coffers searched and had found an incriminating letter.[33] This anonymous chronicler does not specify whether the evidence had been planted or not, but in his account in the *Esposizioni*, Boccaccio leaves no doubt as to the actual falsity of the letters.[34] A Pisan manuscript recounts that Frederick had had Piero blinded and sentenced to death as a fomenter of discord because he had obstinately opposed a reconciliation between the Emperor and the Pope. Again, the story is baseless, for the Pope had adamantly opposed all reconciliatons after deposing Frederick at the Council of Lyons and had aimed at and eventually succeeded in the destruction of the Hohenstaufen monarchy.[35]

In the fourteenth century the tales were to become even more inventive and silly. The Dominican Francesco Pippino relates the rumor that Pier della Vigna had indeed betrayed the Emperor but that the Logothete had had just cause: Frederick had seduced Piero's wife.[36] The Pisan chronicle blithely states the opposite: Piero was punished for coveting the Empress.[37] As the first story is implausible, so the second is impossible. The Empress Isabel of England, Frederick's third wife, had died in 1241 long before

Piero's fall, and the then-sixty-year-old Emperor had never remarried.

The various conflicting versions reflect the number and type of rumors current in Dante's day. That the Logothete was not involved in a plot to poison the Emperor and that he was not in league with the Pope appears clear. The number of documents which Piero drafted on behalf of his prince, the vehemence with which he defended the imperial cause, and the Pope's implacable treatment of his family and estate after his death make it extremely unlikely that a reconciliation with the Papacy, even in secret, was possible.[38] However, that the Emperor's minister had an avaricious nature and that he was engaged in other crimes just as sinister and thus, ultimately, treasonable, is borne out by existing evidence. Piero's greed appears in the methods he used to enlarge his estate in Capua at the expense of a hostel engaged in the care of pilgrims, the poor and the sick, the Ospedale di San Jacopo di Altopascio, the seat of the Order of the Knights of St. James situated on the Via Romea, near the Cerbaia or imperial Tuscan hunting preserve.[39] In February, 1244, an exchange of property took place between the wealthy monastery and the "procurator" of the Emperor, Uberto Gangi. In exchange for ceding their rights to an estate including a church and house near Capua, the Master and Brothers received the income and properties of a nearby smaller foundation in Tuscany, the Ospedale di Santa Maria della Trinità. The reasons alleged for the trade were that the Capuan property was too far away for the monastery to administer properly and that the tithes accruing from it had become too small to be worthwhile. The arrangement would be of little historic interest except that the Capuan property ended up in the personal possession of one whose name appears nowhere in the deed, Pier della Vigna.[40] After his death, it returned to the control of the Crown with the rest of his confiscated property; and later, as we learn from a letter of Innocent IV, the exchange was declared null and void.[41] According to the Pope, Pier della Vigna had used the weight and pressure of the strongest office in the imperial government to force the Ospedale to cede its Capuan property against its will. We also learn from the papal letter that Piero had made himself feared by the poor and the powerful rich alike: "Non solum erat terror humilium, sed sublimium personarum" (p. 317: "Not only was he the terror of the humble, but of the people of highest degree"). Regardless of the inimical motives of the Church and regardless of whether the Logothete forced the exchange with the Emperor's knowledge, ignorance or connivance, the fact remains that Piero was historically capable of appropriating for his own use the possessions of institutions concerned with the sick and needy. With or without the Emperor he had stolen from Holy Church.

Various fragments of the imperial register published by Huillard-Bréholles show that Piero was especially involved in imperial finances; many entries deal with the administration of property and the exaction of duties and taxes, but a great number deal with the prosecution of accused traitors and with the confiscation of their belongings.[42] Here, too, Piero had much opportunity to seize property and commandeer it for his own. That he did so is made clear by the Emperor's letter to his son-in-law, Richard, Count of Caserta, from which we learn that Piero's years of embezzlement—which had led the state to the brink of destruction— had been the subject of other missives from the Emperor to his lieutenants; the metaphors show that Frederick saw the crimes as having endangered both his Empire and his person. The document recommends that the greatest care and secrecy be used henceforth in ascertaining the guilt of those accused of treason. It makes clear not only that this care had not been used in the past but that great abuses had been inflicted upon the innocent. Pier della Vigna is used as the negative example of the methods previously employed.[43]

Nineteenth- and twentieth-century historians agree on the nature of Piero's crimes. For Huillard-Bréholles, Piero was guilty of avarice, bribery and embezzlement, the sale of justice, and the abuse of power to enrich himself and his family.[44] Kantorowicz generally concurs but sees the purposeful twisting of justice and the enormous misappropriations of state funds as a veritable betrayal of the Emperor and his trust.[45] The historian and critic, Leonardo Olschki concluded:

[Dante's] representation according to which [Piero] forfeited peace and life—lo sonno e li polsi—in the faithful discharge of his function as highest official and confidant of the Emperor, is, in the light of our knowledge, seen to be a pious fable invented and used by the poet with definite intentions. The Chancellor was one of the astonishingly large number of high officers of state and dignitaries who unscrupulously exploited their position for their own ends, amassed wealth, and in the end turned treacherously against their lord and benefactor.[46]

Friedrich Baethgen, in an essay which makes convincing changes in the interpretation of major individual documents, comes to the same basic conclusion: Pier della Vigna was not guilty of attempted poisoning but of embezzlement.[47] The American historian Van Cleve concludes:

> His "treasonable acts" consisted in cupidity—the avarice of a man already abundantly wealthy for greater wealth and for greater power, to be obtained from selling justice for his own profit. . . . That he was guilty of peculation there can be no reasonable doubt; his trial and the sentence imposed appear to have confirmed his guilt.[48]

Avarice in office, it is agreed, caused the fall of the Emperor's minister.

The literal level of Dante's Poem, at least Piero's own profession of innocence, seems to contradict this consensus. The Wayfarer is left speechless with pity. Dante *poeta*, though, appears, as we will show, to have known the darker sides of the story. Every classical and biblical image in the episode points to a form of violent and rapacious avarice and to its opposite, profligacy. Dante presents two frenzied and unnatural extremes of an Aristotelian mean.

The foul human-faced Harpies, who together with the black bitches act as agents of Divine Wrath in this subdivision of circle seven, form the first composite image. In this metaphor Pier della Vigna plays the role of a classical figure of avarice, Phineus, the Harpies' original victim to whom Piero stands in striking parallel even historically. As the greedy Phineus, who had blinded or killed his sons, was blinded by the irate gods in just retaliation, so Piero was blinded in life by Frederick. Fulgentius begins his "Fabula Finei": "Phineus is taken as a symbol of avarice," and he claims that the name Phineus derives from "fenerando," "practicing usury," "Fittingly he is blind, because all avarice is blind in not seeing what is its own."[49] The Third Vatican Mythographer and the pseudo-Bernardus Silvestris follow him without originality.[50] The Harpies are a just infliction upon the avaricious in the classics and, indeed, Fulgentius etymologizes their very names as signifying acts of rapaciousness.[51] The Third Vatican Mythographer cites Fulgentius' explanation, and tells us:

> The Harpies however are called the hounds of Jove, because they are also said to be Furies. Whence also they are said to snatch food

from banquets, because this is the work of Harpies. Here also the avaricious are made to suffer the Furies, because they abstain from [using] their share.[52]

"Bernardus" also repeats Fulgentius' explanations for the Harpies' names, form, and virginity, but he further allegorizes their swollen bellies: "A gluttonous belly is a voracious rapacity for money."[53] The aptness of God's *contrapasso* in the *Inferno* is apparent in the smallest detail: the avaricious Piero is tormented by symbols of his shameful greed and rapine. Benvenuto da Imola, in fact, noted in his *Comentum* on the *Comedy*, "Figuratively a Harpy represents avarice," and later "Avarice and prodigality most of all lead a man to despair."[54]

A second major classical allusion can help us understand the structure of the episode. Actaeon, the prototype of the profligate, chased and torn by his own hounds, forms the antithesis of the first image in an Aristotelian balance, for as Dante knew, the Philosopher had called profligacy a type of self-destruction in the fourth book of the *Nicomachaean Ethics*.[55] Fulgentius interprets the tale as that of the prodigal who wastes his substance on his hounds; though too old for the hunt, Actaeon cannot bear to be parted from his pack, and ruins himself to feed them.[56] The allusion also helps us to see that the two bestial agents of torment, the Harpies and the black hounds of Dante's thirteenth canto, are, in some way, one. They form a unity partly recognized by the early commentators: not only were the Harpies the "hounds of Jove," but one of Actaeon's bitches was named "Harpyia."[57]

Lastly, the central image of the speaking tree inspired by the Polydorus episode in the *Aeneid* actually cuts with a double edge, a fact so far unnoticed. In the received interpretation, Pier della Vigna suffers the unjust fate of Polydorus: the innocent son of Priam, entrusted to the care of Polymnestor, King of Thrace, is killed by the latter precisely because of Polymnestor's avarice for Polydorus' riches.[58] The aptness of the parallel is at once apparent. Fra Salimbene, hinting that Frederick II had ruined his faithful minister in order to seize the latter's fortune, twice attributes the following cynical dictum to the Emperor: "Never did I feed a hog, from which I did not extract lard."[59] It would appear too that Dante *poeta* would have us see Piero at first in his role as victim and sufferer — that is, until we explore the traditional allegorization of the Polydorus episode familiar to the Poet. In the pseudo-Bernardus Silvestris' interpretation of

the *Aeneid*, this "victim" plays quite a different role. Polydorus is seen
bewilderingly as a grasping entrepreneur wrapped up in his greed, coldly
and calculatedly absorbed in the efforts of gaining wealth:

> Now Polydorus signifies "much bitterness," for "doris" in Greek
> is "amaritudo" in Latin. . . . This Polydorus is buried in Thrace
> because much bitterness is wrapped in avarice: for what can be more
> bitter than the avaricious man who "seeks and like a wretch abstains
> from what he has found and fears to use it?" What can be more
> bitter than that "he manages everything fearfully and coldly"? Than
> the fact that "love of money grows as the money itself grows," and
> that "the greedy man is always poor"? Polydorus, then, makes Aeneas
> flee from Thrace because the bitterness and toil of seeking and holding
> on to money often frighten a man away from the pursuit of money.[60]

May we not see in "Bernardus' " interpretation some ironical grist for
Piero's profession of devotion to office: "such that for it I lost both sleep
and life?" Regardless of the overly discussed differences between the
Polydorus episode and Dante's creation, the fact remains that Piero *is* the
type of Polydorus.[61] The Logothete is changed into a tree not only because
he may have been the victim of another's avarice but because he was
avaricious himself.

Our appreciation of the fittingness of such a transformation is strengthened further by Bersuire in his *Ovidius moralizatus*. Though this writer
is later than Dante, his view reveals the traditions and significance surrounding this type of metamorphosis. Discussing the similar fate of
Phaeton's sisters, he states that the avaricious were regularly turned into
trees as a matter of course![62]

Perhaps independently of its use by the Mythographers, the metaphor
of greed as a tree was used in the Church Fathers. St. Gregory the Great
discusses the "root of the juniper" of Job 30:4: the tree, whose root is
allegorized as avarice, has thorny spines instead of leaves:

> For the juniper tree has spines instead of leaves, for so bristly are
> those which it puts forth that like thorns they can pierce anyone
> who touches them. Now a thorn is all sorts of sin, because while
> it draws the mind into delight, as it were, by piercing, it wounds
> it. . . . What then is there denoted by the "root of the juniper" but

avarice, from which the thorns of all the sins are produced? Concerning this it is said by Paul: "For the desire of money [*cupiditas*] is the root of all evils" (I Timothy 6:10, Douay). For that springs up covertly in the mind, and brings forth openly the spines of all sin in practice.[63]

Since Polydorus' bush in *Aeneid* III.23 is not a naturally bristling thorn but a myrtle darted with javelins, "densus hastilibus horrida myrtus," at least part of Dante's inspiration may have come from such passages as St. Gregory's.

Inescapably and conclusively we begin to perceive that the images point to the "root of all evil," the love of money, and its consequent outgrowths. The major allusions of the episode of Pier della Vigna are thus in perfect consonance with contemporary historical records. Both reveal what Piero's words would hide: a grasping and avaricious nature. The episode in Cantos XIII and XIV.1–3, in fact possesses a close artistic unity: violent avariciousness leading to the destruction of corporal substance is punished together with violent profligacy engendering the wasting of worldly substance.

We must now turn to the immediate puzzle of why Dante, having "disposed" of the misers and squanderers in *Inferno* VII, would place so much emphasis on covetousness or avarice here. The answer may be had not only from the biblical and patristic notion of sins engendering more serious sins, but also from the rhetoric of Frederick's court, from contemporary opinions about Pier della Vigna, and from the traditional typology of avarice in the Church Fathers and in Christian art.

The metaphors in which the Emperor and his Curia regularly wrote of the concept of sovereignty are of a religious or even sacrilegious nature. The monarch's authority, as Dante would later echo in the *De monarchia*, derived solely from the Godhead.[64] Frederick conceived of himself as the Deity's vicar on earth and frequently couched himself as the Messiah. His birthplace, Jesi, for example, becomes "Bethlehem" where his "divine mother gave him life!"[65] The Popes' inexorable campaign, including the deposing of the Emperor, two excommunications, and the proclamation of a crusade against him, made Frederick feel that he was repeating the passion of Christ. Such imagery appears in many letters. In March or April of 1249, most probably from Cremona, Frederick wrote to the King of France bitterly complaining of the persecution; his Kingdom is the Holy

Land; he himself is on the Cross.[66] If, in the rhetoric of the King and
Court, Frederick is the Son of God, then the pursekeeper among his
ministers, the breaker of his trust, must be Judas. And thus is Piero styled
in the Emperor's letter to the Count of Caserta referred to above. Here
Frederick sees embezzlement of temporal funds as one with ecclesiastic
simony, and he accuses Piero of the crime. The Logothete's greedy pecula-
tions evoke the avaricious crimes and thefts of the traitor Judas in John
12:6: "Fur erat et loculos habens ea quae mittebantur portabat" ("He was
a thief and, having the purse, carried things that were put therein"), and
John 13:29: "Loculos habebat Judas" ("Judas had the purse"):

> You will be able to recall through other documents something of
> the base advice and various scandals [scandali multiformis] of Petrus,
> that is, of this Simon, still another betrayer, who, so that he might
> have the purse, or that he might enrich himself, turned the rod of justice
> into a serpent, so that he might by means of his usual lies bring
> this empire into peril by which we might have perished in the depths
> of the sea, one with the Pharoah's army, like the Egyptians' chariots.[67]

Interestingly, Papal documents use similar metaphors. The writer of the
Vita Gregorii IX, perhaps Giovanni di Ferentino, refers to Piero as a "new
Ahitophel."[68] These same images, used in rival Church and Imperial sources,
curiously find a parallel in those which form the iconography of Inferno XIII.

Judas Iscariot was more than the betrayer of Christ: he had misap-
propriated money from the poor and he had taken his own life. The fallen
apostle's descent to betrayal led by degrees from covetousness through
theft and hypocrisy. Of the four Gospels, Matthew (26:15) most emphasizes
the avarice of Judas as the primary motive of his treachery: "Quid vultis
mihi dare et ego vobis eum tradam et illi constitutuerunt ei triginta
argenteos?" ("What will you give me, and I will deliver him unto you?
And they assigned him thirty pieces of silver"). Describing the anointing
at Bethany, the Gospel of John recounts that the apostle's complaint over
the extravagant "waste" was occasioned by excessive love of money: when
Judas suggested that the ointment should be sold and the proceeds
distributed among the poor he did so hypocritically and only as an opportunity to embezzle (John 12:4–6). The Evangelist calls Judas a thief, "fur
erat," who would steal what was put into the common purse entrusted
to his safekeeping. St. Augustine glosses:

Harken to the true witness: "Now he said this, not because he cared for the poor; but because he was a thief and, having the purse, carried the things that were put therein (John 12:6, Douay)." "Carried" or "carried off?" Nay, but by office he carried, by theft he carried off. . . . Behold among the Saints is a Judas! Behold he is a thief, this Judas! And that you make not light of that, a thief and sacrilegious, not any common kind of thief! A thief who stole from the purse, yea, but from that of the Lord! From the purse, yea, but from the sacred purse! If in the courts of law a difference is made between the crime of common theft and peculation, for it is called peculation when it is the stealing of public property and the stealing of private property is not judged so heinous as that of stealing public property, how much more sternly shall that sacrilegious thief be judged who has dared to rob, not in any common way, but to rob the Church! *He who steals ought from the Church is one with Judas the lost.* (My italics.)[69]

As we would expect, the fallen apostle is thus a familiar *figura* of avarice in the Fathers of the Church. St. John Chrysostomos warns the avaricious to consider his punishment. Judas lost everything, including his immortal soul through greed: "Judas is set forth as an example to the avaricious."[70] Regularly in their comments on Judas' sins, the Fathers cite I Timothy 6:10: "Cupidity [love of money] is the root of all evil," (often the passage is cited as "Radix . . . est avaritia"), and Ecclesiasticus [Sirach] 10:9: "Now nothing is fouler than an avaricious man."[71] Besides St. John Chrysostomos, other Fathers such as Origen, St. Cyril of Jerusalem, and Rabanus Maurus all ascribe the main motive of Judas' wickedness to avarice.[72] St. Jerome even interprets Judas' second name in the same light: "No matter how you interpret it, Iscariot means money and price."[73] Most illuminating for our purposes, however, is St. Thomas Aquinas' article on the patristic doctrine of the "daughters of avarice" in the *Summa theologica* showing the progression of the sin toward violence and beyond:

The daughters of covetousness are the vices which arise therefrom, especially in respect of the desire of an end. Now since covetousness is excessive love of possessing riches, it exceeds in two things. For in the first place it exceeds in retaining, and in this respect covetousness gives rise to *insensibility to mercy*, because, to wit, *a man's heart is not* softened by mercy to assist the needy with his riches. In the second place, it belongs to covetousness to exceed in receiving, and in this respect covetousness may be considered in two ways. First as in the thought (*affectu*). In this way it gives rise to *restlessness, by hindering man with excessive anxiety and care*, for "a covetous man shall not be satisfied with money" (Eccles. 5:9). Secondly, it may be considered in the execution (*effectu*). In this way *the covetous man, in acquiring other people's goods, sometimes employs force, which pertains to violence.*

St. Thomas continues listing worse sins until he concludes with treachery "as in the case of Judas, who betrayed Christ through covetousness."[74]

Judas' earthly end as described in Matthew 27:3–5 is our most important concern here. Too late the remorseful apostle, rebuffed by the high priests, tosses his blood money into the temple. In despair he hangs himself from a noose, "laqueo se suspendit"—tradition said from a tree.[75] This final act was for St. Jerome and other Church writers far worse than even his betrayal. Commenting on Psalm CVIII [CIX], the saint writes: "The repentance of Judas became worse than his sin. How so? He went out and committed suicide by hanging himself; he who became the betrayer of God became his own hangman. In regard to the clemency of the Lord, I say this, that Judas offended the Lord more by hanging himself than by betraying Him."[76] St. Gregory echoes the concept: "Thus the reprobate Judas, when he inflicted death upon himself to spite sin, was brought to the punishment of eternal death, and repented of sin in a *more heinous way than he had committed sin*." (My italics.)[77] Evidently for the Fathers of the Church, Judas was at least as important as an example of avarice and suicide as he was a symbol of betrayal.

Of the early commentators on *Inferno* XIII, only Dante's son, Pietro Alighieri, mentions Judas in reference to Pier della Vigna and his sin of despair: ·

Despair is said to be a sin against the Holy Spirit if it is committed out of contempt and malice, because it is not forgiven in this life— that is, not without difficulty—nor in the life to come, *as in the case of Judas*. It must be construed to mean that such a wood—*that is, the state and reputation of those who are desperate*—is trackless, because our thought is not able to proceed by consideration of such a case.

And the fronds are dry because their memory is dead. Thus he tells how they come to be plants there, and the reason why they will not have their bodies. With regard to this it is said in the *Decreta*: "*Judas* sold the Redeemer of all men, and having soon after hanged himself from a noose did not keep that Redeemer's grace" — and rightly so, because no one is able to retain that which he has sold. (My italics)[78]

Maddeningly, Pietro Alighieri stops here, never to pick up the thread again nor to tie his suggestions to the context. And no modern commentator has yet thought to take his comparison seriously.

In *Inferno* XIII, however, it *is* as *Judas*, a body hanging from a tree surrounded by wingèd demons with human faces, the claws of birds and swollen stomachs that Dante has Pier della Vigna visualize himself after the Last Judgment (vv. 103–8). For this image, Dante drew not only from Patristics but from the Christian pictorial and sculptural tradition which

Fig. 3
Death of Judas. *Ivory relief on small chest. Northern Italy, ca. 420–430.*
Courtesy of the Trustees of the British Museum.

Fig. 5
Death of Judas. *Ivory Diptych. Carolingian of eighth or ninth centur*
Tesoro del Duomo, Milan. Photo: the author.

Fig. 4
Death of Judas. *Detail of back of "Lipsanotheca," ivory reliquary casket. Northern Italy,*
perhaps Milan, fourth century. Museo dell'Età Cristiana, Brescia. Photo: Anderson.

depicted a lifeless body hanging from a tree to represent both the death of Judas and the more general image of the despair of self-destruction.[79] Such depictions are legion. The suicide of Judas occurs together with the first known realistic portrayal of the crucifixion on an ivory box in the British Museum, made probably in southern Gaul about A.D. 400. This first representation is notable especially because of one detail: a bird feeds its young in a nest in the gallows-tree (fig. 3). The same figure appears carved on the back of the Brescia Lipsanotheca, a North Italian ivory chest of perhaps the third quarter of the fourth century (fig. 4),[80] and on an ivory diptych preserved in the Tesoro del Duomo in Milan (fig. 5). A hanging Judas with a bird, perhaps plucking out his eyes, is the subject of a miniature in the Stuttgart Psalter (ca. 820–830) (fig. 6).

Important later variants depict the devil or demons taking the soul of the betrayer: the fiends commonly have human faces and birds' claws and wings, such as those on the Cathedral doors of Benevento made towards the end of the twelfth century (fig. 7). Most striking is Gislebertus' pilaster capital from Autun Cathedral (ca. 1125–1130) which dramatizes the scene vividly: Harpies with wings, swollen bellies and human faces with gaping, hungry mouths surround the lifeless body of the betrayer as it hangs from a heavily foliaged tree (fig. 8). An earlier capital in the Church of Saint-Andoche at Saulieu (1115–1120) is similar, showing Judas hanging from a tree with an open-mouthed devil with birds' talons.[81] The sandstone tympanum (ca. 1275–1280) of the central West Portal of Strasbourg Cathedral includes the death of Judas among other scenes of its Passion Cycle.[82] In another stone relief on the tympanum in the porch of Freiburg Cathedral, almost coeval (ca. 1290–1310) with the *Commedia*, Judas hangs with tormenting monsters carved above his head.[83] Such images were also being created by major artisans and artists in contemporary Italy; they appear in the mosaics of the Poet's beloved "bel San Giovanni" (ca. 1271–1300) and in Giotto's frescoes for the Scrovegni Chapel of the Arena in Padua (ca. 1305) (figs. 9, 10). Clearly such traditional depictions formed Dante's conception of the suicides' state of soul after death.

The artists who made the early miniatures of the *Divina Commedia* generally limited themselves to depicting the visual form and action of the cantos, the thorn bushes, the harpies and their nests, Virgil's watching Dante plucking away a branch. In a few cases, however, the actual content of Piero's speech is illustrated. A manuscript in the Bibliothèque Nationale in Paris (MS, it. 78, f. 66r) has a sketch of a body of a suicide

Fig. 6. Death of Judas. *Illustration to Psalm 7:12–16. Stuttgart Psalter,*
St. Germain-des Pres, ca. 820–830. Stuttgart, Bildarchiv Foto Marburg, 236839.

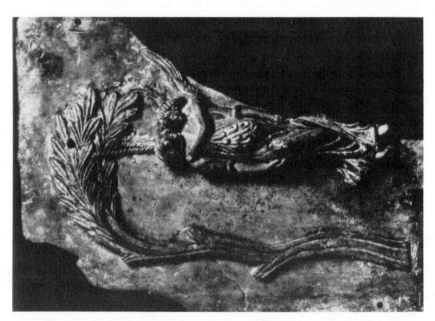

Fig. 7. Death of Judas. *Detail of right-hand leaf of Main Door (row 4, pl. 3),*
of Benevento Cathedral: illustration shows plaque in its present post-World War II state.
Photo: Valerio Gramignazzi Serrone, courtesy of Ferdinando Grassi.

Fig. 8. Death of Judas. *Pilaster capital by Gislebertus, ca. 1125–1130 in the Cathédrale Saint Lazare, Autun. Musée Lapidaire, Salle Capitulaire. Photo: Lauros-Giraudon.*

impaled in the branches (fig. 11). Another in the Biblioteca Nacional in Madrid (MS. 10057, f. 25r) presents a more interesting drawing of a body hanging by a rope from a branch (fig. 12), a clear allusion to the iconographic *topos* of the sins of despair and suicide originating in the death of Judas who hanged himself from a noose for grief.[84]

For the Middle Ages, the traitor and suicide, Ahitophel, was the Old Testament prefiguration of the New Testament Judas.[85] In II Kings [Samuel] 16–18, we read that in answer to King David's prayer, the advice of Ahitophel, the chief counsellor to the usurper Absalom,[86] was turned

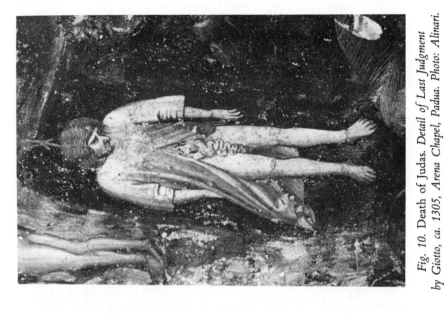

Fig. 10. Death of Judas. Detail of Last Judgment by Giotto, ca. 1305, Arena Chapel, Padua. Photo: Alinari.

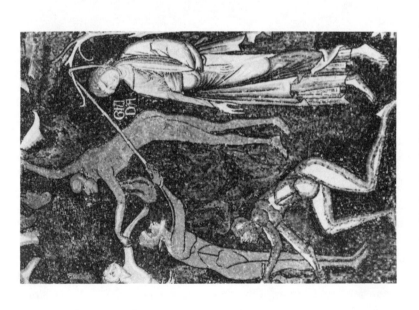

Fig. 9. Death of Judas. Detail of Last Judgment, Florentine Baptistry, ca. 1271–1310. Photo: Museo dell'Opera del Duomo.

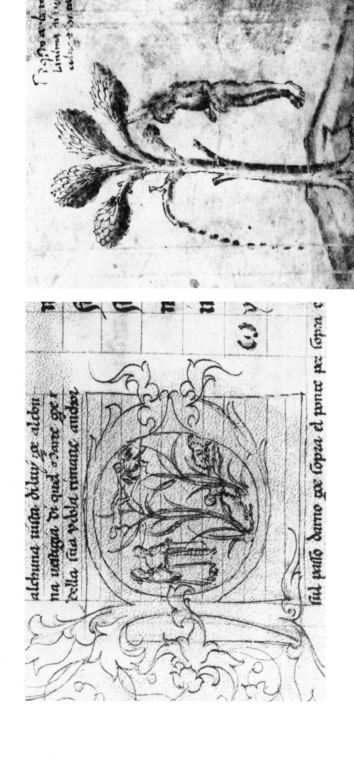

Fig. 11. Pier della Vigna's Body Impaled on a Tree.
Drawing for initial "P" from MS of Divina Commedia,
Cristoforo Cortese, first half of fifteenth century, Venice.
MS B.N. it. 78, f. 66ʳ, Bibliothèque Nationale, Paris.

Fig. 12. Pier della Vigna's Body Hanging From a Tree.
Drawing, MS of Divina Commedia, Italian, mid-fifteenth century.
MS 10057, f. 25ʳ, Biblioteca Nacional, Madrid.

to foolishness and ignored; Ahitophel, seeing that his advice was not followed, committed suicide in his own house: "But Achitophel seeing that his counsel was not followed, saddled his ass, and arose and went home to his house and to his city. And putting his house in order, he hanged himself" (II Kings 17–23, [Douay]).

The two suicides, Judas and Ahitophel, were traditionally joined in the interpretation of the so-called "Judas" Psalm 108 [109]: David's plea and malediction upon Absalom and Ahitophel was interpreted verse by verse as being that of Christ upon the Betrayer. In his *Breviarium in Psalmos* St. Jerome begins his exegesis on Psalm 108 thus:

> "Unto the end, a psalm of David." "Unto the end" is a sign that the message of the psalm pertains not to the present but the future. If, moreover, the prophet speaks of the future, the prophecy concerns Christ. "O God, be not silent in my praise." Christ is saying: "Judas betrayed me, the Jews persecuted and crucified me and thought they were putting an end to me, but you, O God, be not silent in my praise."[87]

St. Augustine returns to the theme in his *Enarrationes*:

> Everyone who faithfully reads the Acts of the Apostles (1:15–26), acknowledges that this Psalm contains a prophecy of Christ; for it evidently appears that what is written here, "let his days be few, and let another take his office," is prophesied of Judas, Christ's betrayer.[88]

And Rabanus Maurus in his gloss on II Kings [Samuel] continues the tradition.[89]

Many moralized Bibles give a pictorial parallel of the two suicides: Judas is depicted hanging from a tree while Ahitophel, represented in an architectural setting, makes a gibbet of his house (fig.13).[90] Many manuscripts present both Judas and Ahitophel hanging from halters inside a building.[91] In an especially noteworthy example (fig. 14), Judas represents those who are ensnared by the noose of simony, who accept the dignity of office only to lose their souls.[92] A related metaphorical use of Ahitophel's story occurs in Richard of St. Victor's *De eruditione hominis interioris* where Ahitophel serves as an example of "affectatio auctoritatis," the ambitious

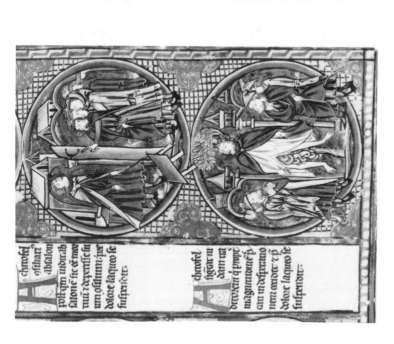

Fig. 13. Judas and Ahitophel. *Moralized Bible,*
illustration to II Regum 17:23, thirteenth century.
MS Oxford Bodley 270b, f. 158. Bodleian Library.

Fig. 14. Judas and Ahitophel. *Moralized Bible.*
Cod. 2554, f. 47ᵛ, Österreichische Nazionalbibliothek, Vienna.

and vain striving after authority: "Affectation of authority is when a man now strives to seem to all to be a man of great advice and sanctity, and that matters which are to be determined or defined depend upon his counsel or opinion. . . . He who speaks of Achitophel shows us what ambition for authority can do in such people. . . ."[93] The parallels to the ambitious counsellor, Pier della Vigna, are obvious. The final words of the second, Florentine, suicide centering upon the concept of "city" and "house" and concluding with "Io fei gibetto a me de le mie case," ("I made me a gibbet of my own house"), bear so close a resemblance to the death of the biblical Ahitophel that they must have drawn from it their inspiration and intended allusion: "And he went *home* to his *house* and to his *city*. And putting his *house* in order, he hanged himself" (II Kings 17:23, Douay) (my italics). The sublime unity of poetry, art, and theme is now apparent.

Seeing Judas as a prototype and pattern for the episode also helps us to explain many other exegetical difficulties, especially that of the Wayfarer's ignorance and the Poet's conviction of Piero's real guilt. The Church Fathers make much of the fact that Judas' avarice was hidden from the other Apostles, and, in a special way, hidden also from Christ himself. St. Thomas' explanation of the problem of divine prescience and of Jesus' unknowing can also permit us to glimpse and grasp the interior workings of Dante's poem modelled on that same distinction between the limits of human intellect and the knowledge of God's *invisibilia*: "The wickedness of Judas was known to Christ *qua Deus*; it was unknown to Him *qua homo*."[94] Similarly, Piero's guilt is concealed from the Wayfarer and from the reader on the literal level, but revealed when we look beneath to the second, spiritual sense. Within the fiction of the poem, the Poet who has glimpsed the sight of God and returns to write of it as a "scribe of God" knows of Piero's real guilt and hidden avarice; Dante, the Wayfarer, does not.

The recognition of Judas as a main element of unity in the episode also casts more light on the probable identity of the second, Florentine, suicide. Just as there is a clear parallel between the discarded minister Ahitophel and the discarded minister della Vigna, so there is a parallel between Judas' selling the Innocent Blood for money and Piero's love of money leading him to embezzle from the state and persecute the innocent for gain. The Logothete who, as Guido da Pisa notes, "was . . . a great master and doctor of laws, and first judge in the High Court of Frederick the Emperor," had in Frederick II's words, "turned the rod of justice into a serpent."[95] Important too is the fact that the image of the Tree of Jesse, parodied in the post-Judgment state of the suicides, *is itself a figuration of Christ come to judge*: "And there shall come forth a rod out of the root of Jesse: and a flower shall rise up and out of this root . . . *he shall judge the poor with justice*, and shall reprove with equity for the meek of the earth. And he shall strike the earth with the rod of his mouth: and with the breath of his lips he shall slay the wicked. And justice shall be the girdle of his loins. . . . (Isaias 11:1–5 [Douay]).[96]

Further, the seventh circle of Hell, in which the suicides hold central place, marks the beginning of the lower realm of those sins which have injustice as their end:

> D'ogne malizia, ch'odio in cielo acquista,
>   *ingiuria* è 'l fine, ed ogne fin cotale
>   o con forza o con frode altrui contrista.

(*Inf.* XI.22–24:"Of every malice that gains hatred in Heaven the end is injustice; and every such end, either by force or by fraud, afflicts another.")

The very suicides, who extend their violence even to robbing themselves of the world (*Inferno* XI.43), view their own sin as an injustice to self:

> L'animo mio . . .
>   *ingiusto* fece me contra me giusto.

(*Inf.* XIII.70–73: "My mind . . . made me unjust against my just self.")

Thus in the context of justice and its perversion, between the traditional identifications of the second suicide, rather than Rocco de' Mozzi, the rich man who hanged himself rather than face poverty, we must choose, for reasons of motive, logic, artistic balance and unity, the *judge* and avaricious *professor iuris*, Lotto degli Agli, who, as the Ottimo tells us, "Having given a false sentence for money, he hanged himself to avoid poverty and shame."[97]

The question of the tree-souls' speech, so well examined stylistically by Leo Spitzer, must receive a new dimension when the figure of Judas

is seen behind Dante's concept of an avaricious Piero. Origen was the first
Church writer to note that the surname "Iscariot" meant "suffocated":
"I heard someone explaining that the town of the betrayer Judas is named
according to the Hebrew words 'from suffocation.' If this is so, a great
fittingness can be discovered between the name of his town and the way
he died, since indeed, by hanging himself from a noose he fulfilled, through
his suffocation, the prophecy of the name of his town of provenance."[98]
Roman B. Halas has traced the allied traditions whereby "Iscariot" derives
from 'as^{e}kara', "death by strangulation": "Furthermore, the Rabbis and
Jewish medical books claim that 'as^{e}kara' is the same as mḥnq (suffocation) mentioned in Job 7:15. Death resulting from this disease is swift
and painful, for the narrow cavity situated in the neck tends to obstruct
the normal flow of air passages and causes instantaneous suffocation. [Since
he was] afflicted with this disease in childhood, his parents began to call
[Judas] 'as^{e}karayòtq'. . . . He ended his earthly existence by suffocation as
a just punishment from God for the sin of betrayal."[99] Dante's is thus
not only a visual but an auditory depiction of the suicide as Judas. The
language of the episode with its coughing sibilants, and the straining speech
of the plants with its painful, hissing issuance must take on a different
interpretation. The suicides imitate forever the point of death of the rapacious apostle, the hanging "man of suffocation."

The stress that the Poet, through the character Piero, places on the notion of "root" ("le nove radici") seems merely a grotesque concentration
on the souls' metamorphosis until it is realized that the "root" of Piero's
sin was the love of money, the *radix malorum, avaritia* or *cupiditas*. The
soul of the sinner has been reduced essentially to the root of its sequence
of sins. Piero thus swears an odd fealty to his lord with a pledge of such
ambiguous resonance.

Comparison with the Circle of Avarice in the *Purgatorio* substantiates
our reading. Hugh Capet, the major representative of the sin in the fifth
girone, identifies himself using the same imagery familiar to the reader from
Inferno XIII:

> Io fui radice de la mala pianta
>   che la terra cristiana tutta aduggia,
>   sì che buon frutto rado se ne schianta.

(*Purg.* XX.43–45: "I was the root of the evil plant that overshadows
all the Christian land so that good fruit is seldom plucked from it.")

In retrospect can we understand even more clearly that Piero's bush reflects perversely a *genealogical* tree, as we noted above. The various uses in the *Commedia* of the verb "schiantare," meaning "to break off" or "pick" twigs or fruit, also comfort our typological and iconological interpretation. The word is used of the fruits of Eden in *Purgatorio* xxviii.120, and of the Tree of Life and Justice in *Purgatorio* xxxiii.58.[100] This last usage puts Piero's inverted state and outrage ("Perché mi schiante?") into clear perspective. By perverting justice, by denial of life in casting asunder the image of the Redeemer in his own person, the Logothete is punished by a metamorphosis into a barren inversion of Christ as *arbor salutifera*. Piero is torn as he once tore figuratively the Tree of Justice.

Again in the purgatorial Circle of Avarice, the major images appear: Polymnestor and his victim Polydorus figure again among the examples:

> ed in infamia tutto 'l monte gira
> Polinestor ch'ancise Polidoro

(*Purg.* xx.114–15: "and in infamy the name of Polymnestor who slew Polydorus circles all the mountain.")

The figure of Judas returns in reference to the greed of Charles of Valois. Charles Lackland's ("Carlo Sanzaterra") "lance of Judas" is avarice, as the context reveals: his "lancia" bursts the swollen belly of Florence's greed (we recall the swollen paunches of the Harpies):

> Tempo vegg'io, non molto dopo ancoi,
>   che tragge un altro Carlo fuor di Francia,
>   per far conoscer meglio e sé e' suoi.
> Sanz'arme n'esce e solo con la lancia
>   con la qual giostrò Giuda, e quella ponta
>   sí, ch'a Fiorenza fa scoppiar la pancia.

(Lines 70–75: "A time I see not long from this present day which brings another Charles out of France, to make both himself and his own the better known. Forth he comes unarmed save only with the lance with which Judas tilted, and he so couches it that he bursts the paunch of Florence.")

Dante was only too grimly aware that Charles had given free rein to his own cupidity in abetting the Black leader, Corso Donati, in pillaging and plundering the property of White Guelphs in 1301.

Most important, avarice is also seen as an absorbing sin which leads to the *neglect of one's own flesh*. Hugh Capet laments:

> O avarizia, che puoi tu più farne,
>   poscia c'ha' il mio sangue a te sì tratto,
>   *che non si cura de la propria carne?*

(Lines 82–84: "O Avarice, what more can you do to us, since you have so drawn my blood to yourself that it has no care for its own flesh?")

With these observations on the historical facts and on the significance of the major images of the episode, we must reread Piero's protestation of innocence in a different light: that he was not guilty of sheer treachery seems borne out both inside and outside the poem, and on both the literal and symbolic levels, for Dante placed Piero not in the ninth circle of Hell among the traitors but in the seventh among the violent. However, that the course of his sins led him by degrees to the same earthly end as Jesus' betrayer there can be no doubt, and it is clear that Judas' other attributes taken collectively form the unifying basis for the imagery of *Inferno* XIII and *Inferno* XIV.1–3. The shameful comparison does little for Piero's worldly reputation. The cantos give nothing of the near-wholesome greatness and magnanimity that romantic and neo-romantic readers believe they see. Beneath the letter lurks the Logothete's grasping avarice, willing to seize from the weak or innocent, ready to sacrifice the poor and humble for cash. Dante, obviously aware of many of the varied tales told of della Vigna's misdeeds and death, reflects in his poetry the murky, dubious nature of the Logothete's sins by a similar ambiguity and conflict between the different levels of the text itself. What Piero's own protests deny, the imagery pitilessly reveals: a greedy, violent, tyrannous character who kills himself in shame and despair after persecuting the innocent and stealing from the common coffers. Dante's didactic subtlety is exquisite. Piero is indeed a new Judas.

Notes

1. Leo Spitzer concentrated brilliantly on the stylistics of the text in "Speech and Language in *Inferno* XIII," *Italica*, XIX (1942), 81–104; republished in *Romanische Literaturstudien 1936–1956* (Tübingen: Max Niemeyer, 1959), pp. 544–68.

Others have demonstrated or refuted that the diction of the canto is a portrait or parody of the major figure: Francesco Novati, "Pier della Vigna," in *Con Dante e per Dante* (Milan: Hoepli, 1898), esp. pp. 17–18, 31; Francesco D'Ovidio, "Pier della Vigna," in *Nuovi studii danteschi* (Milan: Hoepli, 1907), esp. pp. 229–38; C. H. Grandgent, *Companion to the Divine Comedy*, ed. Charles S. Singleton (Cambridge, Mass.: Harvard University Press, 1975), pp. 60–61; Spitzer, pp. 544–45, 555–68.

Others have reentered the worn lists of a *querelle des anciens et des modernes* to prove the superiority or inferiority of Virgil's achievement in the *Aeneid*'s Polydorus incident in comparison with Dante's creation in the wood of the suicides: Ireneo Sanesi, "Polidoro e Pier della Vigna," *Studi medievali*, NS 5 (1932), 207–16. Giovanni Patroni, "L'Episodio virgiliano di Polidoro ed i Dantisti," *Rendiconti dell'Istituto Lombardo di Scienze e Lettere*, LXXI (Milan, 1937), 59–72.

And many have argued without decision over the identity of the unnamed Florentine suicide at the end of *Inferno* XIII: D'Ovidio, pp. 325–33; Spitzer, pp. 563–68; Sebastiano Aglianò, "Lettura del canto XIII dell'*Inferno*," *Studi danteschi*, XXXIII (1955), 141–86, here, 183–85; Gino Masi, "Fra savi e mercanti suicidi del tempo di Dante," *Il Giornale dantesco*, NS 9, XXXIX (1938), 199–238.

Among useful articles not otherwise appearing in the footnotes are the following: Marcello Camilucci, "Il Canto di Pier delle Vigne," in *Letture dell'Inferno*, a cura di Vittorio Vettori, Lectura Dantis Internazionale (Milan: Marzorati, 1963), pp. 115–39; Ettore Bonora, "Il canto XIII dell'*Inferno*," *Cultura e scuola*, IV (1965), 446–54; Étienne Gilson, "Poésie et théologie dans la Divine Comédie," *Atti del Congresso Internazionale di Studi Danteschi* (Florence: Sansoni, 1965), pp. 197–223; Umberto Bosco, "Il canto dei suicidi," in *Dante vicino* (Caltanisetta and Rome: Salvatore Sciascia, 1966), pp. 255–73; Ignazio Baldelli, "Il canto XIII dell'*Inferno*," *Nuove letture dantesche* (Florence: Le Monnier, 1968), II, pp. 33–45; Ettore Paratore, "Analisi 'retorica' del canto di Pier della Vigna," in *Tradizione e struttura in Dante* (Florence: Sansoni, 1968), pp. 178–220; Georges Güntert, "Pier delle Vigne e l'unità del canto," *Lettere italiane*, XXIII, n. 4 (1971), 548–55; Daniel Rolfs, "Dante and the Problem of Suicide," *The Michigan Academician*, IV (1974), 367–75; David H. Higgins, "Cicero, Aquinas, and St. Matthew in *Inferno* XIII," *Dante Studies*, XCIII (1975), 61–94. In the text I have offered my own translation for the foreign language quotations. Where a full English rendering exists for a work, I have so noted it, but I have not always followed the wording of these published translations.

2. Leonardo Olschki ("Dante and Peter de Vinea," *Romanic Review*, XXXI [1940], 105–11) affirms the Protonotary's historical guilt but believes that Dante invented

the "pious fable" of innocence because he identified himself with Piero: both had been charged with corruption in office. Olschki thus believes that Dante intended to "rehabilitate" the notary "as a fellow sufferer" (pp. 105, 110), an untenable interpretation, as we will show. Friedrich Schneider ("Kaiser Friedrich II. und Petrus von Vinea im Urteil Dantes," *Deutsches Dante-Jahrbuch*, XXVII, n.f. 18 [1948], 230–50) concludes erroneously that the *Divina Commedia* is "eine historische Quelle ersten Ranges, die Petrus von Vinea unschuldig erklärt" (p. 250).

Other major studies include: Ernst Kantorowicz, *Kaiser Friedrich der Zweite*, vol. I (Berlin: Georg Bondi, 1927), *Ergänzungsband* (Berlin: George Bondi, 1931); (both vols. reprinted Düsseldorf and Munich: Helmut Küpper vormals Georg Bondi, 1963); the *Ergänzungsband* contains a vast bibliography. The study, without the second volume, appeared in English as *Frederick the Second, 1194–1250*, trans. E. O. Lorimer (London: Constable, 1931). Important also is the bibliography in Thomas Curtis Van Cleve, *The Emperor Frederick II of Hohenstaufen: Immutator Mundi* (Oxford: Clarendon Press, 1972), pp. 543–98, and the book by Antonio Casertano, *Un oscuro dramma politico del secolo* XIII: *Pietro della Vigna* (Rome: Libreria del Littorio, 1928). The most useful, penetrating and convincing study on Piero's historical guilt is by Friedrich Baethgen, "Dante und Petrus de Vinea: eine kritische Studie," *Sitzungsberichte der Bayerischen Akademie der Wissenschaften, Philosophisch-historische Klasse* (1955, Heft 3), 3–49.

3. Cf. *De Monarchia* I. 8: "De intentione Dei est ut omne causatum in tantum divinam similitudinem representet, in quantum propria natura recipere potest. Propter quod dictum est, 'Faciamus hominem ad ymaginem et similitudinem nostram'; quod licet 'ad ymaginem' de rebus inferioribus ab homine dici non possit, 'ad similitudinem' tamen de qualibet dici potest, cum totum universum nichil aliud sit quam vestigium quoddam divine bonitatis" (*Opere di Dante Alighieri*, a cura di Fredi Chiappelli [Milan: Ugo Mursia, 1965], p. 339).

4. Arthur Watson, *The Early Iconography of the Tree of Jesse* (London: Oxford University Press, 1934), pp. 52–54, 87. Gertrude Schiller, *The Passion of Jesus Christ*, trans. Janet Seligman, Vol. II of *Iconography of Christian Art* (Greenwich, Conn.: New York Graphic Society, 1972), pp. 134–37.

5. Dante Alighieri, *The Divine Comedy*, trans. with a commentary by Charles S. Singleton, Bollingen Series, LXXX (Princeton, N. J.: Princeton University Press, 1970–1975), 3 vols. in 6; here *Inferno Commentary*, p. 626. All references to the *Commedia* are made from the Petrocchi text republished in Dr. Singleton's volumes. For the symbolism of the Tree in the description of Satan (*Inferno* XXXIV), see John Freccero's article, "The Sign of Satan," *Modern Language Notes*, LXXX (1965), 11–26. One should also bear in mind that Dante is probably alluding to the legend which stems from the Second Book of Esdras 5:5, viz., that all trees bled in sympathy with the Redeemer on the Tree of the Cross: "Blood shall drip from wood, and the stone shall utter its voice."

6. Similarly, though death has come to the wastrels, they obstinately yearn for the annihilation of their souls: "Or accorri, accorri, morte!" (*Inferno* XIII. 118). By a contemporary pun, the wasting of their "substance" was one with the destruction

of the single "substance" of body and soul. For Aristotle, in the *Nicomachaean Ethics*, iv.1, profligacy was a form of self-destruction (ed. Martin Ostwald, Library of Liberal Arts [Indianapolis and New York: Bobbs-Merrill, 1962], p. 83).

7. See, for example, the absurd tale told by Giacomo d'Acqui (ca. 1334) in A. Huillard-Bréholles, *Vie et Correspondance de Pierre de la Vigne* (Paris: Plon, 1864), pp. 67-68. Huillard-Bréholles' study, which contains many primary sources in the section "Pièces justificatives," will be cited hereafter as *Pierre*.

8. See the letters published in *Pierre*, pp. 289-91.

9. Schiller, Vol. ii, pl. 442; Watson, p. 61.

10. St. Augustine, *In Joannis Evangelium*, Tractatus lxxx (*PL*, 35, col. 1839); my italics. Saint Augustine, *Homilies on the Gospel According to St. John and his First Epistle*, A Library of Fathers of the Holy Catholic Church Anterior to the Division of the East and West (Oxford: John Henry Parker, 1849), ii, p. 825. St. Thomas Acquinas, *Catena aurea super quattuor Evangelistas* (Basel: Michael Wenssler, 1476), Joannes XV, 1. *Catena Aurea* (Oxford and London: James Parker, 1874), vi, p. 474. The theme of Christ as vine forms the central metaphor of the *Vitis mystica seu tractatus de passione Domini* (*PL*, 184, col. 635-740) formerly ascribed to St. Bernard of Clairvaux but now attributed to St. Bonaventure. If Dante knew the treatise, it probably formed many of the fundamental images of *Inferno* xiii.

11. "An forte quis ambigat Dei esse *plantationem* bonum hominem? Audi sanctum David de viro bono quid canat: 'Erit,' ait, 'tamquam lignum quod *plantatum* est secus decursus aquarum, quod fructum suum dabit in tempore suo, et folium eius non defluet.' Audi Ieremiam eodem spiritu concinentem, et hisdem pene verbis: 'Erit tanquam lignum,' inquit, 'quod *plantatum est* secus decursus aquarum, quod ad humorem mittit radices suas, et non timebit cum venerit aetus.' Item Propheta: 'Iustus ut palma florebit, et sicut cedrus Libani multiplicabitur.' Et de seipso: 'Ego autem sicut oliva fructifera in domo Dei.' " *Sermo* xxiii *in Cantica Canticarum*, in Sancti Bernardi, *Opera*, ed. J. Leclerq et al., i (Rome: Editiones Cistercienses, 1957), pp. 141-42.

12. *Catechiesis* xx, *Mystagogica* iii (*PG*, 33, col. 1082-84). Cited by Jean Daniélou, *The Bible and Liturgy*, ed. Michael A. Mathis, Liturgical Studies (Notre Dame, Indiana: University of Notre Dame Press, 1965), p. 45.

13. *Moralia in Job*, xx, 21 (*PL*, 76, col. 150).

14. *PL*, 112, "spinas," col. 1056; "ramos," col. 1037.

15. Watson, *Tree of Jesse*, pp. 167-68; Schiller, i, 15-22.

16. Schiller, ii, 135, 136-37. Other examples include two panels in the Galleria dell' Accademia in Florence: the first a Tree of Jesse by Pacino di Buonaguida (cat. no. 8459) shows instead of a dove, a red pelican feeding its young with its own blood; and second, a Crucifix attributed only to the "Scuola fiorentina" from the beginning of the fourteenth century, bears a white pelican feeding its young above the head of Christ (cat. no. 436).

17. For example, Peter Damian begins his *De exaltatione Sanctae Crucis*: "De verga Jesse devenimus ad virgam crucis, et principium redemptionis fine concludimus" (*Sermo* xlvii, 1; *PL*, 144, col. 761). Watson, *The Tree of Jesse*, pp. 52-53.

See also George Ferguson, *Signs and Symbols in Christian Art* (New York: Oxford University Press, 1961), p. 39.

18. Related to the Tree of Jesse and an offshoot of the "daughters of avarice" doctrine, to which we will return later, was the common parable of the two trees of good and evil (Galatians 5:19-23; Matthew 7:17-20). Adolf Katzenellenbogen (*Allegories of the Virtues and Vices in Medieval Art* [New York: Norton, 1964], pp. 63-68; pl. 64, 65, 66 and 67) describes several important examples, among them the following: "The original of the *Liber floridus Lamberti*, the illustrated encyclopedia written about 1120 by the prebendary of St. Omer shows the reader the 'Arbor bona' as a symbol of the 'Ecclesia fidelium' . . . Beside [it] the 'Arbor mala', also named 'Synagoga', gives an impression of deadness and coldness ('Haec arbor autumnalis est infructuosa, bis mortua, eradicata, cui procella tenebrarum conservata est in aeternum'). *Cupiditas* is the root, and twelve vices, some of which were enumerated by St. Paul as the works of the flesh (Gal. 5:19 ff.) are the evil fruits (p. 65). . . . [A copy of the Pseudo-Hugo, *De fructibus carnis et spiritus* contrasts] the 'Arbor vitiorum' and the 'Arbor virtutem'. Numerous inscriptions interpret in full detail the meaning of the two pictures. The growth of destruction, designated as 'sinistra,' is given the place befitting all depravity, the left ('Stirps, flos, fructus, odor sanctis fuga, sontibus error—Mortis ab hac stirpe vicii genus effluit omne')"(p. 66).

19. Pier della Vigna's life as based on existing documents is found in *Pierre*, pp. 1-90. For the events in the light of his fall, Kantorowicz, *Kaiser Friedrich*, I, 606-9; Baethgen, pp. 3-11; Van Cleve, pp. 519-23.

20. *Pierre*, p. 11.

21. *Pierre*, p. 12.

22. *Pierre*, p. 14.

23. Van Cleve, pp. 256, 323.

24. The closing sentences of the Latin text of the *Constitutiones* declare that the Emperor had commanded his Justice of the High Court to codify the laws: "Accipite gratanter, o populi, constitutiones istas . . . quas per magistrum petrum de Vineis Capuanum, magnae curiae nostrae judicem et fidelem nostrum, mandavimus compilari" (J.-L.-A. Huillard-Bréholles, *Historia diplomatica Friderici Secundi*, vol. IV, pars I [Paris: Plon, 1856; rpt. Turin: Bottega d'Erasmo, 1963], p. 176. *Pierre*, p. 15. James M. Powell, *The Liber Augustalis or Constitutions of Melfi Promulgated by the Emperor Frederick II for the Kingdom of Sicily in 1231* (Syracuse, N.Y.: Syracuse University Press, 1971).

25. The Norman Kings of Sicily had borrowed the term "logotheta" from the Greeks to designate the minister who drew up the laws and edicts. In his *Cronica* (a cura di Giuseppe Scalia, Scrittori d'Italia, No. 232-33 [Bari: Laterza, 1966], II, p. 501), Salimbene de Adam defines it thus: "*De logothéta, quid sit*: Componitur quoque logós cum theta, quod est positio; et dicitur hic et hec logothéta, qui sermonem facit in popolo vel qui edictum imperatoris vel alicuius principis popolo nuntiat." Huillard-Bréholles notes that his duties were in the main fiscal (*Pierre*, pp. 49-51). Baethgen, p. 6.

26. Francesco Pippino describes the painting: Frederick personifying "Justitia,"

was seated on a throne pointing his finger towards Pier della Vigna seated below; in the foreground kneeling subjects appealed for justice. The following legends were inscribed: [Populus:] "Caesar amor legum, Friderice piissime regum/ Causarum telas nostrasque resolve querelas." [Fridericus:] "Pro vestra lite censorum juris adite: / Hic est: jura dabit vel per me danda rogabit. / Vinee cognomen Petrus judex est sibi nomen." (*Chronica*, cap. 39; in Ludovico Muratori, *Rerum italicarum scriptores*, IX [Mediolani: Typographia Societatis Palatinae, 1726], col. 660.) Guido da Pisa also transcribes these legends in his *Commentary* (*Expositiones et Glose super Comediam Dantis* or *Commentary on Dante's Inferno*, ed. Vincenzo Cioffari [Albany, N.Y.: State University of New York Press, 1974], p. 249). Guido's text differs only in small details.

27. Guidonis Bonati, *De Astronomia Tractatus X*, pars 1ª (Basileae: s.n., 1550), col. 210. Domenico Guerri, "Un astrologo condannato da Dante," *Bullettino della Società Dantesca Italiana*, XXII (1915), 200–54, *Pierre*, pp. 69–70.

For the Frederician gold *Augustalis*, see Van Cleve, pp. 277–78; illustrations of the coin, nos. 4 and 6.

28. "Ascendit ad tantum dignitatem, quod beatus reputabatur, qui poterat fimbriolam aliquam habere gratie ipsius; et quicquid ipse faciebat, imperator habebat ratum, ipse autem multa retractabat et infingebat de his que faciebat imperator." Guido Bonatti, col. 210.

29. *Pierre*, pp. 87–88. Kantorowicz, *Ergänzungsband*, p. 246. Antonio Casertano, *Un oscuro dramma politico*.

30. The physician was condemned to death (*Historia Diplomatica*, VI. 708; Baethgen's edition, pp. 42–44); no mention is made in the document of *two* assassins. Historians have proved that this missive does not refer to Pier della Vigna (*Pierre*, pp. 80–82; Baethgen, pp. 12–16).

31. Matthaei Parisiensis, Monachi sancti Albani, *Chronica Majora*, ed. Henry Richard Luard, Rolls Series, V (London: Longman et al., 1880), pp. 68–69; "Fretheriscus letiferam potionem evadit a Petro de Vinea paratam:" "Petrus: 'O domine mi, pluries dedit iste meus phisicus salutarem vobis potionem, quare modo formidatis?"

32. Salimbene de Adam, *Cronica*, I, pp. 288–89. *Pierre*, pp. 38–39. Baethgen, p. 26.

33. The Emperor learned that, "Messires Pierres de la Vigne l'avoit traï a la [sic] Pape et le sot par unes letres, qui furent trouvées en ses coffres;" (*Ex historiis anonymi remensis*, ed. O. Holder-Egger, in *Monumenta Germaniae historica, Scriptorum* tom. XXVI [Hannover: Hahn, 1882], p. 536, para. 240). Baethgen, p. 26.

34. "Gli era da molti baroni e grandi uomini portata fiera invidia; e stando essi continuamente attenti . . . avvenne, che, avendo Federigo guerra con la Chiesa, essi con lettere false e con testimoni subornati, diedero a vedere allo 'mperadore questo maestro Piero aver col papa certo occulto trattato contro allo stato dello 'mperadore e avergli ancora alcun segreto dello 'mperadore rivelato." Giovanni Boccaccio, *Esposizioni sopra la Comedia di Dante*, a cura di Giorgio Padoan, in *Tutte le opere di Giovanni Boccaccio*, VI (Milan: Mondadori, 1965), p. 610. Similarly Giovanni Villani (Lib. VI, cap. 22) had asserted della Vigna's innocence, but his words betray a vagueness concerning the facts: 'Lo 'mperadore fece abbacinare il savio uomo maestro Piero dalle Vigne, il buono dittatore, opponendogli tradigione, ma ciò gli fu fatto per invidia

di suo grande stato, per la qual cosa il detto per dolore si lasciò tosto morire in pregione, e chi disse ch'egli medesimo si tolse la vita" (*Cronica*, compilata da Francesco Gherardi Dragomanni [Florence: Sansone Coen, 1844], I, p. 244).

35. "Tanquam pacis turbatorem cum candenti ferro fecit exoculari." (Flaminio dal Borgo, *Dissertazioni sopra l'istoria pisana* [Pisa: Giovanni Paolo Giovannelli, 1761], tom. I, parte 1, Dissertazione IV, p. 211); *Pierre*, p. 66.

36. Pippino, "De magistro Petro de Vineis," *Chronica*, cap. 39: "Sed quum in honore esset Petrus, non intellexit; nam ex proditionis nota, ut aliqui ferunt, ab Imperatore carceri trusus atque coecatus, horrendo squallore misere vitam finivit. Male enim tractasse dicitur super discordia inter Imperatorem et Papam. Aliqui ad hanc infidelitatem perductum esse ferunt, quod nudatus imperator thesauris suis ex ipsa discordia, ipsum Petrum magno thesauro privaverit. *Nonnulli referunt, quod in vitula eius arabat*," (Italics added); Baethgen, pp. 27–28; and *Pierre*, p. 67.

37. dal Borgo, *Dissertazioni*, tom. I, parte 1, Diss. IV, p. 212. Baethgen, p. 27.

38. In 1246 the pope rewarded conspirators who escaped prosecution by the Emperor, and cared for their families, but in 1249 the Pope deprived Piero's nephew Giovanni of the benefice of his Church of San Pietro *ad cellas* in the diocese of Teano and awarded it to one of his secretaries. Innocent IV's letters are published in *Pierre*, pp. 315–16 ("Pièces justificatives," nos. 16 and 17). The Pope disposed of Pier della Vigna's belongings as an enemy of the Church (*Pierre*, pp. 62–64, and for the pertinent papal letters, pp. 318–19).

39. I follow Baethgen's careful consideration of the affair; see especially pp. 23–25. The primary sources on la Cerbaia are published by Fedor Schneider, "Nachlese in Toscana," *Quellen und Forschungen aus italienischen Archiven und Bibliotheken*, XXII (1930–31), 31–86.

40. The deed is published by Fedor Schneider, p. 80.

41. The letter is published in *Pierre*, p. 317 ("Pièces justificatives," no. 17.).

42. Baethgen, p. 32, n. 80. The records concerning prosecution of traitors and confiscation of their property are published by Huillard-Bréholles in *Historia Diplomatica*, V, pp. 435, 564, 756, 767, 805, 833, 835, 910, 915.

43. The text of the letter is edited by Baethgen, pp. 44–47.

44. *Pierre*, p. 79.

45. Kantorowicz, *Kaiser Friedrich*, I, 607–10. Kantorowicz calls Pier della Vigna "Judas" but nowhere notes that Pietro di Dante had used the comparison, nor does he note its implications for the *Divina Commedia* (Petri Allegherii, *Super Dantis Ipsius Genitoris Comoediam Commentarium*, curante Vincentio Nannucci [Florentiae: Angelum Garinei, 1844], pp. 158–59).

46. Olschki, p. 106.

47. Baethgen, esp. pp. 29–34. Van Cleve, p. 522.

48. Van Cleve, p. 521.

49. *Fabii Planciadis Fulgentii V. C. Opera Accedunt Fabii Claudii Fulgentii V. C. de Aetatibus Mundi et Hominis et S. Fulgentii Episcopi Super Thebaiden*, recensuit Rudolfus Helm, addenda adiecit Jean Préaux (Stuttgart: B. G. Teubner, 1970), p. 79 [*Mitologiarum liber III, 11*]. *Fulgentius the Mythographer*, trans. Leslie George Whit-

bread (Columbus, Ohio: Ohio State University Press, 1971), p. 98; Pietro Alighieri, Guido da Pisa and the Anonimo allegorize the Harpies after Fulgentius (Petri Alleghierii, *Commentarium*, p. 160; Guido da Pisa, *Commentary*, p. 247; *Commento alla Divina Commedia d'Anonimo Fiorentino del secolo XIV*, a cura di Pietro Fanfani [Bologna: Gaetano Romagnoli, 1866], I, 319-20).

50. "Phineus igitur, a fenerando dictus, in modum avaritiae ponitur." *Scriptores Rerum Mythicarum Latini Tres, Romae Nuper Reperti*, ed. Georg Heinrich Bode (Cellis: E. H. C. Schulz, 1834), p. 173; cited hereafter as Bode.

[Pseudo-Bernardus Silvestris] *The Commentary on the First Six Books of the Aeneid of Vergil Commonly Attributed to Bernardus Silvestris*, ed. Julian Ward Jones and Elizabeth Frances Jones (Lincoln and London: University of Nebraska Press, 1977), p. 73, 1.24; all quotations are taken from this edition.

51. "Arpage enim Grece rapina dicitur—ideo virgines, quod omnis rapina arida sit et sterilis, ideo plumis circumdatae, quia quicquid rapina invaserit celat, ideo volatiles, quod omnis rapina ad volandum sit celerrima. Aello enim Grece quasi edon allon, id est alienum tollens, Oquipete id est citius auferens, Celenum vero nigrum Grece dicitur, unde et Homerus prima Iliados rhapsodia: . . . 'Statim niger tuus sanguis emanabit per meam hastem—hoc igitur significare volentes quod primum sit alienum concupisci, secundum concupita invadere, tertium celare quae invadit.'" *Mitologiarum liber I*, IX (Helm, pp. 21-22; Whitbread, p. 52-53); Pietro Alighieri, pp. 161-62; and Guido da Pisa, *Commentary*, p. 247; Anonimo, I, pp. 319-20.

52. Bode, p. 173. See also the First Vatican Mythographer, 27 (pp. 9-10); and the Second, 13, [Harpies] and 142 [Phineus], pp. 78, 124; Fulgentius, *Mitologiarum liber III*.

53. Reading "rapacitas" for Jones' "capacitas." *Commentum*, p. 74.

54. Benevenuti de Rambaldis de Imola, *Comentum super Dantis Aldigherij Comoediam*, curante Jacopo Philippo Lacaita (Florentiae: Barbèra, 1887), I, pp. 427 and 447.

Francesco D'Ovidio, after expressing his own difficulty in seeing the connection between the Harpies and suicide, patronizingly mocks Benvenuto's gloss that they symbolize avarice: "Benvenuto, sedotto da vere e da supposte etimologie, fa le Arpie simboli di avarizia, e arzigogola artificiosi rapporti tra questa e il suicidio" (p. 179). Vincenzo Presta similarly fails to see the intimate moral and artistic unity which the Harpies have with the rest of the Canto: "Proprio a canto finito ci si accorge di come la *imitatio virgiliana* delle Arpie non sia più che una semplice suggestione culturale che, pur se investita di contenuto allegorico, non supera la mera enunciazione e resta quindi senza un vero sviluppo narrativo." ("In margine al canto XIII dell'*Inferno*," *Dante Studies*, XC [1972], 15).

55. See above, n. 8.

56. "Omnem suam substantiam perdidit." Fulgentius, *Mitologiarum liber III*, 3 (Helm, p. 62; Whitbread, p. 85). Bode, pp. 103, 198-99. For Renato Serra ("Su la pena dei dissipatori," *Giornale Storico della Letteratura Italiana*, XLIII [1904], 278-98), the chase in Hell was drawn from the "wilde Jagd" legends of folklore.

57. For "canes Jovis" see n. 51 above. For Actaeon's "Harpyia" see *Metamorphoses* III. 215 (ed. and trans. Frank Justus Miller, Loeb Classical Library [Cambridge,

Mass.: Harvard University Press; London: William Heinemann, 1966], 2 vols.).

58. See for example, William J. Kennedy, "Irony, Allegoresis, and Allegory in Virgil, Ovid and Dante," *Arcadia: Zeitschrift für vergleichende Literaturwissenschaft*, VII (1972), 115–34, esp. 123–29. Kennedy follows the conventional interpretation of the cantos in which the Poet exonerates and rehabilitates Pier della Vigna, the innocent victim of the Emperor's unjust persecution.

59. Salimbene, *Cronica*, I, pp. 288, 635–36. Van Cleve, p. 522.

60. Pseudo-Bernardus Silvestris, *Commentum*, pp. 18–19.

61. Dante has Virgil say expressly:

> "s'elli avesse potuto creder prima,"
> rispose 'l savio mio, "anima lesa,
> *ciò c'ha veduto pur con la mia rima*,
> non avrebbe in te la man distesa."

(*Inferno* XIII.46–49): "If he, O wounded spirit, had been able to believe before," replied my sage, "what he had never seen save in my verses, he would not have stretched forth his hand against you.")

62. "Cum sorores Phaetontis plangerent eius mortem: subito *in arbores sunt conversae* . . . . *Talis mutatio videtur quotidie in avaris* . . . processu temporis: ipsi efficiuntur arbores id est avari: terrae admodum arboris adhaerentes. Nam pes id est affectio efficitur radix inquantum in terra id est in bonis terrenis infigitur per amorem. Cortex etiam exterioris malae conversationis et malae consuetudinis eos operit: et sic in arbores id est viros incompatientes et insensibiles diabolus eos vertit. Unde isti sunt sicut arbor mala quae non facit fructus bonos: quae merito comburi praecipitur [Matt. 3:10]." Petrus Berchorius [*Ovidius Moralizatus*], *Reductorium morale, Liber XV*, cap. ii–xv: *"Ovidius Moralizatus" naar de Parijse druk van 1509*, ed. Joseph Engels (Utrecht: Instituut voor Laat Latijn der Rijksuniversiteit, 1962), p. 50. My italics.

63. *Moralia*, XX.21 (*PL*, 76, col. 150). The *Liber floridus Lamberti* gives an illustration of the effects of avarice: "cupiditas" is shown as the root; and the works of the flesh (Galatians 5:19–23) are depicted as the evil fruits (Katzenellenbogen, *Allegories*, pp. 65–66, pl. 65).

64. See the interesting comments in Van Cleve, pp. 100–102, 120, 125, 162–63, 180, 241, 260, 412, 538; *De monarchia*, esp. Lib. III.

65. "Esium nobilem Marchie civitatem, insigne originis nostre principium, ubi nos diva mater nostra eduxit in lucem. . . . Bethleem nostra terra Cesaris et origo pectori nostro . . . Bethleem, civitas Marchie non minima, es in generis nostri principibus." *Historia Diplomatica*, vol. V, pt. 1, p. 378.

66. "Dum translato quasi vivifice crucis mysterio de partibus transmarinis in Regnum, tanquam iterum in Apulia crucifixus sit Christus. . . ." *Historia Diplomatica*, vol. VI, pt. 2, pp. 710–13. Kantorowicz, *Kaiser Friedrich*, I, 607; *Ergänzungsband*, p. 245.

67. Baethgen edits the letter, p. 46. *Historia Diplomatica*, vol. VI, pt. 2, pp. 700–701.

68. "Achitofel alterum, cujus consilio contemptis principibus majestas imperatoria

regituret respublica gubernatur." *Le Liber Censuum de L'Église Romaine*, ed. Paul Fabre, Bibliothèque des Écoles Françaises d'Athènes et de Rome (Paris: Albert Fontemoing, 1905), vol. i, p. 28, col. 1.

69. St. Augustine, *In Joannis Evangelium*, Tractatus l, 9–10 (*PL*, 35, col. 1761-62). Saint Augustine, *Homilies on the Gospel*, ii, pp. 674-75. My italics.

70. Chrysostomos continues: "Audite avari, cogitate quae ille passus sit; quomodo pecunias amiserit, et scelus perpetraverit; quomodo avaritiae fructum non tulerit, et animam perdiderit. Talis est avaritiae tyrannis: nec argento fruitur, nec praesenti vita, nec futura: sed omnia confertim amisit, malamque nactus apud illos famam, laqueo gulam fregit." *In Matthaeum*, Homil. lxxxv (al. lxxxvi), 2 (*PG*, 58, col. 760). Concerning Judas' "Motive of Avarice" see Roman B. Halas, *Judas Iscariot*, Diss., Faculty of the School of Sacred Theology of the Catholic University of America (Washington, D.C.: The Catholic University of America Press, 1946), pp. 80-81.

71. Halas, p. 81. Cf. Origen, *Commentarius in Matthaeum*, Tomus xi, 9 (*PG*, 13, col. 934). St. John Chrysostomos, *Expositio in Psalmum* vi, 6 (*PG*, 55, col. 79); *In Epistolam ad Philippenses*, cap. ii, Homil. vi, 5, (*PG*, 62, col. 225).

72. St. John Chrysostomos, *In Matthaeum*, Homil. lxxxi (al. lxxxii), 3 (*PG*, 58, col. 733); Homil. xxviii (al. xxix), 4 (*PG*, 57, col. 356); Origen, *Commentarius in Matthaeum*, xi, 9 (*PG*, 13, col. 13, 934); xvi, 3 (*PG*, 13, col. 1390); St. Cyril, *Cathechesis*, xiii, 6 (*PG*, 33, col. 779). Rabanus Maurus, *Commentaria in Libros duos Paralipomenon*, Lib. ii, 27 (*PL*, 109, col. 406). St. Thomas Aquinas, *Summa theologica*, ii–ii, qu. 118, art. 8. Halas, p. 81.

73. "Caeterum quomodocumque interpretatus fueris, merces interpretatur et pretium." *Breviarium in Psalmos: Psalm.* cviii (*PL*, 26, col. 1157). *Homily 35 on Psalm 108* in *The Homilies of Saint Jerome*, i, trans. Sister Marie Liguori Ewald, The Fathers of the Church, 48 (Washington, D.C.: The Catholic University of America Press, 1964), p. 260. Similarly, in his *Commentaria in Evangelium S. Matthaei*, i.10: "Vel a vico aut urbe in quo ortus est, vel ex tribu Isachar vocabulum sumpsit: ut quodam vaticinio in condemnationem sui natus sit. Isachar enim interpretatur 'merces,' ut significetur pretium proditoris" (*PL*, 26, col. 62). Cf. Isidore of Seville: "Issachar enim interpretatur *merces*, et significaretur pretium proditoris, quo vendidit Dominum" (*Etymologiarum*, lib. vii, cap. ix "De Apostolis," *PL*, 82, col. 290). See Halas, pp. 11-21.

74. *Summa theologica*, ii–ii, qu. 118, art. 8, trans. by the Fathers of the English Dominican Province (New York: Benziger Brothers, 1947), ii, 1691 (italics added). In his commentary on *Inferno* xiii, Benvenuto da Imola writes: "Avaritia et prodigalitas maxime inducunt hominem ad desperationem" (*Comentum*, i, p. 447). Cf. *Purgatorio* xxviii.82-84. The "daughters of avarice" were often depicted as the "mala arbor" or "arbor vitiorum"; see n. 18 on the "mala arbor" above.

75. For a useful discussion of the conflicting reports of Judas' death in Matthew 27:4-5 and Acts 1:18 and how various Church writers reconciled them, see Halas, pp. 145-70, bibliography, pp. 193-206.

76. *Breviarium in Psalmos: Psalm.* cviii (*PL*, 26, col. 1157). *Homily 35 on Psalm 108* (*Homilies*, pp. 258-59).

77. *Moralia*, xi.12 (*PL*, 75, col. 959). *Morals on the Book of Job*, A Library of Fathers of the Holy Catholic Church Anterior to the Division of the East and West (Oxford: John Henry Parker, 1845), ii, 9.

78. Pietro Alighieri, *Commentarium*, pp. 158–59.

79. Schiller, ii.76–78. Reference to hanging appears not only in Pier della Vigna's speech but also in that of the second suicide, *Inferno* xiii.151. Giotto's frescoes for the Scrovegni Chapel of the Arena in Padua depict *desperatio* as a hanging woman accompanied by a wingèd devil (*L'Opera completa di Giotto*, presentazione di Giancarlo Vigorelli, apparati critici e filologici di Edi Baccheschi [Milan: Rizzoli, 1966], p. 107).

It might be mentioned here that the medieval "lives" of Judas Iscariot—merely elaborations on the legendary tales of Moses, Ruben, Oedipus and Secundus the Silent Philosopher—were of absolutely no influence upon Dante's episode of the suicides. For a review of such tales see Edward Kennard Rand, "Medieval Lives of Judas Iscariot," *Anniversary Papers by Colleagues and Pupils of George Lyman Kittredge* (Boston and London: Ginn, 1913), pp. 305–16.

80. André Grabar, *Christian Iconography: A Study of its Origins*, Bollingen Series xxx, 10 (Princeton, N.J.: Princeton University Press, 1968), p. 137; pl. 337.

81. Schiller, vol. ii, pl. 279.

82. Schiller, vol. ii, pl. 15.

83. Schiller, vol. ii, pl. 280.

84. Peter Brieger, Millard Meiss and Charles S. Singleton, *Illuminated Manuscripts of the Divine Comedy*, Bollingen Series lxxxi (Princeton, N.J.: Princeton University Press, 1969), i, 276–79 [Madrid], 316–18; ii, pl. 171a [Paris]; the authors do not publish the important Madrid illustration.

85. For this section of my essay I wish to express my especial thanks to my research assistant, Miss Nona Flores, who took such care and effort in helping me research the relation of Judas and Ahitophel in the Spring of 1977. Her invaluable aid and time was made available to me by a generous grant from the Research Board of the Graduate School of the University of Illinois.

86. Absalom also may be related to the image of the suicides after the Last Judgment. After his defeat in battle by David's army, Absalom flees into the forest on a mule; his hair is caught in an oak tree so that he dangles from it ("adhesit caput eius quercui et illo suspenso inter caelum et terram" [ii Regum (Samuel) 18:9]) and is transfixed by Joab's spear. Miss Flores kindly pointed out to me that Bertran de Born's reference to Ahitophel in *Inferno* xxviii is also reflected in the line "e'l capo tronco tenea *per le chiome*" (v. 121). Like Ahitophel, Bertran parted father from son.

87. St. Jerome, *Breviarium in Psalmos*, Psalm cviii (*PL*, 26, col. 1155); *Homily 35 on Psalm 108 [109]*, (*Homilies*, p. 255).

88. St. Augustine, *Enarratio in Psalmum* cviii [cix], 1 (*PL*, 37, col. 1431). See also *Enarratio in Psalmum* vii (*PL*, 36, col. 97).

89. " 'Achitophel etiam consiliarius regis.' Quid per Achitophel, qui quondam David consiliarius fuit, et postea, cupiditate depravatus, cum Absalon de nece ipsius tractabat, nisi Judas Scarioth, qui de apostolatus culmine in proditionis foveam cecidit,

insinuatur? Quod bene vocabulum Achitophel exprimit; interpretatur enim 'frater meus cadens,' sive 'irruens,' seu 'tractans.' Hic enim inter caeteros apostolos familiaritatis locum cum ipso Salvatore habuit; sed postea cum Judaeis avaritia seductus, mortem Domini meditando, perpetuo mortis sibi ruinam ascivit. Unde et Achitophel (sicut in libro Regum narratur [II Reg. 17]) videns suum consilium infatuatum, in domo propria laqueo vitam finire elegit. Similiter et Judas, Evangelio testante, videns quod Jesus ad mortem damnatus esset, poenitentia ductus retulit triginta argenteos principibus sacerdotum et senioribus, dicens: 'Peccavi tradens sanguinem justum. At illi dixerunt: Quid ad nos? tu videris. Et projectis argenteis in templo recessit, et abiens laqueo se suspendit' (Matt. 27)." Rabanus Maurus, *Commentaria in Libros duos Paralipomenon*, Lib. II, 27 (*PL*, 109, col. 406).

90. The thirteenth-century Moralised Bible, MS Oxford, Bodl., 270b, fol. 158; Alexandre de Laborde, *La Bible moralisée illustrée conservée à Oxford, Paris, et Londres*, Société française de reproductions de manuscrits à peintures (Paris: Pour les membres de la Société, 1911–1927), vol. 1, pl. 158. Artists' depictions of a hanging Judas with pendent viscera reflected a conflation of the differing accounts of the betrayer's death in the Vulgate (Matt. 27:5, and Luke's account in Acts 1:18. "Suspensus crepuit medius et diffusa sunt omnia viscera eius"). See Giotto's depiction, fig. 10.

91. Such as those in the Österreiche Nazionalbibliothek, Vienna, Codex 1179, f. 109v (Laborde, vol. IV, pl. 681), Codex 2554, f. 47v (Laborde, vol. IV, pl. 755), and the Codex of Toledo Cathedral, vol. I, f. 126 (Laborde, vol. IV, pl. 628).

92. The British Library, Harley 1527, f. 56 (Laborde, vol. III, pl. 527).

93. *PL*, 196, col. 1360.

94. *Summa theologica*, III, qu. 81, art. 2.

95. "Equitatis virgam vertebat in colubrum." Guido da Pisa, *Commentary*, p. 249. Frederick's letter to the Count of Caserta is published in Baethgen, p. 46.

96. Following St. Augustine, Dante recognized *cupiditas* or greed as the antithesis of justice "quod iustitia maxime contrariatur cupiditas" (*De Monarchia*, 1.11).

97. *L'Ottimo Commento della Divina Commedia*, a cura di Alessandro Torri, I (Pisa: Niccolò Capurro, 1927), p. 258. While the second suicide's role as a representative of all of Florence (Jacopo Alighieri, Jacopo della Lana, Boccaccio, Leo Spitzer) cannot be completely ruled out, he was obviously meant to be recognizable *personally* to his contemporaries. As Manfredi Porena aptly puts it, "Non é un X qualunque" (*La Divina Commedia* [Bologna: Zanichelli, 1951], I, p. 125). Graziolo de' Bambaglioli glosses v. 151: "Iste florentinus fuit dominus Loctus iudex de Aglis de Florentia, qui secundum quod fertur, ex dolore premmio cuiusdam false sententiae quam protulerat . . . se ipsum suspendit" (*Il Commento dantesco dal "Colombino" di Siviglia con altri codici raffrontato*, contributi di Antonio Fiammazzo all'edizione critica [Savona: s.n., 1915], p. 39). On Lotto degli Agli see Guido Zaccagnini, "Personaggi danteschi in Bologna," *Giornale storico della letteratura italiana*, LXIV (1914), 1–47, esp. 24–25. Ferdinando Neri, "Il suicida fiorentino," *Studi medievali*, NS 2 (1929), 205–07. On Rocco de' Mozzi: Gino Masi, "Fra savi e mercanti suicidi del tempo di Dante," *Il Giornale dantesco*, NS 9, XXXIX, (1938), 199–238. Eugenio Chiarini, "Mozzi, Rocco," *Enciclopedia dantesca*, IV, 1052. R. Kay, "Rucco di Cambio de' Mozzi in France and

England," *Studi danteschi*, XLVII (1970), 49–57. Vincenzo Presta, "In margine al canto XIII dell' *Inferno*," *Dante Studies*, XC (1972), 13–24.

To base the identification upon the gallicism "gibetto" and to affirm that Rocco de' Mozzi's claim is better because of French family and business connections is nonsense. The word "gibetto" is not used by the *historical* Lotto or Rocco but by the historical Poet, Dante Alighieri. It might be added that the present writer often uses "hara kiri" and "kaputt" in allied contexts but this in no way suggests that he has Japanese or German commercial associations, regrettably.

98. Origen, *In Matthaeum Commentariorum Series*, 78 (*PG*, 13, col. 1727).

99. Halas, pp. 22–23. It is possible that Dante meant to echo the idea of suffocation also in his use of the word "soffiare" (although the word possibly derives from Latin *subflare*); the word applies to both suicides:

> Allor *soffiò* il tronco forte, e poi
> si convertì quel vento in cotal voce

(*Inferno* XIII.91–92: Then the stub puffed hard, and soon that breath was changed into his voice. . . .)

> . . . Chi fosti, che per tante punte
> *soffi* con sangue doloroso sermo?

(*Inferno* XIII.137–38: Who were you, that through so many wounds blow forth with blood your doleful speech?)

100. For a full identification of the Tree as justice see Dr. Singleton's note to *Purgatorio* XXXII.37–39 (*Purgatorio Commentary*, pp. 784–85).

Purgatorio XIX: Dante's Siren/Harpy

ROBERT HOLLANDER

THE SECOND DREAM OF PURGATORIO, while not nearly so confusing as the first (*Purgatorio* IX. 19–33), is difficult enough when compared with the last (*Purgatorio* XXVII.97–108). Although the fact has not to my knowledge been heretofore observed, all three dreams centrally reflect what we today might want to call "love triangles" (IX. Procne–Tereus–Philomela, Juno–Jupiter–Ganymede, Ulysses–Achilles–Thetis; XIX. Beatrice–Dante–Siren; XXVII. Leah–Jacob–Rachel).[1] Such schematic triangulation of desire asks the reader to acknowledge that love, in its various permutations, may be directed toward worthy or unworthy objects, a message which is the burden of the discourses of Marco Lombardo and Virgil in *Purgatorio* XVI–XVIII. Further, the very fact that these are *sogni*, Macrobian veiled dreams which require further elucidation,[2] prepares the reader to analyze the nature of the various loves which they represent. I will not here restate my own sense of the significance of the various dreams, nor of their relation to the classical amatory material which is summoned up to serve as background to Dante's first perception of Matelda.[3] My purpose here is only to suggest a source for Dante's *dolce serena* (*Purgatorio* XIX.19).

The seed of what follows was planted eleven years ago by Carl Frankel, then a student at Princeton University. The nature of his contribution will shortly be clear. In the brief compass which is pardonable only in

such a partial treatment of a complex part of a complex whole, let me
first present our text:

> mi venne in sogno una femmina balba,
>   ne li occhi guercia, e sovra i piè distorta,
>   con le man monche, e di colore scialba.
> Io la mirava; e come 'l sol conforta
>   le fredde membra che la notte aggrava,
>   così lo sguardo mio le facea scorta
> la lingua, e poscia tutta la drizzava
>   in poco d'ora, e lo smarrito volto,
>   com' amor vuol, così le colorava.
> Poi ch'ell' avea 'l parlar così disciolto,
>   cominciava a cantar sì, che con pena
>   da lei avrei mio intento rivolto.
> "Io son," cantava, "io son dolce serena,
>   che ' marinari in mezzo mar dismago;
>   tanto son di piacere a sentir piena!
> Io volsi Ulisse del suo cammin vago
>   al canto mio; e qual meco s'ausa,
>   rado sen parte; sì tutto l'appago!"
> Ancor non era sua bocca richiusa,
>   quand' una donna apparve santa e presta
>   lunghesso me per far colei confusa.
> "O Virgilio, Virgilio, chi è questa?"
>   fieramente dicea; ed el venìa
>   con li occhi fitti pur in quella onesta.
> L'altra prendea, e dinanzi l'apria
>   fendendo i drappi, e mostravami 'l ventre;
>   quel mi svegliò col puzzo che n'uscia.
> Io mossi li occhi, e 'l buon maestro: "Almen tre
>   voci t'ho messe!" dicea, "Surgi e vieni;
>   troviam l'aperta per la qual tu entre."[4]
>
> (*Purg.* XIX.7–36)

(there came to me in dream a stammering woman,
   squint-eyed and crooked on her feet,
   with maimed hands and of pale complexion.

I gazed on her; and as the sun strengthens
　　cold limbs made heavy by the night,
　　thus did my look make nimble
her tongue, then made her wholly erect
　　in a moment, and then to her bewildered countenance,
　　as love desires, so it gave color.
As soon as her power of speech was thus set free
　　did she begin to sing, in such a way that with difficulty
　　I might have turned my purpose back from her.
"I am," she sang, "I am the sweet Siren,
　　who leads mariners astray in mid-sea,
　　such pleasure do I give when I am heard!
I turned Ulysses, eager on his way,
　　to my song; and whoever becomes accustomed to me
　　rarely departs, so thoroughly do I content him!"
Her mouth was not yet closed again
　　when a lady appeared, holy and alert,
　　alongside of me, to put that other to confusion.
"O Virgil, O Virgil, who is she?"
　　she said sternly. And he approached
　　with his eyes fixed upon that honorable one.
The other one he seized, and opened her up in front,
　　rending her garments, and showed me her belly;
　　this awakened me with the stench that issued forth.
I turned my glance and my good teacher said, "At least
　　three times have I called thee! Arise and come:
　　let us find the opening by which thou mayst enter.")

Clearly the reader is expected to wonder who these two female presences
are. More particularly, we would like to know what literary text might
authorize Dante's association of the Sirens (rather than Circe) with Ulysses
and thus have some better sense of what she represents. And surely we
also wish to understand the identity of the *donna . . . santa e presta* who
opposes the *serena*. In my opinion the second task presents little difficulty: Beatrice is the presence who informs the actions of the dream's holy
lady. Dante's dream should be seen as recreating the offstage encounter
of Virgil and Beatrice as this was narrated by his *autore* in *Inferno* II, carefully
incorporating Virgil's charge, as this was enunciated by Beatrice. While
Hermann Gmelin has also argued for this solution,[5] that simple and best

hypothesis may not yet be said to have achieved common acceptance, even
if most commentators do take note of the obvious echo of this passage
in Beatrice's reproach to Dante in *Purgatorio* XXXI.45, an echo which clearly
underscores Beatrice's presence in Dante's dream here—especially when
we remember that in *Purgatorio* XXX.134, Beatrice says that she has previously tried to call Dante back to herself *in sogno*, a passage which helps to
make it certain that this dream recounts the fact of his backsliding from
her in order to give himself to another.

Accepting this hypothesis, whom or what shall we call this adversary
of Beatrice? The problem is familiar to all *dantisti* and I shall not here review
its tortuous history. As Giorgio Padoan, offering the most recent new
hypothesis, has pointed out, Benvenuto da Imola, the first of Dante's commentators to know "Homer," was also the first to object to Dante's claim
that Ulysses was held by the Sirens ("Sed contra Homerus XI Odysseae
dicit quod Ulixes vitavit Sirenes").[6] Many have been the attempts after
Benvenuto to whiten Dante's "blotted" page: Dante has conflated Circe
and a Siren (to which understanding Padoan sagely replies, following Manfredi Porena, that Dante knows full well [*Inferno* XXVI.92] that Circe's
abode was not in "mid sea," adding that Dante's Ulysses spent his year
and more with Circe *before* he left on his *folle volo*—the two points are
equally telling since the Siren turns Ulysses from his *cammin*, that is, from
a journey initiated after he has left Circe's island behind); he does not
really mean one of the Sirens, but only makes a generic reference to some
sort of enchantress; he turned to Cicero for the Homeric matter which
he did not himself possess. The last case was first advanced by Edward
Moore.[7] His treatment (which begins with a delightful *lapsus calami* that
substitutes Dante's name for that of Ulysses) would have it that from *De
finibus* v.18, Dante learned that Ulysses was tempted by the Sirens. Moore's
argument is countered by Padoan on grounds that Dante was unlikely
to have known this text[8] and on what I take to be still better grounds:
Cicero's text only suggests that Ulysses was *tempted* by the Sirens, but
resisted the temptation; in Dante, however, Ulysses is turned from his
course by the Siren. In other words, Cicero is attempting to explain the
capacity of Ulysses to be tempted by the Sirens in the first place and is
not eventually unfaithful to Homer's text. Dante, on the other hand, is
innocently unfaithful to his unknown Homer.

What then is the source of Dante's Sirens and why does he invent the
tale of Ulysses' vulnerability to them? Padoan's new hypothesis, offered

at the conclusion of his article in the *Enciclopedia dantesca*, holds that Dante has conflated not Circe and the Sirens, but Calypso and those ladies. For Dante's knowledge of Calypso he points to Cicero, *De officiis I.*xxxi.113, and to Ovid, *Ars amatoria* ii.125–44, proceeding to argue, ⸗ "E' tutt' altro che improbabile che Dante abbia identificato in quel nome Calipso, che poco gli diceva, una sirena." ("It is altogether likely that Dante understood by the name Calypso, which meant little enough to him, the name of siren"). And he cites the similar solution proposed by Benvenuto: "dici potest quod poeta loquitur de Circe et de Calypso, quae vere sirenes detinuerunt Ulixem, Circes per annum, Calypso per multos" ("It may be that the poet speaks of Circe and of Calypso, which sirens did indeed detain Ulysses, Circe for one year, Calypso for many"). But if Benvenuto, knowing Leonzio's Latin Homer, quite naturally fell victim to the desire to have Dante's account accord with Homer's, we should probably resist such an impulse, allowing that in this detail, as in so many others (the salvations of Cato, Statius, Ripheus; Virgil's prior descent to Hell at the bidding of Erichtho; Adam's first word in Eden — to name some of the more spectacular of our poet's enormous fabrications), the authority which Dante followed was his own.

Yet, if no source we have been able to find puts Ulysses under a Siren's sway, we should nonetheless probably have paid more attention to the sources of Sirenic material which we know Dante had ready to hand, whether or not they associate Ulysses with Sirens. From Virgil, who mentions the Sirens only once and briefly in the final lines of *Aeneid* v, Dante would take only the sense of Aeneas's lack of interest in these creatures. But on their rocks ("scopulos Sirenum") we (and Dante) may see the bones of other sailors who were lost there.[9] If, in Virgil's treatment, Palinurus may be drowned near them, they no longer seem to possess the power which they had in Homer — at least not for Virgil's hero, who seems oblivious to their presence. And thus for Dante, Aeneas, in Virgil's poem, is seen to act in a way that offers an implicit criticism of the behavior of the Ulysses in his own. Ovid, while retelling the *Aeneid*, is faithful to his *auctor* on this score when he reports that Aeneas sailed past "Sirenum scopulos" (Virgil's very words),[10] even if he did lose his helmsman. Thus, if Dante thinks of Ulysses as the negative counterpart of the voyager Aeneas, if he thinks of the Sirens as creatures who attempt to lure sailors from their chosen paths, he would easily have been tempted to concoct, on his own authority, a Sirenic interruption in his concocted last voyage of Ulysses.

Neither Virgil nor Ovid presented Dante with the sharply moralistic view of the Sirens which we find in the *Commedia*. Virgil, in his gloss of Dante's dream (xix.58–60), says she is a *strega* who represents the three sins which are purged on the upper terraces of Purgatory, thus identifying her with excessive love in general and perhaps most directly with the seventh sin, lust. Giorgio Padoan, following a commentary tradition of some standing, cites Boethius's counterposition of the Sirens and philosophically more worthy Muses (*De consolatione* I. 1.35) to help account for the heavily moralizing tone of Dante's treatment.[11] Isidore of Seville's handling, restating the earlier encyclopedic tradition's view and carrying it forward for the later middle ages, seems equally to the point:

> Sirenas tres fingunt fuisse ex parte virgines, ex parte volucres, habentes alas et ungulas: quarum una voce, altera tibiis, tertia lyra canebant. Quae inlectos navigantes sub cantu in naufragium trahebant. Secundum veritatem autem meretrices fuerunt, quae transeuntes quoniam deducebant ad egestatem, his fictae sunt inferre naufragia. Alas autem habuisse et ungulas, quia amor et volat et vulnerat. Quae inde in fluctibus conmorasse dicuntur, quia fluctus Venerem creaverunt.

> (They [ancient poets] have it that the three Sirens were part woman, part bird, having wings and talons; one of them made music with her voice, another with the pipes, a third with the lyre. They led sailors, seduced by their song, to shipwreck. In truth they were actually prostitutes who, since they led passersby to poverty, are portrayed as causing shipwrecks; as having wings and talons because love both flies and wounds. Thus they are said to dwell in the waves, since the waves gave birth to Venus.)[12]

Isidore's treatment, offered in the chapter devoted to monsters, "De portentis," while yielding no trace of Ulysses, does offer a picture of the Sirens themselves which is utterly to Dante's purpose. The whorish creatures (one of whom attracts seafarers by means of song, rather than by instrumental music), part bird and part woman, are seen as morally despicable by Beatrice in *Purgatorio* xxxi. In *Purgatorio* xix Ulysses (and Dante!) are accused of turning to a false singer, to a "whore." I have elsewhere tried to make good the case for understanding that Dante's most troublesome "siren" was in fact the Lady Philosophy of the *Convivio* and will not repeat myself here.[13] In my view Dante becomes (or nearly became, save for the intervention of Virgil and Beatrice) the second "nuovo Ulisse" (Guido da Montefeltro representing the first "new Ulysses," at least in the opinion of Filippo Villani[14]). In Beatrice's later formulation, Dante, no longer a "young bird" ("novo augelletto," *Purgatorio* XXXI.61), should have resisted the Sirens' song. Yet he, Ulysses-like, interrupted his journey toward Beatrice when he heard that false music. Worse, as the testimony of his own dream informs us, he has himself created the loveliness of the creature, who was in fact ugly and deformed until he made her beautiful in his own beholding.

Dante's *femmina balba* is not half-woman, half-bird. Or does some of her original plumage remain in Dante's mind? Padoan claims that by Dante's time the Sirens were thought of rather as mermaids than as bird-girls. Yet Dante was frequently as conversant with the Golden Age as with his own time. And Ovid's description of the Sirens is worth noting:

> . . .vobis, Acheloides, unde
> pluma pedesque avium, cum virginis ora geratis?
> an quia, cum legeret vernos Proserpina flores,
> in comitum numero, doctae Sirenes, eratis?
> quam postquam toto frustra quaesistis in orbe,
> protinus, et vestram sentirent aequora curam,
> posse super fluctus alarum insistere remis
> optastis facilesque deos habuistis et artus
> vidistis vestros subitis flavescere pennis.
> ne tamen ille canor mulcendas natus ad aures
> tantaque dos oris linguae deperderet usum,
> virginei vultus et vox humana remansit.

(But, daughers of Acheloüs, why have you the feathers and feet of birds, though you still have maidens' features? Is it because, when Proserpina was gathering the spring flowers, you were among the number of her companions, ye Sirens, skilled in song? After you had sought in vain for her through all the lands, that the sea also might know your search, you prayed that you might float on beating wings above the waves: you found the gods ready, and suddenly you saw your limbs covered with golden plumage. But, that you might not lose your tuneful voices, so soothing

to the ear, and that rich dower of song, maiden features and human
voice remained.)[15]

Ovid's Sirens are not morally repulsive, as are Isidore's. Yet we should
remember that, given Virgil's lack of interest in describing the Sirens
himself, these twelve lines of Ovid offered Dante his only "canonical"
classical description.[16] In my view Dante has "demetamorphosed" the Ovidian Sirens, leaving only their human traits in his description, while sup-
pressing their avian attributes, Ovid's "pluma pedesque avium." Featherless,
they nonetheless reveal their source. Since Dante's *serena* is a counter-
Beatrice, he was probably wise to suppress overt reference to her original
feathers and feet. Still, it is striking that, as the canto progresses, within
a dozen lines Dante is confronted by a winged creature, the angel who
removes the "P" of sloth from his brow, possessed of "ali aperte, che parean
di cigno" (XIX.46) and feathers ("penne" — 49). The angel comes upon
us as a counter-Siren. The *serena* sings, he speaks; she was part bird, he
is perceived as having her avian characteristics in a benevolent form.[17] His
last words to Dante, reported in indirect discourse, also reveal the poet's
continuing concern with the Siren: those who mourn are blessed, for they
shall have their souls mistresses of consolation ("ch'avran di consolar l'anime
donne" — 51). The locution is a strange one and may be explicated as
follows: those who mourn here their former sloth will be blessed in heaven,
for there their souls shall be "ladies" who give true consolation, that is,
we may add, their *donne* will not be *serene*, will rather resemble Beatrice,
the "donna . . . santa e presta" of the dream.

From Isidore and Ovid Dante knows that the Sirens were part bird,
part woman. From Virgil he knows nothing about their appearance. But
in Virgil's text he finds similar creatures, winged virgins with taloned
hands. In the article "Arpie" in the *Enciclopedia dantesca*,[18] Giorgio Padoan has shown how closely Dante has followed Virgil's description of
the Harpies in his own (*Inferno* XIII.10–15)[19] without considering, in his
later treatment of the Sirens, that the Harpies might inform Dante's portrait of the Sirens as well. According to Isidore, the Sirens are "ex parte
virgines, ex parte volucres"; according to Ovid they have "pluma pedesque avium, cum virginis ora"; Virgil's Harpies are described as follows:

> virginei volucrum vultus, foedissima ventris
> proluvies uncaeque manus et pallida semper
> ora fame.

(Maidenly of face, yet winged most foul / the outpouring of their bellies, their hands taloned, / their faces always pale with hunger.)[20]

Dante's Siren may, "sovra i piè distorta," reflect the pedal condition of Ovid's Sirens, who have "pedes avium," but the rest of her appearance seems to be far more closely related to Virgil's Harpies:

> . . . mi venne in sogno una femmina balba,
> ne li occhi guercia, e sovra i piè distorta,
> con le man monche, e di colore scialba.

The *femmina* is *balba*, that is, she is not "soave e piana" in her speech as is Beatrice, the "anti-Siren," in *Inferno* II.56, but is instead stuttering and unclear in speech. Virgil's Harpies, at least until their leader, Celaeno, offers her dispiriting augury (III.247–57), are decidedly noisy but not particularly verbal. The first sound they make, as they swoop down upon the Trojans' feast, is by shaking their wings (226); subsequently their voices are characterized as unpleasant and ominous, and are associated with their foul stench ("vox taetrum dira inter odorem" — 228); they are noisy if not clear speakers ("turba sonans" — 233). All that I wish to suggest is that the movement in Virgil's passage, like that in Dante's, is from unclear utterance to a clear speech which is meant to deter a noble purpose, Aeneas's journey to Italy, Dante's to Beatrice. More than her speech, her hands and her color show the dependence of Dante's *femmina* upon Virgil's Harpies. Her hands are *monche*. The word appears only one other time in the *Commedia*, appropriately enough in *Inferno* XIII.30, where Dante's thoughts will be "amputated" when he plucks a branch of the thornbush that is Pier delle Vigne. And it seems to me that these hands derive from Pier's fellow denizens, the Harpies, whose hands are *uncae* in Virgil. The Siren's color is *scialba*, pale (from *scialbare*, dependent upon Latin *exalbare*[21]): "et pallida semper / ora fame" is Virgil's formulation. Thus three of the pertinent details which describe the Siren may be seen to reflect Virgil's description of the Harpies. But it is the last and most dramatic detail in Dante's dream, when Virgil reveals, at Beatrice's behest, the true nature of this Siren, that most clearly associates Siren and Harpies. Dante is awakened by the stench that issues from the Siren's belly when Virgil rends her clothing. As Carl Frankel made me and our fellow students see in the autumn of 1968, Dante's "e mostravami 'l ventre; / quel mi svegliò col puzzo che n'uscia" surely reflects Virgil's "foedissima ventris / proluvies."[22]

Thus Dante has made use of all of Virgil's description of the Harpies —
except their birds' bodies and foul hunger — as a guide to our understanding of the nature of his sin in turning aside from Beatrice to the Siren.
For not only was she not beautiful in any eyes but his, she was such a
creature as would have led to despair and death, had he followed her Siren's
song to shipwreck. Ulysses was precisely such a sailor; Dante is so no
longer.

Dante's dream of the *serena* is not only prophetic, as are all three of
the Purgatorial morning dreams, but it also reflects what is transpiring
while the sleeper dreams (as is also true of the first dream, which begins
as Lucia is about to carry the pilgrim up the slope and ends as she sets
him down before the gate). While in the dream the holy lady who mirrors Beatrice calls on Virgil twice ("O Virgilio, Virgilio, chi è questa?"),
thus reinforcing the notion that we should discover just such an ugly female
in Virgil's poem, his guide has called Dante at least three times ("Almen
tre / voci t'ho messe"). John Adams and Christopher McElroy, con-
templating this passage in class with me ten years ago, thought of another
text which, I believe, is also applicable here. In Matthew 26:40–46 Christ
calls on his sleeping apostles three times. They continue to sleep. Just so
does Dante. And, like them, he will eventually rise: "Surgite," Jesus says
to them; "Surgi e viene," says Virgil to Dante. What is said of them (Matthew 26:41) may be said of Dante, drawn in dream by his Siren/Harpy:
"The spirit indeed is willing, but the flesh is weak."

Notes

1. Depending on whether or not we identify "la concubina di Titone antico"
of *Purg.* IX.1, as the aurora of the Moon, we may be able to add yet another "triangle"
to the matter which surrounds the dream of Ganymede. For details of this dispute,
see Charles S. Singleton, *Purgatorio, Commentary,* Bollingen Series, (Princeton, N.J.:
Princeton University Press, 1973), pp. 177–79. If the *concubina* is the lunar Aurora,
Tithonus also is seen as involved in a triangular love affair, with his wife, the solar
Aurora, being the third party.

2. Guido da Pisa's "Expositio lictere" of *Inferno* I gives an interesting summary
of Macrobius' theory of dreams as Guido sees it applying to the *Comedy.* See his
Expositiones et Glose super Comediam Dantis, ed. Vincenzo Cioffari (Albany, N.Y.:
SUNY Press, 1974), pp. 18–20. *Somnium* is characterized as follows: "Somnium

proprie vocatur illa visio que figuris tegitur et ambagibus nubilatur, et que non nisi per interpretationem potest intelligi vel cognosci." Each of the four dreams recorded in the *Comedy* is referred to at least once as a *sogno* (Dante's Italian for *somnium*): *Inf.* XXXIII.45; *Purg.* IX.19; XVIII.145, and XIX.7; XXVII.97.

3. See *Allegory in Dante's Commedia* (Princeton, N.J.: Princeton University Press, 1969), pp. 136–52.

4. The text is that established by Giorgio Petrocchi, as presented by Charles S. Singleton (see n. 1, above). The following and subsequent translations are my own, except where otherwise noted.

5. *Kommentar*, II (Stuttgart: Klett, 1955), 304.

6. "Sirene," *Enciclopedia dantesca*, V (Rome: Istituto dell'Enciclopedia Italiana, 1976), p. 269a; now also available, in somewhat different form, in Padoan's *Il pio Enea, l'empio Ulisse* (Ravenna: Longo, 1977), pp. 200–204: "But against this Homer, in the eleventh book of the *Odyssey*, says that Ulysses shunned the Sirens."

7. *Studies in Dante*, 1st ser. (Oxford: Clarendon Press, 1969 [1896]), pp. 264–66.

8. "Il canto degli Epicurei," *Convivium*, XXVII (1959), 19. I confess that I find Padoan's argument unconvincing. He cites three pages of his earlier study (18–20) as evidence for his view that Dante did not in fact know the last three books of the *De finibus*. But while in those pages he does develop an argument to the effect that when writing the *Convivio* Dante knew only the first book, whereas the *De monarchia* reveals acquaintance with the second, his dismissal of Dante's later knowledge of Books III–V is a mere assertion in a footnote: "Ciò farebbe supporre che Dante non abbia mai conosciuto i libri III, IV, V di quest'opera." Without discussing the validity of Moore's four citations of Books III–V as being known to Dante, one may note that the attack on Epicurus is not confined to the second book (e.g., IV.27), and it is Cicero's attack on that Greek philosopher which Padoan finds lacking in Book I but present in Book II. Indeed, that is the crucial point in his argument.

9. *Aen.* V.864–71.

10. *Meta.* XIV.88.

11. As cited in "Sirene," p. 269a (n. 6 above): "Sed abite potius Sirenes usque in exitum dulces meisque eum Musis curandum sanandumque relinquite" ("But be gone, ye Sirens, sweet unto death, and leave his curing and healing to my Muses").

12. *Isidori hispalensis episcopi Etymologiarum sive originum libri xx*, ed. W. M. Lindsay (Oxford: Clarendon Press, 1971 [1911]), XI.3.30–31.

13. *Allegory in Dante's Commedia*, pp. 136–44, 162–63; again in "*Purgatorio* II: Cato's Rebuke and Dante's *scoglio*," *Italica*, LII (1975), now reprinted in my *Studies in Dante* (Ravenna: Longo, 1980), pp. 91–105.

14. See "The Tragedy of Divination in *Inferno* XX," in *Studies in Dante*, p. 142, n. 28.

15. *Metamorphoses* V.552–63, trans. F. J. Miller, 3rd ed., rev. by G. P. Goold, Loeb Classical Library (Cambridge, Mass.: Harvard University Press; London: Heinemann, 1977 [1916]).

16. It is of interest that it was almost certainly in this Ovidian text that Ulysses' pleasing phrase (*Inf.* XXVI.125) first met Dante's eyes: "super fluctus alarum insistere remis" is the most likely progenitor of "de' remi facemmo ali."

17. Not only is *cigno* a *hapax* in the *Comedy*, no other angel on any other terrace of Purgatory is explicitly compared to a bird (but cf. *Purg.* II. 31–36, for the anti-Ulyssean angel, the "uccel divino" of vs. 37, who is helmsman of the ship bearing the arriving saved souls). According to Isidore (*Etym.* XII.7.18–19), the swan's voice is sweet and he is an auspicious omen to sailors, who, seeing him, know that they will not drown.

18. Volume I (1970), pp. 389b–390a.

19. Lines 13–15 describe their appearance:

> Ali hanno late, e colli e visi umani,
>   piè con artigli, e pennuto 'l gran ventre;
>   fanno lamenti in su li alberi strani.

(Wide wings have they, human necks and faces, clawed feet, large feathered bellies; they make lament atop the strange trees.)

20. *Aen.* III.216–18 in *P. Vergili Maronis Opera*, ed. F. A. Hirtzel (Oxford: Clarendon, 1950 [1900]).

21. *Enciclopedia dantesca*, V.73a.

22. But cf. Giuseppe Toffanin, "La 'foetida Aethiopissa' e la 'femmina balba,' " *Giornale storico della letteratura italiana*, LXXVII (1921), 147–49. Toffanin argues for a source in the *Vitae patrum* (V.5 "De fornicatione"). His argument is interesting but not, I think, ultimately convincing for two reasons: first, we have no sure sense that Dante was acquainted with this text; second, Virgil's text seems still closer to the scene—and in Dante's text it is Virgil himself who reveals the stinking belly.

The Seven *Status Ecclesiae*
in *Purgatorio* XXXII and XXXIII

R. E. KASKE

I N PURGATORIO XXXII, after the Griffon has tied the car of the Church
to the great tree and the tree has burst into new leaf (49–60), Dante
falls into a sleep (61–69), awakens to find the Griffon ascended and
Beatrice sitting "in su la terra vera" surrounded by the seven nymphs
(70–99), and is directed by Beatrice to fix his eyes upon the car (100–8).
What he is then shown is a series of assaults on the car, beginning with
a buffeting by an eagle, an invasion by a she-fox, a return of the eagle
to deposit some of his plumage, and an attack from beneath by a dragon:

> Non scese mai con sì veloce moto
> foco di spessa nube, quando piove
> da quel confine che più va remoto,
> com' io vidi calar l'uccel di Giove
> per l'alber giù, rompendo de la scorza,
> non che d'i fiori e de le foglie nove;
> e ferì 'l carro di tutta sua forza;
> ond' el piegò come nave in fortuna,
> vinta da l'onda, or da poggia, or da orza.
> Poscia vidi avventarsi ne la cuna
> del trïunfal veiculo una volpe
> che d'ogne pasto buon parea digiuna;

> ma, riprendendo lei di laide colpe,
>   la donna mia la volse in tanta futa
>   quanto sofferser l'ossa sanza polpe.
> Poscia per indi ond' era pria venuta,
>   l'aguglia vidi scender giù ne l'arca
>   del carro e lasciar lei di sé pennuta;
> e qual esce di cuor che si rammarca,
>   tal voce uscì del cielo e cotal disse:
>   "O navicella mia, com' mal se' carca!"
> Poi parve a me che la terra s'aprisse
>   tr'ambo le ruote, e vidi uscirne un drago
>   che per lo carro sù la coda fisse;
> e come vespa che ritragge l'ago,
>   a sé traendo la coda maligna,
>   trasse del fondo, e gissen vago vago.

(Lines 109–35: Never with so swift a motion did fire descend from dense cloud, when it falls from the confine that stretches most remote, as I saw the bird of Jove swoop downward through the tree, rending the bark as well as the flowers and the new leaves, and it struck the chariot with all its force, so that it reeled like a ship in a tempest, driven by the waves, now to starboard, now to larboard. Then I saw leap into the body of the triumphal vehicle a fox that seemed starved of all good nourishment; but my lady, rebuking it for its foul offenses, turned it to such flight as its fleshless bones allowed. Then, from there whence it had come before, I saw the eagle descend into the body of the chariot and leave it feathered with its plumage. And a voice such as issues from a heart that is afflicted came from Heaven, and it said, "O little bark of mine, how ill are you laden!" Then it seemed to me that the earth opened between the two wheels, and I saw a dragon issue therefrom, which drove its tail upward through the chariot, and, like a wasp that retracts its sting, drawing to itself its malignant tail, tore out part of the bottom and went its vagrant way.)[1]

I have already suggested briefly in print that these lines form part of an allegorical dramatization of the familiar medieval historical scheme known as the seven *status ecclesiae* or "conditions of the Church";[2] the aim of the present study is to present this argument in fuller form, along with supporting documentation.

The most convenient approach is by way of the early commentators on the *Commedia*. Of the nine who include the *Purgatorio* (the "anonymous Lombard," Jacopo della Lana, the author of *L'ottimo*, Pietro di Dante, the author of the *Chiose anonime*, Benvenuto da Imola, Francesco da Buti, the "anonimo Fiorentino," and Giovanni da Serravalle), all agree that the initial attack by the eagle (109–17) represents the persecutions of the early Church by the Roman Empire; in the words of Benvenuto da Imola, perhaps the most learned and intelligent of them all, "Nunc poeta incipit describere tribulationes ecclesiae, et primo quidem describit figuraliter primam generalem maximam persecutionem quam ostendit per persecutionem unius aquilae fulminantis." ("Now the poet begins to describe the tribulations of the Church, and first indeed he describes figuratively the first general great persecution, which he shows through the persecution of a lightning-like eagle.")[3] The fox (118–23) is identified by seven of the nine as heretics or heresy, and by the other two as Mohammed and the schismatics and/or heretics; Benvenuto explains, "*Poscia vidi una volpe,* idest, versutam astutiam multorum haereticorum, sicut Sabelli, Arii et aliorum. . . ." ("Then I saw a she-fox, that is, the deceitful cunning of many heretics, such as Sabellus, Arius, and others. . . .")[4] The return of the eagle and the gift of feathers (124–29) are unanimously understood as the Donation of Constantine, with the voice from heaven paralleling the voice that in some accounts was heard at the Donation; Benvenuto says that in this image the poet

> tangit dotationem quam fecit Constantinus quam poeta ponit pro magna persecutione ecclesiae, quae generaliter infecit praelatos avaritia quae est fundamentum omnium malorum. . . . Et probat poeta quod dotatio fuit magna persecutio ecclesiae, quia tempore illius prodigae donationis audita est vox de coelis, dicens: "Hodie diffusum est venenum in ecclesia Dei."

(. . . refers to the endowment which Constantine brought about, which the poet represents as a great persecution of the Church, which has corrupted prelates in general with avarice, which is the foundation of all evils. . . . And the poet proves that the endowment was a great persecution of the Church, because at the time of that lavish donation a voice from heaven was heard saying, "Today poison has been poured upon the Church of God.")[5]

The dragon (130–35) is interpreted by six of the nine commentators as Mohammed, by two as the Antichrist, and by one as "il maggiore persecutore, che la Chiesa e il popolo di Dio avesse mai" ("the greatest persecutor that the Church and the people of God ever had"); according to Benvenuto, "Machomettus christianae fidei perfidus adversator, se Dei prophetam mentiens orientales plagas et maxime Arabiam labefecit. . . . Ad literam ergo, poeta describit istum sub figura draconis. . . ." ("Mohammed, the treacherous adversary of the Christian faith, falsely representing himself as the prophet of God, overthrew the eastern regions and especially Arabia. . . . Literally, therefore, the poet describes him under the figure of a dragon. . . .")[6] With all allowance for the tendency of commentators to repeat one another, this total pattern seems to imply that for a late medieval reader, one plausible interpretation of lines 109–35 would be as an allegory of the Church successively harassed by the early persecutions, the early heresies, the Donation of Constantine, and the Mohammedan schism.

The idea of seven *status ecclesiae*, or successive conditions of the Church, is derived from the opening of the seven seals in Apocalypse 6–8:

Et vidi quod aperuisset Agnus unum de septem sigillis. . . . et ecce equus albus . . . [6:1–2]. Et cum aperuisset sigillum secundum. . . . exivit alius equus rufus . . . [6:3–4]. Et cum aperuisset sigillum tertium. . . . ecce equus niger . . . [6:5]. Et cum aperuisset sigillum quartum. . . . ecce equus pallidus . . . [6:7–8]. Et cum aperuisset sigillum quintum, vidi subtus altare animas interfectorum propter verbum Dei . . . [6:9]. Et vidi cum aperuisset sigillum sextum; et ecce terraemotus magnus factus est . . . [6:12]. Et cum aperuisset sigillum septimum, factum est silentium in caelo, quasi media hora [8:1].

(And I saw that the Lamb had opened one of the seven seals. . . . and behold, a white horse. . . [6:1–2]. and when he had opened the second seal. . . . there went out another horse, red. . . [6:3–4]. And when he had opened the third seal. . . . behold, a black horse

. . . [6:5]. And when he had opened the fourth seal . . . . behold,
a pale horse. . . [6:7–8]. And when he had opened the fifth seal, I
saw beneath the altar the souls of those killed because of the word
of God. . . [6:9]. And I saw when he had opened the sixth seal;
and behold, there was a great earthquake . . . [6:12]. And when he
had opened the seventh seal, there was silence in heaven, as it were
for half an hour [8:1].)

The identity of the various *status* differs greatly, of course, according to
the time and historical outlook of the exegetes.[7] The particular scheme
with which we are concerned, apparently dating from the twelfth century, identifies the first *status* as the time of the Apostles, with the Church
in its original condition of innocence; the second as the time of persecutions and martyrs; the third as the time of heretics; the fourth as the time
of "false brothers," or hypocrites; the fifth as a comparatively undefined
time, most often involving consolation for past hardships; the sixth as
the time of the Antichrist; and the seventh as the time of peace following
the death of the Antichrist.

A typical example appears in a thirteenth-century commentary on the
Apocalypse attributed to Hugh of St. Cher:

Et vidi quod aperuisset Agnus [6:1]: Diuiditur autem haec pars tota
in septem partes, secundum quod ostenduntur hic septem status Ecclesiae per septem sigillorum apertionem, quorum apertio est status
Ecclesiae reuelatio. . . . Prima pars [huius capituli] est secundum
primum statum Ecclesiae, qui fuit tempore Apostolorum, qui
designantur per equum album cuius sessor est Christus. . . . *Et cum
aperuisset sigillum secundum* [6:3]: Secunda pars capituli, in qua agit
de secundo statu Ecclesiae, qui fuit tempore Martyrum. . . . *Et cum
aperuisset sigillum tertium* [6:5]:. . . . Quia vidit Diabolus se nihil
proficere interficiendo Martyres, sed magis eorum patientia & virtute Ecclesiam roborari, suscitauit haereticos qui peruerse exponentes
Scripturas, haereses induxerunt. . . . *Et cum aperuisset sigillum quartum, audiui vocem &c.* [6:7]: Quarta pars huius capituli vbi agitur de
quarto statu Ecclesiae, scilicet de persecutione falsorum fratrum, scilicet
hypocritarum, quos tandem Diabolus in Ecclesiam introduxit, & per
eos domesticos eius secretius & familiarius turbare tentauit, vnde &
periculosius. . . . *Et cum aperuisset quintum sigillum* [6:9]: . . . quia

graues, & magnas praemisit tribulationes, ne terrerentur boni qui
in huiusmodi persecutionibus affligendi sunt & occidendi, propterea
consolatur eos hic. . . . *Et vidi cum aperuisset sigillum sextum* [6:12]:
Sexta pars capituli in qua agitur de apertione sexti sigilli, quae nihil
aliud est, quam praeostensio persecutionis futurae tempore Antichristi. . . . *Et cum aperuisset sigillum septimum* [8:1]: . . . Hic ergo
determinatur status futurus post mortem Antichristi, vbi dabitur pax
Ecclesiae, quae tamen parum durabit.

(*And I saw that the Lamb had opened* [6:1]: This whole part, moreover,
is divided into seven parts, in accordance with which there are shown
here seven *status* of the Church through the opening of the seven
seals, the opening of which is the disclosure of a *status* of the Church
. . . . The first part [of this chapter] accords with the first *status* of
the Church, which was in the time of the Apostles, who are
designated by the white horse whose rider is Christ. . . . *And when
he had opened the second seal* [6:3]: The second part of the chapter,
in which he deals with the second *status* of the Church, which was
in the time of the martyrs. . . . *And when he had opened the third seal*
[6:5]: . . . Because the devil saw that he accomplished nothing by
killing the martyrs, but rather that the Church was strengthened
by their patience and courage, he raised up heretics, who, expounding the Scriptures wrongly, introduced heresies. . . . *And when he had
opened the fourth seal, I heard a voice, etc.* [6:7]: The fourth part of
this chapter, where the fourth *status* of the Church is dealt with,
namely the persecution of the false brothers, that is the hypocrites,
whom the devil at length introduced into the Church, and through
them tried more secretly and intimately, and hence more dangerously,
to confound his servants. . . . *And when he had opened the fifth seal*
[6:9]: . . . because he has previously sent heavy and great tribulations, lest the good who have been cast down and destroyed in such
persecutions should be terrified, therefore he consoles them here. . . .
And I saw when he had opened the sixth seal [6:12]: the sixth part of
the chapter, in which the opening of the sixth seal is dealt with,
which is nothing other than a foreshowing of the future persecution
in the time of the Antichrist. . . . *And when he had opened the seventh
seal* [8:1]: . . . Here therefore is defined the future *status* after the

death of the Antichrist, where peace will be given to the Church, which nevertheless will last only a short time.)[8]

The series turns up also in eschatological treatises of the late Middle Ages — as for example in a *Tractatus de Antichristo et eius temporibus* written in 1300 by John Quidort of Paris:

Per apertionem enim primi [sigilli] significatur reuolutio primi status ecclesie, quando tempore apostolorum ecclesia erat dealbata per baptismum, vnde ostenditur in equo albo. Per apertionem secundi sigilli, vbi apparuit equus ruffus, reuelatio status martyrum. Per apertionem tertii, persecutio hereticorum, vnde ibi ostenditur equus niger propter recessum a luce veritatis. Per apertionem quarti, vbi apparuit equus pallidus, persecutio falsorum christianorum & hypocritarum, quorum cetus est falsa religione & astutia palliatus. Per apertionem quinti reuelatur status ecclesie in celo triumphantis, vbi fit mentio de animabus stolas sanctas accipientibus. Per apertionem sexti reuelabitur status ecclesie sub antichristo. Per apertionem septimi reuelatur status uel pax ecclesie post mortem antichristi. Ibi enim dicitur quod factum est silentium in celo, idest pax & tranquillitas, quasi media hora, quia per modicum tempus, quia cito post veniet dominus ad iudicium.

(For through the opening of the first [seal] is signified the coming about of the first *status* of the Church, when in the time of the Apostles the Church was purified through Baptism, whence it is manifested in a white horse. Through the opening of the second seal, where there appeared a red horse, a revelation of the *status* of the martyrs. Through the opening of the third, the persecution of heretics, whence there is shown a black horse for a retreat from the light of truth. Through the opening of the fourth, where there appeared a pale horse, the persecution of false Christians and hypocrites, whose band is cloaked with false religion and cunning. Through the opening of the fifth is revealed the *status* of the Church triumphant in heaven, where there is mention of the souls receiving holy robes. Through the opening of the sixth will be revealed the *status* of the Church under the Antichrist. Through the opening of the seventh is revealed the *status* or peace of the Church after the death of the Antichrist. For there it is said that there was silence in heaven, that is peace and tranquillity, as it were for half an hour, because [it will be] for a little time, because quickly afterward the Lord will come to judgment.)[9]

Ignoring temporarily the first of these seven *status* (that of the Apostolic Church), let us begin by noticing that the second and third *status* (those of the persecutions and the heretics) correspond precisely to the initial attack of the eagle (109–17) and the entry of the fox (118–23) as interpreted by Dante's early commentators. The eagle is of course an inevitable symbol of the Roman Empire, and his smiting the car would allegorize aptly enough the violence of the persecutions; his rending the newly restored tree can, I suspect, be best explained as the first of the abuses to be inflicted on newly reconstituted human nature.[10] The fox traditionally signifies heretics, particularly in commentaries on Canticles 2:15, "Capite nobis vulpes parvulas quae demoliuntur vineas"—for example in that of the twelfth-century Italian exegete Bruno of Asti, who refers also to the effects of heretics on the Church: "Vox adversus haereses: 'Capite nobis vulpes parvulas, quae demoliuntur vineas.' Quid per vulpes, nisi haereticos, vitia et malignos spiritus? . . . Vineam autem hanc vulpes demoliuntur, quoniam Christi Ecclesiam destruunt et dissipant." ("A voice against heresies: 'Catch us the little foxes who destroy the vines.' What [is signified] through the foxes except heretics, vices, and wicked spirits? . . . The foxes moreover destroy this vine, because they destroy and scatter the Church of Christ.")[11] The remark that the fox "d'ogne pasto buon parea digiuna" (120), and the further reference to her "ossa sanza polpe" (123), are convincingly interpreted by the early commentators as allegorizing the heretics' lack of solid doctrine; Benvenuto explains, *"d'ogni buon pasto*, idest, omni bona doctrina, sed omni pravo dogmate pasta" (*"from all good food*, that is, all good doctrine, but fed with every wicked dogma").[12] Her being put to flight by Beatrice offers the equally convincing allegorical meaning of heresy routed by Scripture, theology, or other aspects of divinely revealed or inspired truth.[13]

The second descent of the eagle (124–29), clearly allegorizing the Donation of Constantine, corresponds to none of our *status ecclesiae*. Bypassing it for the moment, I proceed to the attack by the dragon (130–35)—which, as we have seen, is explained by most of Dante's early commentators as the Mohammedan schism, with the dragon representing Mohammed himself. The dragon's pulling out part of the bottom from the car of the Church would certainly be an appropriate figure of schism, and Joachistic commentary on the Apocalypse does provide some basis for an identification of the fourth *status ecclesiae* as the time of the Mohammedan schism; for example, Peter Olivi, in a complex exegesis of the opening of the fourth seal, remarks that "per equum pallidum, cuius sessor est mors, designatur Sarracenorum populus et eius propheta mortiferus, scilicet Machomet. . . ." ("through the pale horse, whose rider is death, is signified the people of the Saracens and its death-bearing prophet, namely Mohammed. . . .")[14] In the scheme of seven *status* that I have proposed as the basis for Dante's passage, however, the fourth *status* is characterized not by schism but by *falsi fratres* or hypocrites; and while I would not press the suggestion too strongly, an interpretation of the dragon as the devil inserting hypocrisy into the Church does seem to me to fit the total image somewhat better than does the interpretation as schism. It would, to begin with, be suggested naturally enough by exegesis of the opening of the fourth seal, which frequently presents the hypocrites as introduced into the Church by the devil:

Quando enim vidit Diabolus quod nec per apertas tribulationes, nec per apertas haereses proficere potuit, sed per has sanctam Ecclesiam robustiorem & cautiorem reddidit, fratres in hypocrisi ambulantes subintroduxit. . . .

(For when the devil saw that he could gain neither through open tribulations nor through open heresies, but that through these he rendered Holy Church stronger and more circumspect, he secretly introduced brothers walking in hypocrisy. . . .)[15]

The representation of the devil as a dragon or serpent is of course a commonplace of the sort that defies meaningful documentation;[16] and the identity of Dante's dragon as both "dragon" and "serpent" is confirmed by Beatrice's later reference to the car as the "vaso che 'l serpente ruppe" (XXXIII. 34: "vessel which the serpent broke"). This very definition of the car in terms of the attack on it by the dragon may, I suppose, give him a certain generic quality, thus contributing subtly to a recognition of him as the master of evil. His appearing immediately after "la terra s'aprisse / tr'ambo le ruote" (130–31: "after the earth opened between the two wheels") strongly suggests that he has come from hell. In line

133 he is said to pull back his tail "come vespa che ritragge l'ago" ("like a wasp that retracts its sting"); though the wasp has few traditional associations of any kind, and none which coincides neatly with any of its possible meanings here, Augustine's interpretation of the *vespas* in Joshua 24:12 (Vulgate *crabrones*, "hornets") as "aerios occultos spiritus, quod in psalmo [77:49] dicit: *per angelos malignos*" ("secret spirits of the air, because in the Psalm [77:49] it says: *through wicked angels*")[17] seems to point in at least the general direction of the devil. The dragon's attacking with his tail recalls inevitably the popular image of the scorpion stinging with his tail, which appears, for example, in the Apocalypse a few chapters after the opening of the seals: "Et [locustae] habebant caudas similes scorpionum, et aculei erant in caudis eorum" (9:10). ("And [the locusts] had tails as of scorpions, and there were stings in their tails.") A standard commentary on a nearby verse associates the scorpion explicitly with the devil and (though the avowed subject is the spreading of heresy) implicitly also with hypocrisy:

> Potestas nocendi in scorpione est in cauda, per quam percutit, et venena diffundit. Similiter diabolus per haereticos venenum suae malitiae diffundit, sicut per caudam suam. . . . Item, similes sunt [locustae] scorpionibus: quia scorpio blanditur in facie sed occulte cauda percutit.

> (In the scorpion the power of harming is in the tail, through which he strikes and pours out the venom. Similarly the devil pours out the venom of his malice through heretics, as if through his tail. . . . In the same way [locusts] are like scorpions, because the scorpion is pleasant in his face but secretly stings with his tail.)[18]

The attack from beneath and the removal of part of the bottom of the car would have a plausible relation to hypocrisy, which can easily be thought of as covertly damaging the very "foundation" of the Church; Anselm of Havelberg, in his elaboration of the fourth *status*, describes the hypocrite himself as "non habens fundamentum" ("not having a foundation").[19] The description of the dragon's departure, "gissen vago vago" (135), may reflect an interpretation relating the *viros . . . vagos* of Judges 9:4 to hypocrisy, found in the *De Antichristo* attributed to William of St.-Amour: ". . . quos homines infructuosos & vagos, ut illis [Antichristus] dominetur, sub

umbra sua requiescere precatur, id est sub simulata hypocrisi. . . ." (". . .
which unfruitful and vagrant men, so that [the Antichrist] may rule over
them, he prays them to rest under his shadow, that is, under false hypocrisy. . . .")[20] And finally, the serpent is a natural and traditional symbol
of hypocrisy—as for example in Christ's extended reproach to the Scribes
and Pharisees in Matthew 23:13-33 (quoted prominently by Anselm of
Havelberg in his account of the fourth *status*), with its repeated refrain,
"Vae vobis scribae et pharisaei hypocritae. . . ." (13, 14, 15, 23, 25, 27,
29), climaxed by the epithets "Serpentes, genimina viperarum. . . ." (33).
("Woe unto you, Scribes and Pharisees, hypocrites. . . . Serpents, generation of vipers. . . .")[21]

So far, I have suggested that the attack of the eagle and the invasion
of the fox dramatize respectively the second and third *status ecclesiae*, and
that the damage inflicted by the dragon dramatizes the fourth *status*—
probably to be thought of as the time of hypocrisy, though an interpretation as the Mohammedan schism, following exegetes like Joachim, Olivi,
and Ubertino, as well as Dante's early commentators, would not be impossible. In constructing this partial pattern, I have temporarily omitted
the first *status* (the Apostolic Church) and the second descent of the eagle
representing the Donation of Constantine; I now propose to make a similar
detour around the fifth *status* (the time of consolation) and proceed to the
sixth and seventh.

Following the growth of the feathers left by the eagle in the car and
the appearance of the mysterious seven heads (136-47), Dante sees the
car occupied by a whore and a giant:

> Sicura, quasi rocca in alto monte,
> > seder sovresso una puttana sciolta
> > m'apparve con le ciglia intorno pronte;
> e come perché non li fosse tolta,
> > vidi di costa a lei dritto un gigante;
> > e basciavansi insieme alcuna volta.

(Lines 148-53: Secure, like a fortress on a high mountain, there appeared to me an ungirt harlot sitting upon it, with eyes quick to
rove around; and, as if in order that she should not be taken

from him, I saw upright at her side a giant, and they kissed each other again and again.)

I have argued elsewhere that the whore is a reflection of the *meretrix magna* or "great whore" in Apocalypse 17, evidently bearing her common exegetical significance as the *ecclesia carnalis* or "carnal Church"—in broad terms, the multitude of the wicked within the Church. The giant who is her lover seems clearly to represent the Antichrist, who appears prominently as a giant in almost all medieval commentary on the famous number 666 in Apocalypse 13:18. The role of the Antichrist in medieval eschatology as both seducer and persecutor of the great whore is reflected in lines 153 and 156, by the giant's first kissing the whore and then beating her. The Antichrist is very frequently portrayed as sitting above or upon the corrupted Church, here represented by the transformed and damaged car on which the giant sits.[22] Such an interpretation, of course, places the action of lines 148 ff. firmly within the time of the Antichrist, which is itself the sixth *status ecclesiae*.

In Canto XXXIII, Beatrice's famous prophecy of the *cinquecento diece e cinque* refers back to both the dragon and the eagle, thus placing the promised savior in the context of the series of vicissitudes suffered by the car in Canto XXXII:

> Sappi che 'l vaso che 'l serpente ruppe,
> fu e non è; ma chi n'ha colpa, creda
> che vendetta di Dio non teme suppe.
> Non sarà tutto tempo sanza reda
> l'aguglia che lasciò le penne al carro,
> per che divenne mostro e poscia preda;
> ch'io veggio certamente, e però il narro,
> a darne tempo già stelle propinque,
> secure d'ogn' intoppo e d'ogne sbarro,
> nel quale un cinquecento diece e cinque,
> messo di Dio, anciderà la fuia
> con quel gigante che con lei delinque.

(Lines 34–45: Know that the vessel which the serpent broke was, and is not: but let him whose fault it is believe that God's vengeance fears no hindrance. Not for all time shall be without an heir the

eagle that left its feathers on the chariot, whereby it became a monster
and then a prey: for I see surely, and therefore I tell of it, stars already
close at hand, secure from all check and hindrance, that shall bring
us a time wherein a Five Hundred, Ten, and Five, sent by God,
shall slay the thievish woman, with that giant who sins with her.)

In my earlier study I interpreted this "five hundred, ten, and five" as Christ
in a future advent, by way of a complex association between its equivalent
in Roman numerals (*DXV*) and the monogram ℧ (*VD*) — used consistently in medieval missals and sacramentaries for the words *Vere dignum*
at the beginning of the Preface of the Mass, and interpreted by medieval
liturgists as a symbol of Christ, with the *V* representing His human nature
and the *D* His divine. Beatrice's prophecy of the killing of the giant by
this *DXV* announces in cryptic form the great eschatological climax of
the killing of the Antichrist by Christ, derived from II Thessalonians 2:8,
"Et tunc revelabitur ille iniquus, quem Dominus Jesus interficiet spiritu
oris sui, et destruet illustratione adventus sui eum. . . ." ("And then shall
be revealed that iniquitous one whom the Lord Jesus shall kill with the
spirit of His mouth, and He shall destroy him with the brightness of His
coming. . . .")[23] The death of the Antichrist will inaugurate a relatively
brief period of earthly tranquillity before the end of the world and the
Last Judgment, which is commonly identified as the seventh *status ecclesiae*.[24]

The addition of these two periods — the time of the Antichrist and the
time after his death — gives us a pattern of correspondences between
Purgatorio XXXII–XXXIII and the second, third, fourth, sixth, and seventh
status ecclesiae, and so allows us to ask seriously whether the first and fifth
may not also be somehow represented. An allegory of the fifth *status*, if
it exists, would presumably have to fall between the attack of the dragon
(the fourth *status*) and the episode of the whore and the giant (the sixth
status) — that is, in lines 136–47:

> Quel che rimase, come da gramigna
>   vivace terra, da la piuma, offerta
>   forse con intenzion sana e benigna,
> si ricoperse, e funne ricoperta
>   e l'una e l'altra rota e 'l temo, in tanto
>   che più tiene un sospir la bocca aperta.

> Trasformato così 'l dificio santo
>   mise fuor teste per le parti sue,
>   tre sovra 'l temo e una in ciascun canto.
> Le prime eran cornute come bue,
>   ma le quattro un sol corno avean per fronte:
>   simile mostro visto ancor non fue.

(What was left was covered again, as live soil with grass, with the plumage, offered perhaps with sincere and kind intent, and both one and the other wheel were covered with it in less time than a sigh keeps open the mouth. Thus transformed, the holy structure put forth heads upon its parts, three on the pole and one on each corner: the three were horned like oxen, but the four had a single horn on the forehead. Such a monster was never seen before.)

As Wilhelm Kamlah remarks of the fifth *status* in Apocalyptic commentary, "einen greifbaren status ergibt es . . . nicht."[25] Within the pattern of *status ecclesiae* with which we have been concerned, it is identified most frequently as a time of consolation for the evils of the preceding three *status*[26] — a characterization manifestly at odds with Dante's picture of the car covered with feathers and the sprouting of the seven heads, all of which, whatever their precise meaning, clearly allegorize some form of corruption. In medieval eschatology, however, the seven *status ecclesiae* derived from the opening of the seven seals are accompanied respectively by seven great *ordines praedicatorum* or "orders of preachers," derived from the sounding of the seven trumpets in Apocalypse 8–10, who preach against the evils of their respective *status*; and it is in exegesis of the sounding of the fifth trumpet (9:1–12) that the evils of the fifth *status* are more often described. In the words of the *De Antichristo* attributed to William of St.-Amour, with obvious reference to the friars,

> In hac ergo sigilli quinti apertione [diabolus] praecursores praemittit in fine scilicet hujus pacis ecclesiae, qui exercitum ejus congregent, & vias antichristi in perversorum cordibus praeparent. Unde Johannes . . . describens statum bonorum sub mysterio septem tubarum, correspondentem casum describit malorum, & quinto angelo tuba canente, annuntiatur damnatio eorum, quos diabolus praemittit ad

praeparandas vias ante faciem antichristi. . . .

(Therefore in this opening of the fifth seal [the devil] sends ahead
precursors—in the end, that is, of this peace of the Church—who
are to assemble his army and prepare the ways of the Antichrist in
the hearts of the wicked. Whence John . . . describing the state of
the good under the mystery of the seven trumpets, describes the corresponding situation of the wicked, and when the fifth angel sounds
his trumpet, there is announced the damnation of those whom the
devil has sent ahead to prepare the ways before the face of the
Antichrist. . . .)[27]

The targets of the preaching represented by the fifth trumpet are sometimes
the precursors of the Antichrist (as in the passage just quoted) and sometimes
a miscellany of evils including these precursors, as in the commentary attributed to Hugh of St. Cher:

Et quintus Angelus [9:1]: Postquam singulariter per Iudaeorum aemula-
tionem, per persecutorum crudelitatem, per haereticorum prauitatem,
per falsorum fratrum simulationem & hypocrisim Diabolus impedire
non potuit praedicationem, multa mala simul inducere Ecclesiae ostenditur, vt quod per singula non potuit, per multa conetur facere si
possit, sicut in sequentibus patebit. . . .

(And the fifth angel [9:1]: After the devil was not able to hinder the
preaching through the envy of the Jews, through the cruelty of
persecutors, through the evil of heretics, through the simulation and
hypocrisy of false brothers, employed one at a time, it is shown that
he brings into the Church many evils at once, so that what he could
not accomplish through single evils he may try to accomplish by
many if he can, as will be clear in what follows. . . .)[28]

My suggestion—depending heavily on the framework of status already
established—is that Dante, following the hint that seems offered by exegesis of the fifth trumpet, has adapted the ill-defined fifth status ecclesiae
into a time dominated by pervasive corruption in the Church, allegorized
by the growth of the eagle's feathers and the emergence of the seven heads.[29]
Such a time would grow naturally out of the time of hypocrisy that I

take to be represented by the attack of the dragon, and would lead naturally into the time of the Antichrist that I take to be represented by the advent of the whore and the giant — particularly in view of the precursors of the Antichrist who appear so regularly in commentary on the fifth trumpet. With regard to the dividing-line between "present" and "future" in the sequence we have been considering, I suppose the most obvious distinction is that the events of Canto XXXII are narrated in the past tense while the arrival of the *DXV* is foretold by Beatrice. Within our external pattern of *status ecclesiae*, however, there is a tendency to identify the fifth *status* as the present; an Apocalyptic commentary once attached to the name of Aquinas remarks that "quinque prima [sigilla] respiciunt statum Ecclesiae praesentem et praeteritum: duo sequentia pertinent ad futurum" ("the first five [seals] regard the present and past condition of the Church; the two following pertain to the future").[30] Given the prominence of present ecclesiastical corruption in eschatological literature of the late thirteenth and early fourteenth centuries, and the usual assumption that the Antichrist himself has yet to appear, it is worth asking whether Dante may not intend this picture of the feathered and deformed Church as the "present" in his panorama of New Testament history, with the following episode of the whore and the giant as a vision of the imminent future.

There remains only the first *status*, that of the primitive Church in the Apostolic age. In a previous article I have proposed that the Griffon's tying the car to the dry tree by means of its pole (XXXII. 49–51) and the tree's bursting into fresh bloom (52–60) are to be understood as Christ joining the Church to fallen human nature by means of the Cross, and the consequent "bloom" of re-justification; this cosmic spiritual regeneration is embellished at length in a lavish series of images, including the Zodiacal signs of Pisces and Aries (52–57), the tree's burgeoning into a hue less than of roses and greater than of violets (58–60), the *canticum novum* of Apocalypse 5:9 (61–63), the Ovidian tale of Argus put to sleep by hearing the story of Pan and Syrinx (64–66), Christ as the apple-tree of Canticles 2:3 (73–75), and the Transfiguration (76–81).[31] The chronology implied by this interpretation seems confirmed when Dante wakens from his sleep (82), by Matelda's report that "li altri dopo 'l grifon sen vanno suso" (89: "the rest are rising on high behind the griffin"), which so far as I know is generally accepted as a reference to the Ascension. If so, any allegory of the first *status* should appear somewhere in lines 82–105, between Dante's awakening and directing his attention to the assaults on

the car. Two immediately promising details are Matelda's description of
Beatrice, "Vedi lei sotto la fronda / nova sedere in su la sua radice" (86–87:
"See her beneath the new foliage, seated upon its root"), and the picture
of her a few lines later:

> Sola sedeasi in su la terra vera,
>   come guardia lasciata lì del plaustro
>   che legar vidi a la biforme fera.

(Lines 94–96: She was sitting there alone on the bare ground, like
a guard left there of the chariot which I had seen bound by the biform-
ed animal.)

In both these passages, I would suggest for Beatrice a meaning approx-
imating Divine Revelation, that which God makes known directly to
man — in the first passage shown as guardian over newly regenerate human
nature, in the second as guardian over the still pristine Church. Her sitting "in su la terra vera" (which I take to mean "on the very earth," that
is, the bare earth) would be a natural image for the simplicity and austeri-
ty that characterized the primitive Church;[32] and the *sette ninfe* who form
a protective circle around her (97–99), usually explained as the Seven Virtues, would obviously be consistent with this interpretation. Finally, exegesis of the opening of the first seal frequently emphasizes the preaching
during this early time, as for example in a commentary formerly attributed
to Aquinas: *"Veni et vide* [6:1]. Per hoc intelligitur, quod praedicatores
primitivae Ecclesiae convertendos invitabant." (*"Come and see* [6:1].
Through this is understood that the preachers of the primitive Church
invite those who are to be converted.")[33] Can it be that in Beatrice's speech
of reassurance and admonition to Dante (100–105) we are to recognize
an allegorical re-enactment of this early preaching?

We come at last to the second descent of the eagle, the gift of feathers,
and the voice from heaven, "O navicella mia, com' mal se' carca!" (124–29:
"O little bark of mine, how ill are you laden"), clearly allegorizing the
Donation of Constantine and the voice from heaven that accompanied
it: "Hodie diffusum est venenum in ecclesia Dei!" ("Today poison has
been poured upon the Church of God!")[34] Since I can find no example
of the *status ecclesiae* which includes or mentions the Donation, and no
account of the Donation which in any way hints of the *status ecclesiae*,

I am forced to the tentative conclusion that it is an original adaptation by Dante—added presumably because from a medieval perspective the Donation is one of the great critical points of Christian history, and also because it provides a necessary basis for the powerful later image of the car completely overgrown with feathers.

In the preceding pages I have tried to show that *Purgatorio* XXXII and XXXIII contain a highly imaginative allegorization of the great medieval historical pattern of seven *status ecclesiae*, with the passage after the ascent of the Griffon, centered on Beatrice, representing the first *status* or time of the primitive Church; the violent descent of the eagle, the second *status* or time of the persecutions; the invasion of the she-fox, the third *status* or time of the early heretics; (the second descent of the eagle and the gift of feathers, the Donation of Constantine); the attack of the dragon, the fourth *status* or time of the hypocrites; the growth of the feathers and heads on the car, Dante's adaptation of the indistinct fifth *status* into a time of massive corruption in the Church; the whore and the giant, the sixth *status* or time of the Antichrist; and Beatrice's prophecy of the *DXV* in Canto XXXIII, the seventh *status* or time of peace beginning with the death of the Antichrist. The relationship thus created between the Apocalyptic opening of the seven seals and the last two cantos of the *Purgatorio* may be subtly reinforced by a small structural parallel, in which the climactic seventh event of each series is set off from the preceding six. In the Apocalypse, the opening of the first six seals is told continuously in Chapter 6, with the opening of the seventh delayed until the beginning of Chapter 8; in the *Purgatorio*, Beatrice's prophecy of the seventh *status ecclesiae* is similarly separated from the vision of the first six by the beginning thirty-odd lines of Canto XXXIII.

To whatever extent this argument has been convincing, it will in turn support the interpretation of the whore, the giant, and the *DXV* presented in my previous studies. A final question concerns the thematic relationship between this whole figurative survey of Christian history, and the earlier survey of human history that seems embodied in the procession of Sacred Scripture in *Purgatorio* XXIX. 82 ff. If Cantos XXXII and XXXIII do indeed contain the historical pattern I have suggested, why has Dante chosen to duplicate its theme, though in strikingly different imagery, in a part of the poem so closely preceding? If I may repeat a conclusion from an earlier paper, I suspect that what is being dramatized here is the distinction between "history" as it exists in the mind of God, and history as it is allowed to work itself out in a material universe. The Procession of Scripture—unearthly, severely ordered, and using as its major symbols the Books that are themselves the word of God—is history seen, as it were, *sub specie aeternitatis;* the historical survey of Cantos XXXII and XXXIII, allegorical though it is, presents with greater liveliness and variety the vicissitudes and ultimate triumph of this divinely ordained drama when it is put into production on the imperfect stage of earth.[35] Such a relation between these two historical allegories, if it is plausible, would itself reflect the exegetical concept of *recapitulatio*—"la description réitérée des mêmes faits sous des formes diverses"—which plays so prominent a part in medieval commentary on the Apocalypse,[36] and so would embellish further the complex process by which, in the words of Professor Singleton, "a human poem is . . . by analogy participating in a divine poem."[37]

Notes

1. All quotations of the *Purgatorio* are from *La Commedia secondo l'antica vulgata,* ed. Giorgio Petrocchi (Le opere di Dante Alighieri, Edizione Nazionale a cura della Società Dantesca Italiana, 7; Milan: Arnoldo Mondadori, 1966–67), III. English versions of passages cited from the *Commedia* here and *infra* are provided by Dante Alighieri, *The Divine Comedy,* trans. with a commentary by Charles S. Singleton, Bollingen Series LXXX, 3 vols. in 6 (Princeton, N.J.: Princeton University Press, 1970–75). In line 135, I have replaced Singleton's translation of *gissen vago vago,* "made off, all content," with the traditional rendering, "went its vagrant way."

2. "Dante's '*DXV*' and 'Veltro',", *Traditio,* XVII (1961), 220–21; and "Dante's *Purgatorio* XXXII and XXXIII: A Survey of Christian History," *University of Toronto Quarterly,* XLIII (1974), 196–98 and 211.

3. *Benevenuti de Rambaldis de Imola comentum super Dantis Aldigherij Comoediam,* ed. J. P. Lacaita (Florence: G. Barbèra, 1887), IV, 257; the interpretation is developed at length on pp. 257.-58. See also the anonymous Lombard (ps.-Jacopo Alighieri), *Chiose di Dante le quali fece el figliuolo co le sue mani,* ed. F. P. Luiso (Florence: G. Carnesecchi e figli, [1904]), II, 158–59; *Commedia di Dante degli Allagherii col commento di Jacopo della Lana,* ed. Luciano Scarabelli, Collezione di opere inedite o rare, 39 (Bologna: Tipografia Regia, 1866),II, 387; *L'ottimo commento della Divina Commedia,* [ed. Alessandro Torri] (Pisa: Niccolò Capurro, 1827–29), II, 572; *Petri Allegherii*

super Dantis ipsius genitoris Comoediam commentarium, ed. Vincenzio Nannucci (Florence: Guilielmus Piatti, 1845), p. 527; *Chiose anonime*, [ed. Vincenzio Nannucci], *Chiose sopra Dante* (Florence: Tipografia Piatti, 1846), p. 508; *Commento di Francesco da Buti sopra la Divina Commedia*, ed. Crescentino Giannini (Pisa: Fratelli Nistri, 1860), II, 793–94; *Commento alla Divina Commedia d'anonimo Fiorentino del secolo* XIV, ed. Pietro Fanfani, Collezione di opere inedite o rare, 14 (Bologna: Gaetano Romagnoli, 1868), ii, 518; and Giovanni da Serravalle, *Translatio et comentum totius libri Dantis Aldigherij* (Prato: Giachetti, 1891), pp. 800–801. Selections from commentary on lines 109–23 are assembled by G. Biagi et al. (ed.), *La Divina Commedia nella figurazione artistica e nel secolare commento* (Turin: U.T.E.T., 1924–39), "Purgatorio," pp. 704–6. On the commentary of the anonymous Lombard (not included by Biagi), see Bruno Sandkühler, *Die frühen Dantekommentare und ihr Verhältnis zur mittelalterlichen Kommentartradition*, Münchner romanistische Arbeiten, XIX (Munich: M. Hueber, 1967), pp. 116–31.

4. *Benevenuti de Rambaldis*, IV, 258, with the further discussion on p. 259. Heretics or heresy: anonymous Lombard, II, 159; Jacopo, II, 387; *Chiose anonime*, p. 508; Buti, II, 794–95; anonimo Fiorentino, II, 519; and Giovanni da Serravalle, p. 801. Mohammed and schismatics and/or heretics: *L'ottimo*, II, 572–73; and Pietro, p. 527.

5. *Benevenuti de Rambaldis*, IV, 259–60. Other commentators, *loc. cit.* Selections from commentary on lines 124–41, Biagi, *ed.cit.* pp. 707–9.

6. *Benevenuti de Rambaldis*, IV, 260–61, with the further discussion on p. 262. Mohammed: anonymous Lombard, II, 160; Jacopo, II, 387; *Chiose anonime*, pp. 510–11; Buti, II, 796–97; and Giovanni, p. 802. Antichist: Pietro, p. 528; and anonimo Fiorentino, II, 519. "Maggiore persecutore. . . ": *L'ottimo*, II, 574.

7. Several versions are discussed by Wilhelm Kamlah, *Apokalypse und Geschichtstheologie: Die mittelalterliche Auslegung der Apokalypse vor Joachim von Fiore*, Historische Studien, 285 (Berlin: Emil Ebering, 1935), pp. 61–70; and see Henri de Lubac, S. J., *Exégèse médiévale: Les quatre sens de l'Écriture* ([Paris]: Aubier, 1959–64), II, 1, 521–27. For present purposes, Joachistic versions of the seven *status* seem less relevant than the traditional scheme presented below. See for example Joachim of Flora, *Expositio in Apocalipsim* (Venice: Franciscus Bindonus and Mapheus Pasinus, 1527), fols. 113^V–120^r and 123^r, and the summary by M. Reeves and B. Hirsch-Reich, "The Seven Seals in the Writings of Joachim of Fiore," *Recherches de théologie ancienne et médiévale*, XXI (1954), 216, with a text of the short Joachistic tract *De septem sigillis* on pp. 239–47; and Peter Olivi, *Postilla in Apocalipsim*, MS Florence, Bibl. Laurenziana, Conventi Soppressi 397, fols.75^V–90^V (old 73^V–88^V) and 101^V–102^r (old 99^V–100^r), and the summary quoted by Étienne Baluze, *Miscellanea* (Lucca: Vincentius Junctinius, 1761–64), II, 258. Ubertino da Casale, *Arbor vite crucifixe Iesu*, v, i (Venice: Andreas de Bonetis of Pavia, 1485; repr. Turin: Bottega d'Erasmo, 1961), fols. 204^r–205^r and pp. 409–11 respectively, enumerates many different schemes of "seven *status ecclesiae*."

8. Hugh of St. Cher, *Opera omnia in universum Vetus et Novum Testamentum* (Lyon: 1645), VII, fols. 385^r–387^r and 390^r; according to B. Smalley, "John Russel

O. F. M.," *Recherches de théologie ancienne et médiévale*, XXIII (1956), 305, this work "seems to be of doubtful authenticity." For the same pattern of *status*, see the *Glossa ordinaria* and the interlinear gloss in *Biblia sacra, cum Glossa interlineari, ordinaria, et Nicolai Lyrani Postilla . . .* (Venice: 1588), VI, fols. 248^V–250^r and 252^r; Anselm of Havelberg, *Dialogi*, I, 7–13 (*PL* 188, cols. 1149–60); Richard of St. Victor, *In Apocalypsim Joannis*, II, 4–10 (*PL* 196, cols. 760–76); Martin of Leon, *Expositio libri Apocalypsis* (*PL* 209, cols. 334–45); ps.-Albertus Magnus, *In Apocalypsim B. Joannis*, ed. A. Borgnet, *B. Alberti Magni . . . opera omnia* (Paris: Vivès, 1890–99), XXXVIII, 574–83 and 600; ps.-Aquinas, *Expositio I super Apocalypsim*, ed. S. E. Fretté and P. Maré, *Thomae Aquinatis . . . opera omnia* (Paris: Vivès, 1874–89), XXXI, 538–60; and ps.-Aquinas, *Expositio II in Apocalypsim, ibid.*, XXXII, 171–211. Bede, *Explanatio Apocalypsis*, I, 6–8 (*PL* 93, cols. 146–54), and Anselm of Laon, *Enarrationes in Apocalypsin* (*PL* 162, cols. 1522–29), present somewhat similar interpretations; and a *Commentum . . . in Apocalypsi*, MS Berlin, Deutsche Staatsbibl., Phillipps 1728, fols. 25^V–28^r and 33^r (attributed in the manuscript to Anselm of Canterbury, but probably by one Menegaudus), differs only in explaining the *equus pallidus* of the fourth seal as (fol. 27^r) "omne genus diabolice persequutionis" ("every kind of diabolic persecution").

9. Printed with *Expositio magni prophete Joachim in librum Beati Cirilli de magnis tribulationibus et statu sancte matris Ecclesie . . .* (Venice: Lazarus de Soardis, 1516), fol. 49^V. (Since the completion of the present article, a new edition and translation of the *De Antichristo* has been completed by Sara Beth Peters Clark, "The *Tractatus de Antichristo* of John of Paris: A Critical Edition, Translation, and Commentary" [Dissertation, Cornell University, 1981]; the text of our passage is on pp. 56–57, the translation on pp. 110–11.) The scheme appears also in a treatise possibly by William of St.-Amour, *Liber . . . de Antichristo et ejus ministris*, II, 1 (seals 1–5), I. 10.3, and III. 3.4 and 8.7 (seal 6), and IV. 12.9 (seal 7), ed. E. Martène and U. Durand, *Veterum scriptorum . . . amplissima collectio* (Paris: Montalant, 1724–33), IX, 1336–40 (seals1–5), 1313, 1372, 1388 (seal 6), and 1439 (seal 7); the edition mistakenly ascribes the work to Nicolas Oresme. Ubertino, *Arbor vite*, V, 1, includes these seven *status* (though with the fourth represented by the Saracens rather than by hypocrites) as parts of three of his many "sevens" (*status* 1–3, fol. 204^r or p. 409, second column, lines 24–29; *status* 3–6, fol. 204^V or p. 410, second column, lines 33–39; *status* 7, *ibid.*, first column, lines 3–4); these passages appear also in a popular compendium *De septem statibus ecclesie*, ch. 1, printed with *Expositio magni prophete Joachim in librum Beati Cirilli*, fol. 55^{r-V}. Parts of our basic sequence can of course be found elsewhere—for example in Bernard of Clairvaux, *Sermones super Cantica Canticorum*, XXXIII, 7.14–16, ed. J. Leclercq, C. H. Talbot, and H. M. Rochais, *Opera* (Rome: Editiones Cistercienses, 1957–72), I, 243–45, in an exegesis of Ps. 90:5–6 as four temptations of the Church: persecutions, heresy, hypocrisy, and the Antichrist; and William of St.-Amour, *De periculis novissimorum temporum*, ch. 3, in *Opera omnia* (Constance: Alithophili, 1632), p. 29, explaining the horses of Apoc. 6:4, 5, 8 as "aperti Tyranni" ("open tyrants"), "aperti Haeretici" ("open heretics"), and "falsi fratres" ("false brothers"), *i.e.*, the friars.

10. For my interpretation of the tree's new foliage (52–60), see "Dante's *Purgatorio* XXXII and XXXIII," pp. 200–204. Note ps.-Aquinas, *Exp. I sup. Apoc.*, on Apoc. 7:3, "Nolite nocere . . . arboribus" ("Harm not . . . the trees"), XXXI, 551–52, where the good are described as "arbores fructiferae facientes fructus bonorum operum, habentes folia verborum in medicinam et fructum operis in satietatem, radicati in Christi humilitate" ("fruit-bearing trees producing the fruits of good works, having leaves of words as medicine and the fruit of work as abundance, rooted in the humility of Christ").

11. *Expositio in Cantica Canticorum* (*PL* 164, col. 1249). This interpretation of Cant. 2:15 is of course a commonplace; note also commentary on Judges 15:4–5.

12. *Benevenuti de Rambaldis*, IV, 259; see also Jacopo, Buti, the anonimo Fiorentino, and Giovanni, *loc. cit.* (n. 4 above). Bernard of Clairvaux, *Serm. sup. Cant. Cantic.*, LXV.1.2, *Opera*, II, 173, expounding the foxes of Cant. 2:15, says that a particular heresy "damnis pascitur alienis" ("is fed with the harms of others").

13. Anonymous Lombard, Jacopo, *L'ottimo*, Pietro, *Chiose anonime*, Benvenuto, Buti, the anonimo Fiorentino, and Giovanni, *loc. cit.* (n. 4 above).

14. *Post. in Apoc.*, MS Florence, Bibl. Laur., Conv. Soppr. 397, fol. 77^{r-v} (old 75^{r-v}); see also the further development on fol. 77^v. A later discussion, fols. 81^v–82^r (old 79^v–80^r), begins, "Et hinc est quod abbas Joachim dicit per equum pallidum intelligi regnum Sarracenorum. . . ." ("And hence it is that the abbot Joachim says that through the pale horse the kingdom of the Saracens is to be understood. . . ."); the reference is to Joachim, *Exp. in Apoc.*, fol. 116^r. Note also Ubertino, n. 9 above.

15. Commentary attributed to Hugh of St. Cher, VII, fol. 386^r; note also the quotation at n. 8 above. See also, for example, *Glossa ordinaria*, VI, fol. 249^v; and the *De Antichristo* attributed to William of St.-Amour, IX, 1338. Ps.-Aquinas, *Exp. II in Apoc.*, XXXII, 180, adds, "*Et qui sedebat super eum* [Apoc. 6:8], scilicet diabolus; qui licet sedeat per dominationem in omnibus malis, tamen specialius dicitur sedere in falsis fratribus. . . ." ("*And he who sat upon him* [Apoc. 6:8], namely the devil; who, although he sits by way of domination on all the wicked, nevertheless is more particularly said to sit on false brothers . . .").

16. Note particularly the *draco/serpens* of Apoc. 12, along with its medieval commentaries.

17. *Quaestiones in Heptateuchum*, VI, 27, in *Opera*, CCL 33 (Turnhout: Brepols, 1958), V, 330; repeated by Rabanus Maurus, *Comment. in librum Josue*, III, 15 (*PL* 108, col. 1101).

18. Ps.-Albertus, *In Apoc. B. Joan.* on Apoc. 9:3, XXXVIII, 615; the passage is found also in many of the other commentaries cited in n. 8 above. (Cf. also the portrayal of Geryon in *Inf.* XVII, 1–27.) If this interpretation of the dragon as the devil is convincing, it may be worth recalling that the car of the Church has twice been referred to as a ship (*nave*, 116; *navicella mia*, 129), and that any such reference must rest ultimately on the great commonplace of the Ark as a type of the Church. If so, there is a tantalizing correspondence between the dragon's sticking his tail through the bottom of the car, and a widespread folk-motif in which the devil breaks

a hole in the Ark and a serpent sometimes sticks his tail through it. See a thirteenth-century Viennese chronicle by Jansen Enikel, *Weltchronik*, 2571-74, ed. Philipp Strauch, *Jansen Enikels Werke*, MGH, Scriptores qui vernacula lingua usi sunt: Deutsche Chroniken und andere Geschichtsbücher des Mittelalters, 3 (Hanover: Hahn, 1900), p. 50; the fourteenth-century English *Queen Mary's Psalter*, ed. George Warner (London: British Museum, 1912), p. 57 and fol. 7, pl. 12; and for a general account, Oskar Dähnhardt, *Natursagen: Eine Sammlung naturdeutender Sagen, Märchen, Fabeln, und Legenden* (Leipzig: B. G. Teubner, 1907-12), I, 277-79. I am grateful to N. R. Havely of the University of York for calling my attention to this motif.

19. *Dialogi*, 10 (*PL* 188, col. 1154).

20. II, xi, 4, *ed. cit.*, IX, col. 1363.

21. Anselm, *Dialogi*, 10 (*PL* 188, col. 1153). See also, for example, the comment by Hugh of St. Cher, VI, fol. 74^r, repeating ps.-Chrysostom, *Opus imperfectum in Matthaeum*, XLV, 33 (*PG* 56, col. 889).

22. For the complete argument, see "Dante's 'DXV' and 'Veltro'," pp. 193-95 and 205-11; abridged, with some important additions, in "Dante's *DXV*," in *Dante: A Collection of Critical Essays*, ed. John Freccero (Twentieth Century Views; Englewood Cliffs, N. J.: Prentice-Hall, 1965), pp. 127-32, and summarized in "Dante's *Purgatorio* XXXII and XXXIII," pp. 195-196. In the translation of line 152 (above), I have changed Singleton's rendering of *dritto* as "standing" to "upright."

23. For the complete argument, see "Dante's 'DXV' and 'Veltro'," pp. 187-93, 196-98, and 211-19; abridged, with additions, in "Dante's DXV," pp. 123-27 and 132-36, and summarized in "Dante's *Purgatorio* XXXII and XXXIII," pp. 194-96.

24. See "Dante's 'DXV' and 'Veltro'," pp. 245-48; and for a brilliant analytical survey of medieval opinions about this period of earthly tranquillity, Robert E. Lerner, "Refreshment of the Saints: The Time after Antichrist as a Station for Earthly Progress in Medieval Thought," *Traditio*, XXXII (1976), 97-144. With reference to the duration of this final period—traditionally 45 days—and the possible contradiction that might be found between an arrival of the *DXV* so close to the end of time and Virgil's prophecy of a future reform under the *Veltro* in *Inferno* I. 101-11 ("Dante's 'DXV' and 'Veltro'," pp. 227-47), I take this opportunity to add that by Dante's time it could be thought of as extending over centuries. Lerner, p. 140, notes that the chronological reckonings in a prophecy of around 1305 attributed to one Frater Columbinus "provided grounds for the conclusion that the wondrous last age would endure for 220 years"; for example the early fourteenth-century Hugo de Novo Castro, *De victoria Christi contra Antichristum* ([Nuremberg: Joh. Sensenschmidt], 1471), Bk. II, Ch. 27, reports Columbinus, "totum tempus septimi signaculi videlicet CC & XX anni" ("the whole time of the seventh seal will indeed be 220 years"). I am indebted to Professor Lerner personally for a great deal of help and encouragement in the present study.

25. *Apokalypse und Geschichtstheologie*, p. 68.

26. See generally the works cited in nn. 8-9 above.

27. II, i, 14, *ed. cit.*, IX, col. 1340.

28. VII, fol. 393^r, followed by an extended elaboration on fols. 393^r–394^v; the reference to the "ministri Antichristi" ("ministers of the Antichrist") is on fol. 394^r. For other such interpretations, see Richard of St. Victor, *In Apoc. Joan.* (*PL* 196, col. 783); Martin of Leon, *Exp. lib. Apoc.* (*PL* 209, cols. 349–53); Menegaudus, *Comm. in Apoc.*, MS Berlin, Staatsbibl., Phill. 1728, fols. 36^r–38^r; ps.-Albertus, *In Apoc. B. Joan.*, XXXVIII, 613–20; and ps.-Aquinas, *Exp. I sup. Apoc.*, XXXI, 573. For interpretations emphasizing the precursors of the Antichrist, see *Glossa ordinaria*, VI, fol. 253^v; ps.-Aquinas, *Exp.* II *in Apoc.*, XXXII, 231; the *De Antichristo* attributed to William of St.-Amour, II, ii, 2, *ed.cit.*, IX, cols. 1340–1341; and John Quidort, *De Antichristo*, fol. 49^v (Clark, ed. and trans., pp. 57, 111).

29. For my hesitant conjecture that the four single-horned heads may represent the corruption resulting from the misuse of man's natural emotions, and the three two-horned heads the deeper corruption resulting from more deliberate evils like hypocrisy, see "Dante's *Purgatorio* XXXII and XXXIII," pp. 198–99.

30. Ps.-Aquinas, *Exp.* II *in Apoc.*, XXXII, 172. Note also the tenses of the verbs in the long quotations at nn. 8 and 9 above. Herbert Grundmann, *Studien über Joachim von Fiore* (Leipzig, 1927; repr. Stuttgart: B.G. Teubner, 1966), p. 94, concludes that Anselm of Havelberg's fifth *status* is "seine Gegenwart."

31. For the full interpretation, see "Dante's *Purgatorio* XXXII and XXXIII," pp. 199–210, supplemented by my article " 'Sì si conserva il seme d'ogne giusto' (*Purg.* XXXII, 48)," *Dante Studies*, LXXXIX (1971), 49–54.

32. *L'ottimo*, II, 571, offers the compatible explanation, ". . . Beatrice, la quale si sedea in sulla terra vera, cioè verace e ubbidiente al suo Fattore. . . ." (". . . Beatrice, who was sitting on the very earth, that is, true and obedient to her Creator. . . ."); note also Buti, II, 790–91. A different interpretation of these two actions of Beatrice, which I now find less convincing, is suggested in "Dante's *Purgatorio* XXXII and XXXIII," p. 210.

33. Ps.-Aquinas, *Exp.* II *in Apoc.*, XXXII, 173. See also *Glossa ordinaria*, fol. 249^r; the commentary attributed to Hugh of St. Cher, VII, fol. 385^r; ps.-Albertus, *Exp. in Apoc. B. Joan.*, XXXVIII, 575; the *De Antichristo* attributed to William of St.-Amour, II, i, 5, *ed. cit.*, IX, col 1336; and, of course, all commentaries on the related sounding of the first trumpet in Apoc. 8:7.

34. For references to the voice at the Donation, see J. J. I. von Döllinger, *Die Papst-Fabeln des Mittelalters* (Munich: J. G. Gotta, 1863), pp. 100–101; and especially Gerhard Laehr, *Die Konstantinische Schenkung in der abendländischen Literatur des Mittelalters bis zur Mitte des 14. Jahrhunderts*, Historische Studien, 166 (Berlin, 1926; repr. Vaduz: Kraus, 1965), pp. 72, 76, 103, 122, 143–44, 172–75, 177, and 180–81.

35. Repeated from "Dante's *Purgatorio* XXXII and XXXIII," p. 211.

36. On *recapitulatio*, see for example Kamlah, *Apokalypse und Geschichtstheologie*, pp. 23–24 et passim; and A. Feuillet, "Les diverses méthodes d'interprétation de

l'Apocalypse et les commentaires récents, "*L'Ami du clergé*," LXXI (1961), 259–60. The quotation is from Feuillet, p. 259.

37. Charles S. Singleton, *Dante Studies 1: Commedia, Elements of Structure* (Cambridge, Mass.: Harvard University Press, 1957), p. 59.

Words and Images in the *Paradiso*:
Reflections of the Divine

JOAN M. FERRANTE

I N THE PARADISO, Dante attempts and achieves the impossible. He describes an experience which occurred and which remains beyond the scope of human language.[1] Protesting all the while that not even the memory, let alone speech, can retain or recapture what he has seen, Dante conveys the essence of his vision by stretching his medium to its limits, by using words that do not exist, images that contradict each other, by distorting sequential and logical order, and by ignoring the boundaries of separate languages. He draws on the complex nature of his subject to furnish the style as well as the structure of his description: his language and imagery reflect the essence of the divine.

Dante approaches his task with a mixture of diffidence — telling us again and again that what he has seen cannot be recounted[2] — and assurance — accepting, in the first canto of the *Paradiso*, the identification with Paul as God's vessel which he had rejected at the beginning of the *Comedy*.[3] It is this sense of himself as God's tool which gives Dante the confidence to do what cannot be done. In fact, even in his statements of inadequacy, one finds hidden qualifications:

> non perch'io pur del mio parlar diffidi,
> ma per la mente che non può redire

sovra sé tanto, *s'altri non la guidi,*

(XVIII.10–12: Not only because I distrust my own speech, but
because of memory, which cannot return on itself so far unless
Another guides it,)[4]

but another *is* guiding it and therefore it will be done. In Canto X.43ff.,
he tells us that his wit and art could not so describe the shining of the
sun within itself that others could imagine it; our fantasies cannot go so
high because the eye has never gone beyond the sun—but Dante's eye
has. Towards the end of the *Paradiso*, he falls back on the lyric cliché of
the lover's inability to describe his lady, but with a new twist: because
there is no way to describe Beatrice's smile (XXIII.55ff.), the "sacred poem"
must make a leap and move on to an even harder subject, Mary; and in
Canto XXX, he announces that the quest begun in the *Vita Nuova* is over,
that he now leaves Beatrice to a "maggior bando / che quel de la mia
tuba" (XXX.34–5: "greater heralding than that of my trumpet"), which
is coming to the end of its difficult work, that is, he is about to describe
the final vision of God. Dante is clearly playing with the lyric hyperbole—he
cannot describe his lady's beauty but he can describe the Trinity, with
the image of God-made-man within it, the most inaccessible mysteries
of Christian theology.

Dante describes these mysteries with the tools of poetry—image and
sound—in a language which is still alive and can be twisted to his will.
"Trasumanar significar *per verba* / non si poria," ("going beyond the human
state cannot be expressed *in words*"), he tells us in the first canto (I.70–1),
using the Latin phrase perhaps because it is precisely in Latin words that
one cannot do it. He must use not only exempla rather than words, but
the words of a living poetic language (Italian), rather than of learned prose
(Latin).[5] Many of the plays with meaning and sound that are so essential
to the success of the *Paradiso* are not possible in Latin: the repetition of
the same sounds for different shades of meaning, particularly different grammatical forms, e.g., "luce la luce di Romeo" (VI.128: "shines the light
of Romeo"), where the same word is both verb and noun, so that essence
and action are one—Latin would require "lucet lux"; or the same sound
for totally different meanings, e.g., homonym rhymes, which often turn
out to be closer in meaning than they appear;[6] but, especially, the freedom
to create new words in order to lift the mind to a higher level

of perception by inducing intuition rather than by guiding understanding.

It is in these revolutionary uses of language that Dante comes closest to imitating the communication of Heaven where the mediation of human speech is not necessary, where perception is immediate because there are no obstacles to it. The souls in Paradise, like the angels, reflect God's light directly; they receive his thought according to their capacity, by intellection not rational expression. The joy of Heaven is expressed in sounds and sights that do not need and cannot be reduced to words, in music and in light, which Dante imitates with harmonies of sound and with visual symbols (the circles, cross, eagle, ladder, garden, and rose, which convey whole bodies of meaning without explanation); these symbols are extremely important to the poetic and didactic force of the *Paradiso*, but I restrict myself in this paper to the effects of language and imagery. Just as religious writers have recourse to metaphors and symbols, because the normal patterns of discursive language limit or impede the expression of transcendent concepts, Dante often uses images rather than explanations, but he also violates standard rules of speech and thought in order to enable and compel us to perceive concepts beyond normal human experience. He extends the possibilities of human language without sacrificing the ability to communicate meaning, his freedom always controlled by the rigid rhyme scheme and metrical count. In this he imitates the ideal operation of desire and free-will as they are described in the middle cantos of Purgatory; in so doing, he glorifies the tool whose inadequacy he so laments.

Dante justifies the liberties he takes with language by having Adam, in *Paradiso* xxvi, describe speech as a man-made product, constantly changing, not bound by divine laws but by human needs.[7] If those needs are often corrupt (abuses of language are catalogued in Canto xxix), the basic impulse to speak remains pure and God-given. God created the universe in order to share the joy of existence, so that his splendor could *say* "I exist," "perché suo splendore / potesse, risplendendo, dir 'Subsisto' " (xxix.14–15). The souls in Heaven are now beyond the need for human speech, though they must use it to communicate with the pilgrim Dante. Nonetheless, they sometimes have an impulse to express themselves in a form of speech: Cacciaguida "speaks" things that are beyond human conception (xv.37–42); he is not therefore speaking either to Dante, who cannot understand him, or to God and the other souls, who already know his thoughts, but his feeling is so strong that only the most natural human form of expression, speech, can give vent to it; only after he has satisfied that need can he continue in words suited to Dante's comprehension: "quando l'arco de l'ardente affetto / fu sì sfogato, che 'l parlar discese / inver' lo segno del nostro intelletto" (xv.43–45: "And when the bow of his ardent affection was so relaxed that his speech descended toward the mark of our intellect . . ."). The sound made by the souls in Saturn which so disturbs Dante (xxi.140–42) is interpreted by Beatrice as a prayer for revenge (xxii.13–14), a desire so strong they must express it, although again Dante cannot understand it and the others do not need to. As Cacciaguida tells Dante, the souls in Heaven look in a mirror in which thought is mirrored before it is thought (xv.62–3), so they know what Dante will say; nonetheless his voice must utter his desire in order to fulfill God's will (xv.64–68). God does not need man's words to know his thoughts, but the expression of those thoughts in words is a commitment to their meaning.[8]

If speech is man's natural, and peculiar, form of expression, it must reflect his moral state. Thus in Hell, language is misused, distorted so that it fails to communicate any meaning and drives men apart. In Purgatory, it draws men closer to each other and to God through prayers and messages of love. In Paradise, where the souls are already one with God, Dante's language reflects that union and draws us into it by creating harmony in sound and new forms for meaning. Dante is working towards a poetic expression of "quella favella / ch'è una in tutti" (xiv.88–89: "that speech which is one in all men"), the pure expression of thought. One of his techniques is to incorporate Latin words and phrases into the Italian, but not in separate lines and quotations from other texts, as in Purgatory, where although they are fitted into the rhyme scheme they remain distinct elements carefully set apart (e.g., "*In exitu Isräel de Aegypto*, / cantavan tutti," ii.46–47). In the *Paradiso*, they are rarely perceived as foreign, and they bring a wealth of added meaning, e.g., "ma già volgeva il mio disio e 'l *velle*" (xxxiii.143: "but already my desire and my *will* were revolved"), where *velle* has philosophical implications which an Italian word would not carry.[9] Apart from one line in Justinian's praise of God (vii.2), and the three lines with which Cacciaguida greets Dante in imitation of Anchises, the only lines in the *Paradiso* that are entirely in Latin are sarcastic references to the greed of the modern church (xii.93) and the futile arguments of philosophers (xiii.100). Even the quote from Solomon that is spelled out by the souls in Jupiter, "Diligite justitiam . . . qui judicatis terram" (XVIII.91 and 93), is divided by a line in Italian, and then disappears, the final letter, M, giving way to the far more powerful visual symbol of the eagle.

If, on the one hand, Dante seems to be moving back towards man's original language—he goes furthest in this direction at the beginning of Canto VII, where Justinian praises God in a combination of Latin and Hebrew, the two sacred languages—on the other hand, he is moving forwards toward a new language which retains what is useful in Latin but which can be created as need dictates. The medium of poetry and the tool of language are stretched beyond their normal limits in various ways, but the most striking is the formation of neologisms.[10] By far the greatest number of coined words are verbs, which Dante creates from nouns, adjectives, and pronouns, to extend or violate our sense of time and place, and to suggest the fusion of separate beings. The unusual verb forms emphasize the active and continuing nature of the experience: *trasumanar* (I.70) and *sempiterni* (I.76) in the first canto immediately direct our minds to a realm beyond normal experience, where it is possible to pass beyond the human condition or to become eternal, not simply to *exist* beyond it or to *be* eternal—such is the force of the verb form.

Most of the verbs Dante creates are based on prepositions in combination with nouns or pronouns, stressing the movement *into* another essence: *inciela* (III.97), "inheaven" ("perfetta vita e alto merto inciela / donna più sù," "perfect life and high merit inheaven a lady higher up"—in other words, make her one with heaven, not just place her in it); *s'india* (IV.28), "inGods" ("D'i Serafin colui che più s'india," "of the Seraphim, the one who most inGods himself"). In the heaven of Venus, where human love is the dominant force, pronoun verbs appear, suggesting the fusion of beings.[11] When Dante speaks to Folco, he uses three such verbs, in the first and last lines of his address: "Dio vede tutto, e tuo veder s'in*lui*a . . . s'io m'in*tu*assi, come tu t'in*mi*i" (IX.73 and 81: "God sees all, and your seeing in*him*s itself . . . if I in*you*ed myself as you in*me* yourself"). Succumbing to the feeling of the region, Dante's language reflects his identification with the souls and suggests their direct communication without the need of speech. In the heaven of the sun, where the Trinity is alluded to (X.1-3, XIII.26-7, XIV.28-30), discussed (XIII.55 ff), and reflected (a third circle forms around the first two, XIV.74-75), verbs are formed from numbers to convey the incomprehensible essence of three beings in one: "quella viva luce . . . che non si dis*una* / da lui né da l'amor ch'a lor s'in-

trea, / per sua bontate il suo raggiare ad*una*" (xiii.55–58: "that living light . . . that does not dis*one* itself from it [its Lucent Source] nor from the love that in*threes* itself in them, through its goodness at*ones* its raying"). *Aduna* is not a neologism; it is a verb meaning "gather," "bring together," but in this passage its number root is stressed.[12]

Aduna is really a pun in this passage, as is *s'interna* in xxviii.120, where it means not "internalizes," but "in*threes*." The form is presumably dictated by the rhyme scheme (with *sempiterna,* and *sberna,* 116 and 118), but *sberna* is itself an unusual word, literally "unwinter,"[13] and the whole passage plays with the concept of three, presenting the nine angelic orders in groups of three: "il primo *ter*naro *ter*minonno" (xxviii.105: "they terminated the first triad," with a pun in the verb); "l'altro *ter*naro . . . in questa primavera sempi*ter*na" (115–16: "the other triad . . . in this eternal spring"); "con *tre* melode che suonano in *tre*e / ordini di letizia onde s'in*ter*na" (119–20: "with three melodies which sound in the three orders of bliss in which it [the triad] in*threes* itself"). Both *tre*e and *inter*na are rhyme words, as is *tri*pudi (124), which means "dances," but again contains a pun on the three in *tri.* This kind of punning is particularly effective in the *Paradiso* because of the number of neologisms which raise our expectations for new meanings: "tu credi che a *me* tuo pensier *me*i" (xv.55: "you think that your thought pours into me"); the echo of *me* in *me*i, recalling the "inme" verb in ix.81, suggests a particularly close connection between Dante and Cacciaguida. Consider the series of verbs which pun on *donna,* "lady": *indonna,* "dominates," and *donnea,* "courts," verbs which indicate the two extremes of Dante's relation to Beatrice, and which always appear in the emphatic position of rhyme words, e.g. "quella reverenza che s'in*donna* / di tutto me" (vii.13: "that reverence which is wholly mistress of me") which rhymes with *donna* (vii.11); "a Grazia, che *donne*a / con la tua mente" (xxiv.118: "the grace that holds amorous discourse with your mind"); and "la mente innamorata, che *donne*a / con la mia *donna* sempre" (xxvii.88–89: "my enamoured mind which ever pays court to my lady"). Sometimes the pun indicates a difference where there should be similarity, as in *travasa,* which describes the increasing corruption of cardinals ("quel cappello / che pur di male in peggio si tra*vasa*," [xxi.126: "that hat which ever *passes down* from bad to worse"]) in contrast to Paul ("il gran *vasello*," [xxi.127: "the great vessel"]); unlike Paul and Dante, the cardinals refuse to be God's instruments.

The mystic union of separate beings, which is implied by the created

words and by many of the puns, is what gives poetic force to these and
other techniques, like repetition and equivocal rhymes, which, though
not peculiar to Dante, take on dimensions in his poem they do not seem
to possess elsewhere. By repetition, I mean the same word repeated within
the line or in the following line, having apparently the same meaning.
There are a number of variations on this technique, including repetition
of the same word with slightly or entirely different meanings (as in equivocal
rhymes and puns), repetition of the same word with the same meaning
but leading to a new meaning, and repetition of different words with
similar sounds which are connected in meaning.[14] The effect of the repeated
sound is always to create a sense of harmony, even if, or particularly if,
the meaning is different. The device of repetition reflects two of the
philosophical principles of Paradise, one, the Aristotelian idea that the end
of motion is to achieve rest and perfection (the repetition of sound brings
the divergent meanings together into a oneness that lies beyond meaning), and the other, the neo-Platonic view that all created beings are reflections of the creator. Dante uses the imagery of mirrors throughout the
Paradiso to convey the relation between God and the souls: God is a mirror in which souls see others' thoughts, xv.62–63; and the souls are mirrors of God's mind, xviii.2. Repetition is a mirroring in language—like
the heavenly mirrors, the words are apparently but not perfectly identical. Consider the two examples of *voce / voce*: "render voce a voce in
tempra" (x.146: "render voice to voice with harmony"); "come in voce
voce si discerne" (viii.17: "as a voice within a voice is distinguished").
In the first phrase, the two "voce" are equal, in perfect balance; in the
second, they are in harmony, but one can be discerned within the other,
because one is moving and the other is not. The repeated word gives the
sense of difference as well as of similarity. Compare ii.39, "se corpo in
corpo repe" ("if body enters body"); because they are similar in having
material substance, it is impossible to conceive of one *corpo* being able to
receive the other. It is, of course, the essence of Dante's Paradise, in which
the souls are petals of a single flower but do not lose their individual features,
that beings should be at once identical and distinct. When he describes
the Rose, Dante has recourse to the same kind of repetition:

> . . . così di soglia in soglia
> giù digradar . . .
> vo per la rosa giù di foglia in foglia.

> ...
>
> e altri fin qua giù di giro in giro.

(xxxii.13–15,36: Thus from rank to rank downward . . . I go
downward through the rose from petal to petal . . . and others
as far down as here from circle to circle.)

In each case the word is the same, the rank and leaf and circle is apparently identical, but in fact, each is less in intensity of grace than the one above,
that is, the repetition emphasizes the difference.

Dante often combines a series of simple repetitions and builds to a climax
of meaning through the series, rather than in the separate cases, as in
iii.79–85:

> Anzi è formale ad esto beato esse
>   tenersi dentro a la divina *voglia*,
>   per ch'una fansi nostre *voglie* stesse;
> sì che, come noi sem di *soglia* in *soglia*
>   per questo *regno*, a tutto il *regno* piace
>   com' a lo *re* che 'n suo *vol*er ne 'n*voglia*.
> E 'n sua *vol*ontade è nostra pace.

(Nay, it is the essence of this blessed existence to keep itself within
the divine will, whereby our wills themselves are made one; so
that our being thus from threshold to threshold throughout this
realm is a joy to all the realm as to the King, who draws our
wills to what He wills; and in His will is our peace.)

Here the repeated words and sounds culminate in God's will which
swallows them all like "that sea to which all moves" (iii.86) and makes
them one. In xii.6–7: "e *moto* a *moto* e *canto* a *canto* colse; / *canto* che *tanto*
vince nostre muse . . . " ("and matched motion with motion and song
with song: song which . . . as much surpasses our Muses"), the first line
is one of perfect identity and harmony, the second moves on through the
added repetition of *canto* and the rhyme with *tanto* to the superiority of
this song over earthly song. A similar repetition, that suggests both harmony and supercedence, by implied comparison with every other form
of existence, occurs in xxx.39–42:

> . . . al ciel ch'è pura *luce*;
>   *luce* intellettüal, piena d'*amore*;
>   *amor* di vero ben, pien di *letizia*;
>   *letizia* che trascende ogne dolzore.

(. . . to the heaven which is pure light: light intellectual full of love, love of true good full of joy, joy that transcends every sweetness.)

In another passage, Dante plays on the phrase *in te*, "in you," repeating the sounds in other words:

> O luce etterna che sola *in te* sidi,
>   sola *t'inte*ndi, e da *te inte*lletta
>   e *intende*n*te te* ami e arridi!

(XXXIII.124–26: O Light Eternal, who alone abidest in Thyself, alone knowest Thyself, and, known to Thyself and knowing, lovest and smilest on Thyself!)

so that the oneness of God's essence is presented in a perfect harmony of sound continually coming back on itself and intensifying.

Dante uses a similar combination of repeated words and sounds in various ways: " 'Ave / Maria' *cantando* e *cantando vanio*" (III.121–22: "singing Ave Maria, and singing, vanished"); the *a*, *i* sounds of *Maria* are repeated in *vanio* on either side of the repeated "singing" so that the singing seems to disappear. In XX.94–99, Dante repeats the words *vince* and *vinta* in conjunction with the alliterating sounds of *violenza, viva, volontate,* and *vuol,* to convey the paradoxical thought that God's will is conquered by human will because it wills itself to be conquered:

> 'Regnum celorum' *violenza* pate
>   da caldo amor e da *viva* speranza,
>   che *vince* la di*vina vol*ontate:
> . . .
>   ma *vince* lei perché *vuole* esser *vinta*,
>   e, *vinta, vince* con sua beninanza.

(*Regnum celorum* suffers violence from fervent love and from living hope which vanquishes the Divine will . . . but vanquishes
it because it wills to be vanquished, and vanquished, vanquishes
with its own benignity.)

This passage echoes and reverses IV.73–78, where human will allows itself
to be conquered because it lacks the force to resist ("violenza . . . volontà, se non vuol, non s'ammorza / . . . / se mille volte violenza il torza").

In Canto XXX, Dante repeats different forms of the same word, *vidi*,
for his last vision of Beatrice:

> Dal primo giorno ch'i' *vidi* il suo *viso*
> in questa *vita*, infino a questa *vista*

(XXX.28–29: From the first day when in this life I saw her face,
until this sight)

and his first of God:

> O isplendor di Dio, per cui io *vidi*
> . . .
> dammi virtù a dir com'io il *vidi*!
> Lume è là sù che *vi*sibile face
> . . . .

(XXX.97–100: O splendor of God whereby I saw . . . give to me
power to tell how I beheld it! A Light is there above which makes
visible. . . .)

The alliteration with *vita* in the first passage suggests the "vita nuova"
that the vision in each case heralds; the rhyming of *vidi* with itself in the
second (it is the only word that rhymes with itself in the *Paradiso* apart
from *Cristo*), focuses on the concept of vision (we were told in
XXVIII.109–11 that vision must precede love) and also connects Beatrice,
the sight of whom started Dante on the journey to God, with the God
to whom she has now brought him. That Beatrice is also a Christ figure
is not coincidental. Dante rhymes *Cristo* with itself four times, in Cantos
XII, XIV, XIX, and XXXII. In three of the four, the repetition emphasizes

Christ's presence in Dominic (xII.71–75), in the crusaders (xIV.104–8), and in Mary (xxxII.83–87); the remaining time, however, the repetition indicates his absence by a startling contrast between those who do not know Christ and yet believe in him, and those who profess to follow him, but do not. The word itself occurs four times in the pattern of a cross:

xIX.104		Cristo	
106	Cristo		Cristo
108		Cristo	

the first and last time in negative phrases ("chi non credette in Cristo," and "tal che non conosce Cristo") which are positive in effect because they refer to people who will be saved, although they did not know Christ. The repeated word in the middle line is the cry of those who claim to believe ("molti gridan 'Cristo, Cristo!' ") but who use the name for their own purposes, and they will be damned. Thus, even with the name of God, the repetition can indicate diversity within identity.

Although neither the *vidi* nor the *Cristo* rhymes are homonymic, the sound effect is similar and Dante does use homonym rhymes quite often in the *Paradiso*. He also uses them in Hell, but in Hell they are usually the same words with very different meanings (see *Inf.* 1.34–36, II.44–48, II.116–18, etc.), whereas in the *Paradiso*, though they are mostly paired verbs and nouns, apparently with different meanings, in fact they are almost identical, for example, *porti*, in I.112 and 114: "onde si [tutte nature] muovono a diversi *porti* / . . . / con istinto a lei dato che la *porti*" ("all natures move towards different *harbors carried* by their given instincts"). The final "harbors" to which they move are all one, God, who is also the source of the instinct which "carries" them, so the two *porti*, verb and noun, both refer to God. Note II.143–46: "la virtù mista per lo corpo *luce* / . . . / Da essa vien ciò che da luce a *luce* / par differente" ("the mingled virtue *shines* through the body . . . thence comes what seems different between *light* and *light*"); the light seems different, but in fact it is the *virtù*, the capacity of the receiver that is different, not the light. *Voto* in III.28–30 is a homonym rhyme meaning "vow" and "what is empty": "ma te rivolve, come suole, a *vòto*; / vere sustanze son . . . / qui rilegate per manco di *voto*" ("but turns you, after its wont, to *vacancy*; these . . . are real substances, assigned here for failure in their *vows*"). It is the failure in the vow that renders it empty and makes the souls Dante sees appear to have no substance, so that he too is led to turn away from true being to emptiness. The pun is repeated in the plural a few lines later— "fuor negletti / li nostri *voti*, e *vòti* in alcun canto" (III.56–57: "our *vows* were neglected and *void* in some particular"), where the second *voti* negates the meaning of the first. In IX.121–23, *palma* is both the palm branch carried as a sign of victory, and Christ's hands which bear the holes that are a sign of his victory. *Pianta*, IX.127–29, is both the devil's "plant," Florence, the source of corruption in Italian politics, and the "lamenting" caused by the devil's envy. The verb, *aduna*, "gather"—all good is gathered, brought together in Mary (XXXIII.20)—rhymes with the adverbial phrase *ad una ad una* (XXXIII.24), the spiritual lives Dante has seen "one by one" at Mary's behest, and which are finally (at least those who are saved[15]), gathered in her rose. All but one of these examples differ in grammatical form but are intimately connected in meaning.

An unusual variation on homonym rhyme occurs in XXIV.14–17, where Dante is discussing optical illusion. He rhymes *mente* with *differente-mente*:

> . . . il primo, a chi pon *mente*,
> quieto pare, e l'ultimo, che voli;
> così quelle carole, differente—
> mente . . .

(. . . to one who gives heed the first seems quiet and the last to fly, so did those carols, dancing severally . . .)

and divides the word between two lines, causing an inner rhyme from the end of one line to the beginning of the next but within the same word, the only time, I believe, Dante splits a word at the end of a line. Since the adverbial *mente* not only rhymes with, but is identical to, the noun *mente* in the earlier line, it seems likely that the second instance is a pun, that the *mente* of the adverb includes the sense of "mind," in other words, not just "differently" but also different to the mind or the perception. Other variations on homonym rhyme occur in Canto XXXII: the rhyme words in succeeding lines (28 and 29) are *scanno* and *scanni*,[16] referring to Mary's seat and the seats of the souls below her; and in 122 and 123, they are *gusto* and *gusta*, referring to Adam's "tasting" which left such a bitter "taste" to mankind; *gusta* rhymes with *Agusta* (119), Mary, who closed the wound which Eve, by her tasting, had opened (cf. XXXII.4–6).

With such repeated words and homonym rhymes, Dante conveys the sense of harmony through diversity which is yet another underlying principle of Heaven and of the ideal society it represents:

> Diverse voci fanno dolci note;
>   così diversi scanni in nostra vita
>   rendon dolce armonia tra queste rote

(VI.124–26: Diverse voices make sweet music, so diverse ranks in our life render sweet harmony among these wheels.)

—so Justinian tells us in the heaven of Mercury. In Venus, Charles Martel lectures Dante on the need for "diversi offici," different functions on earth (VIII.119 ff); and in the Sun, Dante is shown how different modes of perceiving truth—the souls, whose intellectual positions were often antithetical, together form the figure which symbolizes the essence of God, the circle.

Dante applies this principle of reconciling opposites not only in his language, but also in his images.[17] He conveys the paradoxical nature of his material by images which are jarringly irreconcilable: the moon is like a cloud (II.31), a diamond (33), a pearl (34) and water (35). The mind cannot picture a substance which is solid, diaphonous, transparent and opaque at the same time, and yet that is how Dante insists we conceive of the moon. The sound of the eagle speaking in Canto XX is like a stream pouring over rocks (XX.19–20), formed at the neck, as in a lute (where pitch is determined by pressing a string, 22–3), or a bagpipe (where it is the result of wind passing through a hole, 23–4); thus we have sound produced by one substance pouring freely over another, by the activation of a string, by wind through a pipe, all to suggest the sound made by a creature which exists only as the composite of many others, and whose "neck" is not a hollow tube but an optical illusion. When Dante hesitates between two questions he wants to ask (IV.1–6), he describes his desires in a series of conflicting images: like a hungry man, unable to choose between two foods (the subject of the analogy is an aggressor out of need), like a lamb caught between two wolves (the subject is the prey), and like a dog between two hinds (again the aggressor, but by instinct more than need). When he talks about the nuns who have been forcibly taken from the cloister, he compares them to Alcmeon who murdered his mother in order not to wrong his father; the analogy is startling, but it forces us to see how terrible it is to renege on a vow to God. Dante combines military with love imagery for Francis and Dominic, the great champions in the fight to renew the Church, and also the "lovers" of Poverty and Faith; similarly, the Rose, which is the whole body of the blessed, is both a "milizia santa," and the spouse Christ wed with his blood (xxxi.1-3), because the love of God means continual war with evil. (God himself uses two stringed instruments, one musical, the lyre (xv.4-6), the other military, the bow.) The Rose, the culmination of all heavenly symbols, is at once a flower of innumerable petals (xxx.117), and amphitheatre with its seats nearly filled (xxx.131), and a city (xxx.130).

These conflicting images reflect the paradoxes that run through man's conception of the divine: the justice that appears unjust by human standard, how the nuns in the Moon can be blamed for what others forced on them, how those who never knew Christ can be condemned, how a just revenge can justly be avenged.[18] Paradise is the realm of resolved paradoxes in the answers to such questions and in major figures: Adam is the father to whom every bride is daughter and daughter-in-law; Mary is virgin and mother, daughter of her son, humble and high, in whom her creator made himself her creature, a torch in heaven, a fountain on earth (xxxiii.1-12). God, of course, is the ultimate reconciliation of opposites, containing everything within himself: he is the source and goal of all the motion in Paradise, at once the archer and the target. The analogy with the archer is not explicit, but the image recurs frequently and in each case only God can be the archer: Dante talks about the bow that shoots all creatures (i.118-20) and about providence as the end at which the bowstring aims (i.121-26); he is himself the arrow that strikes before the cord is quiet (v.91-93); and the elements of creation, form, matter, and their combination, are three arrows shot from a three-stringed bow (xxix.22-24), a startling image which evokes the Trinity. More unusual, perhaps, from a logical point of view, is the description in Canto ii of the bolt's action: "in tanto in quanto un quadrel posa / e vola e da la noce si dischiava" (ii.23-24, "and perhaps in that time that a bolt strikes, flies, and from the catch is released"), like a film run backwards. This may be meant to convey simultaneity, but it certainly conveys circularity as well—the source is the end, the object is returning to its origin.[19]

This is, of course, what Dante's journey in the Comedy is: on the one hand a return to God, the source of all life, on the other, in Paradise, a poetic recapturing of an experience which begins at the end; "La Gloria di colui che tutto move," (I.1: "the Glory of the All Mover"); is "l'amor che move il sole e l'altre stelle" (XXXIII.145: "the love which moves the sun and the other stars").[20] God is himself portrayed as a circle, or a series of circles: "tre giri / di tre colori e d'una contenenza" (XXXIII.116–17: "three circles of three colors and one magnitude"). That final vision is adumbrated in the sun, where a third circle of souls begins to form around the other two (XIV.73–75). God is both center and circumference, the core and the boundaries of the universe. Although Dante uses the common names and attributes of the Trinity, he describes it more often by numbers and circles which move in and out from each other:

> Quell'uno e due e tre che sempre vive
>   e regna sempre in tre e 'n due e 'n uno,
>   non circunscritto, e tutto circunscrive

(XIV.28–30: That One and Two and Three which ever lives, and ever reigns in Three and Two and One, uncircumscribed, and circumscribing all things)

moving in and out as the circles do in the final vision:

> e l'un da l'altro come iri da iri
>   parea reflesso, e 'l terzo parea foco
>   che quinci e quindi igualmente si spiri.

(XXXIII.118–20: and one seemed reflected by the other, as rainbow by rainbow, and the third seemed fire breathed forth equally from the one and the other.)

This image recalls one in Canto XII which described the first two circles formed by the souls in the sun, as "due archi paralleli e concolori / . . . / nascendo di quel d'entro quel di fori" (XII.11–13: "two bows, parallel and like in color . . . the one without born of the one within"); the double rainbows were further compared to an echo, then to the rainbow that signaled the pact between Noah and God, and finally back to the two circles of souls. This motion, in towards the center and out again, like the "one and two and three which ever lives, and ever reigns in three and two and one,"[21] is echoed in Dante's description of his own understanding:

> Dal centro al cerchio, e sì dal cerchio al centro
> movesi l'acqua in un ritondo vaso,
> secondo ch'è percosso fuori o dentro.

(xiv.1–3: From the circle to the rim, and so from the rim to the center, the water in a round vessel moves, according as it is struck from without or within.)

The action of Dante's mind in absorbing Thomas' lesson reflects and foreshadows the movement of the three circles in his vision of the Trinity.

It is not only in the structure of thirty-three cantos, and the rhyme scheme of terza rima, then, that the *Paradiso* reflects God, but in all the poetic techniques of language and imagery—verbs and nouns with the same form, homonyms connected in meaning, Latin and Italian words joined in one phrase, two words fused to form a third. Dante, in his poetic expression, reflects the harmony which is achieved through diversity, the reconciliation of opposites, the resolution of paradoxes, and the mystic union of separate beings. Not only the final lines, but the whole *cantica*, describes the vision of God, which occurred in a moment outside time, to which the normal rules of logic and grammar do not apply. All of Paradise exists in the mind of God; all existence and motion begin and end in him; every aspect of the poetry reflects him.

Notes

1. Many current critics have spoken of the technical difficulties Dante faces in the *Paradiso*: John Freccero in "The Final Image: *Paradiso* xxxiii.144," *MLN*, lxxix (1964), 14 and in the Introduction to *The Paradiso*, trans. John Ciardi (New York: New American Library, 1970), p. xi; Irma Brandeis, in *The Ladder of Vision* (Garden City: Doubleday, 1962), p. 212; Marguerite Mills Chiarenza, in "The Imageless Vision and Dante's *Paradiso*," *Dante Studies*, xc (1972), particularly p. 78 and p. 82. Most recently, and taking a different approach, Robin Kirkpatrick, *Dante's Paradiso and the Limits of Modern Criticism* (Cambridge: Cambridge University Press, 1978).

2. See Cantos i.5–9, x.43–48, xviii.8–12, xxiii.55–60, xxx.16–33, xxxi.136–38, xxxiii.106–8, xxxiii.121–23.

3. "Io non Enea, io non Paulo sono," *Inf.*ii.32. Later in the *Paradiso*, Dante identifies with both Aeneas and Paul, implicitly, by comparing Cacciaguida to Anchises

and by having him ask to whom heaven has so opened its gates twice.

4. Dante, *The Divine Comedy*, trans. Charles S. Singleton, Bollingen Series, LXXX (3 v. in 6; Princeton: Princeton University Press, 1970-1975). All citations are from this edition, as are the translations, except in a few instances where I have modified them in order to emphasize a particular word or word-play.

5. Dante uses Latin words frequently in the *Paradiso*, for specialized meanings (see below, pp. 106–7), as well as for dignity (the speeches of Justinian and Cacciaguida) and for conciseness.

6. See below, pp. 113–15. Homonym rhymes are characteristic of Romance poetry, particularly Provençal (*rimas equivocas*).

7. In XVIII.72, Dante speaks of the Latin words written in the sky as "nostra favella," which Singleton translates as "our human language," and glosses as "letters of the alphabet" (*Paradiso*, II, *Commentary*, p. 308).

8. Hence the formal and rather simplistic examination Dante must pass on the theological virtues in the heaven of the fixed stars.

9. Freccero, "The Final Image," p. 26, points out that *velle* is a technical scholastic term, meaning, according to Aquinas, "the unshakeable adherence of the will to its natural end."

10. P. A. Di Pretoro lists 84 neologisms in the *Comedy*, 44 of which are in the *Paradiso* ("Innovazioni lessicali nella 'Commedia'," *Atti della Accademia Nazionale dei Lincei*, XXV [1970], 265); Edward A. Fay, working with slightly different criteria, counts 93 in all, of which 62 are in the *Paradiso* (*Concordance of the Divine Comedy* [Graz: Akademische Druck-& Verlagsanstalt, 1966], p. v). For my purposes, what matters is that the vast majority appear in *Paradiso* (and that most of the new formations are verbs, 70 of Di Pretoro's 84).

11. The technique is very different from those used in *Inferno* XXV to describe the fusion and exchange of thief and snake: step-by-step graphic description and a series of metaphors, both effective in producing horror in the reader.

12. Cf. other verbs formed from numbers: *addua*, "attwo," VII.6, *s'incinqua*, "infive," IX.40, *s'inmilla*, "inthousand," XXVIII.93. I have cited only a few of the many examples of created verbs in this section. Among the more interesting are *t'insusi*, "you inup yourself," XVII.13, *ingigliarsi*, "inlily themselves," XVIII.113; *ingemme*, "ingem," XVIII.117 and *s'inzaffira*, "insapphire," XXIII.102, both meaning to make a jewel of by one's presence; and *m'inventro*, "I inbelly myself," XXI.84.

13. From Latin *exhibernare*, based on the root "winter," and meaning to sing as birds do in the spring. See Singleton, *Commentary*, note to XXVIII.118, and G. Siebzehner-Vivanti, *Dizionario della Divina Commedia* (Florence: Olschki, 1954), p. 504.

14. See Tibor Wlassics, "Nota sull'anadiplosi nella *Commedia*," *L'Alighieri*, XIV, 1 (1973), 23–33, for an informative discussion of certain kinds of repetition in the *Comedy*.

15. Whether Dante means all the souls he has seen in the three realms or only those in Purgatory and Paradise depends on how one reads "lacuna" in line 22. See Singleton's note to XXXIII.22–24, *Commentary*.

16. Wlassics, "Nota," calls these "contiguous rhymes," p. 33. For studies of dif-

ferent aspects of Dante's rhymes, see T. Wlassics, *Interpretazioni di prosodia dantesca* (Rome: Signorelli, 1972) and E. G. Parodi, "La rima nella *Divina Commedia*," *Poesia e Storia nella Divina Commedia* (Naples: F. Perrella, 1920), pp. 85–103.

17. Several critics have noted Dante's use of contradictory elements: Freccero, "*Paradiso* x: The Dance of the Stars," *Dante Studies*, LXXXVI (1968), p. 86; Brandeis, *The Ladder of Vision*, p. 162; Georges Poulet, "The Metamorphoses of the Circle," trans. C. Dawson and E. Coleman, *Dante, A Collection of Critical Essays*, ed. J. Freccero (Englewood Cliffs: Prentice-Hall, 1965), p. 153.

18. The tendency of the human mind to conceive of problems which cannot be resolved in the same context is perhaps best exemplified in the examples Dante cites from geometry: the construction of a triangle without a right angle inside a semicircle (XIII.101–2), two obtuse angles contained within a triangle (XVII.15), and the squaring of the circle (XXXIII.133–34).

19. On simultaneity, see C. H. Grandgent, *Companion to The Divine Comedy*, ed. C. S. Singleton (Cambridge: Harvard University Press, 1975), p. 220; he makes an analogy between this passage and XXII.109, the drawing out and putting into the fire, where speed is clearly the point. Singleton ("The Vistas in Retrospect," *MLN*, LXXXI [1966], p. 64), suggests that the image is meant to convey not great velocity, but teleological movement, motion caused from the end.

20. That the end and the beginning are the same, and that circularity is the structural principle of the Comedy has been pointed out by Poulet, "The Metamorphoses," p. 153, Singleton, "The Vistas," p. 63, Robert Hollander, *Allegory in Dante's Commedia* (Princeton: Princeton University Press, 1969), p. 198, and K. J. Atchity, "Inferno 7: The Idea of Order," *Italian Quarterly*, XII (1969), pp. 19 and 21. Joseph A. Mazzeo makes the same points in *Structure and Thought in the Paradiso* (New York: Greenwood Press, 1968), although he is primarily concerned with other aesthetic and philosophical principles.

21. Aldo Scaglione calls this motion "retrogradus" and notes that it recurs several times in the same episode ("Periodic Syntax and Flexible Meter in the *Divina Commedia*," *Romance Philology*, XXI [1967], p. 20).

Time and Eternity in the
Myths of *Paradiso* XVII

MARGUERITE MILLS CHIARENZA

F EW VERSES IN THE DIVINE COMEDY are as familiar as those in *Paradiso*
XVII describing the hardships and humiliations of Dante's exile and
referring to the part of his life during which he was forced to travel
from court to court dependent on the generosity of the great families of
cities other than his own. Readers have traditionally felt that here, as
perhaps nowhere else in Dante's writings, the poet exposed his innermost
feelings, in particular those of nostalgia for his city and bitterness against
its citizens. While the prophecy canto is an exceptional and revealing document of Dante's personal life, it is a mistake to be so impressed by this
aspect that we neglect to see Dante's poetic purpose in the canto. Attilio
Momigliano, for instance, completely misses Dante's message when, speaking of this canto and the opening of *Paradiso* XXV, from which it is
thematically inseparable, he says:

> Nonostante la sua astrattezza, anche il *Paradiso* è fortemente ancorato
> ai più vitali interessi terreni di Dante: è questo uno degli argomenti
> principali per affermare che il *Paradiso* è mistico solo ad intervalli.
> L'aspirazione al ritorno in patria non è mai così viva come in questa
> cantica; . . . dall'alto dei cieli si leva il sospiro dell'esule verso la cit-
> tà terrena. La corona della patria mortale gli è ancora più cara di
> quella della patria celeste. . . .

(Despite its abstractness, the *Paradiso* too is deeply rooted in Dante's most vital earthly concerns: this is one of the arguments for affirming that the *Paradiso* is mystical only in parts. The desire to return to his land is never so alive as it is in this *cantica*; . . . from the heavenly heights the exile's sigh is raised toward his earthly city. The crown of his mortal home is even dearer to him than that of his heavenly home. . . .)[1]

Momigliano's statement that Dante's heavenly *patria* is less meaningful to him than his lost home on earth is of course completely gratuitous. But Momigliano's reading is only an extreme example of a common tradition which stresses the poet's desire to return to Florence as the great theme of both *Paradiso* xvii and the opening of *Paradiso* xxv. Modern critics view the *Divine Comedy* very differently from critics like Momigliano. However, in the case of particular passages, we do not always have a modern interpretation with which to replace a traditional one of romantic or postromantic inspiration. I believe this is the case in *Paradiso* xvii and hope, with my remarks, to open the way at least to a more objective reading of Cacciaguida's prophecy.

It is commonly accepted that when the poet placed the final prophecy in Cacciaguida's mouth he had forgotten that he had announced twice in the *Inferno* (x.130–32; xv.88–90) that this prophecy would be delivered by Beatrice, or if he had not forgotten he had simply changed his mind. But it is hardly thinkable that in a canto of such great structural and thematic importance Dante would have been so careless. In fact, we need look no further than the *Aeneid* to realize that, though we have an inconsistency, it is an intentional one. Just as the pilgrim is told that Beatrice will meet him and give him a clear account of his future, so Aeneas is told (*Aeneid* iii.458–60) that he will meet the Sibyl who will tell him of the future of Rome. As it turns out, the Sibyl leads Aeneas to his father, Anchises, who is the one who reveals those secrets to him (*Aeneid* vi.756–886). Similarly, Beatrice leads Dante's pilgrim to his ancestor, referred to throughout the episode as a father, and it is he who actually gives the prophecy we had expected from Beatrice. The pilgrim's meeting with Cacciaguida has already been explicitly compared to that of Aeneas with Anchises (*Paradiso* xv.25–27) and there are many other details of the three cantos which contain the Cacciaguida episode that recall Anchises' prophecy in *Aeneid* vi. The strong connection Dante is suggesting between his episode and the one in the *Aeneid*, even to the point of repeating the Virgilian inconsistency, is already an indication that exile, in this context, implies hardships and bitterness which are not in vain, and it leads to some greater end than nostalgia.

The relation between the *Aeneid* and the Cacciaguida episode is not my present subject. However, it is related to it in that I believe the key images of the prophecy canto, the climax of the Cacciaguida episode, are the two myths strategically placed at the beginning of the canto and the beginning of the prophecy, and, therefore, both because of the importance of the *Aeneid* in the background and because of the classical myths which guide the imagery to its Christian goal, this is one of the many parts of the *Divine Comedy* which can only be understood through the background of Dante's classicism. But before turning to my specific subject, the mythological imagery of the canto, it is necessary to discuss, at least briefly, some general aspects of prophecy in the *Divine Comedy*.

Throughout the journey, especially in Hell, the pilgrim has received disturbing prophecies concerning his political future. On the surface, the content of such prophecies does not seem to differ much from that of Cacciaguida's, and yet the pilgrim is told several times that he should expect a fuller and more enlightening prophecy when he reaches Paradise. We have already encountered the subject of prophecy in the circle of Hell where Manto and the other false prophets are held. If Cacciaguida's is the true prophecy—and Dante surely means this to be so—it must be radically different from both the Infernal prophecies and those of the souls damned for their practicing on earth the art of telling the future. And yet the actual facts foretold by Cacciaguida do not differ substantially from those foretold by Brunetto Latini, or Ciacco, or Farinata. Furthermore, there is no indication that the information given by Manto and the others was factually untrue. It would seem that the ability to tell the future is not what distinguishes Cacciaguida's prophecy. Perhaps the backward-turned heads of the false prophets in the *Inferno* suggest, among other things, that to tell the future ultimately means no more than to tell the past, for the true prophet reveals something that, even when the future has become past, can only be revealed through prophecy.

The two series of verses concerning contingency and necessity which serve, in *Paradiso* XVII, as preambles to the pilgrim's and Cacciaguida's words, give us some help in understanding what Dante intends the nature of his prophecy to be. The pilgrim says:

"O cara piota mia che sì t'insusi
  che, come veggion le terrene menti
  non capere in trïangol due ottusi,
così vedi le cose contingenti
  anzi che sieno in sé, mirando il punto
  a cui tutti li tempi son presenti."

(Lines 13–18: "O dear root of me, who are so uplifted that, even as earthly minds see that two obtuse angles can not be contained in a triangle, so you, gazing upon the Point to which all times are present, do see contingent things before they exist in themselves.")[2]

The pilgrim is simply saying that since Cacciaguida, different from us, draws his knowledge from eternity, he knows those things in the future which we cannot know, the contingencies. In fact, what we can predict accurately in the future are logical and natural necessities; what we cannot predict accurately are contingencies which, by definition, may or may not occur. It is interesting, however, that Dante compares God's knowledge of future contingency to our knowledge of necessity rather than, as we might have expected, to our knowledge of past contingency, and that he uses a geometrical example. In a different context, but still speaking of prophecy, St. Thomas uses a similar example. He is discussing the relation of the prophet to the principle of knowledge, which he does not possess though he is enlightened by it:

> Thus, if someone did not know how to deduce the conclusions of geometry from the principles, he would not have the habit of geometry, but would apprehend whatever he knew of the conclusions of geometry as one who believes his teacher. Hence he would have to be instructed on each point. . . . [3]

Though Thomas is comparing the prophet to God and Dante is comparing the ordinary man to the prophet, the point of the examples is not really different. In fact, Thomas is speaking of the prophet insofar as he is also a man, while Dante is speaking of him as the one who has access to the source. Thomas' example helps us to see that, when Dante compares God's knowledge of contingency to our ability to apply geometrical principles, the implication is that our knowledge is as faulty as that of one who knows how many obtuse angles are in a triangle because he has counted them. Although it does not seem that the pilgrim is asking for anything more than a forecast of the future and additional information about the events of his life, both the comparison of God's knowledge of contingency to ours of necessity and the example implying two different ways of knowing the same geometrical facts suggest that God's knowledge, from which the prophecy will be drawn, differs not just quantitatively from ours, but above all qualitatively.

Before beginning his prophecy, Cacciaguida too has some words about contingency and necessity:

> "La contingenza, che fuor del quaderno
> de la vostra matera non si stende,
> tutta è dipinta nel cospetto etterno."

(Lines 37–39: "Contingency, which does not extend beyond the volume of your material world, is all depicted in the Eternal Vision.")

As far as I know, Cacciaguida's statement that contingency does not exist in God's mind is not at all typical of Scholastic thought. The usual Scholastic statement is that contingency is not contingent in God's mind, that is, God knows eternally what will or will not occur. By this I do not wish to imply that Dante's meaning is philosophically original, but rather that he chooses to express a philosophical commonplace in an unusual way. The effect of denying the existence of contingency outside our experience is to stress the irrelevance to Cacciaguida's message of our categories of time, basic to all our experience. Both preambles suggest a radical difference in nature between the view in time, represented by the pilgrim, and the view in eternity, represented by Cacciaguida. The implication is that additional knowledge of time is not the solution to our existence of uncertainty and, therefore, telling the future is not the ultimate goal of true prophecy. But, to clarify this, we must move on beyond the preambles.

Paradiso XVII opens with the comparison of the pilgrim to Phaëthon:

> Qual venne a Climenè, per accertarsi
>   di ciò ch'avea incontro a sè udito,
>   quei ch'ancor fa li padri ai figli scarsi;
> tal era io . . .

(Lines 1–4: As he who still makes fathers chary toward their sons came to Clymene to be reassured about that which he had heard against himself, such was I.)

The opening of the prophecy itself is also a comparison of the pilgrim to a mythological hero, Hippolytus:

> "Qual si partìo Ipolito d'Atene
>   per la perfida e spietata noverca,
>   tal di Fiorenza partir ti convene."

(Lines 46–78: "As Hippolytus departed from Athens, by reason of his pitiless and perfidious stepmother, so from Florence must you depart.")

Dante has an important precedent for the use of Phaëthon and Hippolytus together, a precedent that greatly clarifies the two myths' appearance in this canto. However, before presenting this precedent, I should review the relevant details of the myths themselves.

Besides falling to their deaths from chariots, which caused Hyginus to catalogue Hippolytus and Phaëthon together,[4] they had in common that they owed their deaths to their fathers and to a promise that could not be broken, a Stygian oath. Briefly, Phaëthon, who had heard rumors that his mother's claim to have been loved by Apollo was a lie, went to her for an explanation and for proof of her story. She arranged for him to meet with Apollo, who offered to prove his fatherhood by granting any wish Phaëthon might ask of him. When Phaëthon asked to be allowed to drive the chariot of the sun, Apollo, realizing that this would mean death for his son, begged him to change his mind. Phaëthon was unable to control the horses, who ran off track scorching the heavens and the earth, so that Jupiter, in order to avoid further disaster, hurled a thunderbolt at the young driver, knocking him to his death.[5]

Hippolytus' very different story shares some aspects with Phaëthon's.

Hippolytus was devoted to his horses and scorned the love of women. When his stepmother Phaedra failed in her attempt to seduce him, she complained to Theseus that his son had attempted to seduce her. Theseus foolishly believed his wife's lies and requested from his own father, Neptune, the means to take revenge on his innocent son. Neptune, in fact, had previously promised to grant Theseus three wishes and one of these was still left. Theseus asked that Neptune send a sea moster to frighten Hippolytus' horses and cause them to drag him to a terrible death. Like Apollo, Neptune had no choice but to grant his son's foolish wish. Theseus banished Hippolytus who, as he left the city, was thrown from his chariot and dragged to death by his beloved horses.[6]

The text I believe Dante had in mind when he used these myths is a passage in John of Salisbury's *Polycraticus*. John warns that a promise should not be kept when time has so altered the situation that what was intended to be beneficial may become harmful. His examples of cases in which a promise that should have been broken was foolishly kept involve precisely Hippolytus and Phaëthon:

> Who can be so certain of the future as to be sure that he can some day do what he has put off? . . . what man of wisdom can promise with any assurance that which depends upon the whim of nature, since he may be readily hindered for many a cause? In addition anyone may at times for good reasons change his intention. This is so, for a person may seem deserving of a favor at a given moment and yet as the same circumstances develop, be found undeserving. . . . In such cases to change one's mind is often no fault; on the contrary, a virtue; for, to allow ourselves to be instructed by fable, Theseus would not have been bereft of his only son had he been willing to change his mind. Phoebus, too, under the goad of sorrow at Phaëthon's fall would not have tended the herds of Admetus, had it been permitted him to change the wish by which, under Stygian oath, he had bound himself to his aspiring son.[7]

John of Salisbury goes on to say that making promises is inadvisable in any case for, in the best of circumstances, the promise only diminishes the impact of the favor, just as "iacula quae previdentur feriunt minus" ("spears which are foreseen inflict lighter wounds").[8] The image is, of course, strikingly close to the one the pilgrim uses to illustrate his reason for wanting to know from Cacciaguida what the future holds in store for him: "saetta prevista vien più lenta." It is because of this detail which Dante's and John of Salisbury's texts have in common that I believe Dante had John's text in mind rather than—or, more likely, together with—the passage in Cicero's *De officiis* on which it is modelled:

> Those promises are not binding which are inexpedient to the persons themselves to whom they have been given. To go back to the realm of story, the sungod promised his son Phaëthon to do for him whatever he should wish. His wish was to be allowed to ride his father's chariot. It was granted. And before he came back to the ground he was consumed by a stroke of lightning. How much better had it been if in his case the father's promise had not been kept. And what of that promise, the fulfilment of which Theseus required from Neptune? When Neptune offered him three wishes, he wished for the death of his son Hippolytus, because the father was suspicious of the son's relations with his step-mother. And when this wish was granted Theseus was overwhelmed with grief. . . . Promises are therefore sometimes not to be kept.[9]

Dante certainly knew both texts. His familiarity with the writings of John of Salisbury is demonstrated in many places in his works[10] and, as for the passage in the *De officiis*, he alludes directly to it in *Paradiso* v.64–72. Given the presence of both texts—and perhaps there are others of which I am not aware—we can assume that the association of the two mythological heroes within a certain context was familiar to Dante. It is this association that I believe is the reason for their appearance together in the prophecy canto.

In Cicero's and John of Salisbury's reading, both are stories of the tragic death of a young hero, brought about, though not intended, by the hasty action of a father. Had Apollo known what his son would ask he would not have made him a blind promise; had Neptune known what his son's third wish would be neither would he have promised anything; had Theseus known he was to regret bitterly his impulsive action he would not have forced his father to help him. In both stories a commitment was made with the intention of benefiting and showing love to a son, but, because of developments which could not be foreseen at the time of the commitment, what was intended as beneficial became tragically harmful. Cicero and John of Salisbury suggest that not only is the future unknown, but it is capable of reversing our understanding of what was thought to be known and they advise that, since man cannot know the future, he should be cautious in his commitments and, when necessary, ready to go back on them. Theirs is a piece of moral philosophy based on man's situation in time, a situation which can be alleviated by caution but not solved. Indeed, even the gods of their examples are ignorant of the future. Their conclusions are Dante's starting point.

Dante too presents us with a scene between a father — actually an ancestor playing the role of a father — and a son. As in the fables, danger lurks in the son's future. The scene is compared to the one which led up to the meeting of Phaëthon and Apollo. Originally, Phaëthon went to his father to gain certainty ("per accertarsi") about the past, but as it ended it was Apollo's ignorance of the future that led to Phaëthon's fall. In Dante's scene we sense that the comparison to Phaëthon and Apollo is in view of somehow correcting the mistakes portrayed in that story. In fact, the father in Dante's text, unlike Apollo or humanity in general, has clear and certain knowledge of the future, and it is to this knowledge that the pilgrim appeals in the hope of avoiding a complete disaster such as Phaëthon's. He appeals to Cacciaguida as one who knows "le cose contingenti anzi che sien in sé" and asks for information about the future as a kind of fortification against it. In his first request, which concerns his future as a man, he says:

> "dette mi fuor di mia vita futura
>   parole gravi, avvegna ch'io mi senta
>   ben tetragono ai colpi di ventura;
> per che la voglia mia saria contenta
>   d'intender qual fortuna mi s'appressa:
>   chè saetta previsa vien più lenta."

(Lines 22–27: ". . . heavy words were said to me about my future life, though I feel myself truly foursquare against the blows of chance; so that my will would be well content to hear what fortune is drawing near me, because an arrow foreseen comes slower.")

During his request for information and guidance concerning his poem's future he explains:

> "Ben veggio, padre mio, sì come sprona
> lo tempo verso me, per colpo darmi
> tal ch'è più grave a chi più s'abbandona;
> per che di provedenza è buon ch'io m'armi,
> sì che, se 'l loco m'è tolto più caro,
> io non perdessi li altri per miei carmi."

(Lines 106–11: "I see well, my father, how time spurs toward me to give me such a blow as is heaviest to whosoever is most heedless; wherefore it is good that I arm myself with foresight, so that if the dearest place be taken from me, I lose not all the rest by reason of my songs.")

The pilgrim speaks as one who is aware of the lesson taught by the fables as Cicero and John of Salisbury read them, a lesson of caution toward the unknown future. Of course, within that context, if man could know the future, he could avoid those mistakes which might generate or aggravate danger to come. The pilgrim, because of Cacciaguida, finds himself in just such a privileged position, and so he asks what he should know in order to act in such a way as to alleviate misfortunes hidden in the future.

However, the pilgrim's request, already described as essentially superfluous by Beatrice (lines 7–12), merely sets the stage for the real point of the canto, Cacciaguida's prophecy, which, different from the pilgrim's petition, does not stress a revelation of the future, but rather an interpretation of it within a larger context: ". . . queste son le *chiose* / di quel che ti *fu* detto" (Lines 94–95: ". . . these are the glosses on what was said to you").[11] The ancestor's words, drawn from eternity and neglectful of matters of concern in time, seem oblivious to the pilgrim's anxiety and unconcerned with providing the kind of fortification he had asked for. Cacciaguida's knowledge consists of something beyond the simple certainty the pilgrim had sought, and his point of view is so radically different from the pilgrim's that he compares his vision of the painful experiences in store for his descendant to a "dolce armonia" (lines 43–45: "sweet harmony".) and announces them joyfully, "chiuso e parvente del suo proprio riso" (line 36: "hidden and revealed by his own smile"). He speaks of positive value to be drawn from the very events most feared:

> ". . . a te fia bello
> averti fatta parte per te stesso."

(Lines 68–69: ". . . it will be for your fair fame to have made you a party by yourself.")

> "Questo tuo grido farà come vento,
>   che le più alte cime più percuote;
>   e ciò non fa d'onor poco argomento."

(Lines 133–35: "This cry of yours shall do as does the wind, which smites most upon the loftiest summits; and this shall be no little cause of honor.")

And most of all, he speaks of a further overturning of events, following the pilgrim's misfortunes, and bringing justice and triumph:

> ". . . ma la vendetta
>   fia testimonio al ver che la dispensa."

(Lines 53–54: ". . . but vengeance shall bear witness to the truth which dispenses it.")

> "ella, non tu, n'avrà rossa la tempia."

(Line 66: ". . . their brows, not yours, shall redden for it.")

> ". . . s'infutura la tua vita
>   via più là che 'l punir di lor perfidie."

(Lines 98–99: ". . . your life shall be prolonged far beyond the punishment of their perfidies.")

> "Chè se la voce tua sarà molesta
>   nel primo gusto, vital nodrimento
>   lascerà poi, quando sarà digesta."

(Lines 130–32: "For if at first taste your voice be grievous, yet shall it leave thereafter vital nourishment when digested.")

This vision of triumph behind apparent harm reminds us of the disaster that was hidden behind the apparent benefit of the promises in the fables. But if, as the fables show, the future not only brings the unsuspected but, by bringing it, changes our interpretation of the past, in the case of Cacciaguida's vision of eternity we do not merely have a new interpretation, which in the course of time might be changed by further developments, but a definitive one, a mark of true prophecy.[12] That Cacciaguida's prophecy is definitive in its reading of the events is one of the points which is made by the allusion to Hippolytus at its opening. In fact, as I have shown elsewhere,[13] the allusion is not to the version of the fable that appears in Cicero and John of Salisbury but to its full version in Ovid and Virgil. In the complete version there is a further overturning of events so that Hippolytus' fall, and hence the promise which led up to it, turn out to be finally beneficial, though not in the way originally intended by any of the characters involved.

In fact, to review briefly the story as the Latins told it, after Hippolytus had been banished and dragged to death by his horses, Diana, moved to pity by his innocence and purity, persuaded Aesculapius to gather together again his scattered members and through potent herbs restore him to life. In order to protect him from further harm, she had his countenance changed to that of an old man and his name changed to "Virbius," etymologized by tradition as "bis vir." He was brought to Italy, where he lived with Diana and her followers as a demigod. The allegorizers of this story saw Hippolytus as a hero of Christian virtue and viewed his second and better life as representing the triumph of the Christian soul in Heaven.

By alluding to the whole story of Hippolytus, Cacciaguida not only suggests that he has total and definitive understanding of the pilgrim's life to which he compares this story, but he also illustrates the point he had made about the nature of his understanding, derived from God's, in his preface to the prophecy:

> "La contingenza, che fuor del quaderno
> della vostra matera non si stende
> tutta è dipinta nel cospetto etterno."

(Lines 37–39: "Contingency, which does not extend beyond the volume of your material world, is all depicted in the Eternal Vision.")

Man's concern with the future is based on his uncertainty of what may or may not occur (contingency); the prophet, to whom the future is as certain as the past, is concerned with the final judgment of events beyond their contingency.

The difference between the "quaderno" of our "matera" and God's wisdom where contingency "tutta è dipinta" is somehow paralleled by the difference between looking at Phaëthon's and Hippolytus' stories only up to the moment of their falls, and therefore seeing them as alike, and looking at the full stories and interpreting their entire message. When interpreted fully and judged morally, the two myths are opposite: one hero falls from the heavens to his death, the other is raised from death to immortality; one hero is proud, arrogant, and deserving of his fall, the other pure, innocent, and ultimately triumphant; to the allegorizers the fall of one was a fall from pride reminiscent of no less a fall than that of Lucifer himself, the other portrayed the triumph of the Christian soul in Heaven. In a Christianized reading, one myth is the story of damnation, the other of salvation.[14] And of the two, it is the story of the exiled Hippolytus, Virbius, which matches the pilgrim's.

The traditional association of the two heroes only makes sense within a limited and secular context based on man's position in time and presupposing the fall as the end to be avoided, or perhaps death as the end to be delayed. Cacciaguida transcends such presuppositions and reads the pilgrim's misfortunes in this life as signs of triumph. Just as Phaëthon and Hippolytus appear alike only when we look at them from the point of view of the external causes or contingencies which led to their falls, so the pilgrim's future is only disastrous in terms of a series of hardships which he must endure. Cacciaguida confirms his fall — "tu cadrai in questa valle" (line 63: "you will fall into this vale") — and all the fears with which the pilgrim approached him, while at the same time his tone is consistently reassuring of ultimate triumph somehow beyond the fall. By his indifference to the pilgrim's fears, he shows them to be based on a limited vision, analogous to that which might view Hippolytus' fall as similar to Phaëthon's. Though exile, rejection, and loss of good name, all part of Hippolytus' story as well as Dante's, seem dreadful to the pilgrim, he asks his ancestor in vain for help in avoiding such suffering. Just as the early story of Hippolytus is superseded by the story of Virbius, so the pilgrim's original rational program of caution against the unknown is replaced by Cacciaguida's message of faith in the wisdom of Providence, where alone the true meaning of events is clear and through which the triumph of the innocent is guaranteed. This point is made most strongly not through the scholastic terminology, which does, however, confirm it, but through the mythological imagery of the canto. It is this imagery, in fact, which suggests first the question: "will the pilgrim fall as Phaëthon and Hippolytus did?" and then, as an answer, the correction of the question itself: "As Hippolytus, not as Phaëthon."

A. C. Charity's reading of the prophecy canto points out many aspects of the imagery as connoting conversion.[15] Charity shows that the prophecy unites Dante's life, the journey, and the poem as all "subfulfillments" of Christ's death and resurrection and as all ultimately reflecting the same experience. In a sense, my remarks merely supplement his by explaining other aspects of the imagery in the same light. The journey is a journey from death to life; the pilgrim's life will take him through defeat to triumph; and his poem will taste bitter at first but finally nourish back to life. It is clear that the whole experience, described as hazardous and even destructive, but ultimately triumphant, reflects Hippolytus' death and rebirth, which in turn is a poetic image of Christ's death and resurrection or of its reflection in the individual Christian's conversion. St. Thomas' words on prophecy seem almost to gloss *Paradiso* XVII:

> All things the knowledge of which can be useful for salvation are the matter of prophecy, whether they are past, future or eternal, or necessary or contingent. But those things which cannot pertain to salvation are outside the matter of prophecy.[16]

John of Salisbury's Ciceronian remarks implied that, trapped in time, we cannot even interpret the present or past, for, as time unfolds, it can invalidate our understanding even of what had already occurred. For Christianity there is one event which cannot be invalidated: the death and resurrection of Christ, through which salvation is made possible. Whenever other events truly reflect this central one, their validity is assured beyond time. When the pilgrim came to Cacciaguida he was looking for a solution in time, a way to be prepared for disasters to come. Precisely because Cacciaguida has revealed a pattern of death and resurrection in the future events which seemed so ominous, now the pilgrim should be able to look back with understanding on the words he picked out of the heavenly song which baffled him just before he spoke to Cacciaguida. Those words were, of course, "Resurgi" and "Vinci" (*Paradiso* XIV.125: "Rise" and "Conquer").

Finally, I would like to make a few remarks on a passage in the *Paradiso* which seems almost an echo of the prophecy, the beautiful opening of Canto XXV:

> Se mai continga che 'l poema sacro
>   al quale ha posto mano e cielo e terra,
>   sì che m'ha fatto per molti anni macro,
> vinca la crudeltà che fuor mi serra
>   del bello ovile ov'io dormi' agnello,
>   nimico ai lupi che li danno guerra;
> con altra voce omai, con altro vello
>   ritornerò poeta, e in sul fonte
>   del mio battesmo prenderò 'l cappello;
> però che ne la fede, che fa conte
>   l'anime a Dio, quivi intra' io, e poi
>   Pietro per lei sì mi girò la fronte.

(Lines 1–12: "If ever it come to pass that the sacred poem to which heaven and earth have so set hand that it has made me lean for many years should overcome the cruelty which bars me from the fair sheepfold where I slept as a lamb, an enemy of the wolves which war on it, with changed voice now and with changed fleece a poet will I return, and at the font of my baptism will I take the crown; because there I entered the faith that makes souls known to God; and afterward Peter, for its sake, thus encircled my brow.")

Like Canto XVII, this passage has been read as a moving expression of the poet's longing for his city. As a matter of fact, if we read the passage according to its own syntax, the poet's return to Florence is merely a hypothesis, whose desirability may seem implicit in the tone of certain words and phrases (*crudeltà, fuor mi serra*), but is not stated. As Gian Roberto Sarolli has shown,[17] the word *continga* has the same connotations as the concept of contingency; therefore, Dante's statement is approximately as follows: if, among the things which may or may not occur and which cannot yet be known, although they are already understood by Providence, a return to Florence is to be, then he will not return as the same man who left but as a new and radically changed man; and any triumph which his poem obtains can be granted appropriately only at the site of his baptism, because the faith he entered there has been confirmed in heaven.

Dante does not say that he hopes to return to Florence, he says that if he does return it will be as a new man and to the literal place of his birth as a Christian. In other words, such a return must be read in the light of death and rebirth in the Christian sense, and the reading is certain, although, paradoxically, the event being read is not. Cacciaguida revealed the spiritual center of the pilgrim's experience, and St. Peter has confirmed it. Because of this, the poet claims certainty of the final significance of his life even though the circumstances are still uncertain. Any desirability of a return to Florence would be in the relative solution it would provide to the poet's problems on earth. But everything in this passage, as well as in the prophecy canto, denies the value of such solutions. In fact, Dante presents an eventual triumph in his city as not only uncertain, but as ultimately irrelevant except as a reflection of a truer triumph. The central theme of both the prophecy canto and the opening of Canto XXV is not nostalgia, but rather the superimposition of providential certainty on human uncertainty: the poet's or pilgrim's dealings in this world simply serve to dramatize that uncertainty. Finally, I would question that longing for his city is even a credible mood of the poet whose last words on the subject were his claim to have traveled "al divino da l'umano, / a l'etterno dal tempo . . . / e di Fiorenza in popol giusto e sano" (*Paradiso* XXXI.37–39: ". . . to the divine from the human, to the eternal from time. . . and from Florence to a people just and sane.")

Notes

1. Dante Alighieri, *La Divina Commedia*, ed. A. Momigliano (Florence: Sansoni, 1957), III, p. 769; translation mine.

2. All further translations are taken from Dante Alighieri, *The Divine Comedy*, trans. with a commentary by Charles S. Singleton, Bollingen Series LXXX (Princeton, N.J.: Princeton University Press, 1970–1975), 6 vols.

3. *De veritate*, XII, art. 1, trans. James V. McGlynn, S.J., in *Truth* (Chicago: Regnery, 1953), II, p. 106.

4. Hyginus, *Fabularum libri*, CCL, ed. Staveren (Leyden and Amsterdam, 1742), pp. 358–59.

5. For a full account of Phaëthon's story see Ovid, *Metamorphoses* I.750–79; I.1–328.

6. Cf. Ovid, *Metamorphoses* xv.497 ff.; Servius, *Comm. in Verg.*, ed. Thilo and Hagen (Leipzig: Teubner, 1881–1887), II, pp. 67–68.

7. John of Salisbury, *Polycraticus* III.xi, trans. Joseph B. Pile in *Frivolities of Courtiers and Footprints of Philosophers* (Minneapolis: University of Minnesota Press; London: Oxford University Press, 1938), pp. 188–89.

8. The origin of Dante's image of the arrow has not been fully clarified. Some of the early commentators mentioned Ovid and Solomon (Alessandro Vellutello, *La Comedia di Dante Alighiere* [Venice, 1554]; Bernardo Daniello, *Dante con l'esposizione di Bernardo Daniello sopra la sua Comedia* [Venice, 1568]), but the passages to which they allude are not easily identified. Vincenzo Crescini took up the problem in "Saetta Previsa," in *Atti del Reale Istituto Veneto di Scienze, Lettere ed Arte*, LXXXVI, II (1916–1917), 1207–19. While I must agree with him and other commentators that the expression is no doubt a commonplace, its value within Dante's text is clarified by identifying its direct source as John of Salisbury.

9. Cicero, *De officiis*, III.25, trans. Walter Miler, The Loeb Classical Library (London: William Heinemann Ltd.; Cambridge, Mass.: Harvard University Press, 1961), p. 371.

10. For John of Salisbury's influence throughout Dante's works, cf. Paul Renucci, *Dante disciple et juge du monde gréco-latin* (Paris: Société d'Édition Les Belles-Lettres, 1954), p. 104; Ernst Robert Curtius, *European Literature and the Latin Middle Ages* (New York: Harper and Row, 1963), p. 364.

11. Many of the details of the prophecy seem to negate that its nature is that of a prediction or forecast of the future. For instance, though the pilgrim had mentioned his voyage in its chronological order (lines 112–15), Cacciaguida responds by alluding to the same voyage backward (lines 136–38). Cacciaguida's view from eternity is very close to what Charles Singleton called the retrospective view (cf. "The Vistas in Retrospect," *Atti del Congresso Internazionale di Studi Danteschi* [Florence: Sansoni, 1965]), maintaining that the significance of events is not clear as long as they are still unfolding, whether in time or in literature. Another example may be the pilgrim's choice of the word "provedenza" (line 109), meaning "foresight." Also of interest for this subject is *Inferno* xx, which could be usefully explored in terms of the theme of the partiality of the prophetic view it condemns. The allusion to the cave of Aruns so high in the mountains that "non li era la veduta tronca" (line 51), the correction by Virgil of Virgil's text, the strange verses (29–30) concerning "il giudicio divino," among other details of the canto, are possibly related to the problem of the reversibility of knowledge from any one point to any other point in time, resolvable only in the totality of the view of Providence ("giudicio divino").

12. Cf. St. Thomas Aquinas, *Summa theologiae* II, II, clxxii, art. 1.

13. "Hippolytus' Exile: Paradiso xvII, vv. 46–48," *Dante Studies*, LXXXIV (1966), 65–68.

14. For the classical and medieval interpretations of Hippolytus's story see my article cited above. As for Phaëthon, though Coluccio Salutati finds some sugges-

tion of Man's enterprise and even free will in the fable (*De laboribus Herculis* II, III; ed. B. L. Ullman [Zurich: Artemis-Verlag, 1951], p. 91), all the interpretations up to Dante's time voiced total condemnation of Phaëthon's presumption and arrogance. For typical Christian allegorizations see: *Ovide moralisé* II.689 ff., ed. C. de Boer, *Verhandelingen der koniklijke Akadamie van Wetenschappen te Amsterdam, Afdeeling Letterkunde,* NS, xv (1915), p. 187; Giovanni del Virgilio, *Allegorie Librorum Ovidii metamorphoseos,* ed. F. Ghisalberti, in *Giornale dantesco,* NS XXIV (1931), 47.

15. A. C. Charity, *Events and Their Afterlife: The Dialectics of Christian Typology in the Bible and Dante* (Cambridge: Cambridge University Press, 1966), pp. 227–56.

16. *De veritate* XII, art. 2, in *Truth,* pp. 111–12.

17. Gian Roberto Sarolli, "Dante's Katabasis and Mission," in *The World of Dante: Six Studies in Language and Thought,* ed. S. B. Chandler and J. A. Molinaro (Toronto: University of Toronto, 1966), pp. 80–116.

Jacopo della Lana interprete di Dante

ALDO VALLONE

Jacopo Alighieri e Graziolo de' Bambaglioli fanno quel che possono dinanzi al poema di Dante. La loro prova è generosa e notevole, non tanto perchè sono i primi a misurarsi con un'opera così vasta, quanto perchè dissimulano le loro forze e non ne menano vanto: il primo anzi nascondendo la trepidazione filiale sotto la stringatezza e l'aridità, il secondo coprendo la venerazione con la ricerca di toni distaccati e obiettivi. Gli anni sono difficili. I lettori ufficiali diffidano dell'opera. I lettori comuni sono ancora impreparati: solo dopo si potranno assumere come documento le vicende narrate da novellatori. I lettori borghesi, quando superano i propri interessi e le barriere delle ideologie e non sempre lo sanno fare, si mostrano i più capaci, ma non tanto da rinunciare a dar prova qualvolta di saperla più lunga di Dante. L'occasione, in questo caso, è offerta e stimolata dalla scienza di Dante. Qui è l'origine delle digressioni, volute e ricercate, che riempiono le pagine degli autichi commentatori. È, sì, una sottolineatura di una particolare concezione della poetica tra pieno Medio Evo e Trecento, che Coluccio Salutati concorrerà energicamente ad arginare; ma è anche un modo proprio della mentalità e del comportamento dei letterati borghesi o, se si vuole, di chierici e laici. A raccogliere in un'ideale antologia questi passi di scienza (filosofia, astronomia e così via), assai poco divergenti tra loro, si viene a proporre, netta e lineare, la fisionomia della cultura media e, vorrei dire, totale nella prima metà del Trecento: limiti, natura, qualità e propositi. Quello che impressiona fino a Benvenuto, e forse escludendo proprio Benvenuto, è la scarsa presenza, se non proprio assenza, di fondo ed esperienza giuridica, anche laddove colpe e pene, delitti e punizioni (e basterebbe pensare a *Inferno* XI) avrebbero potuto offrire più di una ragione o almeno un valido pretesto. Qui, se mai, è più evidente e meglio si esperimenta il modulo della parafrasi.

Jacopo della Lana[1] partecipa di tutto questo, nel bene e nel male ma ha qualche cosa in più dei letterati di ambienti colti, cui appartiene, e dei suoi predecessori: Jacopo Alighieri e Graziolo. Ha più signorilità e discrezione, ma soprattutto ha un respiro più ampio, una capacità di visione più globale, una fermezza e un controllo, sempre dinanzi ai risultati conseguiti prima da altri seppure solo di qualche anno. Altro è trattare del solo *Inferno*, altro è leggere, e per la prima volta, tutt'e tre le cantiche. L'ambiente di meditazione e lettura è ancora quasi certamente Bologna. Si è ancora tra lo sgomento per la morte del poeta e lo stupore per l'opera sua nei contenuti, nei personaggi e nella lingua. Si è negli anni della preparazione all'attacco dell'uomo Dante e della sua ideologia, tra Francesco d'Ascoli e Guido Vernani. Non certo si era dissipato, ma anzi velenoso serpeggiava, il disappunto di Giovanni del Virgilio circa un'opera così indubbiamente sovrana, ma scritta in volgare. Gli stessi fermenti ideativi e poetici, che Dante in parte accolse e in parte escluse dalla sua teoria e certo trattò da par suo nell'esercizio diretto dell'arte, si andavano delimitando o rafforzando o ancora orientando ad altri esiti. Era un terreno solo apparentemente pianeggiante e liscio, di fatto scabroso e irregolare. Tutta questa tempesta resta nel sottofondo della pagina di Jacopo ed egli, quasi libero, orgogliosamente affronta tutto il poema. Lo studia, certamente, quando Dante è ancora vivo: e si sa, infatti, che i notari bolognesi ne trascrivevano pezzi e versi via via che scelte e tempo libero lo permettevano:[2] è questa una fascia di tempo estremamente suggestiva per cogliere i germogli della fortuna dantesca! Ne approfondisce lo studio o meglio lo finalizza in una organica esposizione dopo la morte di Dante e forse proprio scosso e illuminato da essa stessa, come ebbe a risuonare negli ambienti colti e universitari nel richiamo della corrispondenza di G. del Virgilio. La data proposta dal Gualandi, a parte ogni discrepanza sull'anno di nascita con i critici venuti dopo, può essere un accettabile punto di partenza, se si guardi soprattutto al *Paradiso*: 1323 circa. Ad ogni modo il commento è ragionevole porlo, per via di elementi e riscontri interni, tra il 1324 e il 1328. Può in tal senso confortare l'esperienza, da trascurare affatto, dei deputati alla correzione del Boccaccio, che, dallo stato della lingua, supponevano accortamente che la stesura fosse da collocare attorno al 1330.[3] La data del 1349, avanzata da Colomb de Batines, nasce da equivoco, posto che Alberico da Rosciate, traduttore del poema, muore nel 1344.[4] Un elemento certo e clamoroso è dato dalla diffusione del commento. In vario modo e sotto diversi nomi, del XIV secolo restano trentadue codici e circa ottanta in tutto! Questo spiega la fortuna dell'opera, in senso assoluto, la sua novità e comunicabilità (e cioè la rispondenza tra "lettore" e lettori), la sua adattabilità al gusto corrente e, infine, la sua assunzione come modello nei commenti che verranno.

La *Commedia* per Jacopo della Lana è l'unità di un tutto, ch'è sapere universale ed esperienza d'arte. Un'opera del genere presuppone un lettore agguerrito: leggere è capire: capire è partecipare. Il commentatore si assume l'ufficio antico e moderno, ma non sempre composto in termini giusti perchè sempre c'è il rischio o il calcolo della sopraffazione, di fungere da tramite. In realtà non si tratta di porre il lettore al livello di Dante, ma di addestrarlo perchè ne intenda la lezione; e che sia lezione, nel senso più pieno della parola, si desume dalla concezione della poesia come verità rivestita dal meraviglioso: segno, e non poteva essere altrimenti, di una poetica che nutre ancora l'arte e che impegnerà, attraverso fughe e lenimenti vari dall'Ottimo al Boccaccio, da Benvenuto a Salutati, la critica di tutto il XIV secolo e ben oltre, seppure sotto assai differenti forme, fino a Landino.

I versi 1-9 di *Paradiso* II offrono a Jacopo occasione propizia per fissare i dati essenziali:

a volere perfettamente intendere la presente Comedia, hae bisogno allo intenditore essere istrutto in molte scienzie, imperquello che lo autore usa molte conclusioni, molti argomenti, molti esempli, prendendo per principii tali cose e diverse, che senza scienzia acquistata non se ne potrebbe avere perfetta cognizione; e perchè poetria non è scienzia a cui aspetti di sillogizzare, sì demostrativamente com'è necessario, non è però la presente Comedia imperfetta s'ella non provi ogni suo principio; ma puossi di licenzia poetica metaforizzare, esemplificare e fingere una per un' altra, sì come è dimostrato e aperto nella composizione delli precedenti capitoli. E però si conchiude, sì com'è detto, che allo intenditore è bisogno d'essere istrutto in molte scienzie. Dato questo, chiaro appare come l'autore accomiata li inscii dallo studio della sua Comedia; e li scienti, per renderli benivoli a tale studio, invita profferendoli due cose: l'una si è veritade; l'altra, meravigliose cose; veritade, in quanto dice che è condotto da Apollo Dio di scienzia e dalle nove Muse, cioè dalle nove scienzie, siccom'è detto, le quali non possono acquistare od ammaestrare altro che 'l vero; maravigliose cose, in quanto descrive lo Paradiso e li gloriosi cittadini di quella santa cittad. E questa si è brevemente la intenzione della prima cosa toccata.[5]

La cultura di Jacopo è adeguata al compito che si è assunto. Non è solo la cultura che circola agevolmente nell'ambiente bolognese, vivo e fermentante quant'altri mai, ma è anche quella acquistata direttamente con proprio impegno e buona attitudine. In più luoghi si chiariscono riferimenti e accenni proposti da Dante e lasciati aperti ad ogni compimento: in altri si inseriscono richiami fatti in proprio, a chiosa di quel che si legge o a suggerimento per il lettore curioso e avveduto.

Di Aristotele si citano: *De Anima, Etica, Fisica, Metafisica, De sensu et sensato, Dialettica, De coelo et mundo*, e qualvolta più volte e diffusamente;[6] di S. Dionisio il *De angelica jerarchia*; di Boezio il *De consolatione philosophiae*;[7] e ovunque: S. Agostino, S. Bernardo, S. Tommaso[8] e così via. Schmidt-Knatz ha presentato una parcella di 124 citazioni dai Padri della Chiesa e 380 allegazioni da S. Tommaso.

E' una cultura che gli permette di affrontare adeguatamente (il che non capita di frequente nei prischi commentatori) i grandi problemi dottrinali della *Commedia*. Basta attenderlo al varco su due di questi, che preparazione dei chiosatori e cautele politiche e morali hanno concorso assai spesso, fino ai postillatori del XVII secolo (tutto un marasma spazzato via da Vico), a rendere confusi o a svilirli in banalità. Il tema dei rapporti chiesa-impero, tremendamente attuale in quegli anni, è presente drammaticamente nella coscienza di Dante. Nel commento a *Purgatorio* XXXII.100 e ss. sono colti con molta perspicacia i singoli elementi e poi tutti insieme sono ricondotti a significazione generale: la rovina della civiltà cristiana. Ognuno per sè e tutti nel totale sembrano coinvolti nell'immane sciagura. La pagina gareggia, nel tono, con i versi di Dante: fonda essa l'universale interpretazione del più famoso episodio storico della *Commedia*. Anche la sintesi esplicativa dei versi ha impeto e forza drammatici. E dentro di questa i particolari: la prima aquila sta per i predecessori di Costantino; la volpe, la Chiesa; la seconda aquila, Costantino imperatore; il drago, Maometto; la puttana, il sommo pastore; il gigante, i reali di Francia. Fissati così i personaggi, pilastri di un palcoscenico enorme, si seguono le loro azioni, si accumulano gli accidenti, si perseguono le intenzioni e le volontà. Tutto si muove e si sommuove, si scompone e ricompone: passato e presente si avviano per determinare il futuro. Allegorie e metafore (i due termini sono usati da Jacopo spesso, ma senza distinzioni apprezzabili) si scompongono e si rifondono ad un tempo. Nell'afferrare il particolare si trova già il bandolo del generale e dell'insieme. Nulla è a sè: tutto è in ogni cosa. Meraviglia la capacità del globale e dell'unità: le fiere dell'*Inferno* rispuntano nello scenario bestiale e selvaggio dell'alto *Purgatorio*. Il respiro è qui, per la prima volta, veramente ampio e potente.

Qui comincia la visione, e dice che vide discendere l'uccello di Jove, cioè l'aquila, nella quale spezia, secondo descrizione poetica, descendea Juppiter in terra, sicome è detto di Ganimede nel capitolo ix del *Purgatorio*. E questa aquila venia rompendo e stracciando l'arbore a che era legato lo carro, poi percosse nel detto carro e fecelo tutto piegare e miselo in simile movimento come mette la fortuna del mare lo navilio. Dopo questo vide una volpe magrissima e brutta salire nel detto carro, ed essendo in esso Beatrice sgridandola e reprendendola, la cacciò via in tanta fuga quanta s'avvenia a tal bestia; la quale avea tale magrezza e tanta, che solo possedea l'ossa senza alcuna carne, ovvero polpa. Poi vide descendere un'altra aquila per la via della prima, e quando fue suso lo carro sì si spennò tutta; delle quali penne lo carro si coverse tutto, e sì tosto come tali penne coversono il carro, ello udio una voce che lamentandosi dicea: Oh nave mia come tu hai malvagio carico! Poi li parve che tra le ruote del carro s'aprisse la terra, e uscissene un drago lo quale menò la sua coda suso per lo carro, e con quella coda trasse del fondo del carro alcuna parte e andossene molto vago, pulito e allegro. Poi dice che vide con le penne, che gli erano rimase, ricovrirsi lo carro tutto con le ruote di subito, e farsi come uno animale senza membra. Poi dice che questo animale si organò di sette teste, delle quali le tre erano sovra lo timone, e le quattro erano suso lo carro in ciascuno canto una; e dice che le tre teste del timone avea ciascuna due corna per teste, le altre quattro avevano pure uno corno per testa. Poi dice che vide suso la ditta bestia una puttana e uno gigante, che stavano abbracciati insieme, e andavansi baciando. Poi dice che la ditta puttana guardò allo autore, e 'l gigante se n'accorse e battella e flagellola dal capo ai piedi, e sicome pieno d'ira disciolse questo animale mostro dalla pianta, e 'l ditto animale avendo addosso la puttana e 'l gigante, fuggio per la selva tanto lungi che no'l discernea se non lo gigante. E fino a questo termine di visione sua si contiene nel presente capitolo come appare nel testo. La quale visione hae a significare per allegoria lo modo del reggimento de' pastori e secolari della Chiesa di Dio in questo modo. L'aquila prima che flagellò la pianta e fece tanto piegare lo carro, significa li predecessori di Costantino imperadore, li quali imperadori funno perseguitori della chiesa di Dio e molto percoteano ne' fedeli e scacciavanli, sì ch'era come la nave che è nella tempesta combattuta. La volpe magrissima hae a significare la Chiesa, la quale venne ne' fedeli, e assomigliala l'autore a volpe; imperquello che è uno animale pieno di vizii quasi a dire che gli argomenti eretici hanno tanto di scaltrimento in sè, ch'elli fanno errare li fedeli; ponela eziandio magrissima e senza carne a mostrare come li detti argomenti sono senza veritate. Poi mostra come per la veritade della scienzia di teologia le dette eresie sono cacciate, infugate e ridotte a nulla; sì come eziandio si fa vendetta delli eretici che si ardeno e non rimane se non la cenere che è la materia che prima era sotto forma dell'ossa. La seconda aquila che discese e spennossi; delle quali penne si coverse tutto lo carro, significa Costantino imperatore, lo quale dotò la Chiesa delle ricchezze temporali. La voce del lamento, ch'elli udio, significa quella che discese dal cielo quando fu per lo ditto Costantino dotata la Chiesa sì com'è detto; la qual disse: *Hodie diffusum est venenum in ecclesia Dei.* Lo drago che uscì dalla terra fra due ruote significa Maometto, il quale ne portò a sua legge grande parte de' fideli della chiesa, e picciola parte ne rimase al carro. Poi quando mette che si coverse lo carro delle penne, hae a significare che quelli fideli che rimasono, accettono e vollono possedere beni temporali e dice: Forse a buon intendimento, cioè elli vollono possedere quello che ad essi è necessario a sostentare sua vita, ma par che tale se lo intendimento fu buono come reo, lo suo effetto fosse pur reo: imperquello che tali penne generano uno animale mostro, come apparirà. Le membra che vide organarsi in lo ditto animale hanno a significare li sette vizii capitali, li quali vizii entronno nella Chiesa sì tosto com'ella possedio ricchezze temporali, li quali sono superbia, ira, avarizia, invidia, lussuria, accidia e gola. E perchè li primi tre peccati offendono doppio, cioè a Dio e al prossimo, sì li figura per quelle tre teste del timone ch'aveano ciascuna due corna. E perchè li altri quattro sono pure diretti contra lo prossimo, si pone a ciascuno pure uno corno. Per la puttana intende lo sommo pastore, cioè il papa, lo quale dee reggere la Chiesa. Per lo gigante intende quelli della casa di Francia, li quali hanno stuprato e avolterato la Chiesa di Dio, puttaneggiando con li papi; e ogni fiata che li papi hanno guardato verso lo popolo cristiano, cioè hanno voluto rimuoversi e astenersi da tale avolterio, li detti giganti, cioè quelli della casa di Francia hanno flagellatoli e infine mortoli, e ridottoli a suo volere, sichè di tale compagnia non è paruto per rettore se non lo gigante, ed esso quella ha guidata a suo piacere e condotta. E questa brevemente è la allegoria della visione dell'autore di quella parte, che è nel presente capitolo.[9]

Toni e sintassi, vorrei dire, si pongono tra le profezie dell'imminente rovina del mondo e i lamenti della patria perduta: ne occupano lo spazio intermedio, danno via libera ad una profonda angoscia morale. Ma se felicità interpretativa Jacopo dimostra nel cogliere un tema storico, un dramma umano che si svolge e s'impianta nella vita dei popoli; non minore duttilità e penetrazione manifesta nel discutere temi filosofico-morali, tra i più ardui, qual è quello della prescienza e del libero arbitrio. Si è fuori dalla parafrasi o dal commento, che, sciogliendo il rigore sintattico della poesia, allunga l'espressione, la raddolcisce e la rende accetta ad ogni intelligenza. Qui si tratta di due cose, soprattutto: interpretare nel suo fondo il pensiero di Dante e poi collegarlo all'impostazione generale della sua visione, cioè al disegno strutturale del poema. L'occasione è data da *Paradiso* XVII.37 ss. Vi si elencano le ragioni, con tipici schemi scolastici, pro e contra prescienza di Dio e libero arbitrio degli uomini. Anche qui l'attenzione è posta a cogliere tra le due tesi, a lungo discusse e chiarite nei loro elementi di per sè inefficienti e controproducenti, la zona intermedia, laddove cioè l'uno e l'altro concetto s'incontrano salvandosi e saldandosi. La spiegazione non esula dalla parola di Dante, ma è dentro compiutamente con tutta una carica di esempi e ragionamenti, in stretta connessione, che dopo, anche con Benvenuto e Buti (a parte Landino) che pure vi indulgono, saranno almeno allentati. Chiarezza sprigiona anche nella connessione di prescienza-libero arbitrio con i concetti di giustizia e non-giustizia e con quello fondamentale, ch'è un po' il perno di tutto, di "necessità". L'aridità scolastica è levigata dal buon uso di esempi presi dalla realtà, perchè anche qui Dante insegna: laddove più astrusa o alta è la materia, più dal reale e dal concreto deve assumersi il confronto.

In prima dalla parte della giustizia di Dio, la quale punirebbe, o remunerebbe non giustamente; imperquello che se di necessitade io sono vertudioso e non per lo mio libero arbitrio, io non meriterei, e s'io non merito lo remunerare non m'è giusto; e simile s'io sono vizioso di necessitade e non per mio libero arbitrio, la pena non m'è giusta; e così seguirebbe non essere giustamente ordinato lo Inferno per punire li peccati, nè 'l Purgatorio per lavarli, nè 'l Paradiso per premiare li meriti, la qual cosa è assurda eziandio contro la fede cattolica. Da parte dell'uomo si seguirebbe inconvenienzie s'ello non fosse libero arbitrio; imperquello che ello non sarebbe animale razionale, che dacchè ello non potesse raziocinando eleggere, e tutto gli avvenisse di necessitade, ello sarebbe privo di tale razionabilitade. Ancora le polizie e gli ordini delle terre sarebbeno fatti invano e indarno, perchè se l'uomo per libertade non si potesse drizzare a virtude e rimuovere da vizii, e tutto fosse di necessitade, la fine a che le dette polizie sono dirette sarebbono vane; ancora ogni intento d'artista sarebbe indarno, imperquello che se 'l fosse di necessitade che una casa dovesse avere due solari e l'uomo la immaginasse tre, non lo porave fare l'arte ch'ella fosse di tre; e moltissime altre inconvenienzie, che sarebbe luogo a dire, da parte dell'uomo. Ancora ogni orazione che l'uomo facesse sarebbe indarno, se di necessitade l'uomo si potesse perdere o salvare. Ancora a negare lo libero arbitrio non è altro che a negare in quella parte la misericordia di Dio, imperquello che se tutto fosse necessario, ello non potrebbe esser misericordioso; le quali cose sono assurde e devie dalla veritate. Or veduto come Dio è perfetto in tutto, ed è per sè *notum* senza altra demostrazione al presente, e veduto come libero arbitrio è di certo, ed ènne tanto detto che dee essere ad ogni intelligente per sè *notum*, appare la difficoltade circa la nostra cognizione come può essere la prescienza di Dio vera, dato che in noi sia libero arbitrio. Or è da sapere che quanta difficoltade appare in questa cosa procede solo dalla nostra cognizione bassa, la quale non può bene comprendere lo modo della scienza che è in Dio, lo quale è tanto eccelso ed altissimo, che da nulla creatura può essere compreso, ma solo da sè medesmo. Ma tutta fiata lo sano intelletto per alcuni esempli può immaginare essere di tale distanzia, e prenderne fede argomentando per li preditti esempli, e puossi fare in questo modo.

Noi vedemo diversitade in la virtude cognoscitiva in li animali, chè uno cognosce più perfettamente che un altro; l'agnello cognosce lo lupo e fuggelo per natura, ed ha tale cognizione da natura; l'uomo cognosce lo lupo più perfettamente, che sa ch'ello è animale sensitivo, e sa ch'ello è furo, e sa ch'ello è animale di mala razza, e similemente ha l'uomo da natura tale cognizione. Or avvegnachè queste cognizioni, cioè dell'agnello e dell'uomo circa lo lupo, siano diverse, pure lo lupo non muta essere, nè è di sè più cognito, nè meno; così a *simili* le cose contingenti sono considerate dalla cognizione dell'uomo più imperfettamente, che dalla cognizione di Dio, e perchè Dio le cose contingenti cognosca più perfettissimamente che l'uomo, le cose contingenti non mutan però essere, nè sono per sè più cognite nè meno. Or Dio sì come perfettissimo e che è sopra lo tempo, vede, dicerne, e sa sì le future cose, come le contingenti, come le presenti, ed eziandio come le passate, sì che sua prescienzia e cognizione non aggiunge nè non minuisce alle cose contingenti fatte per lo libero arbitrio umano o per difetto di naturale corso, chè anche l'avvenimento di Cristo è contingente, ma è la sua scienzia tanto alta e perfetta che vede più che lo intelletto umano e ogni altra creatura. Or l'autore pone nel testo un altro esempio e bello: ello pone andare per uno fiume uno naviglio, lo quale per libero arbitrio del suo nocchiero va da levante a ponente; e pone stare suso la riva uno che veggia quello navilio; ora nelli occhi e nelle pupille del ditto, che è su la riva, sì appare la specia del ditto navilio e si vede e dicerne per la perfezione dell'organo visivo, cioè dell'occhio, la via che fa lo ditto navilio in quello presente tempo. Or tacite dice l'autore: sì come l'occhio di colui che sta su la riva non impone necessità per lo suo vedere al viaggio del navilio, che è secondo lo libero arbitrio dello nocchiero, così la prescienza di Dio non induce necessità alli atti contingenti, li quali sono nello arbitrio di quelli che li fanno. Vero è che questo esempio non è perfetto, imperquello che non si può perfettamente assimigliare la veduta umana con quella di Dio chè, come è detto, Dio cognosce più perfettamente e vede per tutto lo decorso del tempo sì lo presente come lo futuro o passato che non cognosce o vede l'uomo. Ma basti al sano intelletto averne segno od indizio, e così possiamo ricoglierne una regola di quello che è ditto ch'ello si dee circa la cognizione delle cose considerare lo consideratore, e secondo sua perfezione avere quella cognizione per vera sì come è detto le cose considerate non mutan natura, nè elli imposto alcuna necessità.[10]

Non è il caso, qui e altrove, di sottolineare taluni ingorghi o pieghe nello sforzo interpretativo o anche, (e non son lievi) alcuni segni di cattiva lettura; è piuttosto utile richiamare l'attenzione sulla capacità (e i due passi antologizzati sono solo una prova tra altre non meno significative) che ha Jacopo di appuntare lo sguardo su aspetti fondamentali, e qualificanti dell'opera dantesca e, attraverso questa, direttamente sull'uomo-Dante e la sua angoscia dinanzi alla perennità e universalità dei problemi umani.

Questa posizione, che dunque è centrale e dimostra una mente capace ad abbracciare l'universo e la psiche di Dante, si estrinseca soprattutto in due modi: le articolazioni-divisioni e le supposizioni. Sono noie che d'ora in poi non daranno requie ai dantisti, già accennate in Jacopo di Dante e Bambaglioli, esse diverranno elemento costitutivo fino al XVI secolo per poi riaffiorare, dopo le sintesi ideologiche, storiche e morali dell'Ottocento, in molte *lecturae* d'oggi. Ma le articolazioni-divisioni esprimono in Jacopo sia uno stampo d'origine, cioè una provenienza culturale, sia una necessità interna: sono, insomma, attribuibili alla tradizione scolastica, ma sono anche un modo di assettare, ordinare e comunicare l'enorme materia: non certo un espediente retorico e didattico.

Così, a proposito di *Inferno* VIII.88 il demonio inganna l'uomo in quattro modi: confortandolo "ad intenzione che nascano molti mali", "di fare un male sotto spezia d'esser bene", sconfortando "lo bene" e disconfortando "lo malo acciò che si caggia in peggio".[11]

Più esplicito ancora è il caso a proposito degli eretici con elenco di articoli sulla divinità, sei precisamente dalla credenza "che la essenza divina" sia "una" alle "remunerazioni della gloria" e dentro ognuno di essi infinite categorie (dodici per il quarto, ad esempio) con nomi, ragioni e occasioni storiche;[12] ed altro elenco di articoli sulla umanità, sei anche questi, dalla concezione di Cristo all' "avvenimento al giudizio", svolti ed opposti a numerosi errori (undici per il primo, ad esempio).[13]

Questo modulo occupa i *preamboli* ai canti da *Inferno* VI in poi ed è, talvolta, un espediente dottrinale, uno spunto per raccogliere e inserire osservazioni correnti e deduzioni: così in *Inferno* VII si finisce col discettare su prodigalità, avarizia, ira; in *Inferno* VIII su arroganza e superbia; in *Inferno* IX, come si è visto, sugli "errori" degli eretici e così via. Ogni limite è superato da *Paradiso* VI, che ha il preambolo più ricco, lungo e complesso.[14]

Il modulo si ripresenta anche quando Jacopo avanza delle supposizioni. Si integra allora quel che Dante accenna o addirittura si tenta di leggere quello che non è detto: un modo suggestivo che farà straordinaria fortuna nel tempo e che sarà fonte di grossolani errori e di vanissime dilettazioni via via che le ideologie mutavano (e si pensi a quel che si inventò nell'Ottocento e a cui fermissimamente vollero credere molti romantici). Per quel *tacere* (*Inferno* IV.104–5) Jacopo suppone quattro cagioni: "cose di infedelitate" disdicevoli al cristiano, cose di "sottile materia", "cose alla cui recitazione bisognerebbe grandissima dilatazione di parole", cose che parvero "allo autore vanagloria e arroganzia".[15]

Ad altra conclusione ci porta la supposizione interpretativa. Si tratta di una ambivalenza ch'è dentro al testo di Dante e che si traduce nel commentatore in dubbio. Tale tema affiora in Graziolo, ma domina già in Jacopo della Lana e assumerà altri risvolti, talvolta dilettantistici e stucchevoli, via via nel tempo. Un caso classico nella letteratura dantesca è il 'feltro'.

Questo si può intendere in due modi: tra feltro e feltro, cioè tra cielo e cielo, ciò vuol dire per costellazione. L'altro modo tra feltro e feltro, cioè che nascerà di assai vile nazione, che feltro è vile panno. E questo risponde elli a una tacita questione per una oppinione la quale è che di vile padre e madre non può nascere buono e virtudioso figliuolo.[16]

Ad altra conclusione ancora, e tutta positiva, ci portano certi motivi, il cui nucleo è in Dante fermo, perentorio e inequivocabile e le interpretazioni sono ragionevolmente conseguite, portate avanti e arricchite. Si tratta di veri e propri svolgimenti tematici a traccia fissa, di cui Jacopo sa mantenendosi strettamente nel contesto, sciogliere la vigoria sintetica in fluente e prodigiosa analisi. In questo cammino nulla è abbondante o stravagante o arbitrario. Jacopo ha una diversa mentalità di Dante, ma vede e osserva le stesse cose, palpita nello stesso modo, si pone nella condizione di sentire quel che Dante ha sentito, perchè lo ha capito nel modo proprio e ne rispetta il dettato.

Tutto il preambolo a *Purgatorio* IX è un saggio di valida misura interpretativa, che non oltrepassa la parola di Dante ma la fissa e la chiarisce, che non concede nulla alla lusinga delle supposizioni ma la blocca al punto giusto, che non azzarda ipotesi divaganti proprio là dove più istintivamente sembrano proporsi, ma di colpo tutto riduce all'origine e dentro alla verità del testo. Gli stessi richiami culturali non sono sovrapposizioni (nel caso specifico i Salmi, i passi di S. Agostino e così via), ma accorgimenti esplicativi, note di commento, sottolineature del tutto coerenti e inerenti alla parola di Dante e alla sua rappresentazione. Così è che, anche per questa via, i dettagli, pure in sè analizzati e conquistati si coordinano tra loro e formano unità (nel caso specifico i gradini, l'angelo custode, la genuflessione di Dante e così via): un rito perchè sia tale, a cui è sufficiente quel che dice Dante e il modo con cui Jacopo commenta.

In questo capitolo intende l'autore universalmente trattare tre cose, le quali hanno per allegoria a significare lo stato del peccatore nella prima vita, il quale vuol tornare alla via dritta. E primo pone come elli ascese suso per lo monte alla porta del Purgatorio per essere portato da Lucia, cioè dal suo intelletto chiaro e nobile, la qual possanza elli nella presente Comedia appellava Lucia. La seconda cosa descrive la porta come uno ostiario, molto condizionato al Purgatorio sì di vista come eziandìo di vestimenta. La terza cosa notifica l'autorità del detto ostiario, lo qual figura lo ministro della santa Chiesa di Roma e delle sue chiavi. E così entrando con licenzia del predetto ostiario nella città del Purgatorio, compie lo presente capitolo.

Circa la prima parte si è da sapere che 'l peccatore, quando va per torre penitenzia de' peccati, che ha commessi, dee andare puro e netto e chiaro di cuore e intelletto al penitenzieri, e a lui confessare ogni peccato con tutto lo quore, siccome è scritto nel Psalmo: *Confitebor tibi, Domine, in tote corde meo* etc. e piangere li peccati fatti, e guardarsi da commettere quelli, che li dessero cagione di piangere, sicome dice Augustino in libro *De confessione*: —*Plangere facta et plagenda non committere*; confessandosi umilmente ricevere quella penitenzia, e poi ridurla in atto che al suo confessore parrà convenire. E però l'autore volendo poeticamente figurare tale disposizione essere in lui in persona del peccatore introduce nel poema una aquila, che poi elli l'appella Lucia, la quale lo conduce alla porta del Purgatorio a parlare con l'ostiario di quella.

Alla seconda cosa è da sapere ch'elli pone tre gradi innanzi la porta del Purgatorio, de' quali lo primo era di bianco marmore, molto pulito e lucido, lo secondo era oscuro, livido e fesso, lo terzo era d'un porfido rosso e fiammeggiante; li quali tre gradi hanno a significare tre cose, *vel* condizioni che bisognano al confitente, quando accede al ministro per lavarsi. La prima pel primo grado hae a denotare la recognoscenza, che dee avere il peccatore fra sè medesimo

de' peccati, che ha commessi, e venirsi pensando e specchiandosi fra
sè medesimo de' suoi vizi, e farli così palesi per confessione al prete
come lo pulito marmo e lucido palesa la figura del vizio che vi si
specchia dentro. La seconda condizione pel secondo grado notifica
la contrizione, che dee avere circa li suoi peccati lo peccatore, la quale
dee essere tale e tanta nel peccatore, ch'ella lo dee contristare e afflig-
gere e renderlo dolente tanto e in tal modo, ch'ello per le fessure
in esso fatte da tal doglia, getti sospiri e lagrime da ogni parte. E
perchè tale condizione è ardua, scura, ruvida e crepata, però pone
lo autore lo secondo grado essere così fatto. La terza condizione per
lo terzo grado hae a denotare quanto e come dee essere fervore e
rigidezza del peccatore circa la vertude dello amore della carità del
Creatore ad addurre in atto ogni penitenzia a lui commessa, sichè
la giustizia di Dio sia contentata e satisfatta. E perchè l'amore di
caritate è accendevole, sì lo pone l'autore in colore rosso. In quanto
a gravezza e arduità lo figura anco sanguinolento.

Sichè brevemente per li predetti tre gradi abbiamo tre condizioni,
che bisognano a piena penitenzia: per lo primo *oris confessio*, per lo
secondo *cordis contritio*, per lo terzo *operis satisfactio*, sicome è trattato
nella esposizione del XXVII capitolo dello Inferno, dove si tocca *De
sacramento penitentiae*. E pone l'autore suso lo terzo scalino, *vel* grado,
essere uno ostiario, il quale parea essere di simile colore come lo
diamante; il quale è una fortissima e infrangibile pietra; ponelo vestito
d'una veste di colore cenerigno, ed avente in mano una spada molto
affocata e lucida. Il quale ostiario hae a significare il prete, il quale
dee avere queste condizioni: primo essere diamante, cioè fermo e
costante e infrangibile circa li articoli santi della Chiesa; secondo dee
avere vesta cenerigna, cioè abito umile, e così procedere umilemente
nel suo officio; terzo dee essere pulito e induto di giustizia e di ragione,
sichè elli veramente rappresenti quello Signore di che elli è vicario,
e segua le sue vestigie. E soggiunge l'autore, seguendo il suo poema,
come umilemente si gettò ai piedi del detto ostiario, a denotare che
'l peccatore con umiltà dee andare al confessore, e misericordievilmente
addomandare assoluzione e imposizione di penitenzia de' suoi peccati.

Alla terza cosa è da sapere che l'autore pone che quello portinaio
trasse fuori due chiavi, le quali per allegorìa hanno a significare le
chiavi della Chiesa, che sono due, imperquello che alla potestade
giudiziaria è necessario due cose, cioè l'autoritade di cognoscer le colpe,

e la potestade d'assolver ovvero condannare; e queste due cose sono le chiavi della Chiesa, cioè *scientia discernendi*, e *potestas ligandi, et absolvendi*, le quali Christo commise a santo Piero, sicome scrive santo Matteo 16:19: *Tibi dabo claves regni coelorum*, etc. E non solo è da intendere che elle fosseno commesse pure a san Piero solo, ma a lui e alli suoi successori, imperquello che se tale sacramento fosse pure a lui solo commesso, elli non sarebbe durato se non per la vita di san Piero, e così non sarebbe istituito perfettamente come li altri sacramenti, che dureranno fino al dìo del giudizio.[17]

Esempi di questo genere sono frequenti, perchè l'orientamento della chiesa non è un modulo artificiosamente riprodotto e stampato nella mente di Jacopo, ma è un atto proprio e genuino di vedere e considerare le cose. Se si può parlare di storia, in tal senso, il primo commento storico e documentario di Dante è proprio questo di Jacopo della Lana. Lo si può cogliere in un altro momento-chiave, ch'è dato da *Purgatorio* XXIX. L'articolazione è in dodici parti, entro cui si raggruppano e si propongono come nucleo unitario quelle che vanno dalla quinta all'undicesima. Pezzo pezzo si snoda la processione: ognuno vale per sè: tutti valgono l'insieme: il tutto è la chiesa: i dettagli la conformano e la istituzionalizzano: i sette candelabri, i ventiquattro seniori, i quattro animali, il carro con grifone e ruote, i due vecchi, i quattro dottori, il veglio dormiente. Rito e scenografia passano felicemente da Dante a Jacopo: dopo Jacopo nulla c'è da mutare.

I significati sono acquisiti: la critica se li propone, li convalida; se li ripudia, ingenera stramberie e banalità. La persuasione nasce dalla ragione, dal vedere così rispettati i dati particolari e dall'intenderli perfettamente nelle loro immediate corrispondenze. Si prendano le due ruote del carro: l'una sta per la via contemplativa con le tre donne in rappresentanza delle virtù teologali; l'altra sta per la vita attiva con quattro donne in rappresentanza delle virtù cardinali. Sono logici i simboli in sè, sulle loro correlazioni e nelle loro unità. La giustificazione del perchè di questi simboli scaturisce direttamente dalla cosa rappresentata, è anzi nella cosa stessa. E così fissati, sempre nell'interno del nucleo, i distinti valori, si passa ad altri, che costituiscono un altro nucleo. Il grifone "volatile" e "quadrupede" che tira il carro è Cristo dalla duplice natura, divina e umana. Nè basta, perchè anche i colori (oro e bianco-vermiglio) hanno il loro linguaggio in relazione alla natura del grifone e alla figura di Cristo. Anche qui il passaggio è diretto sia nel proprio sia nel figurato. Sono pagine persuasive, limpide e densissime e vanno rilette perchè determinano le basi di una interpretazione che rimarrà nella sostanza tale e quale nel tempo. Quel che vide Jacopo della Lana poteva non esser visto o visto diversamente da Boccaccio e certo, sperduto e distorto, da Landino. Resta quello ch'è detto: il dopo ne dovrà fare i conti.

La quinta, la sesta, la settima, l'ottava, la nona, la decima e l'undicesima, introduce l'autore per figurare la Chiesa di Dio, lo fondamento e 'l suo processo, siccome apparirà distinta ciascuna sua parte per sè sola. Per la che necessario fue all'autore trattare dopo la felicità umana, che si può acquistare l'uomo per li suoi naturali, la Ecclesia di Dio; la quale è porta, strada, e indutta di quella contemplazione e sommo bene e felicità perfetta, alla quale è dritta e ordinata ogni operazio virtuosa; e solo s'adovrano, per grazia di quella, ed essa solo si desidera per sè medesima, e non è drizzata nè ordinata ad altro. E primo introduce l'autore sette candelabri, li quali siccome istrumenti ignei hanno a significare li sette doni dello Spirito Santo, li quali abbisognano che siano in ogni fedele cristiano, e se non li possiede, impossibile è ch'elli abbia piena fede; li quali doni non solo elli sono preparazione alla fede, ma eziandìo oppognono e contrariano li vizii, siccome apparirà. Lo primo dono è pietà, lo quale oppone all'invidia; lo secondo dono è timore, lo quale oppone alla superbia; lo terzo dono è di scienzia, lo quale oppone all'ira; lo quarto dono è di fortitudine, lo quale oppone all'accidia; lo quinto dono è di consiglio, lo quale oppone ad avarizia; lo sesto dono è d'intelletto, il quale oppone alla lussuria; lo settimo dono è di sapienzia, il quale oppone alla gola. Li quali doni necessario sono bisognevoli all'uomo, che vuole essere fedele cristiano, imperquello che essi sono tutti ordinati alle tre virtudi teologiche, ed esse si hanno sìe ad insieme per concessione che chi perde l'una perde tutte, chi acquista l'una acquista tutte, siccome appare per santo Tommaso nella *Prima Secundae*; e perchè sono li detti doni preparazione in vizio e principio della Chiesa, la quale è congregazione di fedeli, sì li introdusse l'autore in prima; e questo basta alla quinta cosa.

Alla sesta cosa è da sapere che san Giovanni Evangelista nella visione dell'Apocalissi sì vide questi XXIV vecchi vestiti di bianco, li quali figurano li ventiquattro libri della Bibbia del vecchio testamento, sopra li quali si è fondata la fede cristiana, e sono questi: *Genesis*,

Exodus, Leviticus, Numeri, Deuteronomium, Josue, Judicum, Regum, Samuel, Isaias, Jeremias, Ezechiel, Duodecim prophetae, Esdras, Paralipomenon, Judit, Ester, Daniel, Job, Baruch, Thobia, Psalterio, li *Libri di Solomone* che sono computati uno, ch'enno la *Cantica,* lo *Ecclesiastes, Liber Sapientae, Parabole,* e *Proverbii*; poi lo *Libro de' Maccabei*. E però che l'autore similemente vuole descrivere la Chiesa, si introdusse li predetti ventiquattro signori.

Alla settima cosa si introduce quattro animali, li quali figurano li quattro Evangelisti, che figurò Ezechiel profeta, e poi san Giovanni Evangelista. Vero è che l'autore pone che secondo li detti de' predetti, fosse alcuna diversitade; ma quanto quello che è bisogno alla presente intenzione, basta che quelli quattro animali figurino li quattro Evangelisti, li quali sono quattro colonne della fede cristiana: l'uno aquila, l'altro uomo, lo terzo lione, lo quarto bue. Ora, descrivendo lo modo della figura d'essi, sì pone ch'elli aveano sei ali, le quali erano così piene d'occhi come fue quello d'Argo, del quale trattano li poeti ch'avea cento occhi, come apparirae nella esposizione del testo. Le quali sei ali hanno a significare che per ogni dimensione la Scrittura santa per quelli si estende in altezza, in larghezza, e in profonditade. L'esser piene d'occhi hae a demostrare, sicome l'occhio è organo che distingue la singolaritade, così la evangelica scrittura distingue, e declara ogni particolaritade; e però si segue che, poichè tale Scrittura occupa e comprende ogni dimensione, e condiscende ad ogni particolaritade, che in essi sì è ogni perfezione e compimento. E nota che fino quie sieno queste metafore invente per altri, cioè per Ezechiel profeta e per san Giovanni Evangelista.

Alla ottava cosa si è da sapere che l'autore metaforizza per propria intenzione in questa parte. Ello introduce un carro con due ruote, siccom'è detto, lo quale figura la Chiesa di Dio fondata sovra due vite, l'una attiva, l'altra contemplativa; e attorno la ruota, che figura la vita contemplativa, sono tre donne, che figurano le virtudi contemplative, cioè fede, speranza, e caritate. La fede figura ello una donna bianchissima, imperquello che la fede è virtude senza alcuna mistione, candida e nitida. La speranza figura ello una donna verde, imperquello che la speranza riduce l'uomo così a vita, e tienlo, come la verdura fae frondificare l'alboro, e mantienlo vivo. La carità figura ello una donna rossa, che siccome colui che possiede tale virtude, è in ardore e in voglia continua di proficere a Dio e al prossimo, così figurativamente la detta nona si dimostra in colore di fuoco. Or soggiunge l'autore ch'alcuna fiata è retta e drizzata quella ruota della bianca, e alcuna fiata della rossa, lo qual cambiamento ello intende che figuri che molte fiate l'uomo diventa contemplante per indutta di fede, e molte fiate per indutta di caritate, principalmente; di speranza non, imperquello che essere non può senza l'una delle predite due, che l'uomo non può isperare senza fede diquello ch'ello spera, o senza voglia di quello ch'ello intende ed ha speranza. Attorno alla seconda ruota pone quattro donne, cioè quattro virtudi morali, le quali sono nella vita attiva, cioè prudenzia, giustizia, fortitudo e temperanza, e descrive solo la prudenzia ch'ello li pone tre occhi in capo, che siccome colui ch'avesse tre occhi vederebbe più che quello che n'ha due, così colui ch'è vestito di tale vertude antivede per comparazione agli altri; e ponele tutte vestite di porpora, quasi demostrando ch'elle erano circa li atti umani, li quali sono vari e diversi. E pone l'autore che quello carro era menato da uno griffone, il quale figura Jesu Cristo, che è capo e sommo sacerdote della Chiesa; e siccome in Cristo fue due nature, divina e umana, così quanto può figurare in lo griffone si è due nature, l'una volatile, l'altra quadrupede. A mostrare siccome lo carro era menato e tirato da quello griffone, così la Chiesa era menata e tratta da Jesus Cristo, e pone che quello griffone in quanto era uccello, era d'oro che figurava la divinità, e in quanto era altro animale, lo pone bianco misto con rosso a descrivere la umanità che poi fue tinta di vermiglio con lo sangue, ch'ello sparse nella sua passione. Pone che le sue ale ello istendea in suso, le quali occupavano li sette radiarii, che faceano li candelabri, e per questo fatto da chi si procedea tale occupazione nulla di quelli si dannificava; quanto a dire che le sue ali erano esso medesimo Spirito Santo, da chi si procedea quelli sette doni, de' quali è detto.

Alla nona cosa si è da sapere che questi due si era l'uno San Luca e l'altro San Paolo; San Luca fue medico nella prima vita, e così fu medico nella scrittura sua, imperquello ch'esso parla più misericordia che li altri Evangelisti; e però dice l'autore che elli li parea de' famigliari d'Ippocras, che scrisse in medecina. Santo Paolo fu allo mondo uomo d'arme e perseguitatore fue de cristiani, finchè elli fue infedele, e così nelle sue scritture parlò più di giustizia sanza alcuna remissione, e però lo figura così una spada in mano e con lo viso ostero. E soggiunge che avvegna ch'essi fossero in apparenzia diversi, elli erano ad una intenzione drizzati, mostrando che la fine di loro scritture era in Dio, lo qualo è sommo, giusto e misericordioso.

Alla decima cosa si è da sapere che per la Chiesa di Dio sono autenticati principalmente quattro dottori, li quali hanno esposto e dichiarato quello ch'è detto per li precedenti, e cotanto quanto hanno compilato nuove sentenzie e argomenti, li quali sono santo Augustino, santo Gregorio, santo Jeronimo e santo Ambrogio.

Alla undicesima cosa si è da sapere che, sì come nuovo modo fue quello per lo quale santo Joanni Evangelista fe visione e scrissela poi ch'è appellata Apocalipsi, così l'autore lo predetto santo Giovanni in nuovo modo lo introdusse, cioè dormendo e vecchio, a mostrare ch'ello in visione vide queste figure in grembo a Cristo nella cena, e poi quando fu più innanzi nel tempo sì le messe in scritte.

La quale visione, com'è detto, figura la Chiesa di Dio.[18]

La ricerca dei simboli, com'è in genere in tutti gli antichi commentatori (e si son visti Jacopo di Dante e Graziolo) per tutto il XIV secolo e gran parte del XV, è immediata. Lasciando fiere, donne benedette, fiumi ecc., si guardi più in là, alle sette mura quali scienze liberali, al fiumicello come "disposizion dello intelletto umano"[19] e così via. E Jacopo ci dà il perchè: "li poeta quando voleano trattare o descrivere alcuna cosa elli parlavano fingendo ed esemplificando".[20] E se ne ha un po' ovunque pratica applicazione, come per *Purgatorio* I.10: "Descrivono li poeti per sue allegorie che in Grecia era un monte. . . . Or li poeti *methafisice* parlando esemplificavano che suso questo monte era uno templo".[21] E' la chiave per leggere nella poetica, ch'è, nel suo insieme, quella corrente nel tardo Medioevo e in fase preumanistica e a cui Dante largamente attinge facendola propria nell'arte e teorizzandola nel *De vulgari eloquentia* e *Convivio*. Quando la corrispondenza realtà-simbolo, rappresentazione-allegoria non è piana, Jacopo si ferma, parafrasa o tace. Non meno loquaci allora sono questi silenzi. Si può pensare a oscurità del testo e, di conseguenza, a incapacità di lettura; ma si può anche pensare a rispetto di quel vago e generico ch'è in Dante stesso e che anzi Dante volutamente volle imprimere, nella poesia come dato essenziale della visione. Il Veltro ad esempio, è semplicemente uno "signore" che "reggerà lo mondo a tanta largezza, che questa avarizia non sarà nel mondo": e se si oppone lupa a Veltro è, innanzitutto, "perchè è naturale contrarietade malivolenzia tra i lupi e i cani".[22] Così in *Paradiso* XXVII.1–3 non si corre a individuare personaggi ed episodi, resta qual è, libera e imminente la profezia, nella sicurezza, com'è per il Veltro, che "Dio resisterà a tanto disordine e soccorrerà in tale modo, che tanto male sarà punito e castigato".[23] La vaghezza della profezia, propria del Medioevo, si salva con la forza della fede: e si è dentro allo spirito di Dante. A dare rilievo a questo aspetto concorre proprio il contrario, cioè la denuncia e la identificazione (con nome e qualifica del personaggio) del vago o inespresso qualora non rientra nella profezia. E' il caso di "colui che fece per viltà il gran rifiuto" (*Inferno* III.59–60) perentoriamente indicato in Celestino V, in quanto, come già si legge in Graziolo per *Inferno* XIX.55–57 (e i passi sono assai vicini), "fraudolentemente Bonifacio fece rifiutare a papa Celestino lo papato".[24] Ugualmente accade in *Paradiso* XVI.88 ss., laddove alle casate, fustigate da Dante, Jacopo accoppia (ma non sempre purtroppo!) il nome del singolo. E v'è ragione, perchè "chiaro appare dove l'autore specifica li nomi non è mestiere esponere, imperquello che si dee intendere parentati o schiatte così chiamate; quelli che o per armatura, o per singolare atto virtudioso o vizioso sono nomati, latendo over ascondendo sotto tale parlatura lo singolare nome, qui dichiareremo acciò che nullo ascosto trapassi che potesse indurre ammirazione allo studente".[25]

In sostanza il comportamento è rigorosamente scientifico, in assoluto, e rispettoso, nella lettera e nella sostanza, delle intenzioni di Dante: laddove aleggia la profezia, tutto si lascia nell'indeterminato; laddove si inquadra un momento storico, tutto si cerca di cogliere con dati più precisi. Ma non si creda tuttavia che grande progresso si faccia in questo settore. Jacopo dà più volte l'impressione che bene intende il valore della storia e la realtà documentaria dei tempi di Dante, ma resta quasi sempre al di qua di essi. Talvolta la via per tracciare e seguire le linee degli avvenimenti è giusta, ma si arresta al momento introduttivo. Così la Firenze dugentesca è colta bene nel suo insieme, ma non illustrata nelle posizioni, nei propositi e negli interessi: "Nel tempo dello autore la città di Firenze si reggeva per una condizione di cittadini, ch'erano di mezzano essere, non da quelli grandi e nobili e superbi, che vogliono sempre tiranneggiare, e non da quella brucamaglia di popolo, che non distingue bene da male . . .; erano persone che amavano lo buono stato della città. . . . Avvenne che questi così fatti rettori tornonno tutti fuorausciti".[26] Ma sono cose che invano si chiedono a Jacopo della Lana e agli altri antichi commentatori. La storia antica c'è e con essa leggende e miti, come si trasmettevano nelle scuole e negli ambienti di cultura.[27] La storia del presente invece è pericolosa: va trattata con discrezione. L'audacia può essere scambiata per insolenza:

i potenti sono ancora vivi e in piedi le istituzioni. Nessun commentatore ha l'animo di Dante. Jacopo, e dopo uno alla volta anche gli altri e financo Boccaccio, ai tempi di condanne piene e severe, ricorre ai ripari e cerca di dividere la sua opera di "minimo intendente", che pure ha l'orgoglio di avere capito "lo intelletto dello autore" (e questo va sottolineato), dall'opera di Dante.

> La sopradetta esposizione, chiose overo postile hoe scritto secondo che a me minimo intendente pare che fosse lo intelletto dello autore; e però ogni esemplo, argomento, opinione, conclusione, allegoria, sentenzia o vero alcuno ditto, che in essa hoe scritto, inteso od assegnato, s'ello si conforma ed assomiglia al senso e al tenère della santa madre Ecclesia Cattolica Romana affermo, approvo ed hoe per bene detto; se deviasse, discrepasse, avero cantradicesse, al predetto senso e tenere della santa chiesa, sì ho per vano e non per bene detto, e però lo casso e vacuo e tegno per da nessuno valore, sì come cristiano puro, fedele e verace.[28]

Eppure questo senso della storia, qualunque esso sia o comunque si giudichi dinanzi al testo dantesco, può spiegare certa felicità narrativa e quasi discorsiva del commento di Jacopo. Il taglio di certi dialoghi, introdotti quasi a documentazione, dà vivacità letteraria, esprime buon gusto e, soprattutto, abilità inventiva. Un piccolo assaggio è nel pezzo dedicato a Federico II, che vede respinto dai cardinali il proclamato diritto di aver più di una moglie: un più completo panorama si ha invece con l'"infamia di Creti" (*Inferno* XII.17), una pagina gustosamente studiata in passaggi legati tra loro e tesi ad una accorta finalizzazione. Ma questo episodio costituisce una pagina cara a gran parte degli antichi commentatori. Del resto, in più luoghi del commento, Jacopo denuncia una chiara conoscenza della retorica (il primo segno è dinanzi a *Inferno* III.1 ss., ove si definisce il "parlare effettivo"),[29] come anche una diretta intelligenza della poesia, del suo uso e delle sue modulazioni. *Grieve* (*Inferno* v.8) è spiegato con "fastidiosa e malanconica"; *appuzza* (*Inferno* XVII.3) con "impiagato di peccato e di malizia"; *disviticchia* (*Purgatorio* x.118) con "discerni, diparti e distingui";[30] e così via. Sono piccoli spunti linguistici, nel gusto e nei limiti dei tempi, spesso legati ad una matrice psicologico-morale, che tuttavia danno un'idea più completa delle attitudini interpretative sperimentate da Jacopo, allo scoperto e senza nessun sostegno di raffronti esegetici. Il commento è, sì, legato al fondo dottrinale filosofico-teologico del tempo, per cui tutto è gerarchia ordinata *ad unum* (di qui la trecentesca visione del verticalismo della visione dantesca); ma dà anche l'impressione di validità nell'affrontare i grandi temi e di trattarli con adeguata misura e libertà di giudizio, di sostare sulle singole cose e di proporle nella loro giusta luce e, infine, di una capacità di dire le cose che vanno dette, anche nel molto e nel farraginoso, per capire e ritrovare la genuina voce di Dante.[31]

Note

1. Jacopo di Cione di Filippo di Cambio di Oliviero della Lana (v. A. Gualandi, *Giacomo della Lana bolognese primo commentatore della Divina Commedia* [Bologna: Tipi Fava e Garagnani, 1865]) è nato intorno al 1290 (Gualandi, p. 24) o dopo il 1278 (Mazzoni, *Enciclopedia dantesca*, III, p. 563); dopo un soggiorno a Venezia, rientrò e visse a Bologna (e su questo concordano Gualandi, Rocca e Mazzoni). Muore, forse, nel 1365 (Gualandi, p. 42). Il suo commento apparve la prima volta in stampa, ma attribuito a Benvenuto da Imola, in edizione vindeliniana (Venezia, 1477) e subito in edizione nideobeatina (Milano, 1478). L'edizione fu fondata sui codici 1005 della Riccardiana di Firenze e 5.94 dell'Ambrosiana di Milano (trad. lat. di Alberico da Rosciate che, tra l'altro, precisa: "Et quia in ipsa Comedia transtuli de vulgari tusco in gramaticali scientia litterarum ego Albericus de Rosciate dictus utroque jure peritus pergamensis"). Per L. Rocca, cfr. *Di alcuni commenti della Divina Commedia composti nei primi vent'anni dopo la morte di Dante* (Firenze: Sansoni, 1891), pp. 127–227.

2. G. Livi, *Dante, suoi primi cultori, sua gente in Bologna* (Bologna: Cappelli, 1918), passim.

3. Gualandi, pp. 33–35; F. Mazzoni, "La critica dantesca del secolo XIV", *Cultura e scuola*, XIII–XIV (1965), 292–93; L. Scarabelli, I, pp. 21–22 (v. nota 5).

4. E. Cavallari, *La fortuna di Dante nel Trecento* (Firenze: Società anonima editrice F. Perella, 1921), p. 185.

5. *Comedia di Dante degli Allagherii*, a cura di L. Scarabelli (Bologna: Tipografia Regia, 1866–67), III, p. 28. Si segue soprattutto il cod. Riccardiano 1005 (sec. XIV) e, in parti minori, i codd. Plut. XL. 36 (sec. XIV) e Strozz. 166 (sec. XIV) della Laurenziana. Valido è per il *Paradiso* il cod. Braidense A. G. XII.2 (già A. N. XV. 19). L'edizione dello S. è estremamente difettosa: le riserve furono e sono molte. In una copia conservata alla "Casa di Dante" di Roma (G. 51) già di proprietà di C. Giannini è trascritto a penna il seguente severissimo giudizio: "Dei volumi pubblicati dall'ex-professore Scarabelli a Bologna occorre appena dire che non ho potuto fare

verun uso, essendo essi, come ad ogni studioso di Dante è noto, così pieni zeppi di strafalcioni, lezioni errate e falsificazioni, che ad ogni lezione ci vediamo costretti a dubitare se la sia veramente la lezione del relativo Codice e non piuttosto uno strafalcione ed una falsificazione di un editore ignorante sventato e senza coscienza. Gazzabugli come gli scarabelleschi recano grave danno alle lettere che sono un insulto alla scienza. Va senza dire che la scienza Dantesca severa non può prendere notizia di scarabocchi scarabelleschi. . . ." E invero, a parte tutto, a tanto autorizzava l'incauto editore anche in più passi della sua premessa (v., ad es., p. 19). E attendiamo con fiducia la n. ed. a cura di A. Menichetti. F. Schmidt-Knatz presenta in facsimile il cod. Arci B in *La "Commedia" col commento di Jacopo della Lana dal codice francofortese Arci B* (Frankfurt-am-Main, 1939).

6. Cfr. rispettivamente in Scarabelli: I, pp. 138, 168, 211; I, 154, 170, 225 (a lungo), 298; I, pp. 171, 218, 230, 266; I, p. 219; I, p. 225; I, p. 234; I, p. 266; ecc. Ma si vedano anche le molte citazioni nel Preambolo a *Inf.* IX.

7. Ibid., I, p. 119; I, p. 254. Per F. Schmidt-Knatz, cit. (v. nota 5).

8. *Comedia*, a cura di Scarabelli: cfr. rispettivamente I, pp. 152, 276; I, p. 170; I, pp. 172, 217, 276, ecc.

9. Ibid., II, pp. 386–88.

10. Ibid., III, pp. 266–67.

11. Ibid., I, p. 187.

12. Ibid., I, pp. 191–97.

13. Ibid., I, pp. 197–200.

14. Ibid., III, pp. 85–106.

15. Ibid., I, p. 144.

16. Ibid., I, p. 114.

17. Ibid., II, pp. 98–99.

18. Ibid., II, pp. 345–47.

19. Ibid., I, p. 144.

20. Ibid., III, p. 206.

21. Ibid., II, p. 12.

22. Ibid., I, p. 115.

23. Ibid., III, p. 409.

24. Ibid., I, p. 330.

25. Ibid., III, p. 259.

26. Ibid., III, p. 364.

27. Ad esempio a proposito di Federico II (ibid., I, pp. 219–21), di Fetonte (I, p. 307), di Icaro (I, pp. 109–308), dell'infamia di Creti (I, pp. 237–41), di Giasone (I, pp. 317–20), di Proserpina (II, pp. 337 ss.), ecc.; Mazzoni, *Enciclopedia dantesca* III, p. 564, indica spunti novellistici nel proemio a *Par.* XXIX.

28. Ibid., III, p. 515.

29. Ibid., I, p. 127.

30. Cfr. rispettivamente I, p. 163; I, p. 300; II, p. 119.

31. Sommario bibliografico: A. Gualandi, *G. della Lana bolognese primo commentatore della Divina Commedia* (Bologna: Tipi Fava e Garagnani, 1865) — come vari e

fondamentali documenti; C. Hegel, *Über den historischen Werth der älteren Dante-Commentare* (Leipzig: S. Hirzel, 1878), pp. 10–17; C. Witte, "Commentari von Dante's *Göttlichen Komödie*: G. della Lana," in *Dante Forschungen* (Heilbronn: Gebr. Henninger, 1879), I, p. 382 ss.; L. Rocca, *Di alcuni commenti della Divina Commedia composti nei primi vent'anni dopo la morte di Dante* (Firenze: Sansoni, 1891), pp. 127–227; G. Livi, *Dante e Bologna* (Bologna: Zanichelli, 1921), pp. 36–43; E. Cavallari, *La fortuna di Dante nel Trecento* (Firenze: Società anonima editrice F. Perella, 1921), pp. 185–901; *La "Commedia" col Commento di Jacopo della Lana dal codice francofortese Arci B*, a cura di F. Schmidt-Knatz (Frankfurt-am-Main, 1939) e dello stesso, "Jacopo della Lana und sein *Commedia* commentar", in *Deutches Dante-Jahrbuch*, XII (1930), 1–40; F. Mazzoni, "La critica dantesca del secolo XIV", in *Cultura e scuola*, XIII–XIV (1965), pp. 292–93, e "Jacopo della Lana e la crisi nell'interpretazione della Divina Commedia", in *Dante e Bologna nei tempi di Dante* (Bologna: Commissione per i testi di lingua, 1967), pp. 265–306; *Enciclopedia dantesca*, III, pp. 563–65; B. Sandkühler, *Die frühen Dante Kommentare...* (München: Hueber, 1967), pp. 192–205; J. Mortari, "Da Jacopo della Lana all'Anonimo Fiorentino", *Psicanalisi e strutturalismo di fronte a Dante* (Firenze: Olschki, 1972), I, pp. 471–501.
(Nota. Questo saggio fa parte dell'opera, in corso di stampa, *Storia della critica dantesca dal XIV al XX secolo* (Milano-Padova: Vallardi-Piccin), voll. 2).

EDITORS' APPENDIX

English Translation of Passages from Jacopo della Lana

N.B.: Each passage is identified by its footnote number in the text.

5. . . . to wish to understand perfectly the present Comedy, one must be well-informed in many fields of knowledge inasmuch as the author uses many propositions, arguments, and examples, and adopts as principles a variety of things that could not be fully known without learning. Since poetry is not a science requiring syllogistic reasoning presented as clearly as possible, the present Comedy is therefore not imperfect if it fails to prove all its principles. Instead through poetic license it uses metaphors and exempla, and exchanges one thing for another, as was demonstrated and explained in the preceding chapters. One must thus conclude, as was said, that he who would understand the work must be learned in many fields. This being the case, it is clear that the author excludes the unlearned from the study of his Comedy, and invites knowledgeable readers to be well-disposed to such study by offering them two things: the first is truth; the second wonderful things: truth, in that he states that he is inspired by Apollo, god of knowledge, and by the nine Muses, that is, by the nine fields of learning, as they are called, which can convey or teach only the truth; wonderful things in that he describes Paradise and the glorious citizens of that holy city. This is, briefly, the intention of the first matter treated.

9. Here begins the vision, and he (Dante) says that he saw the bird of Jove descend, that is, the eagle, a species in which, according to poetic tradition, Jupiter descended upon the earth, as is said of Ganymede in the ninth canto of *Purgatory*. And this eagle came, breaking and tearing down the tree to which the chariot was bound. It then struck the said chariot and made it crumble, making it move like a ship struck by the anger of the sea. After this, he saw a very lean and ugly fox climb into the chariot. Since Beatrice was in it, she reproved and reprimanded it, making it flee with a speed appropriate to such a beast so terribly lean that it was all bones without flesh or substance. Then he saw another eagle descend along the path of the first one, and when it was above the cart it plucked itself of its feathers which covered the entire chariot. And as soon as these feathers covered the chariot, he heard a voice which, lamenting, said: "O ship of mine, what an awful cargo you hold!" It then seemed to him that the earth opened between the chariot's wheels, and there emerged a dragon that swung its tail onto the chariot, dragged with the tail certain parts from the bottom of the chariot, and departed very charmingly, neatly and joyfully. He then says that the entire chariot was suddenly covered, wheels and all, with the remaining feathers, and became like an animal without members. He then says that this animal assumed seven heads, three of which were on the shaft and the other four on each corner of the chariot; and adds that of the three heads on the shaft each had two horns apiece while the other four had one apiece. He then says that he saw on the beast a whore and a giant, embracing and kissing. Then he says that this whore looked at the author, and the giant noticed this and beat her and whipped her from head to foot, and full of anger he untied this monstrous animal from the tree, and the said animal with the whore and the giant aboard fled so far into the forest that one could see only the giant. His vision reaches this point in the present canto as may be seen in the text. This vision must signify allegorically the behavior of the secular and clerical people of God's Church in the following manner. Before striking the tree and twisting the chariot, the eagle signifies the predecessors of the Emperor Constantine who had been persecutors of God's Church and had smitten and ejected the faithful like a ship stricken in a storm. The very lean fox must signify the Church which penetrated its faithful, and the author compares her to the fox since it is an animal full of vices as if to say that heretical arguments contain so much cunning that they mislead the faithful. He further describes her as very lean and without flesh to show how the arguments contain no truth. Then he shows how said heresies are cast out, routed and reduced to nothing through the truths of the science of theology; just as in like manner vengeance is taken upon the heretics when they are burned and nothing remains but the ashes which are the substance previously appearing in the form of bones. The second eagle, that descended and shed its feathers, covering the entire chariot with them, signifies the Emperor Constantine who endowed the Church with temporal wealth. The lamenting voice he (the poet) heard signifies the one that descended from heaven when the Church received Constantine's aforementioned donation, saying: "Today poison is spread throughout the Church of God." The dragon that emerged from the earth between the two wheels signifies Mohammed, who brought to his laws a large number

of the church's faithful, leaving but a few on the chariot. When he then writes that the chariot was covered with feathers it must mean that the remaining faithful accept and wish to possess temporal goods, adding, "perhaps with good intention"; that is to say, they wished to possess what was necessary for them to sustain their lives, but it appears that, if such an intention was as good as it was evil, its effect was only evil, inasmuch as the feathers generate a monstrous animal as will appear. The members he saw appearing in the animal must signify the seven capital vices which entered the Church as soon as she possessed temporal wealth. These vices are pride, anger, avarice, envy, lust, sloth, and gluttony. And since the first three sins offend doubly, that is God and one's neighbor, he pictures them as the three heads on the shaft, each with two horns. Since the other four are also directed against one's neighbor, each one is likewise given a horn. He then signifies in the whore the supreme shepherd, that is to say the pope, who must rule the Church. In the giant he signifies those of the house of France who have raped and perverted God's Church by prostituting themselves with the popes; and each time that the popes have glanced toward the Christian people, that is , have wanted to avoid and ab-stain from such perversion, the giants, that is, those of the house of France, have beaten and finally killed them or forced them to do their bidding. This is why only the giant seemed an appropriate leader of such a group as he led and reduced her to doing his pleasure. This is in brief the allegory of the author's vision in that sec-tion included in the present canto.

10. First, with regard to God's justice which would punish and reward unjustly, it follows that if I am virtuous of necessity and not through my free will, I would not deserve a reward, and if I am not deserving, the reward would not be just. Similarly, if I am sinful of necessity and not because of my free will, the punishment would not be just. Whence it would follow that Hell is not justly ordered to punish sins, nor Purgatory to cleanse them, nor Paradise to reward merits. This is absurd as well as contrary to the Catholic faith. With regard to man, difficulties would follow if he did not have free will inasmuch as he would not be a rational animal. Since he could not choose rationally and all things would happen to him out of necessity, he would be deprived of such rationality. Furthermore, the police forces and other governing bodies of the world would be rendered vain and useless, for if man could not achieve virtue and avoid sin through freedom, and if all occurred through necessity, the purposes of such forces would be voided. In addition, every artistic undertaking would be in vain inasmuch as if it were through necessity that a house were to have two terraces and a man fancied three, art could not bring about three. There are many other inconveniences to man that could be mentioned here. All sermons that men might deliver would be in vain if man could be damned or saved through necessity. What is more, to deny free will is nothing more than to deny the mercy of God, inasmuch as He could not be merciful if everything were to happen by necessity. Such things are absurd and stray from the truth. Seeing that God is perfect in all things and is known in and of Himself without need of further proof here, and seeing that free will exists with certainty and has been dealt

with at such length that it is known to every man with intelligence, there remains
the difficulty of our knowing how the foreknowledge of God can be true since we
possess free will. Now, one must know that whatever difficulty arises in this matter
results only from our insufficient intelligence which cannot easily comprehend the
kind of knowledge that is in God, who is so exalted and lofty that He can be
understood by no creature, only by Himself. Nevertheless, a sound intellect can
through certain examples imagine being at such a distance and can find confirma-
tion by reasoning from those examples in the following manner.

We see in animals differences in cognitive power since one knows more perfectly
than another. The lamb knows the wolf and flees him by nature, and it has such
knowledge from nature. Man knows the wolf more perfectly, for he knows that
it is a sensitive animal, a thief, and an animal of an evil species. Man likewise possesses
such knowledge from nature. Now although these cognitions of the lamb and of
man concerning the wolf may be different, nevertheless the wolf does not change
his being, nor is it in itself better or lesser known. Thus, by analogy, contingent
things are by man's power of cognition considered more imperfectly than by God's.
Since God knows contingent things much more perfectly than does man, contingent
things still do not change their being and are not in themselves better or lesser known.
Now just as God who is perfect and beyond time sees, discerns, and knows future
things even as He does contingent ones, those present and even those past, so that
His foreknowledge and knowing does not add to or diminish contingent things
caused by man's free will and by the defect of nature's course (even the coming
of Christ is contingent), nevertheless His knowledge is so lofty and perfect that
it sees more than human intellect and more than any other creature. Now the author
places another fine example in the text. He depicts sailing on a river a boat which
through the helmsman's free will goes from east to west, and he imagines standing
on the shore a person who sees that boat. In the eyes and pupils of this person on
the shore there appears the form of that boat, and he sees and discerns through the
perfection of the organ of sight, that is, the eye, the path taken by the boat at that
particular time. And now the author quietly says: just as the eye of the man standing on the shore does not through its seeing impose necessity on the voyage of the
boat which depends on the helmsman's free will, so God's foreknowledge does not
impose necessity on contingent acts which depend on the free will of those performing them. The fact is that this example is not perfect, inasmuch as one cannot
perfectly compare man's sight with God's since, as we have said, God knows more
perfectly and sees throughout the course of time, the present as well as the future
or past which man does not know or see. But let it suffice for the sound mind to
have signs or indications of this so that we may arrive at a rule concerning what
has been said, namely, that with regard to the knowledge of things one must consider the person involved, and according to his perfection hold that knowledge true
which says that the things considered do not change their nature, nor are they subject to any necessity.

16. This may be understood in two ways: between *feltro* and *feltro*, that is, be-

tween one heaven and another, with reference to the constellation. The other way is between "felt" and "felt," that is, that he will be born of very low people since "felt" is of low worth. This is his response to an unspoken question because of the opinion that holds that a good and virtuous son cannot be born of a base father and mother.

17. In this canto the author intends to deal with three general matters. Allegorically, they signify the state of the sinner in his first life who wishes to return to the straight road. First he shows how he ascended the mountain to the gate of Purgatory, being carried by Lucia, that is, his clear and noble intellect, a power which in the present Comedy he called Lucia. Secondly, he describes the gate with a guardian very much in keeping with Purgatory both in appearance and dress. Thirdly, he conveys the authority of the guardian who stands for the keeper of the Holy Church of Rome and her keys. And so, entering the city of Purgatory by leave of the aforesaid gatekeeper, he ends the present canto.

Concerning the first part, one must know that the sinner, when he goes to do penance for the sins he has committed, must proceed pure and clean with sincerity of heart and mind to his confessor. He must confess to him every sin with all his heart, as is written in the Psalm: "I shall confess to Thee, O Lord, with all my heart," etc. He must be sorry for all his sins and beware of committing those that might cause him grief, as Augustine says in his book *On Confession*: "To repent of sins committed and not to commit sins to be repented." In his humble confession he must receive that penance which seems appropriate to his confessor, and then convert it to deeds. Wishing to depict poetically that such a disposition was in him in the person of a sinner, the author introduces into the poem an eagle which later he calls Lucia, who takes him to the gate of Purgatory to speak to its keeper.

Concerning the second matter, one must know that he places three steps before the gate of Purgatory; the first was white marble, very polished and shiny, the second dark, ashen, and cracked, the third of red and flaming porphyry. The three steps must signify three things, namely, the conditions needed by the penitent when he approaches the priest for cleansing. The first condition signified by the first step must mean the awareness that the sinner must have within himself of the sins he has committed. He must approach pensively and see his vices reflected in himself, and he must make them as clear in his confession to the priest as the polished and shining marble reveals the image of vice that is mirrored within it. The second condition signified by the second step suggests the contrition that the sinner must feel regarding his sins. This must be such in the sinner that it must sadden and afflict him and render him so sorrowful that he profusely emits sighs and tears through the fissures created by such sorrow. Since such a condition is arduous, dark, harsh, and fissured, the author depicts the second step as made in this way. The third condition signified by the third step shows what and how great must be the sinner's fervor and steadfastness with respect to a powerful love of the Creator's charity that converts into action every penance directed to Him, so that God's justice may be satisfied. Since the love of charity is readily enkindled, the author depicts it as red in color. As for its heaviness and hardness, he also depicts it as bloody.

Thus in the aforesaid three steps we have in brief three conditions necessary for thorough penance: in the first, *oris confessio*; in the second, *cordis contritio*; in the third, *operis satisfactio*; just as we find developed in *Inferno* XXVII where the sacrament of penance is treated. On the third step or level the author places a gatekeeper who seemed to be of a color similar to a diamond, which is a most strong and unbreakable stone. He has him dressed in a robe of grayish color and holding in his hand a very fiery and polished sword. This gatekeeper is intended to signify the priest, who must possess these qualities: first, he must be like a diamond, that is, firm and constant and unbreakable concerning the sacred articles of the Church; secondly, he must wear an ashen robe, that is, a humble habit, and thus proceed humbly in his office; thirdly, he must be pure and endowed with justice and reason so that he may truly represent that Lord whose vicar he is, and follow in His steps. Proceeding with his poem, the author describes how he humbly threw himself at the feet of the gatekeeper, to denote that the sinner must approach the confessor with humility, and seek absolution as one deserving of mercy, together with the imposition of penance for his sins.

As regards the third matter, one must know that the author has that gatekeeper draw forth two keys, which allegorically must signify the keys of the Church which are two since two things are necessary for juridical power: the authority to recognize faults, and the power to absolve or to condemn. These two things are the keys of the Church, that is, "the knowledge to discern and the power to bind and to absolve" which Christ committed to St. Peter, as is written in St. Matthew 16:19: "To you I give the keys of the kingdom of heaven," etc. And not only must one understand that they were entrusted to St. Peter himself, but to him and to his successors, inasmuch as if such a sacrament were entrusted to him alone it would have endured only throughout the lifetime of St. Peter, and thus would not be instituted as perfectly as the other sacraments that will remain until the day of judgment.

18. The fifth, sixth, seventh, eighth, ninth, tenth, and eleventh matters are introduced by the author in order to symbolize the Church of God, its foundation and operation, with each of its parts appearing distinct unto itself. For this reason it was necessary for the author, after having dealt with human happiness which man can acquire through natural means, to deal with the Church of God which is a gate, road and pathway to that contemplation, highest good, and perfect happiness to which every virtuous act is directed and ordered. They are accessible only through the grace of that church, which is desired only for itself, and not established nor structured for any other end. The author first introduces seven candelabra which as fiery instruments must signify the seven gifts of the Holy Spirit that must be present in every faithful Christian; and if he does not possess them, it is impossible that he possess fullness of faith. The gifts are not only preparation for the faith, but also oppose and thwart the vices, as will be seen. The first gift is compassion which opposes envy; the second is fear which opposes pride; the third is knowledge which opposes wrath; the fourth is fortitude which opposes sloth; the fifth is

counsel which opposes avarice; the sixth is intellect which opposes lust; the seventh wisdom which opposes gluttony. These gifts are necessary for the man who wishes to be a faithful Christian inasmuch as they are all subject to the three theological virtues, which are possessed together since whoever loses one loses all, whoever acquires one acquires all, as appears in St. Thomas' *Prima secundae*. And since the said gifts are preparation against vice and a basis of the Church which is a congregation of the faithful, the author thus introduced them from the beginning. Let this suffice with regard to the fifth matter.

As for the sixth matter, one must know that St. John the Evangelist in his vision of the Apocalypse saw twenty-four elders dressed in white who symbolize the twenty-four books of the Bible in the Old Testament on which the Christian faith is founded, and they are as follows: Genesis; Exodus; Leviticus; Numbers; Deuteronomy; Josue; Judges; Kings; Samuel; Isaias; Jeremias; Ezechiel; Twelve Prophets; Esdras; Paralipomenon; Judith; Esther; Daniel; Job; Baruch; Tobias; Psalms; the Books of Solomon, which are counted as one, and which are the Canticle of Canticles, Ecclesiastes, Book of Wisdom, Parables, and Proverbs; then there is the Book of Maccabees. Since the author wishes to describe the Church in the same manner, he introduced the aforesaid twenty-four elders.

With the seventh matter are introduced four animals which symbolize the four Evangelists described by the prophet Ezechiel and, later, St. John the Evangelist. It is true that the author asserts that there does exist some discrepancy in the words of these two men. But insofar as the present intent is concerned, it suffices that the four animals symbolize the four Evangelists, who are four columns of the Christian faith: one, an eagle; the second, a man; the third, a lion; the fourth, an ox. Now, in describing their types of figures, it is stated that they had six wings which were as full of eyes as was Argus to whom the poets ascribe one hundred eyes, as will appear in the exposition of the text. These six wings must signify that Sacred Scripture extends through each dimension, height, breadth, and depth. Their being full of eyes must signify that just as the eye is the organ that distinguishes the particular, so Scripture distinguishes and clarifies every particularity. It therefore follows that inasmuch as such Scripture occupies and encompasses every dimension, and deigns to deal with every particular, there is in them every perfection and accomplishment. One must note that, up to this point, these metaphors were invented by others, that is, by Ezechiel the prophet and by St. John the Evangelist.

In conjunction with the eighth matter, one must know that in this section the author consciously uses metaphors. He introduces a chariot with two wheels, as was said, which symbolizes the Church of God founded on two lives, the active and the contemplative; and around the wheel that stands for the contemplative life, there are three women representing the contemplative virtues, that is, faith, hope, and charity. He depicts faith as a lady in pure white since faith is a virtue without any admixture, white and distinct. He depicts hope as a lady in green inasmuch as hope leads man back to life and sustains him, just as greenery makes a tree branch out and keeps it alive. He depicts charity as a lady in red because whoever possesses such a virtue is afire and continually willing to benefit God and his neighbor. Thus the lady referred to is depicted with the color of fire. The author now adds that at times the wheel is directed by the woman in white, and at others by the one in red. By this interchange he means that often man becomes contemplative primarily under the impetus of faith and oftentimes primarily under the impetus of charity; but not of hope inasmuch as it cannot be so without one of the mentioned two virtues since man cannot without faith expect to have what he hopes for, or without will expect to have what he longs and hopes for. Around the second wheel he places four women, that is, the four moral virtues which are to be found in the active live: prudence, justice, fortitude, and temperance. He describes only prudence, to whom he ascribes three eyes since, just as the person who has three eyes would see more than the one with two, so the person who is girt with such a virtue is able to see ahead in comparison to others. He depicts them all dressed in purple as if to demonstrate that they applied equally to human affairs which are various and diverse. The author has that chariot drawn by a griffin which figures Jesus Christ who is the head and highest priest of the Church; and just as in Christ there were two natures, divine and human, so he attempts to endow the griffin with two natures, one winged and the other four-legged. To show how, just as the chariot was led and drawn by the griffin so the Church was led and drawn by Jesus Christ, he says that insofar as that griffin was a bird, it was of gold which symbolized divinity, and insofar as it was another animal, it was made white mixed with red to describe humankind, which was later tinted with red from the blood shed in His passion. He says that its wings were extended upwards and became part of the seven rays formed by the candelabra. Because of the griffin's nature, none of the rays was disturbed, which is to say that its wings were the Holy Spirit itself, from whom those seven gifts, as has been said, proceeded.

As for the ninth matter, one must know that these two were St. Luke and St. Paul. St. Luke was a physician in his early life, and thus reveals himself a physician in his Scripture inasmuch as he reflects more compassion than the other Evangelists. That is why the author says that he seemed one of the followers of Hippocrates who wrote about medicine. St. Paul was in the world a man of arms and a persecutor of Christians as long as he did not have the faith; thus in his writings he spoke more of justice without remission. That is why he depicts him with a sword in his hand and with an austere look. And he adds that although they appeared different, they were headed in one direction, showing that the end of their writings was in God who is supreme, just, and merciful.

Regarding the tenth matter, one must know that the Church of God has primarily recognized four doctors who expounded and clarified what was said by their predecessors, as well as compiled news ideas and arguments. These are St. Augustine, St. Gregory, St. Jerome, and St. Ambrose.

With respect to the eleventh matter, one must know that, just as St. John the Evangelist experienced vision in a new manner and then wrote about it in what is called the Apocalypse, so the author introduced St. John in a new manner, that is, sleeping and old, in order to show that in vision he saw these figures in the bosom of Christ at supper, and that later in time he put them thus in writing. This vision, as has been said, symbolized the Church of God.

28. The aforementioned exposition, glosses, or annotations I have written according to how I, a most humble connoisseur, sensed the intention of the author.
Therefore every example, argument, opinion, conclusion, allegory, meaning, or saying
that I have written, intended, or assigned therein, if it conforms to and is in keeping with the spirit and the tenets of holy mother, the Roman Catholic Church,
I do affirm, approve, and hold to have been well written. Should it deviate from,
distort, or contradict the said spirit and tenets of the holy Church, I have written
it vainly and not for good. I therefore, as a pure, faithful, and true Christian, would
declare it to be null and void and utterly valueless.

The Editors

Petrarch's *Epistola metrica* II.10:
An Annotated Translation

THOMAS G. BERGIN

THE LETTER WE ARE HERE CONCERNED WITH is one of the longest of the *Epistolae metricae* and by no means the least interesting of the collection. Highly personal and even confessional in substance, it tells us more about the state of mind of the recently crowned laureate than he himself realized. It confirms or illuminates passages appearing in other works of Petrarch; it has engaging links, notably but not exclusively, with the *Africa*, the *Rerum memorandarum libri* and some of the *Familiares*. And nowhere in the canon of the poet's works are his notions of the nature and function of poetry more clearly and concisely set forth than in certain lines of this polemical *apologia*. Petrarch seems to have thought well of his remarks on allegory, for he returned to gloss them some twenty years later. It may be that the appeal of the letter has been enhanced rather than diminished by the complex of puzzles it presents, not only with respect to such major matters as the date of its composition and the identity of the poet's provocative correspondent, but also as touching its superscription and even its proper number in the series. As to its genesis we may quote the account of E. H. Wilkins (*Life*, p. 46)* which runs as follows:

---

*For bibliographical details on all publications cited in the various sections of this piece, see "List of works cited," pp. 226–229.

Perhaps about the same time (1344) there came to Petrarch a hostile and insolent letter, written ostensibly by Lancellotto Anguissola, a Lombard noble who was associated with the Visconti. The letter attacked not only Petrarch as an individual but also the art of poetry in general. Petrarch's coronation was said to be undeserved and premature, and his poetry was said to be generally unknown; and poets were called mendacious and mad, and their writings puerile.

To this attack Petrarch replied in a long *epistola metrica*, addressed to Lancellotto. . . .

Perhaps before he had the *epistola* ready to send, perhaps after he had sent it and Lancellotto had received it, a letter arrived from Lancellotto saying that he had not written the hostile letter to which his name had been attached; and either through Lancellotto's letter or in some other way Petrarch learned that the actual writer of that hostile letter was Brizio Visconti, a powerful, cruel, and unscrupulous son of Luchino Visconti, who was at this time one of the co–rulers of Milan (the other being his brother, the Archbishop Giovanni): Brizio had simply chosen to attach Lancellotto's name to the letter that he himself had written.

Petrarch then wrote a brief and grateful *epistola metrica* to Lancellotto (II.13), and a violently sarcastic *epistola metrica* to Brizio (II.17). In later years, when Petrarch was making a collection of his *epistolae metricae*, he included all three of these letters, giving to the first the heading, "To a certain unnamed envious man who had indulged in manifold insults, shielding himself under a name that was not his."

Although Wilkins does not here specifically acknowledge his source, it is clear that he is accepting the findings of P. G. Ricci who, some years earlier (1947), had published an article ("Il Petrarca e Brizio Visconti") convincingly identifying Petrarch's correspondent for the first time and assigning a firm date to the composition of the letter. Ricci's argument is ingenious. He begins by noting that Petrarch in his invective addressed to the Cardinal Caraman (written in 1355, see Wilkins, *Life*, p. 47) refers to an earlier *certamen* in which he had engaged years ago against an opponent, feared in all Italy, who was by no means of "mediocre" talent in letters and who was, furthermore, young, thus implying, of course, that the Cardinal has no such formidable assets. There is no work of Petrarch styled "*certamen*," to be sure, but Ricci believes that Petrarch is using the

word to refer to the exchange of compliments of which our letter is
Petrarch's portion. Clearly it must have been composed a long time before
1355 and internal evidence indicates that it was written in Parma, some
time after the death of Robert of Naples (1343). Arguing further from
statements in the invective against the cardinal, Ricci establishes that the
only individual in Petrarch's ambiance within that time span who could
meet the requirements of power, literary talent, and youth was Brizio
Visconti. A son of Luchino—though illegitimate—Brizio enjoyed his
father's confidence, was named *podestà* of Lodi in 1339, and subsequently
was given supreme command of the Milanese army. Ricci (p. 341) quotes
a chronicler who called him "*secundus Mediolani dominus.*" Brizio was
something of a poet, too, of sufficiently enduring distinction to merit the
attention of Croce and Sapegno in our times; the latter published some
lines of the warrior-poet in *Il Trecento*, p. 494. Ricci (p. 336) calculates
that Brizio must have been some five years younger than Petrarch, who
therefore might reasonably call him "*juvenis.*" The case for Brizio is further supported by the fact that Lancellotto Anguissola was a dependent
of the Visconti and possibly a military subordinate of Brizio, who would,
on either count, have had no hesitation in signing Anguissola's name to
his malicious letter.

There is yet another—and clinching if somewhat oblique—argument
for Ricci's identification. As Wilkins noted (*supra*) Letters ii.10 and 17
were addressed to the same individual. In the "definitive edition" prepared
by Petrarch both *epistolae* have anonymous salutations; in the printed editions both are addressed to "Zoilus." But Ricci (p. 338, n. 3) finds that
in two manuscripts that predate Petrarch's "editing," Letter ii.17 is addressed baldly "Ad Brutium Vicecomitibus mediolanensem"; it is logical
to assume that ii.10 had the same target. (Diana Magrini, p. 124, had
already noted that ii.17 bore that heading in the *laurenziano-strozziano*
manuscript but had refrained from drawing a definite conclusion.) Further considerations lead Ricci to establish 1344 (when Petrarch was residing
in Parma) as the date of the epistolary exchange.

With regard to the number assigned to our letter, it should be noted
that some scholars refer to it as ii.11; Rossetti, for example (ii, p. 211),
and, rather surprisingly, Ricci in the article we have cited. The ambiguity derives from the circumstance that the eighth letter of Book ii contains, as an appendix, an epitaph for King Robert of Naples. Since the
epitaph bears its own heading it is easy to think of it as no. 9; this would

of course affect the numbering of all following *epistolae*. Yet the epitaph is certainly not a letter in its own right and both Magrini (p. 110) and Wilkins (*The "Epistolae Metricae"*, p. 14) count it as a part of no. 8 and assign to our letter the number 10; the numbers given by Ernesto Bianchi to the letters he edited in *Francesco Petrarca: Rime, trionfi e poesie latine*, pp. 706–803, indicate that he too would have styled our letter ii.10.

Finally, concerning the wording of the title or indication of addressee, as Wilkins noted (*supra*), Petrarch, in editing his *Metricae*—a task begun in 1350 (see Wilkins, *Life*, p. 92)—gave to this letter the cautious heading "Ad convitiatorem quendam innominatum et sub clypeo nominis alieni multiformiter insultantem." (No. 17 has the superscription "Ad invidum rursus innominatum.") If by this time Brizio was no longer to be feared, his father, before his death in 1349, had become a friend of Petrarch (see *Ep. met.* ii.11 and *Fam.* vii.15); perhaps on that account Petrarch would be reluctant to identify his antagonist. If the labor of editing carried through to 1357 (as Foresti, p. 313, seems to suggest), there would have been more cogent reasons for reserve, since by then Petrarch had been a guest of the Visconti for some time. The mysterious Zoilus comes on stage only with the printed editions. His provenance is not clear. The historical Zoilus was a Greek grammarian of the fourth century B.C., notorious for his acerbic criticism of Homer; a sketch of him may be found in Vitruvius, *De Architectura* (7 *Praef.* 8), a book known to Petrarch (de Nolhac, ii.105, 240). I have found no mention of the atrabilious Zoilus in any work of our poet.

My text is based on that of Domenico Rossetti, published in *Francisci Petrarchae poemata minora quae extant omnia*. His text, with facing page translation by the Cavaliere Lorenzo Mancini of Florence, appears in volume ii of that work, pp. 212–41; notes to the poem (by Rossetti) are printed on pp. 407–11 of the same volume.

There are some differences between Rossetti's text as there printed and my version. I have, first of all, adopted the corrections made by Rossetti himself on pp. 272–73 of volume iii of the *Poemata minora*. I have made a few alterations in Rossetti's punctuation; the significant cases are noted. I have ventured to make one slight change in the wording of Rossetti's text; this too I have noted. I have, in accordance with the practice of recent editors of Petrarch's works, following the orthographical guidelines set forth by Vittorio Rossi (*Fam.* i, pp. clxiv–clxix), restored the medieval spelling which Rossetti had recast in classical form. Finally, also in keeping with modern practice, I have capitalized the first letter of a line only when it is an initial in a proper name or in the first word of a sentence.

In the preparation of my translation and notes I have received truly invaluable aid and counsel from Dr. John L. Ryan of Colorado and Professor Gordon Williams of Yale. I am deeply grateful to them. I wish also to thank the late Professor E. T. Silk of Yale for a number of useful suggestions and Mr. Donald Eddy of the Cornell University Library and Professor Dante Della Terza of Harvard for supplying some items of reference not readily available to me.

Epistola metrica II.10–Zoilo S.

Distrahis atque animum curis melioribus aufers

et calami pervertis iter. Fueratque tacere

cautius, at stimulis residem pungentibus urges.

Da veniam, si vera loquor, licet aspera dictu;

cogor enim. Studiis emitur, sequiturque laborem

laurea, perrarum decus atque hoc tempore soli

speratum optatumque michi. Quis nescit agrestum

premia post meritum? Pudet hec dubitata diserto,

si dubitas vere; quod, si tentare libebat,

certe alio tentandus eram tibi fortius ictu,   10

ut quaterer. Quid enim? Lux ergo novissima forte

expectanda fuit, iungendaque pompa sepulcri

ac pretium studii? Si debita fine laborum

laurea, non aliter; non hanc Eneide sacra

Virgilius meruit, non qui Pharsalica Tempe

sanguine complevit Latio; licet ille, negato

calle petens, alia tulerit ratione repulsam.

Cognita commemoro. Quid? quod ceu sponsa decoram

arguor Hemonia lauro gestasse coronam?

Florea virginibus, sunt laurea serta poetis   20

Cesaribusque simul; parque est ea gloria utrisque.

Arguor improprie. Sed quid vir providus addit?

Vidimus ornatum lauro, quem (protinus inquit)

Metrical Letter II.10–To Zoilus

From loftier matters you divert my mind
and turn my pen from its appointed course.
Silence might well have been my best response
but your annoying barbs give me no rest.
Forgive me if I set forth a few truths,
though they be harsh to hear. I have no choice.
The laurel, an adornment rarely won
and longed for and desired in our time
by me alone, is bought with ardent zeal
and follows toil. The husbandman's reward,   10
as all men know, comes after labor. Shame
on you, a scholar, if you doubt that truth!
But do you really doubt? If you were aiming
merely to test me you should have applied
another thrust with strength to shatter me.(10)
What is your argument? Do you suggest
I should have waited for life's final hour
and joined the recognition of my art
to ceremonies of my funeral?
Why, if the laurel must come fittingly   20
when all our work is done and not before,
then Virgil did not merit it with his
divine *Aeneid* nor did he who filled
Pharsalian Tempe with rich Latin blood—
although the latter, following a path
forbidden, had the prize withheld from him
for other reasons. I speak here of things
well known. So next, I am accused of wearing
the garland of Thessalian frondage as
a bride her nuptial wreath. But certainly   30
what flowers are to maidens so the laurel(20)
is to both kings and bards, who share alike
the same renown. I'm wrongfully accused.
But hear—our sage has more to add. He says:
"We see the laurel crown adorning one

non prius audieram. Velut omnia pulcra relatu
audieris! Quam multa michi, licet ampla, tibique
non audita putas? Nam quantula portio rerum
unius ingenii laus est! Decet alta modeste
cernere, seque prius. Sed enim mea carmina nunquam
sunt audita tibi; quid refert? Forsitan illa
non tibi (parce, precor) cecini; legit illa Robertus,   30
concivis meus egregius, quem Iulia nostro
tempore Pariseos studiorum tertia nutrix
suspicit, et toto venerantur ab orbe magistri.
Tuscus et Eneas legit, et Rainaldus in antris
altus Apollineis; ingens legit illa Iohannes,
Barbatus legit illa meus, sociique fideles
auribus excipiunt cupidis et pectore servant.
Ut cunctas livor seu fors obstruxerit aures,
ipse michi Musisque canam; plausorque pudendus
ingenii nec frena mei nec calcar habebit.   40
Cur redit in dubium totiens mea laurea? Nunquid
non satis est meminisse semel? Decuitne per urbes
circumferre nova viridantia tempora fronde?
Testarique greges hominum populique favorem
infami captare via? Laudarier olim
a paucis michi propositum. Quid inertia vulgi
millia contulerint, quid murmura vana theatri?
Ergo ne Trinacrio minor est michi carmine Regi
gloria quam turbe passim placuisse furenti?

of whom I never heard before." As if
all good news in the world came to your ears!
Think you how vast a store of things there are
to hear that are unknown to you and me.
And surely praises of one man of talent   40
make no great stir. Well, one must look at greatness
with modesty and especially at oneself.
So then, you've never heard my songs? What matter?
Perhaps, forgive me, pray, they were not sung
for you. However they are read by Robert,(30)
my famous townsman, whom that third great nurse
of all the arts today, Paris, admires
as do all scholars through the whole wide world.
Tuscan Aeneas reads them and likewise
Rinaldus, nurtured in Apollo's caves;   50
Great John and my Barbatus read them too,
and loyal friends in truth lend avid ears
to hear them and preserve them in their hearts.
But if all ears were stopped by chance or envy,
yet will I sing my notes to please alone
the Muses and myself. However, praise
from an unworthy source shall neither spur
nor rein my genius in. Why must my laurel(40)
so many times be questioned? Is it not
sufficient to have mentioned it but once?   60
Say, would it have become me to parade
through every city with my temples decked
with fronds renewed? Or to have summoned throngs
of witnesses? to seek by shameful means
for popular approval? At that time
my aim was to win praise from but a few.
What profit were there in the ignorant
applause of all the thousands that compose
the herd, or in the vapid murmurings
of idle theatre-goers? Is it then   70
for me less glorious to have pleased the King
of Sicily with my song than to have won
the favor of the raving multitude

regineque minus Capitolia profuit urbis   50

scandere quam vacuas studio lustrasse paludes

avia quam nemorum, rudibus quam rura colonis,

atque inopes sparsasque casas? Incognita vestro

carmina nostra foro. Quid rustica menia nobis

obiiciunt? Quo jure fremunt? satis esse putavi

terrarum petiisse caput. Qui victor in arcem

signa tulit, summa securus sede quiescat;

extremas nisi forte iubes ambire cloacas

figentem obscenis victricia postibus arma.

Noscor ubi placitum. Laudat mea carmina Tibris,   60

Parthenope studiosa probat; nec terra Nasonis

respuit aut Flacci, nec qui Cicerone superbit

cive simul Marioque locus, nec Gallia nostri

inscia, nec Rhodanus. Quid inepta colonia tantis

una nocet titulis fulvi cui gratia nummi,

ventris amor, studiumque gule, somnusque, quiesque

esse solet potior sacre quam cura poësis?

Mantua Virgilium genuit, Verona Catullum

et Plinios, nostrosque aliquot servavit in annos.

Urbs Antenoridum quantos celebravit alumnos!   70

Nunc (quoniam numerare labor quot Cimbria nuper

secula) Pergameum viderunt nostra poetam

throughout the land? Did it avail me less
to mount the steps of the Capitoline(50)
in the Queen City than to make my way
with plodding purpose over empty swamps
or lonely forest trails or through bleak fields
inhabited by loutish yokels, dwelling
in scattered, squalid huts? Your town knows naught   80
of what I've written; why do your crude walls
impede my progress? Let them not complain.
To me it seemed sufficient to seek out
the world's great capital. The victor who
has raised his standard o'er the citadel
may take his rest in all serenity
on that high seat — or would you have him go
to win approval in outlying sewers
and fix the emblems of his victory
on filthy doorposts? I am known where I   90
desire to be known. The Tiber lauds(60)
my verses, which Parthenope the learned
likewise esteems. Nor do the native lands
of Naso and of Flaccus scorn their worth,
nor yet the city that takes rightful pride
in her sons, Marius and Cicero.
I'm not unknown in Gaul nor in the vale
cleft by the Rhone. Can such a store of honors
be tarnished by a stupid colony
whose habit it has long been to prefer   100
the glint of yellow coin and belly lust
and the allures of avarice and sloth
to cultivation of the sacred Muse?
By Mantua was Virgil sired; Verona
was father to Catullus and both Plinys
and host to others down to our own day.
Beyond all reckoning is the progeny
made famous by the town Antenor built.(70)
To chronicle the Cimbrian ages past
would be too wearisome; our times have seen   110
the bard of Bergamo with austere locks

cui rigidos strinxit laurus Paduana capillos,

nomine reque bonum; Latiique in finibus orbis

Pyerios animos alpis tulit ora nivose.

Parma evo collapsa sui monumenta Macrobi

ostentat, vetus usque novo me carmina saxum

nobilitare iubens, nec eadem degener urbe est

Cassius. Has inter, docta urbs tua sola carebat

vate diu proprio, nisi te sibi fata tulissent   80

purgantem patrias calami splendore tenebras,

longaque parvificis abolentem oblivia terris.

Caucaseum Romana iugum transcendere fama

distulit, Europe iam tunc Asieque tremenda?

At mea, quod vestre nondum sit cognita plebi,

ceu tenebris damnata iacet. Si reddita pridem

est ratio, reddenda iterum: nova gloria regum,

Rex Siculus, celo pro me respondet ab alto,

qui modo, dum terris habitat michi muneris autor

maximus insoliti, famam invidiamque relinquit,   90

adiciiens causam; quod opuscula, iudice tanto,

nostra forent tanti. Melius sibi cognita forte

quam tibi; nocturnas studiis gravioribus horas

subripiebat enim, vigilique ingesta lucerne

immemor interdum ceneque somnique legebat.

encircled by a Paduan wreath—in truth
a man as good in action as in name.
The regions of the snow-encrusted Alps
have fathered spirits fired by the Muse
high on the frontiers of the Latin world.
Parma displays a monument, now ruined
by weight of years, of her Macrobius
and urges me with new verse to ennoble
the ancient stone, and of that selfsame town   120
Cassius was no unworthy citizen.
Among all these only your learned city
has lacked a poet she might call her own
for many years and still would want for one
had not kind Fortune given you to her;(80)
the illumination of your pen, I'm sure,
will dissipate the fuscous clouds that veil
your native town and save that region, scorned
for many years, from dark oblivion.
Did Rome's renown, already held in awe   130
in Asia and in Europe, tarry long
before surmounting the Caucasian ridge?
My fame, however, being yet unknown
to your plebeians, must remain condemned
to dwell in darkness. An account once rendered
must here be given again. That recent splendor
shining among the stars, Trinacria's King,
from thence responds for me. While yet he dwelt
on earth he was to me a lavish donor
of gifts uniquely rare; now he has left   140
to me a double legacy of fame and envy,(90)
and therewith given me reason for the hope
that these small works of mine, so highly praised
by such a critic, might be of some worth.
He knew them better, it may be, than you,
for he was wonted from more serious cares
to steal the midnight hours and by the light
of his ne'er darkened lamp peruse my lines,
often indifferent to food or sleep.

Meque, tibi ignotum, tanto dignatus honore est,

ut procerum primis sub regia tecta vocatis

plurima nostrarum caneret preconia laudum.

Vera utinam! Quam vera tamen Rex viderit ipse;

quin etiam, magno pro munere, parva petita est   100

Africa nostra sibi. Memini; suprema benignus

oscula, et heu nunquam fatis iteranda, parabat,

quum duo dona pio placidissimus ore poposcit.

Obstupui; quid enim immenso donare pusillus

posse videbatur? Sed quid, nisi carmina, vellet

largus opum divesque animi et virtutis amator?

Carmina mansure sedem tribuentia fame

hoc petiit primum; pectus calamumque pudenter

excuso, fragilesque humeros sub pondere tanto.

Instat ab adverso; dubio lis fine resedit,   110

concessisse sibi ut videar, michi prima negasse.

Proxima dona libens tribuo; cui dignius aule,

Scipiade, mittendus eras? At perfida et altis

invida principiis illum Fortuna repente

sustulit interea. Nunc, tamquam lumine rapto,

nescius in tenebris liber est quo flectere cursum;

cogitet, et toto nullum videt equore portum.

Heu cineres bustumque petet qui, turbine quanquam

dilatus vario, multos absumpserit annos.

Si foret hic vestram tantum mittendus ad urbem   120

And even though I am unknown to you   150
he so much honored me that he would summon
the highest barons to his royal palace
and publicly commend my works to all.
Would that his words were true! He thought they were,
and asked, as if it were the greatest favor,(100)
that he might have my little *Africa*.
I see him now: as graciously he moved
to offer me the embrace of farewell,
the last the Fates would ever grant, alas!
With gentle voice he asked of me two boons.   160
I was aghast. For what could one so lowly
offer to one so high? Nay, but what else
could such a man so bountiful, so rich
in worldy goods and treasures of the mind
and virtue's votary, desire of me
but verses? So the first request he made
was for some work that might provide a lasting
foundation for his fame throughout the years.
I humbly begged to be excused, protesting
my faulty courage and my feeble pen,   170
my shoulders all too frail for such a charge.
He would not listen and our argument
concluded in misunderstanding: he(110)
believed I had consented; I was sure
I had refused his first request; the other
I granted with glad heart, for to what court,
my Scipiad, could you more fittingly
have been dispatched? Ere it could come to pass,
alas, false Fortune, envious of great lords,
reft him from us. And now, as though a storm   180
had swept away its beacon, my book drifts
in darkness, knowing not what course to choose,
and, tossed by the vast seas, finds no sure haven.
What has consumed so many years, albeit
by varying gales retarded, must, alas,
now seek out ashes and a sepulchre.
No doubt if it could but have found its way(120)

iam satis exornatus erat, michi crede, superque;

sed, dum multa timet, venturaque secula terrent,

heret adhuc tacitus; cuius si laurea serum

expectasset iter (quod mens presaga timebat),

mortis ab insidiis iam circumventa fuisset.

Hinc prior ille abiit, cuius post funera nullum

examen subiturus eram; nam, maxime, nondum

tu michi notus eras. Fateor mea crimina: tempus

anticipasse iuvat; quamvis nec pauca viderem

scripta michi iam tum. Laudati carmina Vari   130

nulla meos feriunt, oculos tamen inclita pectus

fama ferit. Scriptis ego sum tollendus in altum;

his sine nullus ero. Nunquid tamen illa probari

est opus et vulgo? Titulo caruisse poete,

abiecisse graves spoliato vertice ramos

maluerim, et longis latuisse inglorius annis.

Hactenus hec. Nova lis oritur: quo tramite vertar?

Conquerar an taceam? Risumque refellere risu

sufficiat? Risum moveo? Sic vita meretur

nostra quidem, fateor, sed nunquid carmina risum   140

promeruere etiam, lacrimas que sepe severis

extorsere oculis? Sic tristia forte volutant

nunc mea fata vices, ut qui rorantia vidi

inclita Romulei, dum proloquor, ora Senatus,

regis et indomiti frontem pietate remissam,

to your fair city, it would there have won
sufficient and perhaps excessive honor;
meanwhile, as trepidant of many things   190
and of the years to come, it bides in peace
and does not stir. If, as my prescient mind
so rightly feared, its laurel had awaited
a journey long deferred, it would have fallen
into Death's ambush. When the king had gone
after his passing I could not have hoped
to undergo a proper scrutiny,
for you were then unknown to me, O master.
Well, I confess my sin. I'm not displeased
that I advanced the hour of my laurel—   200
though I must say already at that time
more than a few of my works had appeared.
Of Varius, so much lauded, not one line(130)
has met my eyes and yet his wide renown
endears him to my heart. And as for me,
my verses must upraise me; without them
I shall be nothing. But must they then win
the vulgar herd's approval? Nay, I'd rather
forego the name of bard and tear the wreath
of laurel from my brow and, head uncrowned,   210
languish long years, inglorious and unknown.
Now on that subject I have said enough;
another question here confronts me: whither
shall I now turn? Shall I make loud complaint
or bide in silence? Or would it suffice
to counter ridicule with ridicule?
Am I the cause of laughter? I concede
my life deserves it, but when has my song
ever occasioned mirth? Rather, indeed(140)
it often has drawn tears from sober eyes.   220
Has villainous Fortune so much changed my lot
that I, who saw the famous visages
of Roman Senators grow moist with tears
as I addressed them and who marked as well
compassion shade the temples of a king

ridear ignavo (proh sors malefida!) popello?
Altera legitime superest michi causa querele.
Quis modus audendi, queve ista licentia fandi?
Tela fremens Helicone rapis, quibus agmina vatum
impetis, et nostros in nos accingeris enses.   150
Ante alios Flacci; cuius te scripta monere
occiput ut scabitur, tenero nec parcitur ungui,
vate sacrum decies clam castigante poema,
debuerant, rigidamque notis adiungere limam.
Mendaces vocitare quidem insanosque poetas
in primis furor est, mendaxque insania. Vere
vera canunt, aures quanquam fallentia surdas.
Has etenim sprevisse licet. Puerilia vatum
hinc studia appellas? Puerilis ineptia quorsum
impulit errantem calamum? Puerilia Caesar   160
Iulius et toto regnans Augustus in orbe
tractarunt igitur. Quedam divina poetis
vis animi est, veloque tegunt pulcerrima rerum
ambiguo quod non acies nisi lincea rumpat,
mulceat exterius tantum, alliciatque tuentes;
atque ideo puerisque placet, senibusque verendis.
Insanire licet, fateor: mens concita clarum,
seque super provecta, canet. Vulgaria oportet
linquere sub pedibus; magnum hinc subsistere nullum

invincible, must suffer now the scorn
of an untutored rabble? Ah, false Fate!
And yet another cause I find for just
resentment. Say, is there no end to your
impertinence? What warrant do you hold   230
for such brash words? Impassioned, you would seize
arms from Parnassus to assault the ranks
of poets and you charge upon us, girt
with our own swords—and first of all the blade(150)
of Horace, from whose words you should have learned
how it were needful first to scratch the head,
nor spare the tender fingernails, and how
a poet should revise his lines ten times
in private and still to the final draft
apply the rasping file. . . . But worst of all,   240
to speak of poets as madmen is mad,
to call them liars is an arrant lie.
In truth true things they sing, although deaf ears
may fail to hear them; these well merit scorn.
So "childish" you would call the work of poets?
Nay whither has childish fatuity
misled your wayward pen? Must we conclude
that Caesar and Augustus, sovereign(160)
of all the world, paid heed to childish things?
Poets possess a spiritual power,   250
God-given; over precious things they cast
a shifting veil that only Lynceus' eye
could hope to penetrate. This pleasing surface
can yield its own delight and lure as well
the more perceptive; thus it charms alike
children and men of venerable years.
I grant that madness is permissible
to bards; in truth a spirit, high upraised
above itself, pours forth the sweetest song.
Vulgar concerns are left most properly   260
beneath one's feet. On this account the sage,
the first to have bestowed on him that name
by popular acclaim, and who surpassed

censuit ingenium, nisi sit dementia mixta,   170

iudice qui populo docti cognomen habere

cepit et altisonum liquit post terga Platonem.

Dixit idem cunctis: que tanta infamia vatum?

Quo ruis alterius? Media nos pellis ab urbe?

Sed paulum expecta: iam sponte recedimus; amnes

et nemorum secreta placent, turbamque nocentem

odimus, ac leti campis spatiamur amenis.

Hinc quia prospexit, cui primum publica cure

res fuit, adversos populi nos moribus, illum

moribus infestum nostris studioque futurum,   180

discrevit popolo strepitum, rus vatibus almum

solivagis, vacueque bonus dedit otia silve

liberiusque solum; nam (que mixtura?) perennis

hos stupor attonitos alti caligine veri,

hos autem mestos semperque quietis egentes

turbida solliciti tenuissent tedia vulgi.

Consultum hinc illinc igitur: non urbibus acri

pellimur exilio sequimur meliora volentes.

Nonne, Deum primos olim quesisse poetas,

inquit Aristoteles? Non sanctos celitus aura   190

divina afflatos, et munera rara Deorum,

Marcus ait Cicero? Fautorque domesticus omnis

exulet, externi causam tueantur honestam.

Plato of lofty speech, dared to affirm
that there could be no genius in the world(170)
without some touch of madness. This he said
was true of all men; why must poets then
be so despised? To what extremity
are you now rushing? From the city's heart
you fain would banish us? Nay, wait a little;   270
we are already leaving by our choice.
We love the streams and hidden woodland groves
and scorn the madding crowd and are content
to stroll through pleasant meadows. He who first
concerned himself with matters of the state,
knowing we poets would be alien
to habits of the masses, and the folk(180)
intolerant of our manners and our zeal
for study, ruled the masses should possess
the clamorous town, while the calm countryside   280
should be the home of solitary bards.
The good man granted them as well the peace
of woods unpeopled and wide space of land.
Else—dire commingling!—one group would have dwelt
in stupor, dazed and blinded by the glow
of lofty truth, the other, whose desire
was but for peace, disturbed by the disorder
of bored and restless clods, must have perforce
led miserable lives. So the decree,
with due consideration of both sides,   290
means that we poets are not driven forth
into bleak exile but that willingly
we follow better things. Did not of old
wise Aristotle say the poets were(190)
the first to seek for God? And did not Tully
assert that poets were true holy men,
inspired by a breath divine from Heaven,
and precious gifts from the immortal gods?
If all the poets' friends within the walls
were banished, yet would foreigners arise   300
to maintain their just cause. Assuredly

At, nostros nisi forte vetas ad rostra venire,

vicimus haud dubie. Quis preclarissima bella

heroum, moresque graves et nomina nosset?

Quis stimulis animos ageret per mille labores

perque altum virtutis iter? Quis tristia vite

demeret implicite dulci fastidia cantu?

Ora forent quasi muta hominum si spiritus orbi   200

deforet Aonius; virtus ignota lateret

in se clara licet; studiorumque impetus omnis

torperet, lingue nam fundamenta latine

nulla forent, quibus egregie stant sedibus artes,

in quibus omne procul nostris ostenditur evum,

nostraque venturis longum servabitur etas.

Hic tamen occurret Cherilus, vel Aquinius, aut qui

tempus in infami multum posuere libello,

scriptorum plebeia cohors. Sed dic michi, queso,

quenam turba hominum multos non pascit inertes?   210

Rara quidem ingenii bona sunt, semperque fuerunt,

semper erunt. Paucos altum tenuisse videmus.

Aspice Virgilium. Nunquid pueriliter ille

terrarum celique plagas et sidera lustrat?

Ista palam; quam multa latent? Quid fratribus atris

Eolus imperitans, aut quid superaddita moles

montis, et ipse sedens sublimini vertice rector?

Quid pius Eneas, socius quid signat Achates?

Quid Venus ambobus medie velit obvia silve,

quo peregrina virum circumdet corpora nimbo,   220

we cannot lose our case unless perhaps
you bar us from the rostrum. But for us
who would know aught of far-famed heroes' wars
or austere customs—or their very names?
Who else with spurs would move the minds of men
through myriad toils along the road that leads
to virtue? And who mitigates with song
the heavy cares that cloud life's labyrinth?
Take from the world the spirit of the Muse   310
and mankind's voice is stilled. Virtue, although(200)
of itself luminous, would shine unseen;
the zeal for learning would have long since perished
and the foundations of the Latin tongue
would not have stood to offer a firm base
for all the arts of excellence through which
long-vanished centuries are brought to light
and our own times preserved for future years.
But here comes Cherilus to give us pause,
or the Aquinian, or the vulgar throng   320
of scribblers who assiduously toil
to bring forth an ignoble work. What then!—
tell me, what class of men does not include
some inept members? Nay, the gifts of genius(210)
are truly rare; so it has always been
and ever shall be. We have seen but few
attain the summit. But consider Virgil:
is he so childish when his verse surveys
all earth's wide surfaces and all the stars
of heaven? If such matters are apparent,   330
yet how much more lies veiled! What shall we say
of Aeolus who lords it o'er his dark
and sullen brothers, of the added mass
of the great mountain on whose highest peak
the sovereign wind-god sits? What signify
pious Aeneas and his faithful friend
Achates: what is meant by their encounter
with Venus in the middle of the woods?
What is the nature of the mist she throws(220)

qua nubem sub nube tegat? Quid cantat Iopas?

Quid Bithias magno pateram bibat inpiger haustu?

Quid vehat asper equus, misereque incendia noctis

insultansque Sinon, genitrixque affixa furenti

inter tela duci, mox ut digressa per umbras,

apparere Deos, infestaque numina Troiae?

Quo feror? Hic nullum invenies sine tegmine versum;

Preterio reliquos. Quid Flaccus Horatius ardens

an levam destram ne viam monstrare videtur,

et magnum formare virum? Sed nostra relinquo.   230

Orpheus, Amphion, vel natus Apolline Linus

atque parens Museus, et quos mirata Deorum

Grecia subscribit statuis, pueriliter evum

tam longum peperere sibi? Quid protinus alto est

altius Euripide, magno quid maius Homero?

Que loca, quos portus, gemini que littora ponti,

que freta, quas classes, que prelia, quosve ferarum

quos hominum motus oculis, quibus ipse carebat,

non subiecit enim? Mores populique ducumque

pinxit, et e numero plebis secrevit Ulixem,   240

quem michi non vana circumtulit arte, Charybdim

scilleosque canes ut sperneret, atque Cyclopem

Syrenumque modos et amantis pocula Circes.

Quid moror in verbis? Sacri nec dogma Platonis

nec Socrates aliud, titulum nec nacta Sophie

about the bodies of the wayfarers?   340
With what veil does the poet cloak this cloud?
What meaning has the song of Iopas; what
is signified when ardent Bitias
empties the goblet in one mighty draught?
What sense shall we ascribe to the cruel horse
and Sinon's triumph and the mother clinging
close to the frenzied chief amidst the storm
of flying darts; then, as she disappears
into the night, the vision of the gods
in awesome aspect boding ill to Troy?   350
But why go on? Here you will find no verse
without a double sense. I shall pass over
the others. Does not zealous Horace seem
to indicate the pathway first to left
and then to right in order to give form
to greatness? I shall leave our poets now.(230)
Consider Orpheus, Amphion, Linus, son
of Phoebus, and our ancient sire Musaeus,
and those to whom the marveling Greeks in awe
inscribed their statues; was it childishness   360
that won enduring life for them? And more:
who stands above Euripides the lofty,
and who is greater than great Homer? Say,
how many landscapes and how many ports,
how many shorelines of the twofold sea,
how many straits, how many sea-borne fleets,
how many wars and passions of mankind
and even animals does he not bring
before our eyes, having no eyes himself?
He shows the ways of nations and their chiefs   370
and high above the vulgar herd he set
Ulysses, whom, meseems, he has endowed(240)
with rarest cunning that he might evade
Charybdis and foul Scylla and her cubs,
the Cyclops and the Siren's treacherous notes
and amorous Circe's potions. Why waste words?
Divine Plato, his master Socrates

cetera turba docet, quam quod cantare solemus.

Dicet ad hec aliquis: cur per iuga celsa fatiger?

Huc via fert humilis. Mens delectata laborem

spernit: ad hoc, brevitas memorem succincta relinquit

et dulces iterare sonos iuvat usque legendo.   250

Certus abhinc venie, pueros vocitare memento,

O famose senex, atque inclinare caveto

celeste ingenium et vatum vestigia vita:

insanum genus hoc hominum. Piget illa deinceps

vana sequi: vilis nobis ut parcitur hircus.

Nescio cui merces ea sufficit; est michi fame

immortalis honos et gloria meta laborum.

Corniger at quantum tegat hic sub pellibus hircus

quot nescire putas? — Soccos bonus atque cothurnos. —

Premia Musarum tandem statuisse videris;   260

falleris; est habitus quem secula nostra licenter

postposuisse vides, postquam deferbuit ardor

Pyerius, cessitque retro. Quo nomine signer,

respondere iubes? Anne ad pretoria ventum est?

Iure agitur mecum consignatisque tabellis?

Qui sim, quemve sequar callem, stilus ipse, tacente

me, loquitur. Num plura iubes? Sed epistola finem

longa petit. Dabitur, quam si sonuisse putabis

and all the others who have ever won
the fame of sages teach us nothing else
but what we poets are long wont to sing.   380
Of course someone might here be moved to ask:
"Why should I strive, exhausting all my strength,
to reach the heights? There is an easier path."
Nay, but a mind inspired finds delight
in arduous toil. Crisp brevity will leave
a mindful reader; it is furthermore
a pleasure to repeat harmonious notes(250)
in frequently re-reading. So henceforth,
O libelous elder, now that you are sure
of winning pardon, see that you remember   390
to call all poets children; look with scorn
on heavenly genius and stay far away
from paths trod by the insane breed of bards.
Shameful it were to follow such vain lures:
for us a worthless goat is set apart—
or so you say; there may be some, perhaps
content with such a prize; for me the goal
of effort is the everlasting honor
of glorious fame. How many would you think
are unaware of what this hornèd goat   400
conceals beneath his fleece? Why, sock and buskin!
So finally you think you can define
the Muse's prize? You're wrong again; our times—(260)
now that the Pierian ardor, once a-boil
so hotly, has receded and grown chill—
have put aside such ancient usages.
Now you would bid me to respond and say
By what name I'd be known. Has our case then
come to a court of justice; does the law
require my presence and my documents?   410
Nay, who I am and on what path I tread
my pen makes clear, needing no words from me.
What more would you demand of me? Already
this letter is too long. It craves an end
and will be given it. And if you find

altius, excuser, parcant aures oculique.

Gloria nulla etenim verbis optata superbis,   270

nulla petita mihi. Tua me violentia adegit.

Nec loquor ut lesi vindex Heliconis (an ille

hoc eget auxilio tantis armatus alumnis?)

precipue quia, quo secum pugnare parasti,

plumbeus est gladius, facilique retunditur ictu;

nec velut assertor proprii cognominis arma

Musarum pro parte tuli: sed turpiter illas

maiestate sua sacro spoliarier ausu,

quis tacitus perferre queat? Que perlegis autem

non tibi dicta putes, sed qui te bella movere   280

compulit. Agnosco ingenium, Musisque sacratum

pectus; at externe resonant convitia lingue

in scriptis, dilecte, tuis. Illumque profecto,

quisquis erat, mordax (nunquam tibi cognita pestis)

invidia urebat. Sic nobilis Africa surgat,

sic michi virgineus clause penetralia Cirre

rite chorus reseret, faveatque supernus Apollo!

Tu tamen hoc illi nostris, carissime, verbis

dic, precor, ut quotiens alieno invidit honori,

invideat studiis pulcro invideatque labori.   290

my missive somewhat strident, may I be
forgiven and may those who read or hear
indulge me for I did not strive or hope(270)
for glory by employing haughty words;
your violence compelled me to reply.   420
I speak not to avenge bruised Helicon;
defended by so many foster sons,
the mountain hardly needs to call on me—
especially as the sword you have unsheathed
is leaden and may easily be parried—
nor did I to protect myself take up
arms to defend the Muses. But who could
stand by in silence, seeing them despoiled
most foully of their majesty by bold
and sacrilegious hands? You must not think   430
that what I've said here is addressed to you.
It is intended for the eyes of him
who urged you to attack me. Well I know(280)
your genius and I know your heart to be
devoted to the Muses, but, dear friend,
the insults of a voice that is not yours
are audible in what you've written me.
Whoever he may be, he was consumed,
for sure, by gnawing envy, a disease
that you know nothing of. So, to conclude,   440
let noble *Africa* arise and may
the choir of maidens solemnly throw wide
Cyrrha's sealed portals, may Apollo look
on me benignly from above—and you,
most cherished friend, employ these words of mine
to caution that rash man, reminding him
that every time that he is moved to envy
another's honor, he should envy too
his application and his precious toil.

Notes to the Translation

Numbers refer to line numbers of the translation.
The corresponding lines of the original are in parentheses.

3 (2–3) Petrarch will say much the same in his *Invective contra medicum*, written some
nine years after this letter. There, apologizing to the reader for having spoken
too well of himself and too harshly of his antagonist, he adds: "Magnificentius
fateor, fuisset utrunque contemnere sed rara patientia est, quam non penetret acutum
convitium." (*Invective*, IV. 533–35.)

22 ff. (13 ff.) Virgil died, leaving his *Aeneid* unfinished. Lucan, author of the *Pharsalia*, the subject of which is the war between Caesar and Pompey, committed
suicide at the command of Nero, of whom he had been a protégé; he too left
his epic unfinished. He had "followed a forbidden path" in turning against the
emperor; his poem, in its early part laudatory of his patron, becomes increasingly
anti-imperial. Thus, according to Petrarch, the laurel was withheld from him "for
another reason"; i.e., not only because his work was left incomplete but also because
of Nero's hostility. Tempe is the ancient name of a deep gorge in Thessaly through
which the Peneus flows to the sea; it is mentioned in *Rer. mem.* III.82.2. Nearby
stands the town of Pharsalus where Caesar defeated Pompey (48 B.C.). Petrarch
alludes to the battle in *Rer. mem.* IV.4.6 and 7 and elsewhere; in *Africa* II.238
and in Chapter 22 of his "Life of Caesar" in *De viris illustribus*.

32 (20–21) This affirmation is made also in *Africa* IX.103–5.

43–45 (29–30) Rossetti's original text (II, p. 216) reads: "sunt audita tibi; verum
legit illa Robertus." His correction (III, p. 272) adds a line to the poem.

45 (30) *Robert*: this is Roberto de' Bardi, Chancellor of the University of Paris,
a Florentine. Petrarch had met him when he visited the French capital in 1333.
It was Robert who invited Petrarch to receive the laurel crown in Paris; see *Fam.*
IV.4 where Petrarch also refers to Robert as a "concivis."

47 (31–32) *Iulia . . . Pariseos*: *Iulia* because the city claimed to have been founded
by Julius Caesar (*Fam.* I.4); *Pariseos* is an adjective *sine flexu* (Du Cange). The
designation is also found in Boccaccio, see his *Carmen* III.17 (Massèra, p. 96) and
the *Genealogie deorum* XV.6 (Romano, II, p. 760). The phrase "third great nurse"
is a little ambiguous. Probably Petrarch is thinking historically and putting Paris
after Athens and Rome. If he has his own times in mind perhaps he means Rome
and Florence.

49–51 (34–36) Rossetti (II, p. 409, n. 6) identifies the individuals mentioned as respectively, Enea de' Tolomei of Siena, Rinaldo (Cavalchini) di Villafranca (of Verona,
to whom Petrarch addressed *Fam.* XIII.2, *Sine nomine* XI, and *Ep. met.* II.16), Cardinal Giovanni Colonna, and Barbato da Sulmona. One may have some doubts
about the presence of the cardinal in this roll call. Rossetti writes: ("Il cardinale
Giovanni Colonna suppongo essere il terzo perchè a niun altro potea a quel tempo
convenire l'epiteto *ingens*." Friedensdorff (p. 125, n. 4) concurs. But perhaps a

better case can be made for Giovanni Barrili, the alternate suggested by Fracassetti (n. 4 to *Fam.* XIII. 2; *Lettere*, III, p. 204). The happy days spent with him and Barbato only a few years ago must have been fresh in Petrarch's memory and the association of their names would come naturally to him, particularly if, as these verses seem to hint, they had been privileged to see or hear some lines of the *Africa*. In fact, Petrarch frequently couples Barbato and Barrili: both appear in *Buc. carm.* II; they join with Petrarch (*Ep. met.* II.16) to invite Cavalchini to visit Naples—to mention Barbato here and omit Barrili would have been all but offensive. Nor does *ingens* seem too exalted an epithet for a high official of the Neapolitan court; he is already *magnanimus* in *Fam.* IV.8. One may, incidentally, admire Petrarch's graceful and considerate choice of epithets. John (whichever he be) is "great"; Barbato, to whom the *Metricae* are dedicated, receives the intimate *meus* and Rinaldo, of humbler station, is flattered by the reference to his poetry. Petrarch's argument in this passage is in line with Horace's answer to a critic in *Sat.* I.10.79–91, and the substance of lines 56–70 has something in common, too, with *Odes* III.2.17ff. Petrarch states his elitist position even more baldly in *Invective contra medicum* IV.406–7: " . . . optabam ut essem carus illustribus, vulgo ignotus."

75 (50–51) Possibly an echo of Horace, *Odes* III.30.8–9.

80 (53–54) *Your town*; see below, note to line 99.

91 ff. (60 ff.) The Tiber stands for Rome; Parthenope is Naples. Naso (Ovid) was born in Sulmo (now Sulmona); Flaccus (Horace) in Venusia (now Venosa, province of Potenza). Arpinium (now Arpino, province of Frosinone) was the birthplace of Cicero and Marius. The two are linked also in *Buc. carm.* X.216–19, where it is clear that Petrarch thought that Marius the soldier was also a poet, possibly, Martellotti suspects, (*Laurea occidens*, p. 68), assuming that he is the poet Marius mentioned by Ovid, *Ex ponto* IV.16.24.

99 (64) I have changed the capital C of *Colonia* as Rossetti has it to lower case; I am not sure it is a proper name. Petrarch is ostensibly addressing Lancellotto Anguissola, whose home town was Piacenza—which, therefore, must be the *inepta colonia*. Such is the conclusion of Diana Magrini (p. 112) who hazards the opinion that Petrarch's real critic may have been of the same city. Since we now believe that the calumniator is Brizio Visconti, the identification of the *colonia* is less certain. As both the salutation of the letter and the substance of lines 430 ff. show clearly that Petrarch knew the offensive letter was not written by Anguissola, whom he held in affectionate esteem, it is hard to see why he should want to denigrate the home town of a friend. Were it not that *inepta colonia* and *rustica menia* seem inappropriate terms to apply to the largest and wealthiest city in Italy, one might suspect that Milan was the poet's target. At the time of writing this letter, the laureate was no admirer of the Visconti; his friendship with Luchino, fostered, Ricci suggests (p. 345, n. 1), by Paganino da Bizzozzero, lay a few years in the future. Not to press the argument too far, it is worth noting that Milan is conspicuously absent from the catalogue of North Italian cities that have sheltered poets.

105 (68) Catullus is Verona's poet also in *Rime* CLXVI.4 and in a version of "The

Triumph of Fame," III.82–83 (Martellotti, "Appendice," p. 576); he is paired with Ovid in "The Triumph of Love," IV.22.

106 (69) Rossetti (p. 409, n. 9) sees an allusion to Dante here. But to Friedensdorff (p. 127, n. 2) this seems "unwahrscheinlich"; he believes that Petrarch had in mind poets or humanists who wrote in Latin, perhaps Guglielmo da Pastrengo or Rinaldo Cavalchini (see above, lines 50–51). Since, as Rossetti concedes, Petrarch rarely refers to Dante, one is inclined to agree with the German translator.

108 (70) *Urbs Antenoridum*: Padua, founded by Antenor, fugitive from Troy (*Aeneid* 1.242 ff.), Friedensdorff (p. 127, n. 3) speculates that one of the *alumnos* may be Albertino Mussato, author of the *Ecerinis* and crowned poet in Padua in 1315.

109–10 (71–72) Petrarch's Latin is here difficult to follow; the allusions are obscure and the syntax strained. Rossetti comments (II, p. 409, n. 10): "Nell'espressione di *Cymbria saecula* credo abbracciarsi tutti i bassi tempi, e intendersi quindi accennati quei poeti che in Padova si distinsero per la latina poesia; perciocchè vi si soggiungono subito i *saecula nostra* pel bergamasco Bonatino . . . ." Recently Raffaele Argenio ("Per una edizione critica," p. 489) has proposed another reading. He writes: ". . . La città di Padova è ricordata dapprima mediante una perifrasi dal suo fondatore Antenore, 'la città degli Antenoridi.' Il passo latino, malsicuro anche nella lezione, suona così secondo le Stampe:

> Urbs Antenoridum quantos celebravit alumnos
> Nunc quondam numerare labor, quot Cimbria nuper
> Saecula Pergameum viderunt nostra poetam. . . .

Secondo gli altri manoscritti la lezione più sicura è:

> Urbs Antenoridum quantos celebrarit alumnos
> Nunc quondam etc."

Calling Rossetti's interpretation "ingegnosa" but not "esatta," Argenio continues: "L'aggettivo *cimbria*, secondo me, va riferito a *urbs*. . . . La città dei Cimbri sarebbe Vercelli, detta così dai barbari che la irrorarono del loro sangue ai Campi Raudii. Allo stesso modo che, per significare Padova, il Petrarca pensò a un mitico capostipite fuggiasco da Troia . . . così, per indicare la città di Vercelli, potè pensare all'eccidio dei barbari, ad opera di Mario, avvenimento memorando nella storia. Traduco quindi: 'Costerebbe fatica enumerare ora e prima quanti figli abbia celebrato la città degli Antenoridi, quanti la città dei Cimbri. . . .'"

I find Argenio no less ingenious than Rossetti but not quite so convincing. If Rossetti has quietly amended *quondam* to *quoniam*, that would seem to me not an unreasonable alteration; given that licence, his version is acceptable. Textual matters aside, Argenio's parallel of *Cimbria* and *Antenoridum* seems forced and, more seriously, Vercelli, topographically and otherwise, seems out of place in this *galère*, nor can I readily call to mind any number of poetic *alumnos* of that rugged Piedmontese community. . . . However the reader may judge for himself.

111 ff. (72 ff.) *The bard of Bergamo*: Rossetti (II, p. 409, n. 10), citing Tiraboschi,

identifies this poet as Buono da Castiglione, sometimes called Bonatino or Bonet-
tino, who was crowned in Padua. Tiraboschi (v.3.4.513) does indeed supply the
name and mention the coronation (for which he gives no date). He says that
Buono was a contemporary of Mussato and remarks that it is strange that not
a single verse of such a famous poet has survived. Tiraboschi's comment sounds
like a gloss on these lines, to which indeed he alludes. *Nomine reque bonum* is
an obvious play on the poet's name; *Pergameum* is another verbal artifice, designed to give the town a classical association; the historical Latin name for Bergamo
is Bergomum.

114–16 (75) *alpis . . . ora nivose*: i.e., Northern Italy in general.

118 (76) The birthplace of Macrobius, widely known in the Middle Ages for his
Saturnalia and his commentary on the *Somnium Scipionis*, is not known. There
is no evidence to suggest that he was born in Parma, although such may have
been the pious legend among the *parmigiani*. Friedensdorff (p. 128, n. 2) observes
that there is no trace to-day of the *monumenta*; "kein Wunder, wenn es damals
schon verfallen war."

121 (78) *Cassius*: This is Gaius Cassius Parmensis, one of Caesar's murderers. Horace
(*Ep.* 1.4.3) speaks well of his poetry. Friedensdorff (p. 128, n. 3) cautions us
that the flattering phrase *nec degener* alludes to the verse, not to the politics of
Cassius.

132 (84) Following the suggestion of Professor Williams, I have placed a question
mark at the end of line 184; it clarifies the sense of the passage.

135–36 (86–87) The implication is that Petrarch's antagonist is too dull-witted to
understand anything unless it is repeated. So, but more harshly, the poet will
write to the unnamed doctor (*Invective contra medicum* IV.246–47): "unum tibi
satis inculcare nequeo; nec enim decies repetisse sufficiet."

146–53 (93–98) The king's devotion to study as well as his public praise of Petrarch
are recorded in *Rer. mem.* I.37. The latter item is confirmed by Boccaccio in his
sketch of Petrarch (Massèra, p. 240) but his source is probably the *Rer. mem.*
or possibly this letter.

156 (100–101) The king's request is recorded in *Rer. mem.* III.96.3.

161 (104) Virgil uses *obstupui* (or the variants *obstipuit, obstipuere*) seventeen times
as the initial word of a line in the course of the *Aeneid*; eight times in the first
three books, which Petrarch seems to have had before him in writing this letter;
see below, lines 331–50.

166 (109) Petrarch promises the king such a work in *Africa* I, p. 40 ff. Friedensdorff
(p. 130, n. 1) refers us to *Rer. mem.* III.96.3.

200 (128–29) The years will erode the aggressive complacency of this affirmation.
In "The Triumph of Love" IV.80 Petrarch will admit that the laurel came to
him "forse anzi tempo," and writing to Boccaccio in 1373 (*Sen.* XVII.2) will say
he received it "with leaves immature—when I was not ripe in age or mind."

203 (130) *Vari*: the name appears in the genitive; the nominative could be either
Varus or Varius. Given the position of the syllable in the line, the long *a* of
Varus would seem to make him the more likely choice. Horace (*Odes* 1.18.1)
mentions a friend of that name. Much more famous, however, was Lucilius Varius,

a friend of Horace and Virgil and a poet of eminence, although only a fragment of his work survives. He is mentioned several times by Horace; in *Sat.* 1.10.44 he is spoken of as preeminent in the epic and in *Epp.* II.1.247 and in *Ars poetica* LV his name is linked with Virgil's. Ovid refers to him in *Ex Ponto* IV.16.31; in Petrarch's *Buc. carm.* X.295–300 he appears, though unnamed, and Petrarch praises him in *Invective contra medicum* III.369–70. We may agree with Friedensdorff (p. 131, n. 1) who believes that he is the poet Petrarch has in mind here. There are a number of possible explanations for the false quantity.

207 (133) Here the thought, if not the language, is distinctly Horatian; see *Sat.* 1.10.72 ff.

223 ff. (142–45) On the occasion of his coronation, Petrarch had sensed tears welling in the hearts if not in the eyes of his friends (including Senators) as he rose to speak (*Ep. met.* II.1.43–44). No doubt Robert's eyes were bedewed in the course of his conversation with Petrarch cited above.

236 ff. (151 ff.) See Horace, *Sat.* 1.10.70.

248–49 (160–62) The literary tastes and talents of Caesar and Augustus are discussed in *Rer. mem.* 1.12 and 13. For Augustus see also *Invective contra medicum* III.373–74.

250–56 (162–66) The same notion is expressed at somewhat greater length in *Africa* IX.90–102 and Petrarch returns to the subject in *Sen.* IV.5. Lines 253–56 are closely echoed by Boccaccio in *Genealogie* XIV.9; ultimately the source is Horace, *Ars poetica* CCCXXXIII.

262–63 (171) The sage is Aristotle, whose opinion Petrarch found in Seneca, *De tranquillitate animi* XVII.10. Friedensdorff (p. 133, n. 1) adds that the substance of line 257 *supra* is also found at the end of the same Senecan source.

270 (174) The substitution of a question mark for Rossetti's semi-colon at the end of the Latin line seems advisable.

272–74 (175–77) *amnes* for the original *omnes* at the end of line 175 is Rossetti's correction (III, p. 272). In these lines we may hear the music of the *Canzoniere*. *Rime* CXXIX was composed at about the same time as this letter (Wilkins, *Life*, p. 147). On the shared substance and differing manners of the *Rime* and the *Metricae*, see Giovanni Ponti, "Poetica e poesia," p. 215 ff. Ugo Dotti, "La formazione," p. 538, notes the thematic and formal affinities between *Rime* I and *Ep. met.* I.40–70. Raffaele Argenio, "Gli autori congeniali," p. 458, points out the link with Horace's *Epp.* II.2.76–77.

274 (178) The reference here is to Plato, who in his *Republic* (X.605) would exclude poets from his ideal city—a dictum that has always been embarrassing to defenders of the Muse. In *Invective contra medicum* III.274–78 Petrarch calls on Augustine for help in proving that Plato didn't mean *all* poets. Boccaccio, following his master, is sure that Plato would not have barred poets like Homer, Virgil—or Petrarch (*Genealogie* XIV.19).

276–78 (179–80) I have altered Rossetti's *vos* and *vestris* to *nos* and *nostris*. As lines 173–74 of the Latin—and also line 188 below—clearly indicate, Petrarch is including himself among the poets. Mancini's rather free translation evades the problem. Friedensdorff (p. 133), although with no allusion to the text, rightly translates:

> Dass wusste wohl der Weise, der zuerst
> Der Staaten Wohl zu ordnen unternahm
> Dass wir des Volkes Bräuchen, dass das Volk
> Den unsern feindlich sein und bleiben wird.

293 (189) An echo of Virgil: *Aen.* III.188 and XII.153.

294–95 (189–90) The reference is to *Metaphysics* I.3.983b, 28–30. It is also cited by Boccaccio, *Genealogie* XV.8.

295–98 (190–92) Friedensdorff (p. 134, n. 2) refers us to *Pro Archia* VIII.18 and *De natura deorum* II.66.167, noting that the first is quoted from Ennius.

303–4 (195–96) Following Horace *Odes* IV.8 and 9 (especially lines 25–30).

319–22 (207–9) Rossetti's original text (II, p. 232) reads: "Hic tamen occurret Cherilus vel (Aquinus ait) qui." In his "Varianti e correzioni" (III, p. 272), he amends it to read as we have set it here. He adds (n. 3), "Sono indicate tre classi di poeti 1, i bassi adulatori in Cherilo; 2, i satirici in Giovenale (*Aquinius*) [with reference to Aquinium, birthplace of the satirist]; 3, i poeti osceni." This seems a reasonable gloss, although we may note that elsewhere (*Invective contra medicum* III.371) Petrarch speaks approvingly of Juvenal. Mancini, translating Rossetti's original version is rather free: "Ma qui risponde Aquin: laudi e mercedi / Il vate ottenga, e Cherili faranno / Sorgere." Friedensdorff (p. 135, l. 315 and n. 1) seems to be unaware of Rossetti's correction and assumes that *Aquinus* is St. Thomas Aquinas, here speaking for the scholastic philosophy that would condemn poetry as immoral. But, aside from ignoring Rossetti's emendation, a reference to the Angelic Doctor would be unlikely in this context. Choerilus is the poetaster who was rewarded beyond his deserts by Alexander the Great; see Horace *Epp.* II.1.233 and *Ars poetica* 357. Petrarch speaks of him in *Buc. carm* X.171–75.

331–50 (215–26) On this passage see *Sen.* IV.5 in Appendix below.

349 (225–26) Since we know the scene in the *Aeneid* referred to here, a translation is not difficult. But Petrarch's Latin is faulty. Professor Williams suggests a line may be missing as in lines 20–21 of the Latin *supra*.

353 (228) Horace indicates (*mostrare*) these paths as to be avoided, recommending the middle way. I believe that Petrarch has in mind here not only Horatian moderation and discretion in general but specifically as well *Sat.* II.3.50–51: "ille sinistrorsum, hic dextrorsum abit, unus utrique / error, sed variis illudit partibus."

360 (234) The Latin line owes something to Horace; see *Odes* III.24.28.

362 (235) Euripides is mentioned in conjunction with Homer also in *Africa* IX.65–67; in a draft of "The Triumph of Fame" III.58–59 (Martellotti, "Appendice," p. 575) he is bracketed with Sophocles: "duo nobili tragedi." Petrarch knew him only by reputation.

363–69 (236–39) In *Rer. mem.* Petrarch reveals the source of his comment here: Cicero, *Tusculanum* (v.39.14). A similar passage occurs in *Africa* IX.189–99.

371 ff. (240 ff.) On the significance of Ulysses, see *Rer. mem.* III.87.

377–80 (244–46) This is the conclusion to which Petrarch's arguments have been tending: poetry is equated with philosophy. In the happy paraphrase of the cav. Lorenzo Mancini: "Canta il vate / Quel che insegna il filosofo." Boccaccio makes the same statement in *Genealogie* XIV.17 and 18. Petrarch will claim yet more for poetry; writing to his brother Gherardo some four years later (*Fam.* X.4.1) he will affirm: "the fact is, poetry is very far from being opposed to theology. One may almost say that theology is poetry, poetry concerning God." (Robinson and Rolfe, trans., *Petrarch*, p. 261).

389 (252) *famose senex*: If Petrarch's antagonist is Brizio Visconti he can hardly be *senex*. But Petrarch does not know—or affects not to know—whom he is addressing, and the term gives weight to his irony.

395 (255) These lines allude to the belief that the prize for tragedy (goat song) was originally awarded to the winning contestant. See Horace, *Ars poetica* 220, from which comes Petrarch's "vilis . . . hircus." Rossetti's *parcitur* is a correction; his original text reads *pascitur* (II, p. 238); in a note on his alteration he adds that *parcitur* signifies "è riservato, si tiene in serbo per noi."

401 (259) sock and buskin: the light shoe and the heavy boot worn by actors in Greek comedy and tragedy respectively. Here they stand for achievement (or recognition) in the art of poetry.

408–9 (264) Friedensdorff (p. 138, n. 2) refers us to Cicero, *Tusculanum* v.11.33.

425 (275) The leaden sword is also Ciceronian: see *Ad Atticum* I.16 (Friedensdorff, p. 138, n. 3).

430 ff. (279 ff.) Here Petrarch directly addresses his friend Anguissola, implying that he was aware all the time that the letter sent over the latter's signature was falsely signed.

Appendix:

The Letter to Federico

Note: In lines 331–50 (215–26) of *Epistola metrica* II.10, Petrarch is illustrating by example his statement in lines 251–56 (163–66) concerning the dual function of poetry. Undeniably the figures and episodes cited from the first books of the *Aeneid* are of such nature as to delight the simple-minded reader looking for a good story. The truths under the veil, meant for sophisticated students, may not be immediately apparent to readers less acute than Petrarch. They were certainly not clear to his young friend Federico of Arezzo, who, sometime between 1365 and 1367 (Wilkins, *Petrarch's Correspondence*, p. 97) wrote the master, asking for illumination. Petrarch's reply (*Sen.* IV.5) notes apologetically that the kind of exercise Petrarch is here indulging in was current in the poet's time when the classics were read with an eye to their hidden meanings. Such is the mutability of taste that we today readily accept Petrarch's interest in these matters, so embarrassing to Fracassetti. The poet works here, one may say, in the tradition of Fulgentius and Bernard Sylvestris (see Comparetti, chapters 5–8), but the moral meanings he uncovers seem to be his own. Aside from its value as a gloss on *Ep. met.* II.10, the letter to Federico is an excellent specimen of allegory hunting, undertaken with assurance and carried out with scrupulous thoroughness.

The *epistola*, bearing the title "On the moral truths hidden in Virgil's *Aeneid*," begins with a reference to a *carmen* which Petrarch says he wrote years ago, "in haste and the heat of passion"; it had been occasioned by Petrarch's desire to defend Virgil's poetry against the attacks of a certain unnamed "monster of envy." The poet's language suggests that the altercation was originally oral and not epistolary; he says nothing of receiving a falsely signed letter; to be sure, it was a long time ago and Petrarch avows he has forgotten much of what he said. However the text of *Sen.* IV.5 makes it plain that he has the letter to Brizio in mind. After some preliminary matter, interesting in itself but not to our purpose here, Petrarch addresses himself to Federico's questions.[1]

Take up that letter which impelled you to inquire about such matters and, bearing in mind what I remember having written in it, look at Virgil, whose cause I maintained against that calumniator. In that divine poem, the last the poet wrote but recognized as the first and noblest by all whose lips have approached the Castalian spring, he signifies something loftier than what he says. On which account I maintained at the time of writing my letter (nor do I in any way retract my statement now) that in that poet's work there is probably no verse that does not conceal a hidden meaning and, without going into greater length, I shall reply to your questions. If I should happen to add more than you ask for, you may be grateful to my generous spirit; if on the other hand I should omit something, I know that in view of my many concerns you will hold me excused.

Beginning then with those dark brothers whom Virgil speaks of as subject to the command of Aeolus, you must think of them as the winds. They are brothers because all have a common father: the air. They are dark because of the whirlwinds, squalls, dust storms, clouds and hail which they stir up with their contrasting blasts. Brothers they are but ever raging and quarrelsome and rebellious against their father. Now the real Aeolus reigned over the nine islands that are called Aeolian after him; they lie off the coast of Sicily, battered by the incessant fury of the winds. Aeolus, either through experience or some kind of art, is said to have had such knowledge of the winds that he could, by the color and nature of the air, predict the imminent onslaught of the gales from the mountaintops or the soon approaching diminution of their violence. On this account he was held to be, and therefore called, the king of the winds, not only by the ignorant and marveling folk but also even by the poets and first of all by Homer who in an exquisite fiction said that Aeolus had enclosed the winds in a leather pouch and given this to Ulysses as he wandered over the ocean [*Odyssey* x.19–20]. So the natural, historical sense is clear to all. In addition, there are those who look for a moral sense, for every man has his own purpose in mind to which he applies the strength of his intellect; so it falls out that from one same thing, according to the various uses to which it is put, different profits emerge; as Annaeus says, into the same meadow comes the ox in search of grass, the dog chasing the rabbit, and the stork in pursuit of the lizard [*Epp. morales ad Lucilium* 108–29]. To look for both senses in every passage, with the moral and material meaning linked from beginning to end, would be an exhausting task, as assuredly not even the poets who composed the works had any such intention. But, leaving others aside, let us turn to Virgil, the subject of your enquiries.

In my opinion the subject of his poem is the perfect man; this is what his verses are meant to depict. And inasmuch as such perfection, either solely or principally, has its basis in virtue, I believe it is useful to look for the moral sense in his poem, both because this is the most precious thing in life and because a reader who seeks it is following the intention of the poet. And what I say of him I say also of Homer, for with matching stride both follow the same path.

Coming now to your question about the passage aforementioned I shall tell you that it seems to me that those winds are figures of the passions, the impetuous impulses of concupiscence and wrath that, rising from the depths of our hearts, even as a storm that stirs up the quiet sea, arouse a tumult in our emotions and thoroughly disturb the serenity of our lives. Aeolus, as I see him, can stand for nothing other than Reason, determined to restrain our impulses and appetites, for, left unchecked, these would drag blood, flesh and bone (our mortal part) and eventually the soul (of divine origin) to the brink of death, even as Virgil says of the winds: "maria et terras caelumque profundum" [*Aeneid* 1.58]. As for the gloomy caverns in which the winds lurk, what else can they be but the dark and hidden recesses of a man's heart and bowels, where, according to Platonic doctrine, the passions have their seat? The superimposed mass refers to the head, which Plato himself saw as the seat of reason. Aeneas represents the strong and perfect man of whom I spoke earlier. Achates stands for the precious "company" of such men: care, solicitude and industry. This life of ours is imaged in the wood[2] full of pitfalls and shadows and tortuous and treacherous pathways and inhabited by beasts, which is to say beset with many trials and perils, sterile and inhospitable, yet sometimes attractive to those who pass through it or dwell in it since they are deceived and for a while delighted by the greenery of the leaves, the songs of the birds, and the murmurings of the springs—figures and images of our transient hopes and our false and fleeting pleasures. Aye, and the deeper you penetrate, the more thorny and tangled the jungle becomes; as winter approaches it becomes desolate, choked with fallen trunks and bristling with ugly, defoliated branches.[3] Venus, who comes towards you in the very midst of the wood [*Aeneid* 1.314] is lust, which, precisely when we are in the middle of life's journey, tempts and assails us with greatest violence. She has the semblance and garb of a virgin [1.315] and this is to deceive the ignorant for if they could see her in her proper aspect the sight would suffice to drive them away in horror, for as nothing in appearance is more beautiful so in substance nothing is more foul than lust. And she is described as "naked to the knee and with garments gathered in a knot" [1.320] to indicate how swiftly she runs away, for there is nothing more fleeting and evanescent than this passion; considered generally or particularly it very swiftly passes; even its operation lasts but a moment. She is dressed as a huntress because she goes hunting for souls; she flexes her bow while at the same time tossing her hair in the wind [1.318–19] so that she may simultaneously tempt and wound, always flighty and inconstant like the wind. The poet calls her a friend of the Trojans, either because her cult was more devoutly practiced in Troy than elsewhere or because of the kinds of life described by the poets—that of wisdom and study sacred to Pallas, that of power and riches sacred to Juno, and that of lust and licentiousness sacred to Venus—the Trojans had opted for the third. That Trojan who served as judge, as he had shown himself discreet in his dealing with animals, revealed himself unjust and foolish in a matter of graver importance. For, called upon to give his judgment in the famous contest of the three goddesses I have mentioned, he followed passion rather than reason and gave his verdict to naked Venus; for which, as a fitting reward, he obtained a passing pleasure which was followed by long travails, a sequence of countless evils, and ultimately his own death along with that of all his kin and the slaughter of his entire nation. Withal Aeneas is called the son of Venus because even great men are generated through lust or because he had such rare beauty of person that even in exile and poverty he is depicted as pleasing to chaste eyes. And it was Venus too who, having preserved her son uninjured through great calamities, saving him from fire and shipwreck, brought him, veiled in a dark cloud [1.411 ff.] and accompanied only by Achates, into the presence of a beautiful widow. And under that cloud there is hidden also a great truth: that is, that often when the fair renown of a man reaches our ears or when we hear of such a man in need of help, we begin to love him under the pretext of esteem or courtesy or compassion; then, when we perceive his merit, his nobility and his beauty, the veil is torn asunder and our first sentiments turn into shameless love. And sometimes he too will yield; so even the hero Aeneas succumbs because, however great his virtue may be, a man finds it difficult to resist the allures of beauty, especially if he is aware of having aroused love and desire for him. Indeed, as Jerome says, it is impossible that his body's natural heat should not some times assail a man [*Ad Eustochium, Ep.* XXII.7].

Now to answer your question I shall say first that in the banquet given [by Dido] we are shown how subjects are cared for and nurtured as they should be by magnates and kings, whom we see in our own days stripping and devouring them. At this banquet, that is to say, this human association presided over by royalty, three kinds of men are seated: first the kings themselves who should lead everyone in the study of eloquence and doctrine; these are figured in Iopas [*Aeneid*, 1.740–41] who tells the secrets of nature, a function proper to a philosopher, wherefore he is long-haired and likewise he sings and plays the lyre, which is the office of a poet. Next there are places for the lustful and greedy, who are figured to us in Bitias [1.738–39], who gulps a draught from the golden goblet proffered him by the queen, thus indicating how lust, as a stream from a fountain, is poured down from kings to their subjects. At this noisy banquet the heroic and virtuous man also sits; he takes pleasure in the consciousness of his achievements and with magnificent words he delights the audience. He begins as if constrained to speak and the confused babble of the guests suddenly falls still; then he continues while all listen to him in attentive silence [II.1–9]. And what does he speak of? Why, naught else but the offenses of Fortune, the snares of men, the injuries of this mortal life, the subversive stratagems devised by our passions to subject and enslave the spirit. He tells of the idle dreaming of those who lie in slothful slumber in the midst of perils, of schemes frustrated by the sudden appearance of light, of the faith given to false counsel and withheld from the true; of the portal that falls shattered by the battering ram of sin and of the enemies that break in, slain on the threshold, and of the guardians standing watch in defense of the soul. In sum, he depicts life as similar to a dark night which mortals spend in mindless pleasures while Death fiercely strikes, cutting down the lower orders of mankind; mingling with them, the just and the pious also succumb—aye, and great kings as well are carried away in the general slaughter. And [he tells] of how in the midst of this carnage [the hero], facing the gravest dangers, must turn his back on the solaces of his fatherland, now falling to ruin, and he tells of the loss of his first wife (signifying his putting aside the lust that had been his companion in earlier years) and of how armed with his virtue and at first all alone but later followed by many who became his comrades, carrying his old father on his back and leading his little son by the hand, he miraculously survives and happily sets off towards the goal where, adorned by double right with the name of pious, we see him, with felicitous outcome of his trials, ultimately arrive. All this tumult and ruin, this carnage, in which, amidst the flames fired by licentiousness and the swords brandished by wrath, the lustful city is consumed by its own passion—all this is properly figured as taking place at night, signifying the shadows of human errors and the obscurity under which our life, buried in sleep and wine, is submerged in drunkenness and forgetfulness.

And the monstrous horse, full of armed foemen, which in that same dreadful night was brought into the city through open walls and with no impediment of prudence, may be easily explained as signifying the onset of civil discord, always rich in concealed hatreds and source of evils. The ill-omened device was constructed to the destruction of the fatherland by a young man and the justice of youths and adolescents,[4] of itself a destroyer of cities. The holy man Laocoön, striving to prevent the horse being brought into the city, entangled in the coils of serpents and the venomous knots of the envious, is overcome. With his removal, the insane mob with unanimous accord rushes headlong to its own ruin and the ominous monster is placed within the holy citadel, as the place of reason is usurped by passion, than which nothing is more conducive to our ruin. Then at last the fatal horse opens and from it come forth the evils hidden within; among many others Ulysses (hostile cunning) and Neoptolemus (that is, arrogance and the desire for revenge), and Menelaus (that is, the bitter rancor born of the memory of offenses suffered), and finally Sinon himself, custodian of that fatal hiding place and its pestilential advocate (that is, dissimulation and perjury and fraud, breaking into the open with all its wiles and its concealed evils). So in that vast whirlwind of things, with, as I have said, kings and sons of kings brought down along with the people, only the hero manages to escape, either to rest as in the case of Antenor, of whom it was written "placida compostus pace quiescit" [1.249], or to go on to a glorious labor, as in the case of Aeneas, of whom it is written "bellum ingens geret Italia" [1.262] and also "sublimemque feres ad sidera caeli / magnanimum Aenean" [1.259-60].

Now, as he was wandering confused within the walls of the burning city, it befell that by the light of the flames (that is, illuminated by his miseries) [the hero] caught sight of Helen, the first cause of so much woe, and although the verses that tell of this were taken out of the divine poem, we know that Aeneas was preparing to kill her, thus avenging the destruction of his fatherland, when the goddess Venus, appearing before him, stayed his hand and started to make excuses for Helen and Paris.[5] And it is surely no matter for wonder that Venus speaks in defense of venereal pleasures since even rigid censors are often indulgent to love. The goddess also points out to the hero that his purpose is useless because it is too late; it is pointless to remove the cause when the effect has already followed; nor is there, furthermore, any remedy against the inevitable judgment of God. She urges him to think rather of flight than of vengeance;

in desperate straits it is better to yield to Fortune rather than to offer vain resistance. [She adds that] she herself will be his companion in flight until he comes to safety. (This signifies that even heroes love to be rescued from dangers, provided that they have in no way neglected their duty — and likewise that they are saved by love.) So saying, Venus fades from her son's vision because, amidst the dangers and trials of life, lust, the friend of leisure and idleness, has no place. It is true that the goddess returns later and presents herself as his companion on his journey; this, however, is not the earlier Venus but [signifies] rather the wholesome delight that is born of finding oneself in safety and brought to salvation. And as soon as Venus leaves him the hero sees the wrathful divinities, Neptune, Juno, Pallas and Jove, because if the Greeks have triumphed over the Trojans their victory must be credited to their skill in the arts of navigation, their military prowess, their learning and above all to the favor of Jove who protected them. And the hero had well foreseen this when he said "excessere omnes, adytis arisque relictis, / di quibus imperium hoc steterat" [II.351–52]; now with the lifting of the cloud that had blurred his vision he saw clearly with his own eyes what he had earlier divined in thought. This in virtue of the famous affirmation of Plato followed by Augustine and many others that there is nothing that so much distracts a man from the contemplation of God as Venus and a life given over to pleasure. And probably Plato received this true and solemn lesson from another sovereign philosopher, though one of less renown. I mean Architas of Tarentum. I have in mind precisely the discourse he held with Pontius Brennius, father of that Pontius, famed for his prudence, who, as leader of the Samnites, surrounded the Roman army and compelled it to pass under the yoke. Plato was present at that colloquy, as Tully assures us in his *Cato*, and among the many fair observations made on that occasion this one above all is most memorable: where licentiousness reigns temperance is not possible and in the realm of lust there is no room for virtue. [*De senectute* XII.39–41]. And since of that lust spiritual blindness is born we can readily understand that once it is put aside clear vision returns: "apparent dirae facies inimicaque Troiae / numina magna deum" [II.622–23].

Here then is what I have been able to put together by way of answer to your question. Having a lively and perspicacious wit, you will know how to find many other things like these in other parts of the poem.

* * * * * * * * * * * * * *

Notes to the Letter to Federico

1. My translation follows, as best it can, the text of the Basel edition of the *Opera omnia*, 1564, vol. II. pp. 867–74, which abounds in typographical errors and faulty punctuation. Nor does Fracassetti's Italian version (*Lett. sen.* I, pp. 240–58) always provide reliable guidance.

2. In the Virgilian wood of *Aeneid* I there is no atmosphere of menace and no wild beasts. The nature of the forest and its fauna as here glossed strongly suggest another "selva oscura."

3. The notion of a woodland at first attractive and then menacing is developed in Boccaccio's *Corbaccio*.

4. The text reads: "hanc machinam, quam patriae in excidium ephoebus seu ephoeborum atque adolescentium iustitia fabricata est." *Iustitia* is a puzzling word; in the context it can only be ironic. Fracassetti translates it as *malizia*. It may well be that Petrarch actually wrote *inscitia* ("witlessness"). The repetition of *ephoebus . . . ephoeborum* is strange too; one may suspect that *ephoebus* should be *Epeos*, described (II.264) as *ipse doli fabricator*. The fecklessness of youth is apparent in the *pueri . . . innuptaeque puellae* who rejoice as they drag the horse within the walls (II.138–39).

5. The reference here is to the "Helen episode" (II.567–88). These lines are not found in the best MSS, and, according to Servius, were removed from the poem by Virgil's editors after his death. Most modern editors print them, with varying degrees of confidence in their authenticity.

* * * * * * * * * * * * * *

List of works cited
Details of publication are supplied where pertinent.

Argenio, Raffaele. "Gli autori congeniali al Petrarca nelle 'Epistole metriche.'" *Convivium*, XXXIII. 1965, pp. 449–64.

———. "Per una edizione critica delle 'Epistole Metriche' del Petrarca." *Convivium*, XXIX. 1961, pp. 482–89.

Aristotle. *Metaphysics*.

Bergin, Thomas G. *Petrarch's Bucolicum Carmen*. New Haven-London: Yale University Press, 1974.

Bianchi, Ernesto. "Le epistole metriche del Petrarca." *Annali della Scuola*

Normale di Pisa. Serie II, n. 9 (1940), 251–66.

Billanovich, Giuseppe, ed. *Francesco Petrarca: Rerum memorandarum libri*. Florence: Sansoni, 1945.

Boccaccio, Giovanni. *Carmina*; see Massèra.

――――.*Corbaccio*.

――――.*Genealogie deorum gentilium*; see Romano.

Cicero. *Ad Atticum*.

――――. *De natura deorum*.

――――. *De senectute*.

――――. *Pro Archia*.

――――. *Tusculanum*.

Comparetti, Domenico. *Virgilio nel medio evo*. Vol I. Florence: Bernardo Sieber, 1896.

Dotti, Ugo. "La formazione dell' umanesimo nel Petrarca (Le 'Epistole metriche')." *Belfagor*, XXIII, No. 5 (1968), 352–63.

Du Cange, Charles du Fresne, Sieur. *Glossarium mediae et infimae Latinitatis*. Parisiis: Firmin Didot Fratres, 1840–50.

Festa, Nicola, ed. *Francesco Petrarca: l'Africa*. Florence: Sansoni, 1926.

Foresti, Arnaldo. *Aneddoti della vita di Francesco Petrarca*. Brescia: Vannini, 1928.

Fracassetti, Giuseppe, trans. *Lettere di Francesco Petrarca delle cose familiari libri ventiquattro, lettere varie libro unico, etc.* 5 vols. Florence: Le Monnier, 1863–67.

――――. *Lettere senili di Francesco Petrarca, etc.* 2 vols. Florence: Le Monnier, 1869–70.

Friedensdorff, F. *Franz Petrarcas Poetische Briefe in Versen übersetzt und mit Anmerkungen*. Halle a. d. S., 1903.

Horace. *Ars poetica*.

――――. *Epistles (Epp.)*.

――――. *Odes*.

――――. *Satires (Sat.)*.

Lucan. *Pharsalia*.

Magrini, Diana. *Le epistole metriche di Francesco Petrarca*. Rocca S. Casciano: Cappelli, 1907.

Martellotti, Guido, ed. "Appendice ai Trionfi," in *Francesco Petrarca: Rime, Trionfi e poesie latine*. Milan-Naples: Ricciardi, 1951.

――――, ed. *Laurea occidens: Francesco Petrarca Bucolicum carmen* X. Rome: Storia e Letteratura, 1968.

Massèra, Francesco. "Carmina quae supersunt." *Giovanni Boccaccio: Opere latine minori*. Bari: Laterza, 1928.

Mussato, Albertino. *Ecerinis*.

Neri, Ferdinando, ed. *Le Rime* and *I Trionfi*, in *Francesco Petrarca: Rime, Trionfi e poesie latine*. Milan-Naples: Ricciardi, 1951.

Nolhac, Pierre de. *Pétrarque et l'humanisme*, Nouvelle ed. 2 vols. Paris: Champion, 1907.

Ovid. *Ex Ponto*.

Petrarca, Francesco. *Africa*; see Festa.

————. *De viris illustribus*.

————. *Epistole metriche (Ep. met.)*; see Rossetti.

————. *Epistole sine nomine*.

————. *Familiares (Fam.)*; see Rossi, Fracassetti.

————. *Invective contra medicum*; see Ricci.

————. *Rerum memorandarum libri (Rer. mem.)*; see Billanovich.

————. *Opera omnia*. Basel, 1554.

————. *Rime*; see Neri.

————. *Seniles (Sen.)*; see Fracassetti.

————. *Trionfi*; see Neri, Martellotti.

Plato. *Republic*.

Ponti, Giovanni. "Poetica e poesia nelle 'Metriche' del Petrarca." *La rassegna della letteratura italiana*, Serie VII (1918), 209–19.

Ricci, P. G. "Il Petrarca e Brizio Visconti," *Leonardo*, XVI (1947), 337–45.

————, ed. *Francesco Petrarca; Invective contra medicum*. Rome: Storia e Letteratura, 1950.

Robinson, James Harvey, and Henry Winchester Rolfe. *Petrarch; The First Modern Scholar and Man of Letters*. New York: Putnam, 1898.

Romano, Vincenzo, ed. *Giovanni Boccaccio: Genealogie deorum gentilium*. 2 vols. Bari: Laterza, 1951.

Rossetti, Domenico, ed. *Francisci Petrarchae poemata minora quae extant omnia*. 3 vols. Milan: Societas Typographica Classicorum Italiae Scriptorum, 1829–34.

Rossi, Vittorio, ed. *Francesco Petrarca: Le Familiari*. 3 vols. Florence: Sansoni, 1933–37.

Sapegno, Natalino. *Il Trecento*. Milan: Vallardi, 1938.

Seneca. *Ad Lucilium*.

————. *De tranquillitate animi*.

Tiraboschi, Girolamo. *Storia della letteratura italiana*. Rome, 1783.

Virgil. *Aeneid.*
———. *Georgics.*
Vitruvius. *De Architectura.*
Wilkins, E. H. *The "Epistolae metricae" of Petrarch.* Rome: Storia e Letteratura, 1956.
———. *Life of Petrarch.* Chicago: University of Chicago Press, 1961.
———. *Petrarch's Correspondence.* Padua: Antenore, 1960.

The Adynaton in Petrarch's Sestinas

MARIANNE SHAPIRO

I N NEARLY ALL OF PETRARCH'S ITALIAN POEMS, there is a preoccupation
with the forces of nature and their contrast with human mortality.
Although as a Christian writer he invariably defended the idea of a
created universe, from the wealth of argumentation he provides in works
such as the treatise *De sui ipsius et multorum ignorantia* we may infer that
he thought intensively about universal beginning and ending. It is in his
sestinas that Petrarch expresses in form and content the persistence of both
human and universal temporal cycles. For the sestina form contains a very
high proportion of recurrence (*versus!*), that of the rhyme-words and of
their order within strophes. In addition, the very strictness of the form
orients it firmly to the past: that of its invention in Provençal, that of
the accumulated meanings of the repeated rhyme-words, and especially
in the case of Petrarch, the past of the myth the poem is recounting.

The form invented by Arnaut Daniel and transmitted substantially as
he made it constituted a play of homonymic equivalences with a concomitant prevalence of semantic significance over lexical values. It is composed
of thirty-nine lines: six strophes of six lines each and a *tornada* (or *envoi*)
of three lines. The final rhyme-word of each strophe is repeated as the
initial rhyme-word of the following one, for the same set of rhyme-words
is used in a rigorously determined order in six of the seven strophes. The

rhyme-words if numbered 1 2 3 4 5 6 in the first strophe are reordered to form the sequence 6 1 5 2 4 3 in the succeeding one, and so on, each building from the last. The formula is invariant for every strophe. The *Leys d'amor* characterizes as *coblas capcaudadas* all such as these, which repeat the last rhyme-word of a strophe at the beginning of the next one. The complex itinerary of the poem constitutes a dazzling map of variations and permutations of the rhyme-words.

My study is concerned with repetition as a principle of structure in Petrarch's sestinas having wider implications for the whole of the *Canzoniere*. It is my contention that the use of *adynata* — or *impossibilia* — as an important part of figural speech in the sestinas, and particularly at their conclusion, comprises a fundamental aspect of their composition. It breaks through the cycles of repetition (for the sestinas, that of the rhyme-words) to provide an ending that is semantic as well as purely formal in nature. In other words, the *adynaton* becomes in Petrarch the expression of final time and the culmination of the long meditation on the mystery of temporality that is condensed in the sestina form itself. By analogy with the impossibility-figure, especially that of the "sooner-than" type (expressing the thought that the impossible will come true sooner than that which is mentioned in the second part of the figure), the lover's ambition, that of winning Laura, is "impossible." Thus the deployment of the poet's Orphic powers enters the discourse, the better to reverse *in the poem* the implacable course of time. Whereas the *impossibilia* are such within nature, they are possible within the realm of poetic speculation and therefore *sub specie aeternitatis*. Only outside of nature does Petrarch imagine the end of time both as cycle and as linear progression, or replication. In the process of describing and illustrating Petrarch's use of the *adynaton*, which is especially prevalent in the sestinas, I will touch upon two cardinal structures of repetition in the *Canzoniere* which are significantly challenged and end-stopped by *adynata*: the replication of individual words within lines and in identical rhyme, and the theoretically perpetual recounting of the lover's myth.

The procedure of *retrogradatio cruciata* is based on repetition and inversion. The first principle shows the utilization of units representable as 1, 2, inverted by the second principle 1, 2 (2, 1). The layering of the two units 1, 1 and 2, 2 into a crossed figure shows an *emboîtement des structures*, a double dynamic of reversal and layering:

This kind of stepped construction is conducive to a simultaneity of un-folding and recurrence. Now the two complex units 1 2 3 and 4 5 6 may be perceived as super-imposed upon one another in the following order:

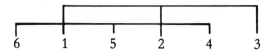

Insofar as the movement of rhyme-words goes in pairs, the strophe is des-tined to remain uncentered. The distribution of rhyme-words from alter-nate ends of the strophe reveals the formation of pairs of digits, each with seven as their sum (6 & 1; 5 & 2; 4 & 3). It is the number of eternity and mutability, of the temporal sublunary world and the world of the eternal Sabbath.

The poem concludes with a half-strophe which manifests all the rhyme-words, generally, but not always, in the order of their first appearance.

The recurrent pattern of rhyme-words in a sestina is often emphasized by endstopped lines. Although enjambment occasionally diminishes the perceived effect of the rhyme-word endings, a sequential reading of the poem produces a recognition of temporal measurement. As the reader picks up new meanings for the rhyme-words, the poem's drive toward its end is semantically both encumbered and accelerated in his expectations. For the troubadour who invented the sestina form, the final half-strophe, or *tornada*, bestowed integrity upon the completed experience of the song. The *tornada* of a Provençal lyric was normally addressed to a listener or listeners who might be the poet's beloved or patron, or both. It generally reproduced the rhymes of the second half of the preceding strophe, and often had an epigrammatic character that conveyed finality or dismissal. It could also affirm nothing but the identity of the song's addressee. The expressive qualities of this ending might imply epistemological attitudes which reach far beyond the specific topics of the poem. Well after the habitual practice of apostrophizing or simply naming the recipient of the poem had ended, the *tornada* survived in the Italian *canzone* and in all sestinas. Through the rhyme-word scheme of its composition, the sestina draws its *tornada* formally and semantically into the rest of the poem. It can recapitulate, contradict or place in doubt the preceding material. And since it had lost its social and pragmatic function essentially before the time of Petrarch, we may posit that it is otherwise pivotal to the sestina's closure. The fact that it is a half-strophe points to an ending, but not a symmetrical one. The circle described by the six full strophes is, thus, not quite closed, for the arrangement of the rhyme-words in no fixed order within the *tornada* betokens a break in the structure. The *tornada* in the Petrarchan sestina is simultaneously the indicator of an ending and the place in which the order of the rest of the poem is dispersed. Petrarch uses it accordingly to concentrate his projections of the "seventh day" (corresponding to the seventh strophe), or of the future. Even as it concludes the linear sequence of the strophes, it is the marker of infinite openness.

In the *tornada*, Petrarch's expression of final time may indeed revolutionize the course of the poem. Though natural imagery may continue to serve as his vehicle, the event of the poem's completion falls out of the cycle. In the *tornada* lies the eschatology of the poem. And the motif of "eternal return," that of the amorous myth echoing Apollo's and Daphne's, as well as that of the sestina-scheme, cedes to the motif of "the end of the world."

The sense of catastrophe often conveyed by this ending is evinced by Petrarch's frequent practice of conferring on the *tornada* the semantic function of the figure *adynaton*. We shall note the presence of *adynata* — "impossibility" figures — elsewhere in his sestinas. Five of the nine poems composed in this form contain them. In two, the *tornada* is occupied by an *adynaton* (XXII and CCXXIX); in another, the *adynaton* occurs in the two lines preceding the *tornada* (CCXXXVII). Petrarch utilizes the "impossibilia" — a daylight filled with stars, breezes gathered in a net — to affirm the fixity of desire over and above external obstacles (such as the cruelty of Laura). In this pattern his imitators are conspicuously inclined to follow suit. The figure, as it occurs in final position, refers to a moment that is impossible within the human understanding of time. Sometimes it could be functionally replaced in a paraphrase by the word "never":

Ma io sarò sotterra 'n secca selva,

> E 'l giorno andrà pien di minute stelle,
> Pria ch'a sì dolce alb' arrivi 'l sole.

(xxii.37–39: But I shall be below earth in dry wood and the day
filled with myriad stars before the sun arrives at so sweet a dawn.)

The above lines refer to the impossibility of Laura's *addoucissement* inasmuch
as it corresponds to that of the reversibility of time. Nevertheless they
also convey, in the magical sense that Jakobson called "the incantatory
function of poetry," an invocation to history to abolish itself *in the future*.

In the New Testament final time is announced to the people via *adynata*,
which are expressed as wonders to come. In prophecies of the end of the
world it is announced that as the end approaches, the year will be shortened,
the month will diminish the number of its days, and the day itself will
contract its length. We are familiar with the notion that chaos is then
to be expected, from the fishes that remain hanging on the limbs of trees
in the myth of Deucalion, to the mountain that is transplanted into the
sea in the Sermon on the Mount of Olives. But in the eschatological context the impossible *becomes possible*. "Impossibility" must then be viewed
(as regards the Petrarchan *adynaton*) only as "improbability within nature."
Petrarch's imitation of the eschatological use of the *adynaton* makes excellent use of residual implications: the "end" will be survived by the continuity of desire and the constancy of the lover.

Dante's one sestina reasserts in an amorous context the impossibilities
that ensued upon Exodus. When Israel came out of Egypt, "The sea saw
it and fled; / The Jordan turned backward. / The mountains skipped like
rams, / the hills like young sheep";[1] The Dantean echo is as follows:

> Ma ben ritorneranno i fiumi a' colli
> prima che questo legno molle e verde
> s'infiammi, come suol far bella donna, de me. . . .[2]

(But the rivers may well return to the hills before this tender green
wood will ever catch fire for me, as beautiful ladies do. . . .)

Taken in itself and as a type of redemption by Christ, the event of Exodus is to be understood as comprising "natural impossibilities" that are
nonetheless realizable *outside* nature. What does not change is the fixity

of the lover's will. For such a love, recompense could only come as part of the destruction of nature and the ensuing abyss followed by another beginning. By implication of their opposites, the parts of an *adynaton* describe what is absent: the normal run of human and natural events. If the world of chaos, or dream, or madness appears like the reflection or the double of the natural world, a tension can emerge between the awareness of "another" possibility (in love and reward) on one hand, and the inability to conceive of the alternative in any way but as a blank opposite of what is already known.

For Petrarch the end of historical, linear time would bring with it the resorption of contending opposites, the disappearance of antithesis. He projects these "possibilities" into the future, the lover's life in the world compelling the postponement of that end. The end of time would entail not just a stoppage of natural activity but its reversal and recommencement (rivers would flow backward, night become day, light pass from the moon to the sun [CCXXXVII.16–18]). Not mere chaos but an actual regression of forms would lead into a mythical, prelapsarian kind of time. But from that point humanity is capable of imagining only a new beginning of linear time. Over and above it, the implication of a *series* points to cycles. Petrarch goes as far as the invocation of new time *following* chaos. It is no accident that he chooses the sestina as a major means of recording his speculation on time, for the form itself shows a twofold motion, both cyclical and sequential.

The Judaeo-Christian context in which he composed provided him with a wealth of speculation on temporal regression. Plato found the cause of cosmic regression and catastrophe in a twofold motion of the universe:

> Of this universe of ours, the Divinity now guides its circular revolution entirely, now abandons it to itself, once its revolutions have attained the duration which befits this universe; it then begins to turn in the *opposite direction*, of its own motion.[3]

This change of direction is accompanied by gigantic cataclysms: "the greatest destruction, both among animals in general and among the human race, of which, as is fitting, only a few representatives remain." This catastrophe is followed by a paradoxical "regeneration": "the white hair of the aged darkens, while those at the age of puberty begin to lessen in stature day by day, until they return to the size of a newborn infant"; then finally, "still continuing to waste away they wholly cease to be." Upon this phase ensues the birth of the "Sons of the Earth" (*gegeneis*).⁴ During the age of Cronos there are neither savage animals nor enmity among animals. Plato gives a description of the Golden Age otherwise renowned in pastoral: the fruits of the earth are taken in abundance, the Sons of the Earth sleep naked on the soil with no need for beds because of the mildness of the seasons. Cataclysm is followed by the myth of the primordial paradise. This scheme corresponds to the lover's wish expressed in two of Petrarch's sestinas by *adynata* (XXII, CCXXXVII).

A spirit of apocalyptic prediction determines the consistent future tense of Petrarchan *adynata* and also links them decisively to a Christian framework. To be sure (as Curtius points out), the Virgilian *adynata* were known in the Middle Ages. In an especially well-known example, a shepherd who has lost his beloved declares: "Now may the wolf of his own free will flee the sheep, the oak bear golden apples, owls compete with swans in song. . . ."⁵ The directness of futurity that we find in Petrarch's *adynata* is missing here. Although he, like Virgil, utilizes the figure to comment on an adverse present, the tone is predictive as well as incantatory:

> ch'allor fia un dí Madonna senza 'l ghiaccio
> dentro, e di for senza l'usata nebbia,
> ch'io vedrò secco il mare e' laghi e i fiumi.
> Mentre ch'al mar descenderanno i fiumi
> e le fiere ameranno ombrose valli. . . .

(LXVI.22–26: For one day my lady will be without her inner ice and her outer, usual cloud, when I shall see the sea and lakes and rivers dry. While the rivers continue their descent to the sea and the beasts love shaded valleys. . . .)

Again:

> Allor saranno i miei pensieri a riva,
> che foglia verde non si trovi in lauro;
> quando avrò queto il core, asciutti gli occhi,

> vedrem ghiacciare il foco, arder la neve. . . .

(xxx.7–9: Then my thoughts will have reached their shore when green leaf is no longer found on laurel; when my heart will be calm, my eyes dry, we shall see fire become icy, the snow catch fire. . . .)

As these examples show, Petrarch did not necessarily situate the *adynaton* in the *tornada* of the sestina. Nor is it always clearly distinguishable as a figure from the antithesis in general. The line between paradox (or two incompatible existents) and *reversal* is sometimes blurred. Here it is to be discovered in the active future tense (*vedrem*), which implies a reversal that can be realized in the imagination and hence is not entirely "impossible."

We are so informed when in sestina CCXXXIX Petrarch declares the autonomy of poetry: "Nulla al mondo è che non possano i versi." This sestina contains the single example in the nine poems of an *adynaton* not given in the future tense. Petrarch here draws on a metaphor of Arnaut Daniel which became Arnaut's hallmark through its recurrence in three of his eighteen known *cansos*.[6] It is transposed into the context of the sestina's *tornada*, anticipated by the last line of strophe vi ("e col bue zoppo andrem cacciando l'aura" [CCXXXIX.36: "and we'll go hunting the breeze with the lame ox"]):

> In rete accolgo l'aura, e 'n ghiaccio i fiori,
> e 'n versi tento sorda e rigida alma,
> che nè forza d'Amor prezza nè note.

(CCXXXIX.37–39: I gather the breeze in a net, and flowers in ice, and in verse I strive for the deaf and rigid soul that values neither the force of love nor notes.)

Arnaut identified himself with this image in one of the relatively rare instances of troubadour signature:

> Ieu sui Arnautz qu'amas l'aura,
> e chatz la lebre ab lo bou
> E nadi contra suberna.

("En cest sonet coind' e leri," 43–45: I am Arnaut who gather the breeze and hunt the hare with an ox and swim against the tide [current].)

Petrarch utilizes *l'aura* "breeze" for a wordplay on the name of his beloved, and his pun extends to the *rete* "net" which would form the second and third syllables of Laura's name (in Provençal, *Laureta*). The borrowing from Arnaut, whose imagery in a number of songs including the "chansso d'ongla e d'oncle" must have seemed to Petrarch like a huge *adynaton*, "impossible" according to poetic *bienséance*, adduces literary authority (albeit in the form of the vernacular) to argue for the limitless powers of verse.

The Arnaldian metaphors from Arnaut are developed and flanked by analogies in a sonnet:

> Beato in sogno, e di languir contento,
> d'abbracciar l'ombre e seguir l'aura estiva,
> nuoto per mar che non à fondo o riva,
> solco onde, e'n rena fondo, e scrivo in vento;
>
> . . . .
> ed una cerva errante e fugitiva
> caccio con un bue zoppo e 'nfermo e lento.

(CCXII.1–4, 7–8: Blessed in dream and content with languishing, embracing shadows and following the summer breeze, I swim in a sea without bottom or shore, I surmount waves, build on sand and write upon the wind . . . and I hunt a wandering, fugitive deer with a crippled, infirm and slow ox.)

It is important to note that the "impossibility" content of the Arnaldian and Catullan images is considerably diminished in the sonnet, although Catullus' allusion to writing in the wind heightens the atmosphere of privileged literariness that Petrarch creates for himself. The source of the diminution is to be found in the qualifier *in sogno* ("in dream"), as well as in the numerous adjectives Petrarch adds to the "ox" images and in his transformation of Arnaut's hare into a deer (suggesting that the previously given objects alone would lack sufficient paradoxical import). Whereas the sonnet posits and frames a special realm of dreaming, the sestina accords privilege to "verse" itself, explicitly describing its Orphic aspect ("e li aspidi incantar sanno in lor note," line 29). The allusion to the miraculous power of poetry is again drawn directly from the matrix of Virgilian *adynata*, the Eighth Eclogue. In accordance with Orphic legend, the pattern of reversal found in the *adynaton* could operate in its most extreme force, as Petrarch says in his double sestina (CCCXXXII), the one most overtly concerned with poetic form:

> Or avess'io un sí pietoso stile
> che Laura mia potesse torre a Morte
> come Euridice Orfeo sua senza rime.

(CCCXXXII.49–51: If I only had so sorrowful a style that I could take my Laura back from Death as Orpheus his Eurydice without rhymes.)

Together with the implicit statement of the power of song to realize impossibilities, there occurs the comparison of the poet with Orpheus and Laura with Eurydice. They are arranged in chiasmus (Io-Laura-Euridice-Orfeo). It is the linkage of mythical possibility with human, historical possibility that shows how "impossible" the lover's wish is. The idea of bringing back the dead is analogous to that of reward from Laura. Within the freedoms accorded by poetry, however, Petrarch is indeed returning Laura from the dead. In the poem all is possible, even to the point of realizing the virtual aspect of his Arnaldian pun: *In rete accolgo "Laura"* (CCXXXVII).

More than this is implied, however, by the mythical link. We have to take into account the far-reaching and diverse connotative power of Orphic legend for Petrarch. Exegesis has always demonstrated the adaptability of the myth to arguments *in bono* and *in malo*, nowhere more evident than in medieval iconography.[7]

A reciprocal influence of the two judgments of Orpheus is, to be sure, to be discerned in Petrarch. As is usual for him, consistent allegoresis is perhaps honored more in the breach, or as a means of reminiscing on his cultural past. Yet the cited passage goes further. It stresses Orpheus' eloquence, which could reverse the process of death (or expunge the impossibility of *adynaton*) while coupling the name of Laura yet again with a projection of the lover's desire ("Laura *mia*") which easily surmounts the obstacle of her death. The aspirations of the lover's wish, however, go beyond these conventional limits, if we read *rime* in its combined medieval acceptance of "poetry" and "rime." The analysis of the entire poem invites a more polysemous interpretation: *rime* is twice opposed as poetry to *versi*, as Latin is contrasted with the vernacular (str. i, iii). In cases other than the cited passage it is bound to generic adjectives or simple prepositions. However, when Petrarch refers to his *roche rime* "raucous rhymes" (line 32), it is to a topos familiar to readers of Dante's *petrose* and of several Provençal "*clus*" poets. Commentators have generally understood *senza rime* to mean only "unrhymed poetry" in the fashion of the Greek verse. Petrarch makes the distinction between Latin and vernacular poetry in the first strophe:

> . . . i soavi sospiri, e'l dolce stile
> che solea resonare *in versi e'n rime*. . . .

(CCCXXXII.3–4: the gentle sighs and the sweet style that used to resound in verses and in rhymes. . . .)

If we read the Orpheus lines on this level, what emerges is a wish to bring Laura back to life *in free verse*, i.e., in a "style" that would presumably convert its immanent obstacles from rhyme to meter. If we read *rime* as only "poetry," however, the multifold meaning gives us "without poetry." The impossible would, then, be accomplished not even by poetry but by an act of overreaching resolution, the arrow of desire hitting its mark without any mediate impediment. In that ultimate impossibility the poem would achieve the realization of the Edenic love whose images hold sway over the poet, though it could not be expressed in words.

The comparison of Petrarch/Laura and Orpheus/Eurydice implies the desire for a reversal of time analogous to the natural cataclysms I have mentioned. The Christian poet, in contrast to the classical philosopher, must write in the everpresent awareness that outside the precincts of classical myth (understood as only fables) resurrection will ensue only upon catastrophe. Petrarch's renowned "ambiguity" operates in his chosen, optative form of verbal expression, "gaining time" (as it were) in the mediating zone of poetic speculation.

But we have seen that the *impossibilia* of the *adynaton* are not to be taken for granted because they are impossible in nature, that *sub specie aeternitatis* they are possible. The pattern is not one of privative opposition but of syntagmatically conceived, sequential *reversal*. It is therefore comparable to the pattern of apocalyptic prediction. No example of non-predictive *adynaton* is to be discovered in the sestinas. The typical form is given in these lines:

> Ma pria fia 'l verno la stagion de' fiori
> ch'amor fiorisca in quella nobil alma,
> che non curò già mai rime né versi.

(CCXXXIX.10–12: But winter will be the season of flowers before Love flourishes in that noble soul that never cared about rhymes or verses.)

The distinction between *rime* and *versi* appears here (as well as in CCXXXII) again, connoting an allied distinction between rhymed and unrhymed poetry and between Latin and the vernacular.

There is more to this pairing than just synonymic repetition. The poet may well have attempted to characterize the status of identical rhyme (rhyming of a word with the same word), the structural basis of the sestina. Elsewhere it is clear that Petrarch, like Dante and his Provençal predecessors, easily accepts identical rhyme within the rhyme-canon. One example:

> Di tai quattro faville, e non già sole,
> nasce 'l gran foco di ch'io vivo ed ardo,
> che son fatto un augel notturno al sole.

(Sonnet, CLXV.12–14: From those four sparks, and not those alone, is born the great fire with which I live and burn, for I am made a nocturnal bird in the sun.)

The semantic association between *faville* "sparks" and one aspect of *sole* "sun" heralds the actual appearance of *sole* in that meaning, actually heightening the phonic redundancy.

The play with sound and sense is as fundamental to Petrarchan poetic language as repetition and recurrence itself. The inability of the lover's *rime* and *versi* to persuade Laura is a recurrent theme in the sestinas (CCXXXVII, CCXXXIX, CCCXXXII), and we have seen it paired with the impermanence of Orphic persuasion. The colligation of *rime* and *versi* keeps the secondary meaning before us: rhyme and free verse, Latin and vernacular, all encompassed in poetry. Still the peculiarity of identical rhyme evades certain characterization as rhyme pure and simple. In the sestina it embodies a state of extreme self-consciousness on the part of the poet. Accordingly, it displays a kind of stress to which the very concept of rhyme is subjected.

A basic poetic function of the rhyme-word is to delineate the architecture of the strophe. It also helps to define the boundaries of the poem. Words in rhyme position invite particular awareness of their semantic (as well as phonetic) sameness and difference. Identical rhyme, however, eludes the evocative processes created in rhyme. It can point to increasingly small differences of meaning, approaching perfect synonymy while retaining a perfect phonetic resemblance of the terms. The role of *syntactic* difference is accentuated, since within the context of exact rhyme syntactic differences appear more marked. The strophes of a sestina would be called, in the terms of the Provençal coiners, *coblas singulars* — "singular" stanzas with "orphaned" rhymes. They point ever outwards toward the other strophes, all of which have the same rhymes, demanding the acceptance of the poem as an unbroken entity.

In rhyme, semantic choice tends to be dissimulated by the identity of sound. This condition tends to suggest a possibly spurious resemblance of objects, an insistently murmuring likeness of substance. Within the poem this linkage (phonetic similarity; semantic difference-cum-similarity) implies the possibility of imaginative association of the two objects rhymed. The connection is no less tenuous, perhaps more, than in punning, which epitomizes one possibility of identical rhyme. There the same spurious objectivity hovers over the phonetic association (whether or not an etymological relationship actually exists).

In the case of identical rhyme, semantic similarity or dissimilarity of the terms reveals itself as a question of degree. It can be invoked in semantic near-blends, or denied, in a context of pure homonymy. The same rhyme does not absolutely represent the same object, concept, or relation but more cunningly invokes it. More than other species of rhyme, identical rhyme plumbs the semantic possibilities of the words involved. Every instance, then, is a self-renewing context, born out of the ashes of a preceding instance.

In the Petrarchan sestina, repetition (both within lines and at their ends) usurps some of the functions normally fulfilled by rhyme. The phonetic identity dominates semantic and lexical traits of the word. Words can, of course, be part of a very great number of descriptive systems (*terra* as "soil," as "planet," as human "clay," for example). But this multiple reference is secondary to the similarity of sound. My point here is that Petrarchan rhyme-words represent gradation rather than simple opposition and equation (although commentators have been largely content to analyze his lexicon in terms of simple contrast or equivalence). The shifting action of different semantic contexts as they are juxtaposed in a poem, and the effect of equivocation issuing from the simultaneous reception of two or more senses of a word, blur over semantic distinctions. (One case not included in a sestina is that of *acque*, whose quasi-Biblical vastness in Petrarchan use engulfs whatever pond or sea we understand as the most specific referent of the moment.) The fact of recurrence is the consistent one and the primary poetic fact regardless of the change of referents.

Nature speaks in Petrarchan song, or at least, it echoes. The speaker in a poem will expect the sonorities of his words to rebound from mountains, valleys, or streams. The echo effects themselves are another species of recurrence. This kind of auditory image is closely associated with Petrarch's preference for forests, valleys, thickets, and other natural enclosures that can serve as echo chambers.[8] We may posit that nature's reply in such cases would be a replication analogous to the repetition of words within the poem itself.

Within a poem, repetition carries an additional, mnemonic value. It helps the words and the poem to be remembered during and after reading. We know that Petrarch's Provençal antecedents placed a very high value on repetition both in stanzas and in whole poems, and that skill in rhyming was fundamental to their success. Now, in the sestina the possibility of grasping the many-sided meanings of the rhyme-word, the featured word, depends on the perception of sameness of sound. The equivocation created by the intertwining of several meanings is contingent upon phonetic identity, spurious with respect to meaning and perfect with respect to sound. A difference of sense in two instances of a rhyme-word is in fact inevitable. And every instance modifies what has gone before.

In addition, since the element of pure coincidence, of simple homonymy, is reduced considerably in the greater number of cases of identical rhyme, the "counterlogical" properties of rhyme[9] generally invite further consideration. The perfect phonetic identity acts to delimit the possibilities of interpretation of the word and its linkages with other rhyme-words. The identical-rhyme-word actually provides an extra measure of information "to go by" since it reduces the number of possible interpretations. Whereas normal rhyme can cement the meaning of either of its terms by their mutual association, identical rhyme reminds us continually of some lost or omit-ted or possible resemblance between the things to which it refers. The reemergence of phonetic identity is crowned by an aura of separate sense. In all of these respects — semantic, mnemonic, hermeneutic — the sestina encourages meditation upon the fact of recurrence itself.

At the same time, the effect of identical rhyme in the sestina is seman-tically cumulative. It can be the repetition or near-repetition of meaning that attracts attention. In other poetic forms, such as the *triolet*, the strict reproduction of a *whole phrase* produces a more static effect (on a scale ranging from the imagined reproduction of a whole poem to that of one word). Therefore, identical rhyme can subserve logical as well as musical recurrence.

A growing and sharpened expectation on the part of the reader discerns correspondences among rhyme-words during the course of the poem. The challenges of the sestina in this regard should not be underestimated. It was created by a poet whom Dante praised for his seamless strophe, that is, for the absence of facile singsong or doggerel-like rhymes. The sestina, like Arnaut Daniel's other songs, defies the ability of any memory that depends excessively on the frequency of rhyme within small units of a poem. The poet's game of suggestion without total satisfaction concen-trates on the word's capacity to multiply its senses, or to put it different-ly, on the word's perpetual otherness of sense. Yet the memory is con-stantly brought into play. As the order accomplishes its shifts, so does the relationship of each rhyme-word to its context.

Through sheer frequency of usage (and the concomitant changes of con-text) the key terms of Petrarch's lexicon are charged with shimmering but distinctive resonances. He shows us how words alone cannot attain fixed value. The recurrent imagery of his living words, as he works with an entire spectrum of connotations, displays the shifting movement be-tween parts and wholes of words. Poems become universes of reciprocal relations. No poet shows better than Petrarch how meanings change, dilate, renew themselves. Memory predominates (together with nostalgia and reminiscence) over much of his poetics, and in his rhymes it is materially embodied. This dominance of Memory entails his choice of nouns over

verbs in key positions and accords rhyme-word status in the sestina only
to nouns. It is important to the subsequent fortune of the sestina that
Petrarch's epigones and followers took his lead in this matter as well.

Since only nouns function as rhyme-words in Petrarch's sestinas, it is
rare, though possible, to find in rhyme-position words belonging to more
than one grammatical class. This feature adds a further restriction on usable
poetic material. That Petrarch chose to restrict himself within the confines
of the sestina form testifies to an initial desire on his part for materially
constraining circumstances when he used the form. The lack of choice
combines with the structures of recurrence in the sestina to create the
most apt poetic form in which a man could reveal his fixity and mutability at once.

Sestina CCCXXXII shows just how deeply Petrarch was able to integrate
the possibilities of intensification through repetition within poetic structure. In this, his double sestina, the point at which the doubling begins
is marked by the repetition of the word *morte*, this time not only in its
rhyme-position: "nè contra Morte spero altro che morte" ("and against
Death I hope only for death," strophe vii.6). Later, in strophe viii, the
whole process itself is repeated to special effect. For the eighth position
signifies a surpassing not only of the usual number (seven) of strophes
comprising the single sestina, but in a semantic sense, "doubles" mortal
life itself:

> Morte m'a morto, e sola pò far Morte
> ch'i' torni a riveder quel viso lieto. . . .

(CCCXXXII.43–44: Death has killed me, and only Death can act so
that I may see again that glad face. . . .)

The paradoxes of these two lines encompass the semantics of Petrarchan
"eternity." The force that outlives death *may* thereby unite the poet with
his beloved, especially if a poetic text can bring into being another gradation of reality.

The patterns of replication continue throughout the double sestina. A
tour de force, it repeats itself, in a "doppiare lo stile," as Petrarch puts it
at a crucial point. That point is the thirty-ninth line, normally the concluding line of a sestina. Petrarch enables *doppiare* to convey the sense of
"doubling" both the poem and the lover's life cycle. There is both a quan-

titative and a qualitative increase.

Petrarch's retelling of myth, its replication, is to be viewed in the same terms. Its form and meaning coincide with his techniques of lexical repetition, on a far greater scale. Petrarch suggests the possibility, in his anniversary poems which deal with the present moment and with his mythicized moment of enamorment, of maintaining a shared status of both "times," in which the historical aspect of continuous time can be elided in order to confer mythical status on the past. But the continuing life of enamorment is claimed to nurture an eternal possibility of repetition. The linear passage of time is challenged, in the words of Bergson, by the memory, "dont le rôle serait de conserver exceptionnellement telles ou telles parties du passé en les emmagasinant dans une espèce de boîte," ("whose role it would be to conserve by way of exception certain parts of the past, collecting them in a kind of box").[10] The revelations of memory are selectively produced and woven into the *bel velo* of poetry. At the same time, we are made poignantly aware of memory's incompleteness as an awareness of something absent. How precariously it is relied upon for information about the past; how incomplete the revelation it affords!

Petrarch transforms this inadequacy into the consoling terms of lyric. As Contini points out, Petrarch's adjectives and verbs acquire a flattened value similar to that of nouns. While adjectives become epithets (not predicates), verbs in their turn have metaphoric import quite devoid of active energy (he cites the examples *tolse, colse, die*). Otherwise they are excluded from any non-lyric context, appearing often in the optative mood or in contrary-to-fact subjunctive clauses or as infinitives. Everywhere existents supplant occurrents, and incisive, stringent raw material is converted into lyrical, fluent discursiveness. The paucity of information conveyed by the poems functions as the very loophole through which a connotative structure recreates and fosters myth. If "la façon la plus simple pour un poète d'imposer ses connotations est evidemment de créer des contextes qui correspondent aux situations qui sont à leur source," ("the simplest means for a poet to impose his connotations is obviously to create contexts that correspond to the situations at the source of those connotations"),[11] then Petrarch's is the prime example of such language. Indeed, it presents us with a linguistic indeterminacy that resides in the improbability of ascertaining the content of just what is signified. The context of an utterance extends to the entirety of the whole *Canzoniere*, the immanent content of any single poem being succeeded by the overarching content of other, prior Petrarchan experience. The quantity of externally identifiable material used is small, in proportion to the number of poetic "signals" that can be decoded with reference to that experience. The crux of Petrarchan language is to be found in its tonality, in the cumulative effect of key terms and turns of phrase which conceal the complex field of semantic values. We can distinguish them not only by frequency but by stress. Thus it is possible to disengage Laura-*l'aura* as a complex "situation" at the core of sestina CCXXXIX, with its subsidiaries *auro, aurora, lauro*, in an unbroken paronomastic series, and simultaneously to perceive these sounds as phonetically symbolic of the beloved ("l'aura de' sospir," line 30). The boundary between allegory and allusion becomes obscured; or we may say that Petrarch understands allegory as allusion, with a resultant depletion of the signified. And yet Petrarch draws from a store of allegorizable scholastic culture, the *Derivationes* of Uguccione da Pisa, to complement his placement of Virgil's hexameters "sed me Parnasi deserta per ardua dulcis / raptat amor . . ."[12] at the "head" of his oration upon receiving the laurel crown: "Daphnes enim grece, ut asserit Ugaccio, latine laurus est." This he does in order to represent the analogy between the myth of Apollo and Daphne and the myth of poetry with its possibilities of a new classical flowering. Prevalent in the dialectic is the sense of *irreversibility*, however, that encompasses poetic activity along with all other human activity, and marks it as unrepeatable.

It is just this irreversibility in nature, realized through his poems, that provides a crucial qualifier to the notion of Petrarch as poet of fixity. Perhaps such awareness underlies the fact that Petrarch reminisces on the lines of another poet of fixity, Arnaut Daniel, in sestina CCXXXIX ("In rete accolgo l'aura," from Arnaut: "Ieu sui Arnautz q'amas l'aura"), but not on lines from Arnaut's sestina, which takes no *self-conscious* account of temporality.

The very same distinction between fixity and repetition must apply to the well-known and much commented upon phenomenon of synonymic (and antithetical) pairs in Petrarch's work. The procedure is extremely common in troubadour poetry from its known inception forward. Contini takes it to be proof of the prevalence of rhythm over semantic value and, therefore, a part of Petrarch's "rhythmic dominant." At the same time it would be appropriate to recall the inseparable connection of words and melody in many of Petrarch's predecessors. The adaptation by Petrarch of the troubadour tradition strongly suggests another motive as well as a different result for his techniques of repetition. It should be recognized that repetition aids not only the memory, but the impression of what it conveys. The emphatic quality of iteration imparts to the poetic line in which it occurs an *intensification* of sense.

Strings of apparent semantic *equivalences*, pairs of synonyms, have seemed typical of Petrarchan poetry. About fifteen percent of his sonnets have a bilateral structure in the last line,[13] which is the place of emphasis. The conclusion has been drawn that Petrarch's system is thus "fundamentally binary." From the viewpoint of rhythm, syntax, and phonetic relations, his persistent schemes of correlation and dichotomy suggest that, for example, since rhymes tend to be nouns there is a strong possibility of another noun in the same line. This kind of relation may be termed a parallelism, but only in the superficial sense that entirely spatializes poetry and determines that it is full of symmetries. For it is not the "sistema equilibrato" of Petrarch's poetry that creates resolution within his works: not simply the enunciation of a pair, but the fact that he can order his dichotomies so that they come under the rule of a third term, the poem. It is true that his presentation of binary schemes seems to predominate over the enunciation of any other kind. It is true as well that he will articulate synonymous or antonymous chains of words in series that appear to be without any nexus, and that pairs are often blurred by syntactic suspension and separation ("Primavera per me pur non è mai," is Contini's famed example). It is only *a posteriori* that the images coalesce into a whole. The demands of the poem on the reader's retrospective ability are tremendous. But once they are met they subvert the equilibrium that it pleases some of Petrarch's most expert readers to discern everywhere in his work. In any event, the temporality of poetry itself militates against the possibility of static correlation, against the establishment of parallelism with pretensions to equivalence.

Perfect equivalence can be said to exist only outside of poetry itself. In the awareness of the temporal movement of language, we can, therefore, posit the presence of an existential judgment of value in the *Canzoniere* taken as a whole; *Cielo* and *terra* each seem to hold an equal share of the poet's mind, but if *cielo* did not have the greater part, it is quite likely that the conflicts reflected in this poetry would not exist at all. *Structures of repetition are also structures of intensification.* The same word is never heard twice, and Petrarch's awareness of this fact lies at the heart of his uncommon success with the quintessential poetic form of repetition, the sestina.

Petrarch's experiments with identical rhyme represent another experiment in the transcendence of duality. It is exemplified in the sestina's "seamless" internal logic. That logic, nevertheless, includes a constant tension between gradations of sameness and difference, never to be resolved in the repose of perfect identification.

It is important, also, that Petrarch's *adynata* follow the pattern of the *reversal* of nature. Reversal would end in neutralization, and all that had gone forward in time would obliterate itself, leaving the only identity he can imagine.

The *adynaton*, then, in its close relation to Petrarch's sestina, denotes a substantial stoppage and reverse movement of nature, whereas in the poem it furnishes end-stoppage for what would otherwise be a perpetual forward movement of separate cycles. Human time, in substance, is linear — in any poem and in the referential context of the Christian poet. Its movement will, therefore, produce history, novelty, and closure, not identity. Whether or not it appears in final position within a poem, the *adynaton* predicts an end. In this respect it epitomizes Platonizing desire superseded by Christian reality. It would be a trivialization of the problem to fail to note that the *adynata* bespeak a nearly total absence of God.

Within the poetic matrix, the futurity of *adynaton* in Petrarch is possessed of a magic force that underscores the special status of poetry as speech act even as it evokes a restricted, myth-bound context. Petrarch reminds us simultaneously of the psychological distance of his implementation of myth from history and of the hospitality of fiction to mythical and permanent resetting. The Ovidian account already makes us aware that the myth-ridden structure of primitive societies is actually at odds with his new retelling. Petrarchan innovations augment that divergence to the next power. It is in keeping with Petrarch's use of *adynata* in the sestina that the overwhelming majority of *impossibilia* in classical poetry produced broad generalities adhering to the discursive principle, enunciated by Ovid: "All things will soon come to pass which I once said were impossible; nothing is incredible."[14]

What is the logical status of the Petrarchan "always?" It has never been proven possible to devise a consistent logical system embodying the assertion that *time will end*. The "end of time" as foretold in Revelations 10 has a mystical truth, to be sure, but no intelligibility. In the Petrarchan sestina the persistent scheme of invariance or fixity encompassing transformation invites speculation on the endlessness of time. It is an invitation that most of Petrarch's followers willingly accepted.

Unlike many classical *adynata*, Petrarch's are based on the interdependence of *two* conditions, both of which he appears to regard as impossible. (The things or conditions assumed to be impossible would prove true sooner than the realization of Laura's love, or his own abandonment of her.) In accordance with Petrarch's apparent poetic schemes of coordination, one part of the figure is balanced against and measured in terms of the other; they thus reveal a strong mutual dependency. Through the resulting coherence, his lover's condition is rendered universal and exemplary. The persistent speculative question of whether temporality can elude linear, historical movement, the nagging consciousness of the fact that, unlike the poem, time has no understandable end, ultimately produces (more than does the absence of an articulated God at the helm of reversal) the sense of unending temporal cycles which no human endeavor is capable of bringing to a close.

The persistent future tense of Petrarchan *adynata* emerges from this knowledge with a particular poignancy. All the modulations of inference, contingency, and conjecture, of a dauntless hope through which consciousness maps the future for itself, emerge from his verbal manipulation of the unknown. Millenarian fantasy provided him with models of a mythical grammar of the future. (At the same time, Dante's Hell would constitute the model of a grammar without futures.) The extension of causality beyond the present does not operate there. But the enunciation of the future by prophets (like those of the Old Testament) could in theory make that future alterable. If man repents and changes his conduct, God can bend the arc of time out of foreseen shape, for there is no immutability except in God's own being. The force and axiomatic certitude of the Old Testament prophet's prediction lie precisely in the possibility that the prediction may go unfulfilled: behind every prediction of disaster there stands a concealed alternative. While Messianic prophecy came to render the will of God enigmatic and the prophet more fully entered upon the function of glossing rather than foretelling what God did, even then the kind of future exemplified in prophecy could not be compared to the lacunae of misunderstanding left by oracular prophecy to the pagan world. The prophesying poet participates in this blending of open message and hermetic code. He can make use of persuasive powers while stressing the optative, indefinite character of the future.

In accordance with the spirit of renewal that is implicit in future-tense propositons, Petrarch's exclusive choice of *adynata* expressed through the future tense is inextricably interwoven with historical awareness, anticipation, and forward inference. Futurity confers upon them a crucial aptitude for survival, what Ibsen called the "Life-lie" — the dynamism of consoling illusion on which the perpetuation of elegiac poetry hinges. Petrarch's *adynata* function within a conception of the future that belongs to the realm of the non-factual utterance. As such, they illustrate the freedom of the poetic word to go beyond and against "that which is the case":

> A qualunque animal che alberga in terra
> Se non se alquanti c'hanno in odio il sole,
> Tempo è da travagliare quanto è il sole. . . .

(XXIII.1–3: For whatever animals dwell on earth, but for the few that hate the sun, while there is sunlight is the time to work. . . .)

The self-perpetuation and life of animals takes place within a constant present. The opening lines of Petrarch's sestina XXII (which first engages the round of terminal words) initiate a contrast of animal with human life that will culminate at last in the *adynaton*. There the presence and presentness of the poet's own certain death provide the poetic occasion to make free of animal and human time and to reverse its course.

Notes

1. Ps. 114:3–4.
2. Dante Alighieri, "Al poco giorno," *Rime* LIV.
3. Plato, *Timaeus*, 33a–e.
4. Loc. cit.
5. Virgil, *Ecl.* VIII. 53–56, cit. E. R. Curtius, *European Literature and the Latin Middle Ages*, tr. Willard R. Trask (New York: Pantheon, 1953), p. 95.
6. For a tracing of the metaphor of the bull and the swimmer through Arnaut's poems, see Leslie T. Topsfield, *Troubadors and Love* (Cambridge: Cambridge University Press, 1974), pp. 210–13.
7. Among the vast number of bibliographical items, see John Block Friedman, *Orpheus in the Middle Ages* (Cambridge, Mass.: Harvard University Press, 1970).

8. For a study of the nature-echo in Virgil, see Phillip Damon, "The *Imago Voci* in Vergilian Pastoral," in his *Modes of Analogy in Ancient and Medieval Verse* (Berkeley: University of California Press, 1961), pp. 281–90.

9. William K. Wimsatt, *The Verbal Icon* (Lexington: University of Kentucky Press, 1954), p. 106.

10. Henri Bergson, *Matière et mémoire,* 13th ed. (Paris: Félix Alcan, 1917), p. 103.

11. André Martinet, "Connotations, poésie et culture," in *To Honor Roman Jakobson,* II (The Hague: Mouton, 1967), p. 1288.

12. Virgil, *Georgics* III.291–92.

13. Damaso Alonso, "Simmetria bilaterale," in his *Pluralità e correlazione in poesia,* tr. M. Rostaing and V. Minervini (Bari: Adriatica, 1971), p. 63.

14. *Tristia* I.8, 5–8.

La pianta più gradita in cielo:
Petrarch's Laurel and Jove

SARA STURM-MADDOX

O F THE MANY MYTHOLOGICAL FIGURES who appear by name or allusion throughout Petrarch's collection of his vernacular lyrics, it is Jove whose name recurs with greatest frequency.[1] Studies of mythology in the *Canzoniere,* however, generally comment only incidentally on the ruling divinity of the pagan pantheon, focusing instead on the Ovidian story of Apollo and Daphne that dominates the collection. The myth of Jove differs from most of the other myths evoked in the *Canzoniere* in that it is composite, encompassed by no single Ovidian narrative, and allusions to the divinity are often dismissed as rhetorical or ornamental components of individual lyrics. Yet the powerful influence of Jove is among the givens of an Ovidian world in which creatures are continually subject to transformation, and the prominent recurrences of his name in the *Canzoniere* suggest that we examine both his independent function in the collection and his relation to the central myth of Apollo and Daphne through which Petrarch slowly elaborated his own myth of the suffering poet-lover.

In his Coronation Oration of 1341, in the famous passage identifying the laurel as a symbol of poetic fame, Petrarch lists a number of singular properties of the tree. The laurel was considered sacred to Apollo, he explains, because it was ever green, "and this gave rise to the story that Apollo loved Daphne, for according to Uguiccione the Greek word *daphne*

has the same meaning as the Latin *laurus*: this story may be read in full
in the first book of the *Metamorphoses* of Ovid."[2] The property of eternal
verdure that prompts this etymological identification is also guaranteed
by "a great and noble prerogative," the immunity of the plant to lightning. This immunity, Petrarch notes, was agreed upon by all authorities
on natural history; it was to be included in turn by other commentators,
among them Boccaccio, who in his *Genealogie deorum gentilium* follows
Petrarch in listing among the properties of the tree that it is not known
ever to have been struck by lightning.[3] While the source of this privilege
is not further developed in Petrarch's Oration, other works of the poet
reveal that he assimilated this naturalistic property of the laurel, like its
evergreen nature, to mythological story: in the Latin epic *Africa* he tells
us that "frondem rapido non fulmine vexat / Jupiter ex cuntis, talemque
meretur honorem / laurus, ab ethereo tanta est clementia rege" ("this leaf
alone Jupiter assaults not with his bolt; the sacred tree deserves the honor,
rightfully enjoying the clemency of Heaven's king").[4] The reference in
the Oration to the plant's immunity to lightning as a "great and noble
prerogative" suggests an anthropomorphic quality that transcends the report
of an unparalleled natural phenomenon, and relates this property closely
to the honor accorded the plant by Apollo.

In the Coronation Oration, then, the laurel's immunity to lightning
is complementary to the favor accorded it by Apollo in assuring its special
status and its permanence. In the *Canzoniere* Jove's protection of the laurel
from lightning is alluded to repeatedly, initially in poem XXIV where the
plant is "l'onorata fronde, che prescrive / l'ira del ciel quando 'l gran Giove
tona" ("the honored branch that protects one from the anger of heaven
when great Jove thunders").[5] The dual components of this figuration of
Jove are both conventional: its emotive aspect of the god's anger, and
the imagistic use of that anger to depict inclement weather. The
iconographical tradition typically depicted Jove armed with thunderbolts,[6]
and Petrarch had abundant classical sources, particularly in Horace, for
his repeated characterization of the deity as *tonante* or "thundering."[7] These
two aspects combine in the first mention of Jove in the collection, in a
reference to the steadfastness of the Colonna family "ch'ancor non torse
del vero cammino / l'ira di Giove per ventosa pioggia" (x.3–4: "whom
even the ire of Jove in the windy rain has not yet turned aside from the
true path"). Recurring throughout the collection, these images of anger,
thunder, and the lightning bolt are subject to multiple recombinations

and to exchange of agents: in Laura's anger Love is seen to "folgorar ne' turbati occhi pungenti" ("lightning in her piercing angry eyes") so that her admirer retreats "come colui che 'l colpo teme / di Giove irato" (CXLVII.8–9: "like one who fears the blow of angry Jove"); in CCII.5–6 the subject is Death and the object the poet, who imagines his adversary "già per ferire alzato 'l braccio, come irato ciel tona o leon rugge" ("his arm already raised to strike, as the angry heavens thunder or as a lion roars").

These conventional figurations of the wrath of the god and their meteorological imagery do not, however, fully account for Petrarch's use of the figure of Jove in the *Canzoniere*. An affective component of the relation of the deity to the favored plant and its extension to Laura herself is suggested by the pair of poems in which the climatological imagery is most elaborately detailed:

> Quando dal proprio sito si rimove
> L'arbor ch'amò già Febo in corpo umano,
> Sospira e suda a l'opera Vulcano,
> Per rinfrescar l'aspre saette a Giove;
> Il quale or tona or nevica et or piove,
> Senza onorar più Cesare che Giano. . . .

(XLI:1–6: When from its own dwelling the tree departs that Phoebus loved in human form, Vulcan pants and sweats at his work in order to renew the harsh arrows for Jove who now thunders, now snows, now rains, without respecting Caesar more than Janus. . . .)

> Ma poi che 'l dolce riso umile e piano
> Più non asconde sue bellezze nove,
> Le braccia a la fucina indarno move
> L'antiquissimo fabbro ciciliano;
> Ch'a Giove tolte son l'arme di mano
> Temprate in Mongibello a tutte prove. . . .

(XLII.1–6: But now that her sweet smile, humble and modest, hides no more its new beauties, the ancient Sicilian smith in vain moves his arms at the forge; for Jove's arms have been taken out of his hand, though tempered in Aetna to all proof. . . .)

These allusions, which demonstrate the interchangeability of laurel and lady in the capacity to soothe the wrath of the god and assure clement weather, are not merely mythological conceits contributing to the often-noted fusion of Laura with the natural world.[8] Jove's affective response to Laura similarly appears in other poems divested of meteorological imagery:

> A me si volse in sì novo colore
> Ch'avrebbe a Giove nel maggior furore
> Tolto l'arme di mano e l'ira morta.

(CXI.6–8: She turned to me with hue so changed that it would have disarmed Jove in his greatest fury, and would have killed his wrath.)

> Non fûr ma' Giove e Cesare sì mossi
> A fulminar colui, questo a ferire,
> Che pietà non avesse spente l'ire
> Et lor de l'usate arme ambeduo scossi:
> Piangea Madonna. . . .

(CLV.1–5: Jove and Ceasar were never so moved, the former to thunder, the latter to wound, that pity would not have put out their anger and shaken them from their accustomed weapon: my lady was weeping. . . .)

The poet is here like Jove, as elsewhere he is like Apollo, in his response to the irresistible attraction of the lady's beauty.

These images of the power of Laura's beauty recall the portrait of another feminine figure, that of Sophonisba in the *Africa*: "Divina quod illis / vis inerat radiansque decor, qui pectora posset / flectere quo vellet, mentesque auferre tuendo, / inque Meduseum precordia vertere marmor" (vv.36–39: "her glance divine cast all around her a compelling charm, and where she wished to turn it she could rouse desire or bend a will however firm or to Medusan marble change the heart of an admirer . . .").[9] The portrait, like many of the *rime*, describes the effect of that beauty on Jove. The rhetorical opening of the passage, declaring that "Stabat candore nivali / frons alto mirando Iovi"(vv. 22–23: "that brow, as white as snow, might stir almighty Jove to wonder"), is followed by an immediate reference to Jove's susceptibility to feminine beauty, and a second reference, to Sophonisba's arms in which the god might desire eternally to be held, is yet more direct. Ugo Dotti, who aptly characterizes the passage as a *ritratto-catalogo* (portrait-catalog) of Ovidian imitation, denies any trace of sensuality in this reference because of its conventional, rhetorical nature.[10] Yet the Sophonisba of the *Africa*, whose portrait contains many components of the depiction of Petrarch's Laura, is both seductive and subversive — like one aspect of Laura herself. This Laura, whom Thomas Bergin terms "Laura-Sophonisba" and whose beauty presents a danger for the soul of her admirer, is "guilty of arousing the poet's carnal desires, which as a true penitent he must quite properly deplore."[11]

It is noteworthy then that the most extensive reference to Jove in the *Canzoniere* occurs in the famed metamorphosis Canzone XXIII, "Nel dolce tempo de la prima etade" ("In the sweet time of my first age"), in which the poet-lover undergoes a series of transformations resulting from his experience of love and desire. Preceded only by brief incidental allusions in Sonnets IV and X, it is also the first major reference to Jove in the collection. In this poem it is not the love-object but the lover whose state is altered, the poet referring specifically to his transformed person, and all of the six metamorphoses alluding to the fate of Daphne, Cygnus, Battus, Byblis, Echo and Acteon represent consequences of the *innamoramento* announced in the proemial stanza. The last of these appears to include the series in a state of suspension; it is also, as Robert Durling observes, the most violent of the six episodes, the least metaphorical, and the least disguised: "it allows the fullest emergence of sexual affect and acknowledges most fully the fear resulting from a sense of taboo."[12]

Yet the metamorphosis *canzone* does not end with Acteon. Unlike the *commiato* of the typical *canzone*, that of No. XXIII extends the series elaborated in the stanzas:

> Canzon, i' non fu' mai quel nuvol d'oro
> Che poi discese in prezïosa pioggia
> Sì che 'l foco di Giove in parte spense;
> Ma fui ben fiamma ch'un bel guardo accense,
> E fui l'uccel che più per l'aere poggia
> Alzando lei che ne' miei detti onoro:
> Nè per nova figura il primo alloro
> Seppi lassar, chè pur la sua dolce ombra

Ogni men bel piacer del cor mi sgombra.

(Lines 161–69: Song, I was never the cloud of gold that once descended in a precious rain so that it partly quenched the fire of Jove, but
I have certainly been a flame lit by a lovely glance and I have been
the bird that rises highest in the air raising her whom in my words
I honor; nor for any new shape could I leave the first laurel, for
still its sweet shade turns away from my heart any less beautiful
pleasure.)

These concluding transformations with which the poet negatively or
positively identifies his own experience are all accounts of metamorphoses
of Jove. Unlike those of the tormented lover of the preceding stanzas,
they are transformations willed by the subject; however, they complement the earlier series in that each is part of an amorous encounter: the
references are to Jove's conquest of Danae, of Semele, and of Ganymede.

However edifying the fate of Jove at the hands of moralizing allegorists
in the late Middle Ages, who often made of the ruling pagan deity a figure
of the Christian God, it is important to recall that the Jove of the *commiato* of Canzone XXIII is the dominant Jove of the *Metamorphoses*. Whereas
most of the metamorphoses recounted by Ovid are those of earthly
creatures, like that of Daphne resulting from the pursuit of Apollo, and
are irreversible, Jove's are multiple, temporary, and undertaken to effect
his sexual conquests. Furthermore, the association of Jove with sexual appetite in *Canzone* XXIII is not unique in the collection. In No. CCCXXV,
the final recurrence of his name in the *Canzoniere*, he is listed along with
other gods as helpless before the powers of Cupid. It is of course the armed
Cupid who initiated both the ill-fated love of Apollo for Daphne and the
love of the *Canzoniere* poet for his equally inaccessible Laura. The reference
in No. CCCXXV correlates further with a passage in the *Triumphus Cupidinis*
in which Jove stands closest to the triumphant boy god; from his guide
the poet learns, as Aldo Bernardo reminds us, that the victims of Cupid
are victims of passion, of a god whose power originates in human idleness
and human lust.[13]

In his depiction of a lascivious Jove, then, Petrarch does not depart from
Ovidian story. But how are we to account for the prominent comparison
of the poet of *Canzone* XXIII with a Jove who is clearly a figure of carnal
desire, in a collection in which the love-experience is primarily that of

progressive sublimation? The third of the allusions to Jove in the *commiato*, "e fui l'uccel che più per l'aere poggia, /alzando lei che ne' miei detti onoro" ("and I have been the bird that rises highest in the air raising her whom in my words I honor"), identifies the poet's activity with regard to the beloved as one of writing, the activity to which he had had recourse when human speech was denied him earlier in the poem: "ond'io gridai con carta e con inchiostro" ("so I cried out with paper and ink"). On this basis the *commiato* may be read as a statement of the "practical" as opposed to the "emotional" theme of the *canzone*, "to illustrate how Petrarch *honored* his love in verse."[14] But the reader familiar with Ovid recognizes that the image of Jove as bird carrying his human prey is laden with sexual connotations, as are the allusions to Danae and Semele that precede it, and the reference to the poet's "detti" or words suggests that at best the writing of love-poetry is a compensatory function for the frustrated lover.[15]

The source of the allusions to Jove in the *commiato* may be suggested by a text dearer to Petrarch than even his classical authors. In Book I of the *Confessions*, describing his own early training in the schools, Augustine writes of the pagan deity as follows: "This traditional education taught me that Jupiter punishes the wicked with his thunderbolts and yet commits adultery himself. The two roles are quite incompatible. All the same he is represented in this way, and the result is that those who follow his example in adultery can put a bold face on it by making false pretenses of thunder. . . . In this way their wickedness would not be reckoned a crime, and all who did as they did could be shown to follow the example of the heavenly gods, not that of sinful mortals." The indictment of pagan mythology as an excuse for human wantonness is then illustrated with a scene drawn from classical literature: "Terence," Augustine reminds us, "brings on the stage a dissolute youth who excuses his own fornication by pointing to the example of Jupiter. He looks at a picture painted on the wall, which 'shows how Jupiter is said to have deceived the girl Danae by raining a golden shower into her lap.' These are the words with which he incites himself to lechery, as though he had heavenly authority for it: 'What a god he is! His mighty thunder rocks the sky from end to end. You may say that I am only a man, and thundering is beyond my power. But I played the rest of the part well enough, and willingly too.' "[16]

In this passage the story of Jove and Danae is offered as an example of the deleterious influence of mythological story. The association is seconded by Boccaccio, who invokes it nonetheless to defend the study of classical poets, not by youths unsteady in the faith, but by mature Christians. "Sinner that I am," Boccaccio declares, "I am not by grace of Christ like young Cherea, in Terence, who by looking at a picture of Jove falling in a shower of gold from the roof to the lap of Danae, was inflamed to the desire of a similar misdeed. Any weak susceptibility of that sort, if it ever existed . . . left me with my youth."[17] It is, of course, this shower of gold, this myth of Jove and Danae, that is explicitly invoked in the first of the three allusions of the *commiato* of Canzone XXIII, in which the "fire" of Jove has clearly sexual connotations.[18]

The use of this allusion in the uncharacteristic boasting comparisons of the *commiato* suggests an analogy between the youthful poet of *Canzone* XXIII and the misguided youth of Terence's account relayed by Augustine. And a further, more comprehensive analogy is implied between the historic Petrarch, author of the poem, and the youthful Augustine of *Confessions* I. Petrarch's use of the Augustinian text as a model for his own self-depiction, notably in the account of his ascent of Mt. Ventoux in *Fam.* IV.1, has been established by a number of studies in recent decades.[19] Specifically with regard to the association of rhetoric and passion Calcaterra identifies the moral correlation that Petrarch apparently perceived between himself and Augustine the rhetorician, the unregenerated sinner devoured by the flame of the senses,[20] and in the *Canzoniere*, as Freccero has noted, the *Confessions* furnishes a fundamental model "for much of Petrarch's depiction of the lover as sinner."[21] In the opening book of the *Confessions*, Augustine's discussion of the fascination of classical story occurs within a general indictment of the misconduct of his own passionate youth; similarly, in *Canzone* XXIII the *innamoramento* is located in the "dolce tempo de la prima etade" ("sweet time of the first age"), a time corresponding to the "primo tempo" ("first season") of CXLII in which the poet seeks shelter from the ardent light of Venus. The Jove to whom the poet compares himself in the *commiato* of No. XXIII is not merely an addition to the catalogue of mythological metamorphoses, but specifically a figure of sexual appetite. The allusion relates the entire series to the erotic susceptibility of youth, the "fera voglia che per mio mal crebbe" ("fierce desire which for my hurt grew") of the opening stanza, and situates the poem within the continuum of experience retrospectively depicted in the narrative movement of the collection as a whole.

The pagan Jove, a figure of Protean desire in the *Metamorphoses*, thus functions to allow expression of the poet's sexual fantasy, affording in *Canzone* XXIII a paradigm of sexual conquest to counter the fatal metamorphoses of unsuccessful lovers. The allusion to carnal passion reappears in the depiction of Laura as the single creature invulnerable to Cupid's attack: in a celebration of her chastity in *Canzone* XXIX she is represented as

> . . . stella in terra, e, come in lauro foglia,
> Conserva verde il pregio d'onestade;
> Ove non spira folgore nè indegno
> Vento mai che l'aggrave.

(Lines 46–49: . . . a star on earth, and as the laurel its leaf so she preserves the worth of chastity. No lightning ever comes, or unworthy wind, to bend her down!)

Immunity from lightning here suggests the virtue of chastity, as the "unworthy wind" suggests sexual passion.[22] And in the story of the poet relayed in the *Canzoniere* it is Laura's chastity that protects her admirer as well as herself, a protection alluded to repeatedly and allegorically detailed in the opening stanzas of CXLII:

> A la dolce ombra de le belle frondi
> Corsi fuggendo un dispietato lume
> Che 'n fin qua giù m'ardea dal terzo cielo; . . .
> Tal che, temendo de l'ardente lume,
> Non volsi al mio refugio ombra di poggi
> Ma de la pianta più gradita in cielo.

(Lines 1–3, 10–12: To the sweet shade of those beautiful leaves I ran, fleeing a pitiless light that was burning down upon me from the third heaven; . . . so that, fearing the burning light, I chose for my refuge no shade of hills but that of the tree most favored in Heaven.)

The heaven from which the laurel affords the young poet protection is that of Venus, and this symbolism is an essential component of the love-experience in the collection, mediating between desire and Christian virtue.[23]

Yet it remains evident, as Durling observes, that transformation into the laurel "is a figure of sublimation, in which desire accepts an object other than its natural one."[24] While the unattainability of the object of desire relates positively to chastity as a Christian virtue, it relates negatively to the anguish of the lover, and the figure of Jove reappears in a direct and vehement reaction to this tension in the final stanza of sonnet LX, "L'arbor gentil" ("The noble tree"), with the exclamation:

> Nè poeta ne colga mai nè Giove
> La privilegi; et al sol venga in ira
> Tal che si secchi ogni sua foglia verde.

(Lines 12–14: Let no poet ever gather from it, nor let Jove favor it, and let it receive the sun's anger so that all its green leaves dry up!)

This threefold exclamation, combining the three principal attributes of the laurel set forth in the Coronation Oration and repeatedly alluded to elsewhere as a defining set,[25] apparently invokes the destruction of the tree. To its rejection by poets, symbolic of the loss of its association with poetic immortality, is added the wrath of Apollo who had conferred on the beloved plant the attribute of eternal verdure; if Jove revokes the privilege he had accorded it, the laurel is rendered vulnerable to his lightning. Because of its harshness of tone and its evident punitive intent, the reader is tempted to dissociate the stanza from the lover's story in the *Canzoniere*; Raffaele Amaturo, for example, considers it a detail relevant not to the account of the love-experience in the collection but rather to its literary stylization, and dismisses it as a literary topos.[26] The poem, however, details the poet's rejection by the lady/ laurel ("fece di dolce sè spietato legno"—line 6: "it turned from sweet to bitter wood") and his consequent loss of hope, both amorous and poetic. As an angry expression of frustration, this final stanza is an essential moment of the "critical tension between contemplative form and sexual content" identified by Durling as a major theme throughout the collection.[27]

Poem LX is unique in the collection in its apparent invocation of the destruction of the laurel. In its images of destruction, however, it is closely related to the laurel stanza of *Canzone* CCCXXIII, "Standomi un giorno solo a la fenestra" ("Being one day alone at the window"), in which Jove's role is again prominent. The pagan divinity appears by name in the initial stanza, in a rhetorical reference which recalls the portrait of Sophonisba in the *Africa* and which functions again to introduce an element of sensuality that is a subdued but essential component of the entire stanza:

> Una fera m'apparve da man destra
> Con fronte umana da far arder Giove,
> Cacciata da duo veltri, un nero, un bianco.

(Lines 4–6: . . . a wild creature appeared to me on the right hand, with a human face such as to enamor Jove, pursued by two hounds, one black, one white. . . .)[28]

Through its reactivation of the associations of Jove with Laura prominent in the earlier components *in vita di madonna*, this allusion prepares the critical passage of the laurel stanza:

> E mirando 'l io fiso
> Cangiossi 'l cielo in torno, e tinto in vista
> Folgorando 'l percosse, e da radice
> Quella pianta felice
> Subito svelse, onde mia vita è trista,
> Che simile ombra mai non si racquista.

(Lines 31–36: And as I gazed on it fixedly the sky around was changed and, dark to sight, struck with lightning and suddenly tore up by the roots that happy plant, whereat my life is sorrowful, for such shade is never regained.)

Of the six visions through which the death of Laura is emblematically depicted in *Canzone* CCCXXIII, that of the fate of the laurel is of particular interest because the laurel alone of the six emblems has a primary association with immortality throughout the collection. In the "draft manuscript" Vat. Lat. 3195 the *canzone* includes several revisions in this section of the laurel stanza, and a parallel development written into the text attests that two alternatives were considered: an ancient woman, fierce in aspect, who uproots the plant, and the eventually favored version of a lightning bolt from an ominously darkening sky.[29] The choice of the lightning bolt may, as Chiappelli suggests, be characterized as that of a "modern" or "naturalistic" alternative in preference to a medieval, allegorical, figurative mode.[30] Yet even in his selection of an evidently naturalistic solution Petrarch apparently hesitated over the means by which to depict the destruction of the laurel. In *Eclogue* x, *Laurea uccidens*, a laurel plant lovingly cultivated by the shepherd Silvano is destroyed in his absence not by lightning but by a violent storm, and a similar reference to Laura's fate is found in *Fam.* viii.3. Here the initial representation of the laurel destroyed by a plague is replaced by the declaration of its destruction by a tempest, a correction evidently representing an attempt at rationalization between fact and symbol.[31]

It is within the broad context of mythological allusion in the *Canzoniere*, then, that we may locate the significance of the poet's choice of the lightning bolt as the means of destruction of his symbolic laurel. Within that context the lightning bolt of *Canzone* cccxxiii is more than a natural phenomenon: it is the act of a god. We may of course explain the destruction of the laurel by the lightning bolt, a bolt from which this plant alone had been immune, as fully consonant with the transitory nature of earthly life and happiness depicted throughout the six visions; in the Coronation Oration Petrarch himself demands, "in the affairs of men what thunderbolt is more terrible than the diuternity of time, which consumes all the works of men, all their possessions, all their fame? Rightly, therefore, since the laurel fears not the thunderbolt, is a crown of laurel given to those whose glory fears not the ages that like a thunderbolt lay all things low."[32] The *canzone*, however, suggests again the meteorological imagery of Jove's anger, the menacing anger that Laura's presence had once been able to dispel. The destruction of the laurel is specifically anticipated by the wish expressed in Poem lx that Jove withdraw the protection he had afforded the tree.

Yet the visions of *Canzone* cccxxiii are related within the context of the *Canzoniere* through the central event of the death of Laura, and while the laurel is subject to the unexplained violence of a pagan deity, Laura and her poet belong to an ordered Christian universe. In the depiction of the ultimate fate of the laurel and of Laura this contrast is sharply focused. Jove's protection of the laurel implies his power to destroy it, and it is as an omnipotent cosmic force that Petrarch relates the ruling pagan deity to the earthly delight and earthly hope expressed through his myth of the laurel. Jove's protection had been essential to the plant's eternal verdure, and it is his lightning that destroys it. With the plant dies also the illusion of earthly immortality as represented by the Daphne myth throughout the collection.[33] And Laura, too, dies, despite the fervent prayers which the poet addresses to God to protect her life. In its Christian finality, however, this death differs radically from its emblematic representation. The death of Laura is not only an end but a beginning: her body perishes, but she reappears in a new guise of immortality, bearing an urgent reminder to the poet to abandon transient earthly images and to seek instead the eternity of a Christian Heaven.

It is in his omnipotence within the Ovidian world of the *Canzoniere*, then, that Jove assumes his ultimate function in the collection as a counterpart to the Christian God. For the association of the two deities a ready model was provided by the moralizing Ovidian commentaries of Petrarch's period.[34] In Poems CXLVI and CLXVI the *vivo* and *eterno Giove*, like Dante's *sommo Giove* of *Purgatorio* VI.18 that precedes them, are readily identified as the Christian deity, and initially suggest a possible syncretism.[35] Jove, however, remains limited to his Ovidian role: further appeals by the poet are addressed directly to God or to an evidently Christian *cielo*, and it is central to the function of classical models in the *Canzoniere* that the Jove of pagan myth and the God of Christian history remain distinct.

To understand this function, we must recall that Petrarch is a Christian poet, for whom the fascination of classical myth is tempered not only by the moralizing allegories of Ovidian commentary[36] but also by Augustine's vigorous critique of pagan letters. Mythological story provides in the *Canzoniere* a rich variety of models to which the poet's own experience may be assimilated, both systematically, in his identification with Apollo as poet-lover, and episodically, as in the series of transformations of the metamorphosis *canzone*. This use of classical myth, however, is subject to an internal critique exemplified for Petrarch by the penitent rhetorician Augustine, and repeated intimations of idolatry recall the spiritual peril inherent in the fixity of his attention to symbolic secular images.[37] The tension inherent in the contrastive mythological and Christian models is initiated in the early poems that describe the *innamoramento* on Good Friday and relate the birth of the beloved to the nativity of Christ. The essential incompatibility of these models for the interpretation of human experience is insistently rendered in the final stanza of CXLII through the repetition of "other," as the sheltering image of the laurel yields to an allusion to the tree of the Cross and the third heaven of Venus is replaced by the Christian Heaven:

> Ora la vita breve e 'l loco e 'l tempo
> Mostranmi altro sentier di gire al cielo
> E di far frutto, non pur fior e frondi.
>   Altr'amor, altre frondi et altro lume,
> Altro salir al ciel per altri poggi
> Cerco (che n'è ben tempo), et altri rami.

(Lines 34–39: Now the shortness of life and the place and the season show me another pathway to go to Heaven and bear fruit, not merely flowers and leaves. Another love, other leaves, and another light, another climbing to Heaven by other hills I seek [for it is indeed time], and other branches.)

In the contrastive evocation of mythological and Christian models central to the poet's story of the *Canzoniere*, the displacement of Jove by the Christian God late in the collection functions within a broad reinterpretation of earthly experience through Christian images that progressively transplant pagan story.

Notes

1. In addition to numerous direct and indirect allusions, the name of Jove occurs eighteen times; see *Concordanze del Canzoniere di Francesco Petrarca* (Florence: Accademia della Crusca, 1971), vol. I.

2. The Coronation Oration is translated by E. H. Wilkins in *Studies in the Life and Works of Petrarch* (Cambridge, Mass.: Mediaeval Academy of America, 1955), pp. 300–313.

3. Giovanni Boccaccio, *Genealogie deorum gentilium*, ed. Vincenzo Romano, 2 vols. (Bari: Laterza, 1951), pp. 363–64. For discussion of this passage in relation to Petrarch's Oration, see Thomas Roche's forthcoming study of Ovid's Daphne, Petrarch's *Can-*

zoniere, and their sixteenth-century commentators.

4. Africa, IX. 117–19, ed. G. Martellotti, in F. Petrarca, Rime, Trionfi e poesie latine (Milan and Naples: Ricciardi, 1951). Petrarch's Africa, trans. and annotated by Thomas G. Bergin and Alice S. Wilson (New Haven and London: Yale University Press, 1977), p. 227. All translations from the Africa refer to this volume.

5. References to the text of the Rime are to the edition of Giosuè Carducci and Severino Ferrari (Florence: Sansoni, 1899), reprinted with an introduction by Gianfranco Contini in 1969. All ranslations of Petrarch's Italian poems are from Petrarch's Lyric Poems: the "Rime sparse" and Other Lyrics, trans. and ed. by Robert M. Durling (Cambridge, Mass. and London: Harvard University Press, 1976).

6. Petrarch follows Albricus in his own description of the pictorial representation of the god in the great hall of Syphax in the Africa: "Jupiter ante alios, augusta in sede superbus / Sceptra manu fulmenque tenens" ("first of all sits Jupiter in pride on his high throne with bolt and sceptre"); see Jean Seznec, The Survival of the Pagan Gods, trans. B. Sessions (New York: Pantheon, 1953), pp. 172–74.

7. The epithet also recurs in Petrarch's Latin works. See Alfred Noyer-Weidner, "Zur Mythologieverwendung in Petrarcas Canzoniere," in Petrarca 1304–1374: Beiträge zu Werk und Wirkung, ed. F. Schalk (Frankfurt-am-Main: Klostermann, 1975), esp. p. 234.

8. See, for example, Gianfranco Contini's Saggio d'un commento alle correzioni del Petrarca volgare (Florence: Sansoni, 1943), and Umberto Bosco's study of "Amore e contemplazione" in Francesco Petrarca (Bari: Laterza, 1961), pp. 23–49.

9. The portrait of Sophonisba occurs in Rime, Trionfi, pp. 638–43 and in Africa, pp. 83–85. For an analysis of Petrarch's verbal portraiture see Ezio Raimondi, Metafora e storia (Turin: Einaudi, 1970), esp. pp. 180–87.

10. Ugo Dotti, "Petrarca: il mito dafneo," Convivium, XXXVII (1969), pp. 9–11.

11. Thomas Bergin, Petrarch (New York: Twayne, 1970), pp. 163–64. This Laura-Sophonisba is a third role in addition to those of Laura-Daphne and a Laura-Beatrice who provides celestial direction.

12. Robert Durling, Petrarch's Lyric Poems, p. 28.

13. Aldo Bernardo, Petrarch, Laura, and the "Triumphs" (Albany, N.Y.: SUNY Press, 1974), pp. 103–4.

14. Dennis Dutschke, "The Textual Situation and Chronological Assessment of Petrarch's CANZONE XXIII," Italian Quarterly, XVIII (1974), 49.

15. John Brenkman observes that these allusions involve "a series of displacements, from the literal to the metaphorical, that betrays the infinite suspension of his desire;" see "Writing, Desire, Dialectic in Petrarch's Rime 23," Pacific Coast Philology, IX (1974), 12–19.

16. St. Augustine, The Confessions, trans. R. S. Pine-Coffin (Baltimore: Penguin, 1961), pp. 36–37.

17. Giovanni Boccaccio, Genealogie deorum gentilium, XV.8, trans. in Charles Osgood, Boccaccio on Poetry (Indianapolis and New York: Liberal Arts Press, 1956), p. 127. As Osgood notes, Boccaccio here probably recalls Augustine's citation of Terence: his "defense" frequently appears as an answer to Augustine's specific charges.

18. Petrarch acknowledges the seductive appeal of this narrative in Fam. XXIV.10

addressed to Horace: "Who would not lend thee a willing ear," he exclaims, "when thou recountest . . . how Danae is deceived by a shower of gold?" Şee Petrarch's *Letters to Classical Authors*, trans. M. Cosenza (Chicago: University of Chicago Press, 1910), p. 130.

19. See especially Bortolo Martinelli, "Del Petrarca e il Ventoso," in *Studi in onore di Alberto Chiari*, II (Brescia: Paideia ,1973), pp. 768–834, and Robert Durling, "The Ascent of Mt. Ventoux and the Crisis of Allegory," *Italian Quarterly*, XVIII (1974), 7–28.

20. Carlo Calcaterra, *Nella selva del Petrarca* (Bologna: Cappelli, 1942), p. 44.

21. John Freccero, "The Fig Tree and the Laurel: Petrarch's Poetics," *Diacritics*, v, No.1 (Spring 1975), p. 34. For a detailed examination of the *Canzoniere* in relation to the *Confessions* see Nicolae Iliescu, *Il Canzoniere petrarchesco e Sant'Agostino* (Rome: Accademia Dacoromena, 1962).

22. See Michele Feo, "Il sogno di Cerere e la morte del lauro petrarchesco," in *Il Petrarca ad Arquà: Atti del Convegno di Studi nel VI Centenario (1370–1970)*, ed. Billanovich and Frasso (Padua: Antenore, 1974), p. 135.

23. See the discussion by Marga Cottino-Jones, "The Myth of Apollo and Daphne in Petrarch's *Canzoniere*: The Dynamics and Literary Function of Transformation," in *Francis Petrarch, Six Centuries Later: A Symposium*, ed. A Scaglione (Chapel Hill and Chicago: University of North Carolina and Newberry Library, 1975), pp. 152–76, and Bernardo's chapter on "Laura as *nova figura*" in *Petrarch, Laura, and the "Triumphs"*, pp. 163–201.

24. Durling, *Petrarch's Lyric Poems*, p. 27.

25. It occurs, for example, in *Eclogues* III and IX.

26. Raffaele Amaturo, *Petrarca* (Bari: Laterza, 1971), p. 274. Amaturo concludes that the poet only apparently invokes the destruction of the tree: "si intende che altro è il pensiero del poeta" (p. 275).

27. Durling, *Petrarch's Lyric Poems*, p. 20.

28. For a discussion of this aspect of the poem see Charles Roger Davis, *Petrarch's Rime 323 and its Tradition through Spenser* (Princeton University dissertation, 1973), pp. 32 and 43: "The flesh-eating dogs," he suggests, are part of a "very medieval and Christian sequence lifting Petrarch's personal world to the level of precept," and they "more than suggest Gula, the lust of the flesh."

29. For a description of the manuscript and a discussion of the revisions see Fredi Chiappelli, *Studi sul linguaggio del Petrarca: la canzone delle visioni* (Florence: Olschki, 1971), pp. 52–53.

30. Ibid., p. 68.

31. See the discussion by Feo, "Il sogno di Cerere," esp. pp. 142–43.

32. Wilkins, *Studies*, pp. 309–12. In the *Secretum* Petrarch avows that "one of the chief reasons why I love the laurel is that thunder will not strike this tree" (ibid., p. 156).

33. With this destruction of the laurel, as Feo points out, we find the end not only of Laura but of the entire myth of Daphne as well; every certainty collapses if Jove, the laurel's greatest protector, turns his bolts against the plant (p. 143). Jose Basile, *Forma simbolica ed allegorica nei "Rerum vulgarium fragmenta" ed altre cose*

(Assisi-Rome: B. Carucci, 1971), comments that the story of Apollo and Daphne in the *Canzoniere* is the allegorical guise of the illusion of hope.

34. For the commentaries see Aldo Bernardo, *Petrarch, Scipio, and the "Africa"* (Baltimore: Johns Hopkins Press, 1962), pp. 137–38. Petrarch's friend Pierre Bersuire, for example, identifies the ruling divinity of the pagan pantheon *naturaliter* as fire (we recall the *commiato* to *Canzone* XXIII "ma ben fui fiamma . . . "), but also *spiritualiter* as the "contemplative virtue of all good" and by further extension as "a figure of the Christian God, especially in his aspect of charity." See also the important study of Don Cameron Allen, *Mysteriously Meant* (Baltimore: Johns Hopkins Press, 1970).

35. Thomas Bergin decries the failure of an apparent attempt at syncretism in the *Africa*: "Petrarch's description of a pagan Jove pompously plotting his own incarnation is simply absurd" (*Petrarch*, pp. 112–13).

36. In his forthcoming study of the *Canzoniere* in relation to the commentators Thomas Roche argues persuasively that "the body of interpretive glosses that accrued to the original text of Ovid from the twelfth century on could not have been ignored by Petrarch in the creation of his myth," and concludes that from the poet's use of the Daphne myth the reader is "meant to be consciously aware of the discrepancy between Petrarch's love for Laura and his love of God" — between *cupiditas* and *caritas*.

37. See especially Robert Durling, "Petrarch's 'Giovene donna sotto un verde lauro'," *MLN*, LXXXVI (1971), 1–20, who sees in the diamond branches of the laurel of sestina XXX an idolatrous counterpart of the cross; see also Freccero, "The Fig Tree and the Laurel," pp. 34–40.

Boccaccio on Interpretation:
Guido's Escape
(*Decameron* VI.9)

ROBERT M. DURLING

ERHAPS MORE THAN ANY OTHER single individual in our time, Charles Singleton has awakened students of medieval literature to the richness and subtlety of the poetic effects available to medieval poets through the use of figural allegory. While other interpreters of Dante were caught in the false Crocean antithesis of *structure* versus *poetry* (or *figura* versus *earthly realism*), Singleton showed how Dante's allegory is the life-blood of the poetry itself, permeating it *usque ad unguem*, to the very texture of the language. Singleton has shown how allegorical interpretation, truly understood, is not at all the imposition of a theological straitjacket but rather a *freeing* of the text from the rigidities of narrowly conceived readings, whether literal or figurative, into the richness of its suggestiveness and of its intertextuality.

It is in the spirit of such an opening up of implication that in this paper I would like to consider Boccaccio's *novella* of the witty retort given by Guido Cavalcanti to the *brigata* of messer Betto Brunelleschi, when cornered by them among the tombs surrounding the Florentine baptistry,[1] as a meditation on the activity of interpretation, especially the interpretation of literary texts. The *novella* repeatedly shows the characters performing interpretation of each others' actions and words, sometimes erroneously; it displays a considerable range of interpretive possibilities from utter incomprehension or error and distortion on the one hand to full comprehension on the other. It shows that the interpreter's motives are a basic factor in the quality of his interpretation. And it has important implications for the interpretation of the *Decameron*, as I hope to make clear.[2]

The "text" taken as exemplary in this meditation is the complex of Guido Cavalcanti's words and actions. Because of their desire to count the noble and socially accomplished Guido among the members of the *brigata*, messer Betto and his friends are pained and puzzled by his refusal or avoidance of them; they form a preliminary interpretation of his conduct, and on its basis they make a playful (but also partly serious and hostile) assault on Guido; he escapes their physical encirclement of him and their verbal aggression, leaving them with a witticism which then becomes a more specific focus of interpretation.

We first see messer Betto and his *brigata* attempting to interpret Guido's reluctance to join them, and there are a number of clues that they are not likely to be able to do so. For one thing, the first paragraph of the *novella* proper, which describes the life of the Florentine *brigate* in general, although it explicitly praises their customs as praiseworthy and contrasts the aristocratic liberality of former times with the now-prevalent avarice, also suggests a side that is less positive; it suggests that they are ostentatious, conformist, and highly competitive.[3] Considerable emphasis is placed on the habit of messer Betto and his *brigata* have of paying honor to individuals by feasting them:

> e così per ordine tutti mettevan tavola, ciascuno il suo dì, a tutta la brigata; e in quella spesse volte onoravano e gentili uomini forestieri, quando ve ne capitavano, e ancora de' cittadini . . . .

> (and so in turn they each provided a meal, each on his day, for the whole brigata; and often they honored in this way both noblemen from elsewhere, when any happened to be in Florence, and ones from the city itself . . . .)

The observation is made casually, but the question as to who—and what —deserves honor lies at the thematic heart of the *novella*. Guido's skill in paying honor is a chief reason the *brigata* want him as a member:

> e a chiedere a lingua sapeva onorare cui nell'animo gli capeva che il valesse.

(and he was able impromptu to pay honor to anyone it occurred
to him deserved it).

In the eyes of the *brigata*, Guido's choices may seem capricious: "cui nel-
l'animo gli capeva che il valesse," but the issue of his superior discernment is implicit here.

For the *brigata*'s attraction to Guido is rather suspect. They are drawn
to him because of his wealth, his social standing, and his social graces.
Although he is "un de' miglior loici che avesse il mondo e ottimo natural
filosofo" ("one of the best logicians in the world and an excellent natural
philosopher"), the *brigata* do not honor him for these accomplishments:
"delle quali cose poco la brigata curava" ("about which things the brigata
cared little"). And not only in his case: they are not interested in the life
of the mind at all. Their way of life may not be actually vicious, but it
involves a disregard of the intellect in favor of social activity. The *novella*
is thus based on the familiar antithesis between the active and the contemplative life: the *brigata* overvalue the active life. And the fact that it
has apparently not occurred to the *brigata* to honor Guido by feasting him,
according to their custom, is part of the suggestion of their lack of
discernment.[4]

Guido's individualism is set over against the rather unthinking conform-
ism of messer Betto's *brigata* as more truly aristocratic and as more serious.
His social accomplishments and his wealth are not belittled; they are asserted
as valuable by the narrator, but they are put in second place. It is striking, of course, that Guido's fame as a poet — and an obscure one — is never
mentioned. Presumably the *brigata* are not interested in poetry either,
though the reference may well be lacking precisely because the *novella* is
also concerned with literary interpretation.

The focus at the outset, then, is on messer Betto and his *brigata*'s interpretation of Guido's reluctance to join them:

Ma a messer Betto non era mai potuto venir fatto d'averlo, e credeva
egli co' suoi compagni che ciò avvenisse per ciò che Guido alcuna
volta speculando molto abstratto dagli uomini divenia; e per ciò che
egli alquanto tenea della oppinione degli epicuri, si diceva tralla gente
volgare che queste sue speculazioni erano solo in cercare se trovar
si potesse che Iddio non fosse.

(But messer Betto had never managed to have him, and with his companions he believed that that happened because Guido often became much abstracted from people in his speculations; and because he held somewhat of the opinion of the Epicureans, it was said among the common people that these speculations of his were exclusively to find out if it could be concluded that God did not exist.)

Messer Betto believes that Guido is taken out of human society—out of the active life, then—by his devotion to speculation (contemplation), and a first anomaly this presents is that of a supposed Epicurean who—in practice, whatever his Epicurean doctrines might suggest—lives more as a contemplative than as an active member of society.[5]

His supposition about Guido's unwillingness to join the *brigata* is, as messer Betto will later conclude, erroneous, or at least only part of the truth; and it is significant that the misinterpretation, which is the basis of the entire mistake of playful aggression against Guido, is associated with the part of the sentence that relates the oversimplification of the *gente volgare*. For the *fact* ("egli tenea alquanto della oppinione degli epicuri") and the *rumor* ("si diceva") are sharply distinguished,[6] and the rumor is related in terms (note especially the *solo*) that emphasize the supposition of the *volgar gente* that they know exactly what Guido thinks.[7]

The *brigata* accept the supposition of the *gente volgare* as a basis for action, and the issue becomes whether they can corner Guido, hem him in, define him. From their point of view, they are attempting to recruit him with their playful aggression, or, failing that, to protest against his unfriendliness. When they see him on foot among the tombs, their cry is, "Andiamo a dargli briga" ("Let's go and give him trouble"). The choice of words, as ever in Boccaccio, is significant. Branca glosses *briga* as *noia*, but the original sense is closer to *quarrel* or *fight*.[8] "Andiamo a dargli briga," then, means something like "Let's try force on him," and there is something utterly characteristic about the word and the act: their way of life, as we have been told, is to impose themselves on the social scene. *Briga*, then, reflects negatively on *brigata*, of which it is the etymon, and the "assalto sollazzevole" (the term *assalto* reminding us of the etymon) casts the group in the role of playful *briganti* as they drive into a corner the dismounted and apparently unarmed Guido.

The members of the *brigata* are hasty and presumptuous, but—perhaps more important—they are governed by anger and a certain degree of malice, which later falls on their own heads. Their desire to force Guido into a corner is the frustrated interpreter's desire to have the text mean one thing, even at the cost of forcing it. Even in the rumor of the *gente volgare*, Guido is not supposed to have succeeded in proving (even to his own satisfaction) that God does not exist.[9] But the *brigata* supposed they know the answer to their verbal challenge in advance, and they imply that his preferring the contemplative life to their company is stupid: "Guido, tu rifiuti di essere di nostra brigata; ma ecco, quando tu avrai trovato che Iddio non sia, che avrai fatto?" ("Guido, you refuse to belong to our *brigata*; but look, when you have found that God does not exist, what will you have done?") The jibe at one level confidently asserts the superiority of the life of *solazzo*; at another it suggests that even if one found through philosophy that God does not exist, the supposed proof would not affect the facts of the matter. The implied answer, then, is *nulla, nothing*.[10]

The *brigata* do not foresee Guido's answer. But just as he knows how to honor men *a chiedere a lingua*, so he knows how to *dir villania* with equal readiness, something the *brigata* have left out of consideration even though it was one of their main reasons for desiring him as a member. And when the answer comes, they do not at first understand it. "Signori, voi mi potete dir a casa vostra ciò che vi piace" ("My lords, you can say to me whatever you please in your own house"), goes utterly over their heads. They suppose that what he has said is meaningless, just as they supposed his speculations were: "cominciarono a dire che egli era uno smemorato e che quello che egli aveva risposto non veniva a dir nulla" ("they began to say that he was witless and that the meaning of his reply amounted to nothing"), because they are in a public place with which they have no more connection than any other citizen, including Guido. They do not understand the metaphor, and they do not understand how it applies to them. They think it means, again, *nothing*.[11]

As messer Betto points out, they are the *smemorati*, the unaware ones, if they have not understood Guido. But clearly they were also *smemorati* in their *assalto*: when they sought to corner Guido among the tombs they were not thinking about the meaning of tombs, but Guido's presence of mind capitalizes in all possible ways on the scene itself. His swiftness of retort and action is such that there is a strong suggestion that he was meditating on the tombs while walking among them.

That the point of Guido's retort must be explained to the *brigata* by their leader is the culmination of the *novella*. Messer Betto takes on the role of authoritative expositor of the text, and his act of interpretation is made the center of attention. He does make two indispensable interpretive steps: he identifies a basic metaphor, and he attempts to apply the metaphor to himself and his friends. Guido's words are, indeed, incomprehensible except in terms of a figurative meaning applied to the tombs; the literalists have failed to make the connection *house: tomb*.

> "Gli smemorati siete voi, se voi non l'avete inteso: egli ci ha onestamente e in poche parole detta la maggior villania del mondo, per ciò che, se voi riguarderete bene, queste arche sono le case de' morti, per ciò che in esse si pongono e dimorano i morti; le quali egli dice che son nostra casa, a dimostrarci che noi e gli altri uomini idioti e non letterati siamo, a comparazion di lui e degli altri uomini scienziati, peggio che uomini morti, e per ciò, qui essendo, noi siamo a casa nostra."

> (P. 564: "You are the witless ones, if you did not understand him: in few words and with great elegance he has given us the greatest insult in the world, because, if you will look well, these tombs are the houses of the dead, since the dead are placed in them and dwell there; and he says that they are our house, to show us that we and other ignorant, unlettered men are, in comparison with him and other learned men, worse than dead men, and therefore, being here we are in our own house.")

Now although messer Betto's explanation is accurate as far as it goes, and although he sets it forth with an assurance that seems to have imposed on most students of the *novella*, it is only partial. It comments only on Guido's words (and only on some of them and only on one aspect of them), not on his actions. Even on the face of it, messer Betto's explanation raises some questions. Why does he so patiently accept the label? If the unlearned are *worse than dead*, that must be because the learned are *more than alive*. This is a clear reference to the familiar idea that Guido and those like him have influence and earn glory that constitutes a kind of immortality. Why is this meaning left implicit?

As we have seen, the *novella* builds a series of interpretations: the *gente volgare*'s, the *brigata*'s initial one, the *brigata*'s incomprehension of the retort, messer Betto's explanation. Why do critics suppose the series is supposed to stop here? For just as we contemplate the difference between the *brigata's* incomprehension and messer Betto's insight, so also we are invited to consider whether there are not further levels of meaning. Messer Betto is quite unaware, it would seem, of the idea of literary immortality, in any case he is quite indifferent to it: surely the reader is not supposed to acquiesce? There is also a lightly ironic tone to the ending of the *novella*: "tennero per innanzi messer Betto sottile e intendente cavaliere" ("from then on they held messer Betto to be a knight of subtle understanding") (I shall return to this clause). Messer Betto and his friends are, as he says, "uomini idioti e non litterati," but the situation has placed messer Betto in a role—that of expositor—usually reserved, in Boccaccio's time at least, to the learned. There is a sly dissonance in his inappropriateness to be the expositor of Boccaccio's wit. And while messer Betto may not be laying claim to actual illiteracy in his phrase "idioti e non litterati," the suggestion is strong that a more careful and less hasty interpreter might see further into Guido's joke. We find, then, three cases (two explicit and one implicit) of a contrast between distorted or oversimple interpretation and more refined interpretation: the unqualified view of the *gente volgare* is explicitly contrasted with the more reliable characterization of him as *alquanto* an Epicurean; the incomprehension of the *brigata* is explicitly contrasted with messer Betto's insight; and messer Betto's incomplete comprehension is implicitly contrasted with the narrator's, the author's, or a reader's fuller comprehension.

To consider first the incompleteness of messer Betto's interpretation in its most obvious respect, and accepting the secular level at which it is pitched, what is the significance of Guido's *action*? Partly, it would seem, that Guido's quickness and resourcefulness have enabled him not only to answer the taunt but also to escape physically as well as hermeneutically from the *brigata's* encirclement. In other words, he has demonstrated a superiority not only in the contemplative sphere but also in the active, and the important implication is that the contemplative life is superior to the active life not only in intrinsic worth but also in being the source of the principles that must guide activity and make it effective. There would also seem to be a corollary in the fact that Guido is physically capable of vaulting over the tombs: this means that he is a trained athlete, and whether or not we are supposed to think of him as concealing his practice in arms and horsemanship (and other accomplishments of his class: "ogni cosa che far volle e a gentile uom pertenente"—"everything that he wanted to do and that pertained to a nobleman"), the *assalto sollazzevole* did not anticipate his agility as a factor in the situation. His escape is particularly successful because it turns the tables neatly on the aggressors: he puts between him and them the very barrier they were relying on to hold him in; partly *because* they are on horseback, they are now blocked by the tombs. Thus it is clear the *briga* is not the only etymon functional in the *novella*; another important one is *cavalcare*: overconfident in their being on horseback, our *briganti* have forgotten that they are dealing with one of the *Cavalcanti*. Hence the reference in the last sentence to messer Betto as a "sottile e intendente cavaliere" acquires an even more ironic tinge.[12]

Not only does messer Betto's exegesis not account for Guido's action, except perhaps implicitly, it only refers to one half of Guido's retort, "Signori, . . . a casa vostra. . . ." The other half, "voi mi potete dire . . .ciò che vi piace" is also important. It brands the *brigata's* taunt not only as gratuitously insulting but also as unthinkingly accepting of the rumors of the *gente volgare*: what pleases the *brigata*, "ciò che vi piace," seems to be the same as what pleases the mob. Like the mob, then, the *brigata* is in no position to know what the goal of Guido's speculations might in fact be; and if they cannot understand his retort, they would not understand even a lucid explanation of a subtle philosophical idea with its manifold distinctions and qualifications. Guido's joke implies, further, that since they are taking advantage of being *at home* in their aggression on him — and since he is thus bound to politeness, by being as it were their guest — he is by the same token released from the responsibility of accounting for his speculations. The presumptuous questioner may be answered with a joke.

Finally, messer Betto focuses exclusively on the negative aspect of Guido's retort. It is because he and his *brigata* have been interpreting Guido in hostility that the situation seems to reverse itself to their disadvantage, so that they consider that they have been punished, labeled irrevocably *worse than dead*. But what they take as condemnation can also be taken as a rebuke, an admonition, even an invitation. Why do they not consider whether Guido is worth *following*? They do not have to be caught among the tombs; if they are willing to learn from him — to make him their *guida*[13] — they can transcend the tomb just as he does. And in reminding them of the inevitability of death Guido may be doing them a valuable service. In the Middle Ages, *memento mori* was often thought to be good advice. Guido *memoratus est mori*, and the featured term *smemorato* is unmistakably related to this familiar theme.[14] Furthermore, the very metaphor on which his joke rests is significantly related to a famous Biblical passage: "Et sepulchra eorum domus illorum in aeternum" (Psalm 48:12). We are not told whether messer Betto is aware of the allusion; presumably he is not, as *non litterato*, but presumably Guido is aware of it, and obviously Boccaccio is.[15] A full interpretation of Guido's words must inquire into the function of the allusion.

But at this point we should pause and draw some tentative conclusions about the view of interpretation taken in the *novella*. Clearly enough, the interpreter is not going to get far if he is hemmed in by his own preconceived notions, if he is hasty or ill-informed, or if his interpretive activity is governed by hostility. And he should not suppose that he can enclose and define (confine) the meaning of a great text. He ought to assume that the writer is more intelligent than he is. And one of the most important interpretive steps would seem to be that of considering how the text applies to himself. In this *novella*, then, Boccaccio has clearly located the problematic of interpretation as much in the interpreter as in the text itself. What ought not, really, to surprise us is that a number of these ideas are very close to points made in the defense of poetry in the *Genealogie deorum gentilium*, Book xiv, whose relation to this *novella* is worthy of further study.[16]

These general implications are extremely important, I think, and I shall return to this question of their applicability to the *Decameron*; but first our attention is claimed by some more particular ones. Boccaccio's character Guido is overtly a reference to the historical Guido Cavalcanti, and we must ask what implications the *novella* has for Boccaccio's view of the historical Guido. But, as the critical tradition has always recognized, the *novella* is also a tissue of allusions to the *Commedia*, especially to *Inferno* x, in which Dante encounters Guido's father and father-in-law. The question of interpretation, then, as Boccaccio has set it forth here, includes not only the function of the biblical allusion but the function of the allusions to the *Commedia*. As must be obvious immediately, the *novella* involves the question of how to interpret the *Commedia*, or at least those parts of it that refer to Guido Cavalcanti. This is partly to say that the *novella* reveals something of how Boccaccio read *Inferno* x, but also much more. For one thing, as we shall see, it shows that Boccaccio interpreted other passages of the *Commedia* as relevant to Dante's view of Guido, passages where Guido is not explicitly referred to at all; the question becomes what importance Boccaccio seems to attribute to the theme of Guido in the *Commedia*. Our *novella* is in fact one of the keys to the understanding of the *intertextuality* of the *Decameron* and the *Commedia*.[17]

For the interpretation of Boccaccio's *novella requires* that its relation to *Inferno* x be accounted for. For one thing, *Inferno* x warns against reliance on the secular forms of immortality: glory and descendants. In particular, it is not through *altezza d'ingegno* that one can overcome the tomb, and it is precisely through the imagery of the tomb that Dante insists on the futility of worldly values. The heretics' reliance on exclusively worldly values, their pessimistic view of human existence, their denial of the immortality of the soul — all are summed up as a choice of the tomb as ultimate goal.[18] They were caught in the tomb in this life, as in a *cieco / carcere* (*Inf.* x.58–59), so that they could not see the light.[19] Since both in its setting and in its action Boccaccio's *novella* unmistakably refers to this set of themes, there must be an accounting for the significance of the reference. For in Dante's terms Guido's superiority — as asserted in messer Betto's interpretation — has already been identified as illusory.

Thus the allusions to the *Commedia* make it impossible for the interpretation of Guido's escape to stop at the level reached by messer Betto. A further step is required by the fact that *Inferno* x is an attack on intellectual pride as well as family pride.[20] One of the possibilities of Boccaccio's story is the ironic one: although Guido can so lightly escape his earthly questioners he will ultimately have to confront the divine Judge, and his intellectual pride will condemn him to the same tomb as his relatives occupy.[21] But Boccaccio has unmistakably used the imagery of *resurrection* in Guido's escape. This would make the irony doubly poignant, of course, but the function of the imagery in the *novella* is more complex. For one thing, it is precisely from the accusation of irreligion that Guido escapes with his figural leap; and messer Betto and company do not consider whether their taunt was fair to the complexity of Guido's mentality. Further, the imagery of resurrection in the *novella* refers also to its presence in *Inferno* ix–x; there the human desire for the secular forms of immortality are identified as themselves expressions of the immortality of the soul, and the heretics act out an abortive resurrection.[22] As Boccaccio knew, the very metaphorical connection *house:tomb* was associated with the theme of resurrection and immortality in the traditional interpretations of Psalm 48:12 and underlies the references to resurrection in *Inferno* x.[23] This amounts to saying that in medieval terms the *primary* suggestion of a leap over the tomb is that of *resurrection* and *salvation*. If the *novella* has been challenging the reader to carry the interpretive arc further, it would seem to lead in this direction. And it is a direction consistent with the subtle way in which the *novella* has discredited the view of Guido as a whole-hearted—that is, heretical—Epicurean (or Averroist) by identifying the *brigata*'s level of understanding with hostile prejudice and unthinking acceptance of rumor.[24] For the *brigata*'s supposition that they live for honor and are the dispensers of honor has been entirely discredited as they reveal their inability to discern to whom honor is due. The suggestion is very strong that if anyone in the *novella* is an Epicurean—*porcus de grege Epicuri*—it is the *brigata* that lives mainly for dressing up, parading, and eating.

And Guido's leap over the tomb contrasts sharply with the actions of Dante's heretics in *Inferno* x. In fact, Boccaccio's *novella* makes Guido parallel to Dante, who moves on, and messer Betto's group parallel to the heretics, who must stay where they are. And this parallel between the *brigata* and Dante's heretics is a fundamental one. For, as Boccaccio saw, *Inferno* x is also a commentary on interpretation: the mistaken philosophy of the heretics is represented by Dante as a systematic *misreading* of the data of experience. Even more to the point for our *novella*, the action of *Inferno* x is a dialogue in which the heretics are shown misinterpreting what is said to them and in which the interpretative mistakes are corrected by the superior interpreter, Dante.[25]

The remark applies to both heretics, Farinata and Cavalcante, but for our purposes the important figure is Cavalcante, Guido's father, who asks a series of questions about Guido. His first mistake is to suppose that it is because of Dante's *altezza d'ingegno* (height of intellect) that he is going through Hell, and the first part of Dante's reply corrects it: he is not on his own but is relying on Virgil's guidance. To the second part of Cavalcante's question (Where is Guido? Why is he not with Dante?), Dante replies with the deliberately obscure line "forse cui Guido vostro ebbe a disdegno" (*Inf.* x.63: "perhaps for one whom your Guido disdained"),[26] one of the most famous cruxes in the poem, one that has elicited volumes of discussion.[27]

Cavalcante misinterprets the halting phrase[28] to mean that Guido is dead, an interpretation of *ebbe* that is pessimistic and paranoid, like messer Betto's interpretation of *a casa vostra*. Although Dante—after clearing up his own confusion about the foreknowledge of the damned—sends word to Cavalcante to correct his mistake ("Or direte a quel caduto / che il suo nato è ancor co' vivi congiunto," *Inf.* x.110–11: "Now will you tell that fallen one / that his son is still conjoined to the living"), he never does explain whatever it was that his own obscure phrase meant. Now of course his reticence here is meant to challenge the reader to be a better interpreter than Cavalcante, but the point is not so much to arrive at the one "correct" meaning of the line as to understand how many different ambiguities and possibilities it is in fact capable of. [29]

By depicting Guido performing an action that iconographically signifies resurrection, then, Boccaccio has raised the question of Guido's salvation. He has put his finger on what is indeed the central question of *Inferno* x: "Mio figlio ov' è?" ("Where is my son?") In other words, Boccaccio has seen that the question of Guido's salvation literally haunts Dante, and he has seen an essential level of meaning of Dante's last message to Cavalcante, that Guido is still conjoined to the living. For just as the connection *house:tomb* is basic to the interpretation of Guido's retort, and just as that connection inescapably implies the dual sense of *tomb* (burial of the body, burial of the soul), so the phrase *co' vivi congiunto* has two senses. If Guido is still literally alive in April, 1300, he may still be spiritually alive; and when Dante is writing the poem years later, the answer to "Mio figlio ov' è?" may still be the same: Guido may be, and Dante must hope that he is, somewhere other than in Hell.[30] In fact, the figure of Guido's father enables Dante to project onto someone else his own agonizing fears about his implication in Guido's death and to cling to a hopeful interpretation of Guido's death. One can go so far as to say that Dante *must not* pretend to know the state of Guido's soul after death; the pretence (and it is only that) of knowing God's judgments has something dangerous about it, and it is with Guido (perhaps also with Dante's father and mother, about whom he is entirely silent in the *Commedia*) that the line is drawn.

One of the most striking conclusions that emerges from these considerations is that Boccaccio seems to have seen that Dante's anxiety about Guido's salvation and about his own role in Guido's death is one of the motives underlying the grand structural pattern of the correlations among the ninth and tenth cantos, the gateway cantos, of the three *cantiche*. In particular he seems to have seen that the long warning against judging the state of souls after death put in the mouth of Thomas Aquinas (*Paradiso* XIII.112–42) is relevant to the theme of hasty judgment in *Inferno* x and especially to the question, "mio figlio ov'è?":

> E questo ti sia sempre piombo a' piedi,
>   per farti mover lento com' uom lasso
>   e al sì e al no che tu non vedi:
> che quelli è tra li stolti bene a basso
>   che sanza distinzion afferma e nega

ne l'un così come ne l'altro passo;
perch'elli 'ncontra che più volte piega
l'oppinion corrente in falsa parte,
e poi l'affetto l'intelletto lega . . . .[31]
Non sien le genti, ancor, troppo sicure
a giudicar, sì come quei che stima
le biade in campo pria che sien mature;
ch'i' ho veduto tutto 'l verno prima
lo prun mostrarsi rigido e feroce,
poscia portar la rosa in su la cima
e legno vidi già dritto e veloce
correr lo mar per tutto suo cammino,
perire al fine a l'intrar del foce.
Non creda donna Berta e ser Martino,
per vedere un furare, altro offerere,
vederli dentro al consiglio divino;
che quel può surgere, e quel può cadere.

(*Par.* xiii.112-20, 130-42: And let this always be lead on your feet to make you move slowly, like a weary man, toward the "yes" and the "no" that you do not see: for he is surely well down among the stupid who affirms and denies without distinction in either case; for it happens that a hasty judgment often bends in a false direction, and then affect binds the intellect . . . Let not the people be too sure in judging, like one who estimates the grain in the field before it is ripe; for I have seen the thornbush seem rigid and fierce all winter and later carry the rose on its summit; and I have seen a ship run straight and swift across the sea for all its voyage, to perish at the end in the entrance to the port. Let not donna Berta and ser Martino believe, when they see one man steal, another make offerings, that they may see them within God's counsel; for the first can arise, the second can fall.)

Boccaccio's messer Betto is a kind of donna Berta or ser Martino who, along with his *brigata*, makes the very faults of judgment warned against here, in judging—of all people—Guido Cavalcanti. He and his *brigata* think of Guido as an Epicurean *sanza distinzion*; they rush to judgment; their judgment is bound by *affetto* (in their case, hostility); they are presumptuous and over-confident (*troppo sicuri*); but although they are on horseback, Guido rises above them (*surge*). [32]

This conclusion has far-reaching implications for Boccaccio's understanding of Dante, at least at the time when he was writing the *Decameron* and probably also when he was writing the *Esposizioni sopra il Dante*. It means that we must give up once and for all the traditional view of Boccaccio as an amiable but essentially dull-witted reader of the *Commedia*; it means that in some respects at least Boccaccio was more advanced in his methods of study than many modern critics of the *Commedia*, for the collation of corresponding cantos of the three *cantiche* is even now only gradually being seen as the fundamental interpretative procedure that it is. It means also that the *Esposizioni sopra il Dante* are very far from setting forth the full range of Boccaccio's understanding of the *Commedia*. But why should we expect them to do so? Why should we expect a medieval poet, committed to the idea that the secrets of the Muses should not be laid bare before the vulgar, to show the full range of his understanding of *any* text in a series of public lectures? [33]

The implications for the study of the *Decameron* may be equally far-reaching. This *novella* is strategically placed in the book as a whole, just after its midpoint, on the sixth of the ten days of storytelling. The topic of the day is "di chi, con alcun leggiadro motto tentato, si riscotessi, o con pronta risposta o avvedimento fuggì perdita o pericolo o scorno" (p. 527). As is seen at once, the *novella* of Guido, in developing the motifs of enclosure and of flight, is close to the root metaphors of this topic. In almost all of the *novelle* of this sixth day, in fact, interpretation is a chief theme, and in most of them the issue is the *use* made by the recipient-interpreter of a rebuke; in most of the *novelle* the characters correctly understand the metaphorical rebuke and modify their behavior (messer Betto is one of the exceptions). Two themes dominate the day—interpretation and, closely allied, the power of eloquence. [34]

Now the *novella* of Guido Cavalcanti and these other *novelle* of the sixth day have important connections with the *novelle* of the first day. Many of them also show characters changing their conduct after being rebuked or otherwise instructed, usually in a metaphorical way, in some cases through a *novella* (Saladino, the king of France, Can Grande, Ermino de' Grimaldi, the king of Cyprus). Particularly important are the connections with the first two or three *novelle*. The deliciously ironic point of the tale of ser Cepparello is that since he has—with his rhetorical skill—persuaded the holy friar that he is a saint, since the friar's eloquence persuades the credulous mob, God forgives the error and accepts prayers made in san

Ciappelletto's name as if he were truly a saint. But the narrator, Panfilo, raises the question, what are we to think of the man himself?

> Così adunque visse e morì ser Cepparello da Prato e santo divenne come avete udito. Il quale negar non voglio esser possibile lui esser beato nella presenza di Dio, per ciò che, come che la sua vita fosse scellerata e malvagia, egli *poté* in su lo stremo aver sì fatta contrizione, che per avventura Iddio *ebbe* misericordia di lui e nel suo regno il *ricevette*: ma per ciò che questo n'è occulto, secondo quello che ne può apparire ragiono, e dico costui più tosto dovere essere nelle mani del diavolo in perdizione che in Paradiso (italics added).[35]

> (Pp. 46–47: Thus, then, lived and died ser Cepparello da Prato, and became a saint as you have heard. I do not wish to deny that it is possible that he is blessed in the presence of God, because, although his life was criminal and wicked, he could, at the very end, have made such an act of contrition that perhaps God had mercy on him and received him into his kingdom: but because this is hidden from us, I speak according to what can appear to us, and I say that fellow must rather be in the hands of the devil in perdition than in Paradise.)

Why has Boccaccio placed at the very beginning of the *Decameron* this consideration of *the state of a soul after death*? Of course it is part of the humorous argument that God accepts the *intention* of the believer in spite of his errors, but it is too easy to say that the question of Cepparello's salvation is merely play. A principal reason is surely because the question of the state of souls after death is a limited case of the problem of interpretation.[36] Here in the very first *novella* of the book we see a naive and hasty interpreter (the friar) led by his own desire to believe into making a radical and presumptuous mistake in interpretation, to which he then becomes attached with all the force of his *affetto*; and he succeeds in imposing his misinterpretation on others so that it becomes the majority view.

An important aspect of this first *novella* is the fact that the main character has two names: his "real" name is *Cepparello*, his new name is *Ciappelletto*. What is striking about the two names is that they reflect the two root possibilities of judgment (Dante's *no* and *sì*, damnation and salvation): Cepparello is from *ceppo* (trunk, the old stock, the old Adam), *Ciappelletto*, as the narrator has emphasized, from the French *chapelet* (hat, wreath, crown, halo). And of course Cepparello *does* deserve the *cappello* that rewards the masterful telling of a beautiful lie. In fact, once the question of the intertextuality of *Decameron* and *Commedia* has been focused, one can see clearly that in the story of Cepparello there is a very characteristic nexus of Dantesque themes. It is the nexus that links *the state of souls after death* with *the injustice of a majority opinion*, and with motifs of *naming, crowning, baptism,* and *eloquence.* One of the clearest cases in the *Commedia*, perhaps in some sense the nucleus of the tale of Cepparello, is:

> Se mai continga che 'l poema sacro
>   al quale ha posto mano e cielo e terra,
>   sicché m'ha fatto per molti anni macro,
> vinca la crudeltà che fuor mi serra
>   del bello ovile ov' io dormi' agnello,
>   nimico ai lupi che li danno guerra;
> con altra voce omai, con altro vello
>   ritornerò poeta, e in sul fonte
>   del mio battesmo prenderò 'l cappello;
> però che ne la fede, che fa conte
>   l'anime a Dio, quivi intra' io. . . .

(*Par.* xxv.1–11: If it ever happens that the sacred poem, to which both Heaven and earth have put their hand, so that it has made me thin for many years, overcomes the cruelty that locks me outside the lovely sheepfold where I slept as a lamb, enemy to the wolves that war on it; with another voice now, with other fleece I will return as poet, and on the font of my baptism I will take the wreath; because there I entered into the faith that makes souls known to God. . . .)

Now there is another famous instance of a change of name that is associated with several of these themes, and Boccaccio has given it an important connection with the *novella* of Guido Cavalcanti. The narrator of this *novella* is Elissa, and, as has long been recognized,[37] her name is associated with Dido, is in fact Dido's *original* name. Here is Servius on the matter:

Dido vero nomine Elissa ante dicta est, sed *post interitum* a Poenis Dido appellata, id est virago Punica lingua, quod cum a suis sociis cogeretur quicumque de Afris regibus nubere et prioris mariti caritate teneretur, forti se animo interfecerit et in pyram iecerit, quam se ad expiandos priori mariti manes extruxisse fingebat (italics added).[38]

(In *Aen*.I.340: Dido was called Elissa earlier, but after her death she was called Dido by the Phoenicians, that is, virago in the Punic language, because, when her allies tried to force her to marry one of the kings in Africa and she was held back by love of her first husband, she strongmindedly killed herself and threw herself on the pyre which she pretended to be setting up to pacify the manes of her dead husband.)

As Boccaccio himself points out in the *Esposizioni*, the fact that Virgil's account of Dido as an adultress prevails as the majority view is a traditional example of the power of eloquence:

La quale oppinione per reverenza di Virgilio io aproverei, se il tempo nol contrariasse. . . . E Macrobio *in libro Saturnaliorum* del tutto il contradice, mostrando la forza dell'eloquenza essere tanto che ella aveva potuto far sospettar coloro che sapevano la istoria certa di Dido e credere che ella fosse secondo che scrive Virgilio. Fu adunque Dido onesta donna e, per non romper fede al cener di Siccheo, s'uccise. Ma l'autore (i.e., Dante) seguita qui, come in assai cose fa, l'oppinion di Virgilio. . . .[39]

(P. 300: Out of reverence to Virgil I would approve that opinion, if the historical period were not inaccurate.. . . And Macrobius in his *Saturnalia* contradicts it entirely, explaining that the force of [Virgil's] eloquence has been such as to make those who knew the true history of Dido suspect it and think that she was as Virgil writes. Dido, then, was a virtuous lady and, so as not to break faith with the ashes of Sichaeus, killed herself. But the author [i.e. Dante] here follows, as he does in many things, the opinion of Virgil. . . .)

Suggested by her name, the connection of Boccaccio's Elissa with Dido is assured by a number of details, as well as by the fact that when she is Queen she tells the *novella* of Guido Cavalcanti. The theme of erroneous majority view is alluded to in Boccaccio's words after she finishes her impassioned song of unhappy love: "Poi che con un suspiro assai pietoso Elissa ebbe alla sua canzon fatta fine, ancor che tutti si maravigliassero

di tali parole, niuno per ciò ve n'ebbe che potesse avvisare che di così cantar le fosse cagione." (Pp. 581–82: "After Elissa, with a very piteous sigh,
had brought her song to an end, although all marveled at such words,
there was no one who could think what might cause her to sing in this
way.") How is this to be understood? Is Elissa secretly in love, is she
perhaps having a liaison with Dioneo (there are some suggestions to that
effect), or is her passion imagined? She is thought to be chaste, is she
unchaste? In various ways, then, the figure of Elissa—even her name itself
(if *Dido* means *manly*, does *Elissa* mean *weak*?)—poses a problem of interpretation parallel to Dido and to Cepparello. Probably its point is that
we are to understand that we do not have enough evidence to be able
to draw a conclusion: *Questo n' è occulto*, and part of discretion is knowing
that is the case. The mystery of Elissa's interiority is preserved.[40]

I do not think one should underestimate the importance to Boccaccio
of the paradox that Dante—the victim of injustice—should accept the
Virgilian slander of Dido, which both Macrobius and Servius acknowledge
to be false.[41] The care with which, in the *Esposizioni*, Boccaccio distinguishes
between what he understands to be historical fact and what he finds in
the *Commedia*, is part and parcel of the concern we find in the *Decameron*
for the difficulty of judging. Of course we are in the realm of fiction in
the case both of Dido and of Cepparello, in the latter also in the realm
of high comedy; but this does not mean that the underlying themes are
not important or serious. *Judge not, that ye be not judged*, then, would seem
to be one of the principles at the heart of the tale of Cepparello; at any
rate, we can certainly say that the naive friar, who so readily renders a
positive judgment on Cepparello, is judged and found wanting.

It is Cepparello's eloquence that beguiles the naive friar, and another
chief function of Boccaccio's raising of the issue of interpretation at the
very outset of the *Decameron* is to insist on the necessity of a critical examination of rhetoric in the book. As in the *novella* of Guido (and as in
Inferno X and *Paradiso* XIII), the naive interpreter is juxtaposed with a better-
informed, more skeptical and sophisticated, more cautious interpreter, who
acknowledges the range of possibilities and avoids a presumptuous and
illusory *sicurezza*. And although Panfilo speaks of ser Cepparello as if he
were an actual person, according to one of the basic fictions of the genre,
an essential point is that he has no existence other than in the words of
the *novella*; the very question of his salvation or damnation is itself in the
realm of play.[42] The case is more complex in the *novella* of Guido

Cavalcanti, but again Boccaccio has deftly kept its implication, both about the historical Guido and about the *Commedia*, in the realm of suggestion, of *the possible*, not *the definitive*. Demanding a univocal meaning from such a text is one of the interpretive traps we see messer Betto and his *brigata* falling into.[43]

A main function of the placing of the tale of ser Cepparello, then, would seem to be that of opening up a space in which things do not have to mean what they may seem to mean, in which fiction and irony are at a premium, where eloquence is marked as suspect, thus a space in which interpretation is clearly necessary but not easy and in which a hasty or naive interpreter will go astray, and where—above all—the burden of interpretation is seen clearly to be on the reader.

The *novella* of Guido Cavalcanti, too, is a little model of the interpretive situation, and it is also clearly about the reader of the *Decameron*, who is being cautioned not to be one of messer Betto's *brigata*, is being invited to see further than messer Betto. It shows messer Betto as making the essential beginning of interpretation by understanding the root metaphor of Guido's joke and by applying it to himself and the *brigata*, but it also shows him as devoid of any desire to *follow* Guido: he accepts the condemnation and does not fundamentally change. As we have seen, the *novella* conveys a strong suggestion that the intertextuality of the *Decameron* with the *Commedia* is an important key to its interpretation, and—since messer Betto and company are shown trying (unsuccessfully) to close things off— Guido's escape suggests that the meanings of a text will always elude such critics: to follow the meanings, interpretation must be light, even winged, as befits an activity whose patron is Hermes. It is by no means incidental that the first and sixth days of the *Decameron* are *mercoledì, Mercurii dies*.[44] The reader is free to stop at the more obvious levels of meaning (and of *sollazzo*), but he is still being challenged to examine his own responses and motives. The "higher" senses of the book, whatever they may be, will only become available to him as he wishes them to do so: *Stant volumina et intelligere volentibus sensus apparent* (The volumes are standing there, and the sense will appear to those who wish to understand).

Finally, like Guido, Giovanni Boccaccio has disappeared, leaving us to ponder his words. Perhaps the pun *Guido: guida*, with its clear roots in Dante, is one of the keys to another puzzling allusion, the subtitle of the *Decameron*, *Prencipe Galeotto*. Like Cepparello and Dido, the book itself has two names, and the second cries out for interpretation. And the parallels between Boccaccio and his character Guido include the question whether the author of the *Decameron* is quite the worldling (Epicurean) that he delights to claim to be.[45] *Questo n'è occulto*, and judgment of others must be cautious and provisional, as our *novella* suggests. And it also suggests that the ultimately important question is, how do *we* use the book?[46]

Notes

1. The dominant trend of modern criticism of this *novella* is well represented by Luigi Russo, *Letture critiche del Decameron* (Bari: Laterza, 1956, 1977), pp. 217–23; Giovanni Getto, *Vita di forme e forme di vita nel "Decameron"* (Turin: Petrini, 1957, 1973), pp. 156–59; Mario Baratto, *Realtà e stile nel "Decameron"* (Vicenza: Neri Pozza, 1970), pp. 336–40 and passim, is a notable step forward. Vittore Branca's annotations provide some essential orientations: *Tutte le opere di Giovanni Boccaccio*, IV: *Decameron*, ed. Vittore Branca (Milan: Mondadori, 1976), pp. 1340; all quotations are from this edition: the text of the *novella* is on pp. 562–64.

2. Except for incidental mention I leave out of consideration Boccaccio's explicit discussions of interpretation (*Genealogie deorum gentilium*, Book XIV), as well as his practice as a commentator in the *Esposizioni sopra il Dante*, etc. Many of these texts may require some reinterpretation in the light of a more profound understanding of Boccaccio's achievement as an imaginative writer. See below, notes 5, 11, 16, 18, 36, 41, 45. As the reader will see, there are a number of points on which my discussion runs parallel—sometimes counter—to Guido Almansi's brilliant (if hasty) discussion of the issue of interpretation in the *Decameron* in *The Writer as Liar: Narrative Technique in the Decameron* (London: Routledge, 1975), pp. 19–54. (See below, n. 39).

3. There is a strong contrast between messer Betto's *brigata* and that of the storytellers of the *Decameron*, whose interest in poetry and narrative is obvious enough, and whose subtlety and agility of mind is constantly being stressed (cf. below, n. 42). I of course take it for granted that the overt statements of any narrator are not necessarily to be taken at face value.

4. The negative judgment of the *brigata*'s lack of discernment is given by the narrator's (Elissa's) description: by calling Guido "un de' miglior loici che avesse il mondo e ottimo natural filosofo," she implicitly asserts (1) that the study of logic and natural philosophy is intrinsically valuable; and (2) that part of her own—and her *brigata*'s—cultural equipment is a secure judgment on Guido's achievements (but cf. note 21). The line of opinion in modern criticism that supposes that Boccaccio validates the *brigata*'s side in the confrontation equally with Guido's (e.g., Getto, Baratto) seems to me to miss the point that Giovanni Boccaccio is making so *onestamente*. For the parallels between this *novella* and the defense of poetry in the *Genealogie*, see below, n. 16. See also Branca's notes 4 and 5 on p. 1342.

5. Cf. Boccaccio's use of the expression *speculatione continua* of poets in *Genealogie*, XIV.11 (see below, n. 16).

6. See below, n. 46 for Baratto's acute remarks on the contrast. That Boccaccio was interested in the *facts* about Guido and was in a position to make some discriminations is established by his interest in Guido's *canzone* "Donna me prega" and the commentary on it by Dino del Garbo. See Antonio Enzo Quaglio, "Prima fortuna della glossa garbiana a 'Donna me prega' del Cavalcanti," *Giornale storico della letteratura italiana*, CXLI (1964), 339–69. Quaglio argues from the references to the poem and commentary in the glosses to the *Teseida* that Boccaccio read them after returning to Florence; he associates Boccaccio's renewed interest—reflected in his copying the *canzone* and the commentary into what is now the Vatican's MS. Chigi L.V. 176—with the adaptations of the commentary in the discussions of love in the *Genealogie* and the *Esposizioni*. Finally, Quaglio argues that when writing the *novella* in the *Decameron*, Boccaccio must have known an oral tradition attributing to Dino del Garbo the retort of *Dinus florentinus* (related by Petrarch in the *Rerum memorandarum libri* II. 60) to a group of taunting old men, analogous in its setting and terminology ("Iniquum hoc loco certamen; vos enim ante domos vestras animosiores estis"). The question of the relation of this *novella* to the *Genealogie* and the *Esposizioni* needs to be reopened.

7. Ed. Branca, p. 1343, n. 18.

8. The *Dizionario etimologico italiano*, ed. C. Battisti and G. Alessio (Florence: G. Barbèra, 1968), gives the following for *briga*: "agitazione, lite; in origine prob. 'forza, vigoria nel combattere,' forse dal celtico *brīga* (cfr. cimrico *bri*, irl. *brīgh*, forza); cfr. lat. medioev. *brīga* (a. 1279). . . ." Cf. Boccaccio's use of the word in *Dec.* x.8 (pp. 915–16): "Dopo non molto tempo per molte brighe cittadine . . . (Gisippo) fu d'Atene cacciato e dannato ad esilio perpetuo" (where one notes the Dantesque—and Cavalcantian—theme of exile). There are a number of occurrences of the word in the *Commedia*; among the most important are *Inf.* v.49, where it is used of the infernal whirlwind; *Purg.* XVI.117, where it is used of the Pope's opposition to Frederick II (cf. also *Par.* XII.108).

9. It ought not, however, to be supposed that the question that is said to preoccupy Guido would have been thought to be philosophically trivial, or necessarily impious. The stringent critique of the alleged proofs of God's existence is Thomistic: Aquinas criticized the ontological proof (*Summa contra gentiles*, I.10 and 11). If Guido could establish that there was *no* proof for the non-existence of God, his skepticism might be considerably affected. See n. 10.

10. In Augustinian as well as Thomistic terms, of course, reason rightly used cannot prove anything contrary to faith; the Paris condemnation of Averroistic (and other) theses in 1277 explicitly forbade refuge in the idea of a truth of reason at variance with the faith. For the historical Guido's Averroism, see Bruno Nardi, *Saggi e note di critica dantesca* (Milan–Naples: Ricciardi, 1966), pp. 190–219 and passim; cf. below, n. 24.

11. For Boccaccio's formal defense of poetry against the charge that it means nothing (*nil*), see below, n. 16. This kind of response is, in his mind, clearly enough, one

of the principal varieties of misreading: not seeing *through* or *beneath* the letter. The parallel ought to suggest that the relevant chapters of the *Genealogie* may be more relevant to the *Decameron* than has been thought. Cf. Boccaccio's remark in the self-defense (Introduction to Day Four): "queste cose tessendo, nè dal monte Parnaso nè dalle Muse non mi allontano quanto molti per avventura s'avisano" (p. 351), and the obviously sly remark in the Conclusion, "elle (sc. le novelle), per non ingannare alcuna persona, tutte nella fronte portan segnato quello che esse dentro dal loro seno nascose [sic] tengono" (p. 962). As Boccaccio says in the *Genealogie* of his own and Petrarch's *Carmina bucolica*, "Stant volumina et intelligere volentibus sensus apparent."

12. If we are meant to consider possible etymologies for the names of the leader of this *brigata*, as all the other etymological play suggests, perhaps we should entertain the possibility that Boccaccio has in mind the famous donkey Brunellus, the main character of Nigellus Wireker's well-known *Speculum stultorum*, which of course would make one of the *Brunelleschi* a relative of an ass (perhaps, as an expositor, even an *asinus in cathedra*); this has the great virtue of symmetry with the play on *cavalcare*. Branca notes that *Betto* is an abbreviation of *Brunetto* (a little dark? cf. *Inf.* VII. 53–54: "la sconoscente — cf. *smemorato* — vita che i fe sozzi / ad ogne conoscenza or li fa bruni"). But my friend Piero Pucci reminds me that *Betto* could also be an abbreviation of *Benedetto*, in which case we would have a character with two names again. The *Speculum stultorum* includes, curiously enough, a story about two cows who allow their tails to be frozen to the ground; the impatient one tears hers off to free herself, but the prudent one — named Brunetta — waits for the ground to thaw. See Thomas Wright, ed., *The Anglo-Latin Satirical Poets* I (London: Longman, 1872); F. J. E. Raby, *A History of Secular Latin Poetry in the Middle Ages*, 2 vols. (London: Clarendon, 1934), II, pp. 94–99. For the haste and violence of centaur-like men on horseback, cf. *Inf.* XII.66, where Virgil says to Nessus, "Mal fu la voglia tua sempre sì tosta."

13. Lest the insistence on etymological play seem farfetched, it should be pointed out that Boccaccio is probably signalling his awareness of its importance in *Inferno* x itself; see my "Farinata`and the Body of Christ," *Stanford Italian Review*, II (1981), 5–35. For Boccaccio in the *Decameron*, *nomina sunt consequentia rerum* has been recognized about many of the characters' names, most notably of the *brigata* of the frame (see Branca, pp. 992–93).

14. *Smemorato* would, strictly speaking, be derived from the verb *memoror, memorari*; cf. Eccles. 7:40: "In omnibus operibus tuis memorare novissima tua."

15. See Branca's note on p. 1340, and see below, n. 23.

16. A preliminary outline of the parallels and points of comparison would include the following: (a) the question of whether the fables of poets mean *nothing*: Cap. x, "Stultum credere poetas *nil sensisse* sub cortice fabularum. Sunt ex his non nulli tantae temeritatis, ut, nulla auctoritate suffulti, non verantur dicere, stolidissimum arbitrari clarissimos poetas sensum aliquem suis *supposuisse* fabellis" (italics added; if the *sensum* is *suppositum*, one must *suspicere*); (b) the issue of the sociability of poets, and the antithesis between the solitude of speculation and the worldliness

of their attackers: Cap. xi, "Dixi hos obstrepentes insuper dicere poetas rura, montes, et silva incolere, eo quod urbanitate et moribus non valerent . . . Quin imo, quos isti blasfemant, tenui contenti victu brevique somno, *speculatione continua* et exercitio laudabili componendo scribendoque sibi famosam gloriam ut per secula duraturam exquirunt" (italics added; here of course is the point, valid in itself, that messer Betto makes); (c) the stupidity of criticizing what one is ignorant of or does not understand, and the motif of the attack returning on the attacker: Cap. xiv, "Stulte damnatur, quod minus sane intelligitur . . . *Stulti militis more* certamen intrant adversarii nostri, qui tanto nocendi hostibus fertur impetu, ut sibi ipsi non videat; ex quo sepe fit, ut, *quos in alterum parat ictus, inermis ipse suscipiat*" (italics added); (d) the lively portrait of the scornful attacker: Cap. xv, " 'Quid has nugas viderimus? Uaph! nec vidimus, nec vidisse volumus, maioribus operam damus! O bone deus, ab eterno opere tuo si velis pausam summere, potes, et, si divinitatis tui apeterent oculi, posses in sumnum ire, si velles, rem tuam isti curant!' . . . O ignave hominum mentes, non advertunt, tam prudentes flocci faciunt, quam misere suam ignorantiam detegant!" (e) the suggestion that instead of attacking poets one should elect them as guides: Cap. xxii., "Poetici nominis hostes orat autor, ut se in melius vertant consilium. . . . Quos (i.e., poetas) si tanti sunt, si adeo venerabiles, non solum non damnare (this is as far as messer Betto and his *brigata* go) debetis, sed eos colere, laudibus extollere, amare, et eorum, ut meliores efficiamini, studere volumina. A quo ne vos retrahat aut etas annosior, aut famosiores audisse facultates, conemini ex vobis ipsis id posse, quod de se non erubuit annosus princeps" (Boccaccio then cites the examples of Robert of Sicily converted by Petrarch to the study of Virgil); (f) an insistence on *distinguishing*: Cap. xv. See also n. 33 below.

17. For the most part the tradition has limited itself to treating the *novella* as a sympathetic evocation of the figure of Guido, to which Boccaccio would have been led by his admiration for Dante and the *Stil novo* and his interest in the historical period. I have not seen any attempt to interpret the *novella* as in any way a commentary on the *Commedia*. Cf. Branca's caution (p. 1343) in glossing the reference to the *arche* around the Baptistry: "*forse* riecheggiamento delle 'arche' in cui Dante pone gli 'epicurei' e Cavalcante (*Inf.* ix.125) sono questa sceneggiatura e questa presentazione" (italics added). Actually Boccaccio calls our attention to something Dante was silent about in *Inferno* ix and x: that the infernal scene itself includes a reference to a once-familiar Florentine scene (connected, through the Baptistry, to the theme of faith and heresy), one that was no longer in existence when Dante was writing. Cf. Branca's note 15, ibid.: "Quelle 'arche,' secondo la tradizione popolare, sarebbero appartenute alle famiglie *dei primi abitatori di Firenze*. Rimosse nel 1296, sono ora in piccola parte nel cortile di Palazzo Medici-Ricciardi e attorno al Battistero" (italics added).

On the general topic of Guido in the *Commedia*, see Gianfranco Contini, "Dante come personaggio–poeta della *Commedia*," and "Cavalcante in Dante," now in *Varianti e altra linguistica* (Turin: Einaudi, 1970), pp. 348–51 and 433–46.

18. See Boccaccio's remarks in the *Esposizioni sopra la "Commedia" di Dante*, ed. Giorgio Padoan in *Tutte le opere di Giovanni Boccaccio* vi (Milan: Mondadori, 1966),

pp. 510–12; and Padoan's "Il canto degli epicurei," *Convivium*, XXVII (1959), 12–38.

19. The allusion, as has long been noted, is to *Aeneid* VI.733–34: "hinc metuunt cupiuntque, dolent gaudentque, neque auras / dispiciunt clausae tenebris et carcere caeco."

20. Boccaccio knows perfectly well how popular a book the *Commedia* is becoming by the time he is writing the *Decameron*; he is one of the leading fans himself, tireless in winning readers to it. It is not possible to read the *novella* as if Boccaccio were unaware that this question would occur to a reader who knew the poem. Even Baratto seems to me to gloss over the matter too quickly: "L'abile contrapposizione svuota di ogni condanna gli stessi richiami danteschi: allusivamente capovolti, mi pare, anche nelle 'arche' tra cui passeggia Guido e nel suo motto enigmatico" (p. 338).

21. Some support is offered to this possibility by the somewhat ominous Dantesque associations of the term *loico* used to describe Guido; cf. *Inf.* XXVII.122–23 (the devil to Guido da Montefeltro): "Forse / tu non credevi ch'io loico fossi!" Giorgio Padoan, "Mondo aristocratico e mondo comunale nell'ideologia e nell'arte di Giovanni Boccaccio," *Studi sul Boccaccio,* II (1964), 148–49, notes the pointed parallel to this same passage in the *novella* of frate Rinaldo (VII.3; pp. 601–2). He comments:

> E' questo un altro chiaro esempio che mostra come lo scrittore avesse continuamente presente la *Commedia*, ma ne trasferisse con estrema libertà situazioni e giudizi dal piano religioso e morale a quello esclusivamente umano . . . . La condanna del narratore c'è: ma è una condanna che proviene dalle esigenze della socialità e della moralità offese . . . ogni accenno al mondo dell'al di là, alle fiamme infernali, rimane implicita e comunque del tutto secondario.

If I am not mistaken, this statement is self-contradictory; in any case there is no effort to explore the *function* of the allusion. I think it is more troubling than Padoan allows.

22. "What is signified by the procreation of children, by the propagation of one's reputation, by the adoption of children, by our diligence in making wills, by our very monuments and tombs and eulogies, except that we are forever concerned about what will happen after our death" (*Tusculan Disputations* I.14.31); according to Cicero, this "tacit proof" given by our natures is the greatest single proof of the immortality of the soul.

23. As E. G. Parodi pointed out in "La miscredenza di Guido Cavalcanti e una fonte del Boccaccio," *Bulletino della Società dantesca,* XXII (1915), 37–47, the tales of Frederick II's Epicureanism purveyed by such Guelf zealots as Fra Salimbene de Adam are in fact derived from the *Dialogues* of Gregory the Great (according to Fra Salimbene, Frederick used to cite Ps. 48:12, Is. 22:15, Sap. 2:5, Eccles. 3:19–22 as proof of the mortality of the soul). For the Pauline and Augustinian background of the Christian polemics against Epicureanism, see my "Farinata and the Body of Christ" (cite in n. 13 above); the main Augustinian texts are the *Enarratio* on Ps. 48 and the *Sermo de scripturis* CL (on Acts 19; Migne, *P. L.* XXXVIII, 810). See also n. 6 above.

24. Parodi (see above, n. 23) notes that the accounts of Guido's Epicureanism that have come down to us derive mainly from this *novella*. More recently the discovery

of a definitely Averroistic treatise dedicated to Guido lends support to the traditional view and to the Averroistic reading of "Donna mi prega" (see P. O. Kristeller,
"A Philosophical Treatise from Bologna Dedicated to Guido Cavalcanti: Magister
Jacopus de Pistorio and his 'Quaestio de felicitate,' " *Medioevo e Rinascimento. Studi
in onore di Bruno Nardi*, 2 vols. (Florence: Sansoni, 1955), I, pp. 425–63. But it is
still a long way from there to establishing that Guido was actually a heretic or that
he died outside the faith. One of the ironies of the history of Boccaccio studies—
and Cavalcanti studies—has been the fact that Boccaccio's *novella*, which so sharply
distinguishes between Guido's agreeing *alquanto* with the Epicureans (or Averroists)
and his total agreement, should have become a principal source of the tradition that
he was a heretic. But there is no doubt that the *novella* offers some evidence—
particularly when placed in juxtaposition with the *Commedia*, where Dante's fears
about Guido are so evident—that Guido *was* popularly regarded as an Epicurean
(or Averroist).

25. The data misinterpreted ranges from the world of external nature, especially
the light of the sun (cf. Romans 1:19), through the words and actions of others
(especially, but not exclusively, in the context, Dante), to the evidences of immortality implicit in their own human nature (see above, n. 2). Against the delusion
and the hasty conclusions of the heretics is set the caution with which Dante carefully
inquires and weighs what he hears before drawing conclusion. I develop this view
in the article cited in n. 13.

26. Citations to the *Commedia* are to Petrocchi's critical text, in the 1975 Einaudi
reprint.

27. For bibliography, see S. A. Chimenz, "Il 'disdegno' di Guido e i suoi interpreti," *Orientamenti culturali*, I (1945), 179–88; and the *aggiornamento bibliografico* by
Francesco Mazzoni to the canto in his edition of the *Inferno. Con i commenti di Tommaso Casini-Silvio Adrasto Barbi e di Attilio Momigliano* (Florence: Sansoni, 1972). The
most generally accepted interpretation is that of Antonino Pagliaro, in *Saggi di critica
semantica* (Messina-Florence: G. D'Anna, 1953), subsumed later in *Ulisse. Ricerche
semantiche sulla Divina Commedia* (Messina-Florence: G. D'Anna, 1967): "Costui
(Virgilio) mi conduce attraverso questi luoghi [forse] da chi [i.e., da *Beatrice*, da
cui] Guido vostro sdegnò, si rifiutò venire" (*Saggi*, p. 368); this involves taking
forse as modifying *cui*, and taking "Guido vostro ebbe a sdegno" as elliptical, i.e.,
as lacking a *di venire*. Most critics seem to have accepted without many qualms the
idea that Dante was assigning his friend to perdition; Bruno Nardi is one of the
few exceptions: "Per questa dottrina (averroistica) intorno all'amore, il figlio di
Cavalcante era forse degno della dannazione eterna, come il padre, e questo ha forse
inteso o temuto Dante, come sembrano pensare taluni? Non oserei affermarlo" (*Saggi
e note di critica dantesca*, [Bari: Laterza, 1966], p. 218).

28. It does not seem to have been noticed that no matter what interpretation
of the line is adopted it can only be read aloud haltingly. If Pagliaro's reading is
adopted, the fact that there is an ellipsis at the end of the sentence must be clearly
indicated, but the reasoning by which Pagliaro seeks to radically distinguish *avere
in disdegno* and *avere a disdegno* is seriously weakened by so many generations of critics
having understood them as identical. *Forse*—the term that indicates Dante's

embarrassment—by definition involves the pause that expresses its tentativeness, and the pause must come either before or after *cui*. In either case the doubt invests the entire line and no easy solution is possible.

29. Cavalcante's error challenges the reader to consider the range of possible meanings of *ebbe* and all the other ambiguities of the line. For details, see my "Farinata and the Body of Christ," pp. 20–26. See above, n. 28.

30. Once we have been taught by Boccaccio's messer Betto to take *life* and *death* always in at least two senses, we cannot miss the reference to the hope of Guido's salvation. Dante is, of course, carefully avoiding any assertion. Bruno Nardi suggested that for Dante one of the uses of dating the journey in April 1300 was precisely that the date allowed him to evade the question of Guido's location in the other world (*Saggi e note*, p. 319—see above, n. 20).

31. I have omitted lines 121–29, which explicitly attribute to hasty presumptuousness the errors of Parmenides, Melissus, Brissus among the ancients, Sabellius and Arius among Christian heretics. The relation to these themes in *Inferno* x could hardly be plainer.

32. Boccaccio might also have been alert to the echoes of Guido's poetry in these lines and to the implicit reference to *Guido* and Buonconte da Montefeltro in lines 134–39. See my "Farinata and the Body of Christ," pp. 25–26, n. 45.

33. While it is certainly the case that the *Esposizioni* represent a Boccaccio older and much more explicitly moralistic than the youthful works, it is easy to demonstrate that they are far from representing Boccaccio's full understanding of the *Commedia*. To take the most obvious kind of example—for Boccaccio it would not have been a trivial one—there is no explicit mention in the *Esposizioni* of numerical symbolism or numerical composition, in spite of the fact that Boccaccio had studied that aspect of Dante's works with some care and, in his own works up to and including the *Decameron* (to what extent in the latter is still being determined), had been a devoted and sometimes fanatical experimenter along similar lines.

Boccaccio's public lectures on the *Commedia* were commissioned by the Commune of Florence in response to a petition, but there were evidently those in ultra-Guelf Florence who believed that the anti-papal Dante should not be explained to the unlearned and who were troubled by the great popularity of the poem. Boccaccio seems to have been nervous about the enterprise from the beginning, and at some time after the lectures were broken off because of his poor health, he wrote a series of four sonnets in which he acknowledged that he had prostituted the Muses by opening their private parts in public (his defense being his poverty and his reliance on others' judgment), vowed never to do so again, accused the "mechanicals" of crass materialism and ingratitude, and rejoiced to have left them in the midst of the ocean without a pilot. There is a striking parallel between the last sonnet and the action of Guido's escape:

> Io ho messo in galea senza biscotto
>   l'ingrato vulgo, e senza alcun piloto
>   lasciato l'ho in mar a lui non noto,

> ben che sen creda maestro e dotto:
> onde el di su spero veder di sotto
> del debol legno e di sanità voto;
> né avverrà, perch'ei sappia di nuoto,
> che non rimanga lì doglioso e rotto.
> Ed io, di parte eccelsa riguardando,
> ridendo, in parte piglierò ristoro
> del ricevuto scorno e dell'inganno;
> e tal fiata, a lui rimproverando
> l'avaro senno ed il beffato alloro,
> gli crescerò e la doglia e l'affanno.

(*Le Rime, l'Amorosa Visione, La Caccia di Diana*, ed. Vittore Branca [Bari: Laterza, 1939], p. 73.)

It is implausible on the face of it to suppose that the *Esposizioni* were ever supposed to leave the plane of an introduction to the poem for the unlearned; the very insistence on the distinction between the literal and the allegorical senses (the latter restricted to the moral sense) may well have been a convenient way for Boccaccio to avoid revealing the secrets of the Muses. Padoan's strictures on the *Esposizioni* (pp. XXVI–XXVIII; cf. also his *L'ultima opera di Giovanni Boccaccio, le "Esposizioni sopra il Dante,"* [Padua: Cedam, 1959]) often seem unfair. One problem has been that we have not learned how to read the *Esposizioni* themselves; for an instance, see my " 'Io son venuto': Seneca, Plato, and the Microcosm," *Dante Studies* XCIII (1975), 95–129, especially p. 129, n. 52. The first text Boccaccio cites in the *accessus* to the *Esposizioni* is Plato's *Timaeus*, whose importance for the understanding of the *Decameron* urgently calls out for investigation. See below, n. 38.

34. One character, Cesca, the niece of Fresco da Celatico, "non altrimenti che un montone avrebbe fatto, intese il vero motto di Fresco, anzi disse che ella si voleva specchiar come l'altre" (p. 527): cf. messer Betto's *brigata*, "quivi dove erano non avevano essi a fare più che tutti gli altri cittadini" (p. 564). Others learn and change: madonna Oretta's knight, Geri Spina, Antonio d'Orso, the Podestà of Prato. See n. 16.

35. Boccaccio's preterites in this passage, especially his *ebbe*, if my interpretation is correct, refer to *Inf.* x.63.

36. Guido Almansi's chapter on *Decameron* VI.1 and I.1 (see above, n. 2) begins: "Perhaps it is true that a book, any book, contains its own inbuilt reader's guide: instructions to the recipient about what to expect, how to interpret what he has before him" (p. 19). Almansi rightly points out, citing Dante, that VI.1 is strategically placed near the center of the book and that it is a *metanovella*, a *novella* about storytelling. His conclusion is that—since it is the unfortunate knight's *manner* of telling the story that is said to disturb madonna Oretta—Boccaccio is saying that in the *Decameron*, *content* is unimportant, *form* all-important. I believe there is an easily perceptible fallacy of undistributed middle in his argument, but in any case a full investigation of the "reader's guide" would have to include the other *novelle* about interpretation. Form is, I should argue, *equally* important with content, as my discus-

sion of vi.9 may suggest. See also Franco Fido's remarks in "Boccaccio's *Ars Narrandi* in the Sixth Day of the *Decameron*," in *Italian Literature: Roots and Branches. Essays in Honor of Thomas G. Bergin*, ed. G. Rimanelli and K. J. Atchity (New Haven: Yale University Press, 1976), pp. 225–42.

Almansi treats I.1 "as an analogue of the literary process" (p. 29), in conformity with the title of his book: "Cepparello, therefore, is not merely an artist and master of verbal inventiveness with a genius for deception, but also a negative print of the writer, who is a master of all deceptions. Cepparello's amazing ability to create a fictitious universe and seat himself at its centre on the throne of sainthood parallels the writer's ability to create the far larger fictitious world of the *Decameron* which shines with the radiance of lying. . . ." This statement (deliberately provocative, of course) seems to me—while it catches an essential aspect of the problematic—to miss another, equally essential point: that *we are not supposed to be fooled by Cepparello* but instead are required to think critically about the whole matter; the necessity of a complex ironic awareness is one of the central serious themes of the book. And one may note that this is an aspect of content, not form. As a matter of fact, in his interpretation of I.1 Almansi seems to me to have fundamentally contradicted his argument about vi.1: the truth or falsehood of the writer's product is a matter of content, not of form. (Thus Almansi—arguing that there is no serious meaning here—puts himself in a position dangerously like that of messer Betto's *brigata*.)

Almansi's playful conclusion is also a mixture of brilliant insight and what I consider radical oversimplification:

> This serene and compelling final formula summing up the life and death of the hero is not a premonition of infernal punishment. The author is not denying the possibility that "God has blessed him and admitted him to His presence." A place for the sinner in Heaven may well be unlikely, but that does not mean it is totally unlikely. Perhaps it is more likely that the scoundrel is down in Hell, in the Devil's hands. *The simultaneous possibility of both alternatives settles the question: there is no way of knowing* Cepparello's precise address in the kingdom of the dead. Whether he is in residence up there or down below does not in the least concern the narrator, who wants to close the story with one last boutade. . . . *He refuses to be the spokesman for a divine condemnation.* Nor is the reader particularly concerned with Ciappelletto's blessedly enjoying the ineffable delights of Paradise: we are merely fascinated by the irony of the suggestion that it might just be the upper of the two. . . . Last but not least, Cepparello himself is indifferent to his fate: his existence came to an end at the ninety-first paragraph of the first *novella* in the *Decameron*, since *his status as a character in fiction does not allow him any extra-textual status whatsoever*, not even in Hell. Instead, the problem of a future Hell might at a personal level concern a reader who has been peering into the scandalous fascinations of the *novella* (pp. 54–55).

This mockery of a certain traditional owlish seriousness is quite salutary. I have italicised the phrases that seem to me to hit the target. What seems to escape Almansi is the magnitude and seriousness of the intertextuality with the *Commedia* here. It is quite true that Boccaccio (or Panfilo) is refusing "to be the spokesman for a divine condemnation"; how strikingly different from the *Commedia*! It does *not* mean that *no* judgment is possible, however, just as it does not mean that Boccaccio's world is exclusively "human" in the sense of excluding all reference to the next life. Nor does the playfulness mean that the theme of *the state of souls after death* is unimportant. Actually the richness of intertextuality with the *Commedia* is one of the ways Boccaccio keeps the issue of the next world alive in a text that seems to the hasty reader to ignore it. For the problem of "lying" and the connections of Cepparello with Dido, see n. 39 below.

Furthermore, why should one assume that Panfilo's remarks exhaust all the possibilities? It is at least worth remembering that one of Cepparello's motives for his deception of the friar is a desire to save the lives of his colleagues, who are liable to be lynched if his true nature becomes known. From Cepparello's point of view, he is forfeiting his last and only chance for salvation for himself, in order to save others. Of course Cepparello has no existence other than the words that define him; as Panfilo's remarks, which speak of him as if he *were* an actual human being, remind us, however, in the case of an actual person it is *not* possible to overhear the dialogue between the soul and God. According to traditional Catholic belief, only in the case of saints is it possible to know beyond any doubt the state of a soul after death; and even belief in any given saint (with the exception of the Virgin) is not an article of faith.

37. Giuseppe Billanovich, *Restauri boccacceschi* (Rome: Storia e Letteratura, 1947), pp. 137–38. See below, n. 39.

38. *Servii grammatici qui feruntur in Virgilii carmina commentarii*, ed. G. Thilo and H. Hagen, 3 vols. (Leipzig, 1881; repr. Hildesheim: G. Olms, 1961).

39. Each time Dido is referred to in the *Esposizioni*, Boccaccio takes care to indicate when the reference is to Virgil's version of the story (pp. 44, 45; 75, 77, 115, 215, 262), in other words, to give an implicit reminder of its fictitiousness. Cf. Padoan's n. 105 (pp. 859–60): "il B. rifiuta qui la versione virgiliana, che nel *De casibus* II, cap. *De Didone regina Carthaginensium* e cap. *In Didonem commendatio* e nel *De mulieribus* aveva del tutto taciuta (mentre in *Genealogie*, XIV.13 difendeva Virgilio dalla pur giusta accusa di mendacio; e v. II.80); ma è evidente che la ragione decisiva di questa scelta nel noto contrasto tra il poeta latino e alcuni Padri è determinata, assai più che da elementi 'storiografici,' da fattori ideologici cattolici e sentimentali (la figura di Didone fedele al marito morto sorrise sempre alla fantasia del B.)." But there are four serious themes here: those of the force of eloquence, the difficulty of interpretation, the unreliability of majority opinion, and the state of souls after death.

The passage from Macrobius referred to by Boccaccio is as follows: after noting that *Aeneid* IV is based on Apollonius,

"Quod ita elegantius auctore digessit, ut fabula lasciventis Didonis, quam falsam
novit universitas, per tot tamen saecula specimen veritatis obtineat et ita pro
vero per ora omnium volitet, ut pictores fictoresque et qui figmentis liciorum
contextas imitantur effigies, hac materia vel maxime in effigiandis simulacris
tamquam unico argumento decoris utantur, nec minus histrionum perpetuis
et gestibus et cantibus celebretur, tantum valuit pulchritudo narrandi ut omnes
Phoenissae castitate conscii, nec ignari manum sibi iniecisse reginam ne pateretur
damnum pudoris, coniveant tamen fabulae, et intra conscientiam veri fidem
prementes malint pro vero celebrari quod pectoribus humanis dulcedo fingen-
tis infudit" (*Saturnalia* v.17.5, ed. J. Willis, Leipzig; Teubner, 1970).
See also Augustine, *Confessions* I.XIII, which juxtaposes the opinions of learned and
unlearned on whether Aeneas visited Carthage or not. As one can see, the passage
from Macrobius lies behind many parts of the *Decameron*, including I.1, VI.9 and
VI.10; Boccaccio is consistently on the side of *critical awareness*, not mere sentiment.
See above, n. 16, 36.

Virgil's Dido is a source of considerable embarrassment to Boccaccio in the
Genealogie, XIV.13, where he devotes a long passage to a defense of Virgil against
the charge of having lied. His embarrassment is the more profound in that he, like
Dante, is used to taking Virgil as a reliable historical source. His defense is that
Virgil's Dido is not meant as anything but a fictional character and that her existence is justified by the poetic functions that she serves in the *Aeneid* (he outlines
four functions served by the episode in Carthage: 1. the exploitation of *ordo artificialis*;
2. the representation of the theme of the conflict of duty and temptation; 3. the
portrait of Aeneas as heroically overcoming temptation — and it must be temptation
worthy of him, queenly — as part of the encomium on the Julian *gens*; 4. the enhanc-
ing of Roman glory in the prefiguration of the Punic wars). See *De mulieribus claris*,
ed. Vittorio Zaccaria in *Tutte le opere di Giovanni Boccaccio* x, (Milan: Mondadori,
1970), pp. 168–82 and notes on pp. 514–15; see also the useful discussion in Robert
Hollander, *Boccaccio's Two Venuses* (New York: Columbia University Press, 1977),
pp. 171–73.

40. Boccaccio gives Elissa particular prominence: when she first inherits the crown,
on the evening of the fifth day, she asks Dioneo to sing and must deal with a whole
succession of obscene double-entendres until he relents and sings an acceptable song;
on the morning of the sixth day she asks Dioneo to adjudge the dispute between
the two servants, Licisca and Tindaro, as to the supposed virginity of brides (he
judges that Licisca is correct in saying there are no virgin brides); she chooses Dioneo
as king for the next day; on the evening of the sixth day she leads the ladies to
the *Valle delle donne* — a landscape calling out for interpretation if there ever was
one; finally, when Dioneo asks her for a song her impassioned song of unhappy
love surprises everyone: "Poi che con un sospiro assai pietoso Elissa ebbe alla sua
canzon fatta fine, ancor che tutti si maravigliassero di tali parole, niuno per ciò ve
n'ebbe che potesse avvisare che di così cantar le fosse cagione" (ed. Branca, pp. 581–82).

41. Giorgio Padoan, "Mondo aristocratico" (see above, n. 21), p. 197, cites Boccaccio's expression of reluctance to judge Dante's habits of *lussuria* (*Vita di Dante*,

xxv.9–10).

42. Cf. Almansi's last paragraph, cited in n. 3 above.

43. Even Baratto, who comes closer than any other critic I have read to seeing that vi.9 is about interpretation, speaks of "closing the circle":

> Il ragionamento di messer Betto è essenziale per chiarire il nodo del contrasto, ma anche per chiudere il cerchio del processo narrativo con quella brigata prima stupita, poi consapevole e pronta a rispettare Guido come a tenere "messer Betto sottile e intendente cavaliere." Quest'ultimo, in primo luogo, e dietro di lui i suoi compagni non sono rimasti immobili: l'avventura determina in loro un progresso, una presa di coscienza, che coincide con l'effetto voluto dal narratore (p. 340).

Cf. Baratto's much more apposite earlier remarks:

> . . . la progressione del testo, nella presentazione di Guido, è calcolata con grande finezza, perché tende insieme a inserire il personaggio in un contesto ambientale e ad isolarlo, all'interno di esso, come problema non solubile per gli altri (p. 337);

and (the *novella*) "è un'indiretta recensione dei luoghi comuni sulla figura del Cavalcante" (but see above, n. 24):

> essa continua, in gradazione discendente, con la voce sull'ateismo di Guido rinviata alla "gente volgare," pure ora anticipata, con una causale prolettica, e distinta dall'osservazione più rigorosa dello scrittore "che egli alquanto tenea della oppinione degli epicuri." . . . Ma l'aneddoto prende luce dalla lenta preparazione di esso (del motto di Guido), dalla sottile disposizione di piani che mette in evidenza, all'inizio e alla fine della lunga sequenza, il valore intellettuale del Cavalcanti: che punta cioè, come su fatti oggettivi, sulle sue indubbie qualità di filosofo, e lascia le interpretazioni soggettive ai vari livelli mentali degli altri (p. 338).

Cf. Almansi's remarks (p. 29): "Perhaps the duty of the critic is not that of clearing the waters by imposing a rigid interpretative scheme on the text with which he is dealing, but rather to muddy things up and suggest a contradictory plurality of readings which draws both the attentive and the careless reader into the realm of hermeneutical delectation." This is much closer to Boccaccio.

For Boccaccio's own views on the varieties of interpretation and on the obscurity of poetry, cf. *Genealogie*, Book xiv, which cites the example of Scripture. Some obscurities are due to the interpreter's inability to see: "nonnulla obscura videri, cum clarissima sint, intuentis vicio (lusco quidem illecescente sole, qui limpidus est, nebulosus videtur aer!)" (there is perhaps a reference here to Leah's *lippitudo*, the type of the active as opposed to the contemplative life); some things are obscure by nature, like the sun; other things, clear in themselves, are veiled by the artifice of poets: "cum inter alia poete officia sit non eviscerare fictionibus palliata, quin imo, si in propatulo posita sint et *memoratu* et *veneratione* digna, ne vilescant familiaritate nimia, quanta possunt industria, tegere et ab oculis torpentium auferre . . . ut labore ingeniorum quesita et diversimode intellecta comperta tandem faciant cariora" (ed. Romano, ii, 715–16; italics added). He then cites a number of passages from Augustine, including: "Et alibi Augustinus idem super Psalmo CXXVI° dicit: Ideo forte obscurius positum est, ut multos intellectus generet, et ditiores discedant homines, qui clausum invenirent, quod multis modis aperiretur, quam si uno modo apertum invenirent" (ibid., p. 716).

44. The second Wednesday, by including striking parallels with the first, establishes a pattern of correlation between the days of the two weeks on which the storytelling of the *Decameron* takes place. Perhaps the most striking case is that of the two Tuesdays—*Martis dies* (days 5 and 10): on the first Tuesday the happy endings of the love affairs are qualified and in some cases (especially *novella* 1) undermined by the prevalence of war and violence; in the stories of the second Tuesday the theme is external war replaced and—in intention at least—transcended in the higher war of generous versus selfish impulse. This implies a kind of *spiral* arrangement that reflects in some measure Boccaccio's study of the ascending correlations among the corresponding cantos of the three *cantiche* of the *Commedia*. It would hardly have escaped Boccaccio that the *Commedia* covers almost exactly a week and that it is a *Mercurii dies* when Dante begins his flight at the beginning of the *Paradiso*. It may be said parenthetically that the appropriateness of the stories of the *Decameron* to the days of the week on which they are told (the appropriateness may be astrological, numerological, etc.) is a subject which has only begun to be investigated. For the importance of astrology in the *Commedia*, see the late Georg Rabuse's indispensable *Der kosmische Aufbau der Jenseitsreiche Dantes. Ein Schlüssel zur Göttlichen Komödie* (Graz: H. Böhlaus, 1958).

45. See above, n. 11. The presumptuous questioner may well, once again, be receiving a joke for an answer.

46. Cf. Almansi's last sentence, quoted in n. 36. In fourteenth–century terms, it is quite plausible to think that Boccaccio might have supposed his readers might have some concern for their own salvation. It is not implausible to think that modern readers have such a concern, in some sense or other.

"Chiuso parlare" in Boccaccio's *Teseida*

VICTORIA KIRKHAM

IN HIS DEDICATORY PROEM TO FIAMMETTA, the author of the *Teseida*
announces that he will tell a long forgotten love story. Hopeful of
regaining Fiammetta's lost favors by appealing to her fondness for
fictional romance, he reports having rendered into Latin vernacular verse,
"una antichissima istoria e alle più delle genti non manifesta, bella sì per
la materia della quale parla, che è d'amore, e sì per coloro de' quali dice,
che nobili giovani furono e di real sangue discesi" ("a very ancient story
and one not manifest to most peoples, beautiful both for the matter of
which it speaks, which is love, and for those of whom it tells, who were
noble youths descended of royal blood").[1] Love, however, is not this
author's only avowed concern, for at the close of the twelfth and last book
of his epic, he proudly proclaims its true subject to be Mars. Bidding the
work farewell, he writes that ever since the Muses began appearing naked
among men, some poets employed the Italian language "con bello stile
in onesto parlare, / e altri in amoroso l'operaro; / ma tu, o libro, primo
a lor cantar / di Marte fai gli affanni sostenuti / nel volgar lazio più mai
non veduti" (*Tes.* XII.84: "with beautiful style in honest speech, and others
put it to amorous use; but you, oh book, are the first to make them [the
Muses] sing the labors borne by Mars, never yet seen in the Latian vernacular").[2] Finally, a pair of postscripted sonnets reveal that at the author's
request, the Muses have delivered his completed book to Fiammetta, who

is to have the honor of giving it a name. She sighed after reading the tale of such valiant heroes, "Ahi, quante d'amor forze in costor foro!" ("Ah, how great the powers of love in them were!"), and has decided to call it "Teseida di nozze d'Emilia" ("Thesiad of Emilia's Nuptials").[3]

Fiammetta's choice is surprising. While the author tells of love in a song inspired by Mars, "nozze" ("nuptials") form the conceptual nucleus in her title. She therefore takes the poem's theme to be marriage. His protagonists are two enamoured knights descended from Theban Cadmus, Arcita and Palemone. Omitting any nominal reference to them, she calls our attention instead to Teseo, Duke of Athens, and Emilia, the Amazon maiden whose affections the Thebans vied to win. The terms in her title, which provide an alternative perspective on the epic, must have been selected for good reason. As we learn from the author's proem, she differs from the unintelligent mob of women generally by virtue of her intellect and knowledge. He has consequently not hesitated to put in his work "né storia, né favola, né chiuso parlare in altra guisa" ("neither story, nor fable, nor closed speech in other guise"). This challenge, alerting Fiammetta to the necessity of looking creatively beyond the letter of the text, invites us to do the same. "Storia," "favola," and "chiuso parlare" all imply an allegorical intent,[4] but the last phrase may refer more specifically to another occult system of literary discourse, namely numerology. The *Teseida* is, in fact, a numerical composition,[5] and one that is particularly rich because it has so many quantifiable elements—books, the "chapters" into which they are separated by rubrics, stanzaic octaves, verses, glosses, and sonnets—all ordered and transcribed by Boccaccio himself on the pages of the Laurentian holograph.[6] Each contributes to the numerological plan of the epic, in which, under the moral guidance of Teseo and Emilia, an arithmetic union signifying marriage secretly joins "amore" and "Marte" at the poem's center.

We may begin our search for the *Teseida*'s symbolic hidden numbers by recalling the author's divisions of its content as outlined for Fiammetta in his proem. He informs her that before relating the tale of Arcita and Palemone's love for Emilia, he will first tell two other stories:

> Dico adunque che dovendo narrare di due giovani nobilissimi Tebani, Arcita e Palemone, come innamorati d'Emilia amazona, per lei combattessero, primamente posta la invocazione poetica, mi parve da dimostrare e donde la donna fosse e come ad Attene venisse, e chi

fossero essi e come quivi venissero similmente, laonde, sì come premissioni alla loro istoria due se ne pongono.

(*Tes.*, p. 247: I say therefore that since I was to tell a tale of two most noble youths, Arcita and Palemone, and how after falling in love with Emilia the Amazon, they fought for her; once I had first set down the poetic invocation, it seemed right to me to show both where the lady was from and how she came to Athens, as well as who the men were and how they similarly came there, wherefore as a premise to their stories I set down two others.)

The poem then opens with a five-stanza invocation to Mars, Venus and Cupid. As the actual narration of events begins, the epic's glossator (none other than Boccaccio himself, feigning yet a different literary persona) reiterates why it was necessary for "the author" to include these two preliminary stories, which occupy respectively Books I and II:

Con ciò sia cosa che la principale intenzione dell'autore di questo libretto sia di trattare dell'amore e delle cose avvenute per quello, da due giovani tebani, cioè Arcita e Palemone, ad Emilia amazona, sì come nel suo proemio appare, potrebbe alcuno, e giustamente, adimandare che avesse qui a fare la guerra di Teseo con le donne amazone, della quale solamente parla il primo libro di questa opera. Dico, e brievemente, che l'autore a niuno altro fine queste cose scrisse, se non per mostrare onde Emilia fosse venuta ad Attene; . . . e il simigliante fa della sconfitta data da Teseo a Creonte, re di Tebe, per dichiarare donde e come alle mani di Teseo pervenissero Arcita e Palemone.

(*Tes.* I.6.gloss: Insofar as the principal intention of this little book's author is to treat of the love of two young Thebans, that is Arcita and Palemone, for Emilia the Amazon, and of the things that came about because of it, as can be seen in his proem, someone could question, and justifiably, the relevance of Theseus' war with the Amazon women, to which the whole first book of this work is devoted. I say, and briefly, that the author wrote these things for no other purpose than to show whence Emilia came to Athens . . . and he does the same for the defeat dealt by Theseus to Creon, king of Thebes,

in order to declare whence and how Arcita and Palemone fell into
Theseus' hands.)

As if these apologetic explanations were not sufficiently clear, he again
alludes to the prefatory nature of Books I and II in his gloss on II.10, "Poscia
che l'autore ha dimostrato di sopra, nel primo libro, donde e come Emilia
venisse ad Attene, in questo secondo intende di dimostrare come Arcita
e Palemone vi pervenissero" ("Since the author has demonstrated above,
in the first book, whence and how Emilia came to Athens, in this second
one he intends to demonstrate how Arcita and Palemone arrived there.")
Boccaccio could hardly be more emphatic. Two accounts precede the third
and main story in the *Teseida*, which begins with Book III. The author
has already announced its subject, "a most ancient story . . . beautiful
for the matter of which it speaks, which is love." So too has the glossator,
"the principal intention of this little book's author is to treat of love."
Now love, the poet's acknowledged main theme, is also given as the
matter most specific to Book III, where his story proper commences. To
document fully the case for an identification between this third book and
love, we must here recall the guiding role played by the sonnets that frame
Boccaccio's epic: a general proemial sonnet summarizing its complete contents, plus a "sonetto particulare" preceding and paraphrasing each single
book, plus the two postscripted sonnets mentioned above in connection
with the book's name. The general proemial sonnet, line 3, announces
love's conquest of the Theban knights, "Nel terzo [libro] amore Arcita
e Palemone / occupa" ("in the third [book] love occupies Arcita and
Palemone"). From the sonnet heading Book III we hear that Mars, who
had motivated Teseo's battle triumphs in Books I and II, will here be allowed
to rest, "Nel terzo a Marte dona alcuna posa / l'autore, e discrive come
Amore / d'Emilia, bella più che fresca rosa, / a' duo prigion con li suoi
dardi il core / ferendo, elli accendesse in amorosa / fiamma" ("In the third
the author allows Mars some repose, and he describes how Love for Emilia,
more beautiful than a fresh rose, wounding the two prisoners in their
hearts with his darts, kindles them to an amorous flame"). Appropriately, the stanzaic octaves of Book III open with an invocation to Cupid,
"con più pio sermone / sarà da me di Cupido cantato / e delle sue battaglie, il quale io priego / che sia presente a ciò che di lui spiego" ("with
more pious voice I shall sing of Cupid and his battles; I pray that he be
present for what I have to reveal about him"). Lest we should have any

doubts about what "di Cupido" means, help is not far away in the commentary, "cioè, d'Amore" ("that is, of love").

Arcita and Palemone, who have so far been suffering supreme sadness in their Athenian prison tower for nearly a year, will soon have reason for more bitter woe because "per Vener, nel suo ciel lucente, / d'altri sospir dar lor fu proveduto" ("through Venus, shining in her heaven, it was ordained that other sighs be in store for them"). Before entering upon the description of their enamorment, which constitutes the longest chapter in the *Teseida* (forty-two stanzas), Boccaccio reports the season, "Il tempo prima, e poi come Arcita e Palemone s'innamorarono d'Emilia" ("First the season, and then how Arcita and Palemone fell in love with Emilia"). He does so with a complex astrological circumlocution condensed into a single stanza that will require the longest astrological gloss in the poem. The stanza in question is III.5, and as we shall see, these numerical signs (3, 5) are significant. Phoebus is rising in Taurus, Venus accompanies him, and Jupiter is in Pisces. The glossator by no means tells us everything he knew about the auspicious and amorous implications of this horoscope, but he does correctly assess its general meaning. The author's purpose here is to "dimostrare il cielo essere ottimamente disposto a fare altrui innamorare" ("demonstrate that the sky was optimally disposed to make people fall in love").[7]

Beneath the stars so favorably configured all terrestrial life reawakens to love. Their joyful celestial influence is felt by plants, flowers, trees, birds, animals, "e' giovinetti lieti, che ad amare / eran disposti, sentivan nel core / fervente più che mai crescere amore" ("and glad youths, who were disposed to love, felt love grow in their hearts more fervent than ever"). The spring brings Emilia into a garden below the prisoners' tower, where one day she sits down to make a garland, "sempre cantando be' versi d'amore" ("singing all the while lovely verses of love"). Arcita espies her and calls Palemone to the window, "vieni a vedere: / Vener è qui discesa veramente!" ("come and see, Venus has verily descended here!"). Palemone looks down exclaiming, "Per certo questa è Citerea!" (This is for certain Cytharea!"). Almost immediately and in quick succession the archer Cupid wounds each knight with a golden arrow shot from the goddess-like lady's eyes. The knights begin to burn; Emilia's image is fixed in their hearts and minds because "Amore, / ladro sottil di ciascun gentil core" ("Love, furtive thief of every gentle heart") and a crueller lord than Teseo, now holds them in his sway. Captives twice over as with the pass-

ing days Cupid's chains bind them ever more tightly, they are given to
copious sighing and can scarcely sleep or eat. Their only comfort is to
watch Emilia for a short while each morning in the garden and praise
her high worth by composing sonnets and *canzoni*. While this fiery desire
increases, so does their suffering, to the point that all recollection of Thebes,
their noble heritage and present humiliating circumstances vanishes. Sighs
yield to tears of grievous lament, leading them to wish for solace in death,
and finally, after Arcita's release from prison, nagging jealousy enters the
heart of his once so loyal companion Palemone. Eventually, Palemone will
escape from the tower to find Arcita and resolve their rivalry, challenging
him to a nearly fatal duel. For that encounter, however, we must wait
until Book v.

Meanwhile, some explanations are in order concerning the abundant
and largely canonical "materia d'amore" of Book III. Why does Boccaccio
postpone the beginning of his love story until this moment in the poem?
He has already defensively justified the delay, affirming that Books I and
II are not irrelevant, as they might seem, because they give needed
background information. But textual clues planted early in the third book
hint at another, unstated reason for reserving it as the narrative locus of
the Theban knights' enamorment. The onset of their passion is attributed
to the operation of "Venus, shining in her heaven." The elaborate
astrological periphrasis following casts a horoscope with Venus ascendant
close to the sun in her lunar house, Taurus, which means that her influence
is maximal. Both passages direct our attention to the goddess of love in
her planetary aspect, "lo bel pianeto che d'amar conforta" ("the fair planet
that prompts to love"),[8] and who shines from the third heaven of the
Aristotelian-Ptolemaic universe.

Boccaccio chose the number 3 for his "book of love" in the *Teseida*
because it is the number of Venus in her cosmic sphere of influence. Dante
was, no doubt, the authority who sanctioned the association for him, but
many others before, of course, had also reckoned Venus as the third planet.[9]
References to the goddess and her heaven elsehere in Boccaccio's early works
echo both the opening of Dante's *canzone*, "Voi che 'ntendendo il terzo
ciel movete" ("O you who move the third heaven by intellection"),[10] and
the context in which this verse is repeated (*Par.* VIII) by Charles Martel,
the first of the souls sheathed in light to address the pilgrim after he and
Beatrice have risen to the star of Venus. Thus in the *Amorosa visione* the
poet-dreamer invokes Cytharea, "O Somma e graziosa intelligenzia / che

muovi il terzo cielo, o santa dea, / metti nel petto mio la tua potenzia: / non sofferir che fugga, o Citerea, / a me lo 'ngegno all'opera presente" ("O highest and gracious intelligence who move the third heaven, O holy goddess, put your power in my breast; do not suffer my mind to fail me, O Cytherea, in the present task").[11] Having consummated his love for Criseida (an event described in the third chapter of the third "Parte" of the *Filostrato*, stanzas 30–39), Troiolo praises Venus ecstatically, "O luce etterna, il cui lieto splendore / fa bello il terzo ciel dal qual ne piove / piacer, vaghezza, pietate ed amore, / del sole amica . . . / sempre sia lodata la tua virtute" ("O eternal light whose joyful splendor gives beauty to the third heaven, from which pleasure, desire, pity, and love rain down on us; friend of the sun . . . praised be forever your virtue").[12] The madrigal composed by Caleon for Fiammetta, queen of the love court held to debate thirteen "questions of love" in the *Filocolo*, is recited by an enamored spirit from the third heaven, "Io son del terzo ciel cosa gentile, / sì vago de' begli occhi di costei, / che s'io fossi mortal me ne morrei" ("I am a gentle thing from the third heaven, so desirous of this lady's beautiful eyes that if I were mortal, I should die of it").[13] When "love's pilgrim," Filocolo, reveals his true identity later in the same romance, Dario will raise his eyes heavenward, expressing wondrous thanks, "O più che altro potente pianeto, per la cui luce il terzo ciel si mostra bello, quanta è la tua forza negli umani cuori efficace!" (*Filocolo* IV.83.1: "O planet more powerful than any other, through whose light the third heaven reveals its beauty, how great is the efficacy of your strength in human hearts!") Two of the *Rime* also assume a bond between love and the third heaven. One tells of an unidentified widow who appears to the poet "accesa con quello splendore / ch'è terza luce nelle rote etterne" ("kindled with that splendor that is third light in the eternal wheels"), and in the other Boccaccio asks Dante to intercede on his behalf with Fiammetta so that she may grant him the mercy of death, "Io so che, infra l'altre anime liete / del terzo ciel, la mia Fiammetta vede / l'affanno mio dopo la sua partita: / pregala . . . / a sé m'impetri tosto la salita" ("I know that up among the other joyful souls of the third heaven, my Fiammetta sees my suffering after her departure; pray her . . . that she quickly grant me the ascent").[14]

Although in the *Teseida* Boccaccio refrains from openly numbering the circle of Venus, he clearly understood it to be the third. Through this connection, the number 3 becomes the arithmetic attribute of the goddess herself and therefore a number signifying "amore." Other triads would, of course, have reinforced the identification, above all the 3 of Trinitarian love that governs so visibly structure and verse form in Dante's *Commedia*. Boccaccio accepts, too, the scholastic distinction defining three categories of love. Mentioned in his *Esposizioni sopra la Comedia*,[15] they are enumerated and discussed by Fiammetta at the center of the love debate in the *Filocolo*.[16] These three types, "amore onesto" ("honest love"), "amore per diletto" ("love for delight"), and "amore per utilità" ("utilitarian love"), seem to reappear symbolically as the three figures crowning the fountain in the garden of worldly vanity in the *Amorosa visione*.[17] The number of Venus is metrically prominent in that cryptographic *tour de force* with three acrostic sonnets preceding a narrative in *terza rima*. Fiammetta's stern lecture on love recalls as well Dante's analysis in the *De vulgari eloquentia* of man's threefold nature (vegetative, animal, and rational), a triplicity determining the great subjects on which worthy poets should write: arms, love, and rectitude. Dante ends this chapter of his treatise with precisely the passage that inspired Boccaccio to compose the first Italian epic, "Arma vero nullum latium adhuc invenio poetasse" ("I do not find, however, that any Italian has as yet written poetry on the subject of Arms").[18]

Since Venus and her number preside over one book in the *Teseida*, we should not be surprised to discover that another is ruled by Mars, the god of whom the poet sings for the "naked" vernacular Muses, "You, oh book, are the first to make them sing the labors borne by Mars, never yet seen in the Latian vernacular." His numerical territory, like hers, depends on the sphere he occupies in the sevenfold planetary hierarchy. With Venus shining in the third position, he has the fifth. Consequently, just as Arcita and Palemone become lovers because of Venus in Book III, so in Book V Mars, "secondo gli antichi pagani iddio delle battaglie" (I.3.gl.: "according to the ancient pagans god of battles"), will compel them to fratricidal combat. The general proemial sonnet announces masculine battle as the theme of the fifth book, "il quinto mostra la battaglia virilmente / da Penteo fatta col suo compagnone" ("the fifth shows the manly battle fought by Penteo and his companion"). The fifth book's "sonetto particulare" then informs us that Mars, "who had been resting too long" — presumably since assisting Teseo with the military campaigns of Books I and II — will now return. His name, twice mentioned here, launches the rhymed résumé:

Marte, che troppo s'era riposato,

> entrato in Palemon novo sospetto
> il suo compagno udendo ritornato,
> dimostra il quinto a lui entrar nel petto;
> . . . .
> Poscia le lor carezze, e'l quistionare
> d'ognun volere Emilia, e 'l fiero Marte
> può chiaro assai chi più legge trovare.

(*Tes.*, p. 382: Mars, who had been resting too long, is shown in the fifth to enter the breast of Palemone, whom suspicion had seized when he heard of his companion's return. . . . Then whoever reads on can find clearly enough their embraces and the dispute over each one's wish for Emilia, and fierce Mars.)

Palemone has learned that Arcita, whom Teseo had released from prison but banished from Athens, is back in the city incognito as Penteo, a servant in the duke's household. The knowledge causes Palemone to fear that Arcita has furtively conquered Emilia's love. Fuming with the same poison of discord that Tisiphone had instilled in the hearts of Eteocles and Polynices (v.13 and gl.), he determines to escape from the tower and "conquistare per arme Emilia" (v.14: "conquer Emilia by arms"). At midnight he goes "armed" to the grove where Arcita, unsuspecting, lies sleeping. Dark, infernal forces continue to stir his passion as he pauses and prays to Luna-Proserpina, "Acciò che per battaglia io possa avere / l'amore di quella sol che m'è in calere" (v.30–32: "so that I may earn in battle the love of the only one who matters to me"). Arcita tries to dissuade him from his "mad plan," but then in resignation agrees to fight. First, however, he recites nine tragic episodes from the history of divine wrath against Thebes: the battle of the men sprung from the dragon's teeth, Actaeon, Athamas, Niobe, Semele, Agave, Oedipus, Eteocles and Polynices, and Creon. Largely based on material drawn from Statius' *Thebaid*, Arcita's declamation, which begins in stanza 55, belongs to the central and longest chapter of Book v. The digression is appropriate in a book dominated by the impulse to strife emanating from Mars because "Mavortia Thebe" ("Martian Thebes") had been the warrior god's city, its inhabitants his children.[19] Arcita and Palemone, "nepoti" ("grandsons") of Cadmus (II,88), are furthermore presumably Mars' descendants since Cadmus had married Harmonia, daughter of Mars and Venus.[20] Arcita sadly concludes, "or resta sopra noi, che ultimi siamo / del teban sangue, insieme n'uccidiamo. / E e' mi piace, poi che t'è in piacere, / che pure infra noi due battaglia sia" (*Tes*. v.59–60: "now it rests upon us, who are last of the Theban blood, to kill each other. And it pleases me, since it is your pleasure, that between the two of us as well there be combat"). We hardly need the glossator to realize, "Vuole qui mostrare Arcita che tutti li suoi predecessori, discesi di Cadmo, facitore e re primo di Tebe, abbiano fatto mala morte, e così convenire fare a loro due che rimasi n'erano, cioè a Palemone e a sé" (*Tes*. v.59–60.gl.: "Arcita wants to show here that all of his ancestors, descended from Cadmus, founder and first king of Thebes, came to a violent death, and so it had to be the same for the two of them who were left, that is Palemone and himself"). After they have been fighting some hours, Emilia arrives (v.77) in a hunting party with Teseo, who adjures the knights in the name of Mars to lay down their weapons. He decrees that each choose a hundred men to fight on his side in a tournament one year hence, and whoever wins shall have Emilia's hand in marriage, "Chi l'altra parte caccerà di fore / per forza d'arme, marito le fia" ("whoever routs the other side by force of arms will be her husband").

Book III thus belongs to Venus and Book v to Mars because 3 and 5 are their planetary numbers. Although for readers today the alternation between amorous and martial matter in the *Teseida* seems to cause awkward, abrupt narrative shifts, it follows a well-conceived plan in which number is a significant ordering factor. This plan also applies to a third major deity in the epic, Diana, patron of its chaste heroine Emilia. On the eve of the tournament that is to decide which of the knights she will wed, the Amazon maiden goes to Diana's temple. Her propitiatory sacrifice, her prayer, and the portents through which Diana communicates an answer are set in three successive chapters of Book VII. The first is announced in the seventh rubric of Book VII, "Come Emilia sacrificò a Diana" ("How Emilia sacrificed to Diana"). This rubric heads a chapter of seven stanzas that begins at VII.70. The following rubric, "L'orazione d'Emilia a Diana" ("Emilia's orison to Diana"), then precedes VII.77. In the next chapter, "Ciò che ad Emilia orante apparve e come ella si partì del tempio" ("what appeared to Emilia as she prayed and how she left the temple"), Diana's chorus speaks, "nel ciel tra l'iddii è fermato / che tu sii sposa dell'un di costoro, / e Diana n'è lieta" ("in heaven among the gods it has been ordained that you be the bride of one of these men, and Diana is delighted about it"). If the first chapter in this three-part sequence has seven stanzas starting at VII.70, the next two, which start with Emilia's prayer at VII.77, contain a total of seventeen stanzas. The entire sequence is placed, moreover, at the structural center — or rather centers — of Book VII. There are actually two: one based on a count of the stanzas, the other on the sum of the rubricized chapters. Since Book VII has 145 stanzas in all, the seventy-third is their mid-point, and VII.73 marks precisely the central octave in the chapter that introduces Diana's temple at VII.70. Reckoning alternatively by rubrics, we find that the reply to Emilia's prayer is announced in the ninth, and as the narrative of Book VII is distributed over nineteen chapters, that ninth rubric falls at the book's "second" center.

The above patterns, coinciding twice over with center in the seventh book, indicate that the number 7 must be Diana's number in the *Teseida*. Her name is not mentioned in the poem proper until the seventh book. Excluded, for example, from Palemone's nocturnal prayer to Luna, which begins, "O di Latona prole inargentata" (v.30: "Oh silvery offspring of Latona"), it appears in that context only as part of the commentary, "Scrivono i poeti che Latona fu bellissima donna, della quale Giove innamorato e avuto a fare di lei ebbe due figliuoli, Apollo e Diana, cioè la luna" (*Tes.* v.30.gl: "The poets write that Latona was a most beautiful woman, by whom Jove, who fell in love and had to do with her, had two children, Apollo and Diana, that is, the moon"). Its first appearance in the octaves themselves comes at the description of the palace of Venus (VII.61), where many broken bows from Diana's faithless nymphs, including Callisto's, hang on a wall as trophies. The sum of the digits designating this stanza ($61 = 6 + 1 = 7$) probably alludes to the goddess of chastity. The last references to Diana form a short sequence starting with the seventh chapter of Book XII, when Emilia protests that she should not marry because the Scythian women had all taken vows of chastity to Diana. Fearing the goddess's vengeance, she prefers to continue obediently serving her. Teseo, however, quickly dispels her resistance, "se Diana ne fosse turbata, / sopra di te verria l'ira dolente, / . . . / la forma tua non è atta a Diana / servir ne' templi né 'n selva montana" ("if Diana were displeased, her painful anger would fall upon you, . . . your beauty was not meant to serve Diana either in temples or mountain forest"). With his speech (XII.43), again in a stanza that could conceal her number ($43 = 4 + 3 = 7$), Diana is dismissed from the poem.

Like the 3's and 5's accompanying Venus and Mars, Diana's number in the *Teseida* is also astrological. Silvery daughter of Latona and sister of the sun Apollo, she is the moon. When Emilia invokes the goddess in her "gran deitate triforme" (VII.80: "great triform divinity"), the glossator remarks, "È questa dea in cielo chiamata luna e ha quella forma la quale noi veggiamo; e in terra è chiamata Diana, dea della castità, allora si figura con l'arco e col turcasso a guisa di cacciatrice; in inferno si chiama Proserpina, e allora si figura come reina perciò che è moglie di Plutone, iddio e re d'inferno" (*Tes.* VII.80.gl.: "In heaven this goddess is called moon, and she has the form that we see there; and on earth she is called Diana, goddess of chastity, and then she is depicted in the guise of a huntress with a bow and quiver; in hell she is called Proserpina, and then she is depicted as queen because she is wife of Pluto, god and king of hell"). In her lunar aspect Diana can be the seventh planet, providing, naturally, we reverse our perspective on the celestial spheres and count them downwards from Saturn.

This alternative system of reckoning the planets was practiced both before and after Boccaccio's time, and he was not the only author to combine the two. Dante, for example, admits that one can number them starting with either the lowest or the highest. In the *Convivio*, adding to the seven revolving heavens a starry eighth and a ninth ("primo mobile"), he correlates each with a branch of learning. To Mars he attributes Music, in part because that planet is at the center and so enjoys an especially harmonious relationship with the others, "E lo cielo di Marte si può comparare a la Musica per . . . la sua più bella relazione, chè, annumerando li cieli mobili, da qualunque si comincia o da l'infimo o dal sommo, esso cielo di Marte è lo quinto, esso è lo mezzo di tutti, cioè de li primi, de li secondi, de li terzi e de li quarti."[21] Chaucer, who surely perceived numerical patterns in the *Teseida*, also counts the orbiting stars both ways. In the *Knight's Tale* he links the number 3 with Venus and her votary, Palamon. Palamon escapes from prison "in the seventh yer, of May / The thridde nyght" (lines 1462–63); before the tournament that Theseus ordains "this day fifty wykes" (line 1850), it was "The thridde houre inequal that Palamon / Bigan to Venus temple for to gon" (lines 2271–72). Similarly, in *Troilus and Criseyde* love's keen shots happen to strike Pandarus "on Mayes day the thrydde" (II.55–58), and amorous Venus opens the *Prohemium* of Book Three, "O blissful light, of which the bemes clere / Adorneth all the thridde heven faire! / O sonnes lief, o Joves doughter deere, / Plesance of love, O goodly debonaire, / In gentil hertes ay redy to repaire!" Conversely, however, it is her mythological and astrological lover who is the lord of this heaven in the *Complaint of Mars*:

> Whilom the thridde hevenes lord above,
> As wel by hevenysh revolucioun
> As by desert, hath wonne Venus his love,
> And she hath take him in subjeccioun,
> And as a maistresse taught him his lessoun,
> Commaundynge him that nevere, in her servise,
> He nere so bold no lover to dispise.
>
> (Lines 29–35)[22]

Chaucer then freely interchanges the spheres of Mars and Venus, accommodating their numbers to the poetic scheme dictated by his different works.

In spite of these alternations, the number 7 had been well-established from antiquity as Diana's defining number. Cicero's *De natura deorum* so counts her, "Diana, *omnivaga* dicitur, non a venando, sed quod in septem numeratur tamquam vagantibus [stellis]."[23] In his *Somnium Scipionis* the moon is also seen as last among the planets by the two Scipios, who gaze from a "lofty perch" in the Milky Way down through the ranks of the underlying spheres in the cosmos, one by one from Saturn to the earth.[24] This planetary perspective logically obtains as well for Macrobius, thanks to whose *Commentarium in somnium Scipionis* the dream fragment from Cicero's *De re publica* was preserved for the later Middle Ages.[25] Scipio the Elder's cryptic reference to the sum of years his grandson will live, "seven times eight recurring circuits of the sun,"[26] requires Macrobius to expound at length on numbers generally. The digit that receives his fullest attention is 7, most venerable in the Pythagorean decad,[27] and the one that motivates the moon, "lunam quoque quasi ex illis [vagantibus sphaeris] septimam numerus septenarius movet cursumque eius ipse dispensat" ("the number seven motivates the moon, which is in the seventh planetary sphere, and regulates its course"). Many proofs, he asserts, can be adduced to demonstrate the truth of this statement. To begin with, the moon completes its cycle in twenty-eight days, and 28 is the sum of the first seven digits $(1 + 2 + 3 + 4 + 5 + 6 + 7 = 28)$: "hiuis ergo viginti octo dierum numeri septenarius origo est. nam si ab uno usque ad septem quantum singuli numeri exprimunt tantum antecedentibus addendo procedas, invenies viginti octo nata de septem" ("seven is the source of this number of twenty-eight, for if you add the numbers from one to seven, the total is twenty-eight"). Then, too, its monthly course can be divided into four quarters of seven days each, "hunc etiam numerum, qui in quater septenos aequa sorte digeritur, ad totam zodiaci latitudinem emetiendam remetiendamque consumit" ("twenty-eight, evenly divided into four quarters, marks the number of days required by the moon to complete its course out and back across the zodiac"). Finally, this mutable body regularly waxes and wanes through seven phases, "similibus quoque dispensationibus hebdomadum luminis sui vices sempiterna lege variando disponit" ("following the same arrangement of seven-day periods the moon also regulates the phases of its light under a fixed law").[28] Other notable authorities, among them Martianus Capella and later Isidore of Seville, reasoned along just these same lines, which compound Diana's number in the planetary hierarchy with the 7's characterizing the lunar cycle.[29] They, like Macrobius, were known to Boccaccio, who therefore preserves a learned tradition by selecting 7 as the number for that goddess in the *Teseida*.

The numerological descent of Venus, Mars, and Diana from their celestial homes to the poetic terrain of the *Teseida* reaches beyond the primary structural areas of influence that I have thus far outlined for Books III, V, and VII. Venus and Mars, who will directly intervene in the tournament on behalf of Palemone and Arcita respectively, also silently determine the hours of its duration. When the two knights march with 100 combatants each into the arena, "già del cielo al terzo salito era / Febo" (VII.104: "Phoebus had already risen to the third part of the heaven"). As Arcita is borne triumphant back to Athens, "Passata avea il sol già l'ora ottava, / quando finì lo stormo incominciato in su la terza" (IX.29: "the sun had already passed the eighth hour, when the pitched battle begun in the third ended").[30] The chivalric contest, stemming from courtly enamorment, begins at a time of day carrying the number of Venus, and it brings an end to the knights' militant rivalry with the victory of Arcita in a period of exactly five hours. Moreover, after setting the rules for this "love battle," Teseo had stated, "Questo sarà come un giuoco a Marte, / li sacrifici del qual celebriamo / il giorno dato" (VII.13: "This will be like a game to Mars, whom we celebrate with sacrifices on the given day"). Referring to Boccaccio's discussion of the commonly accepted astrological relationship between the planets and the days of the week in his *Genealogie*, Janet Levarie Smarr has rightly deduced that the "given day" here in question must be "martedì" ("Tuesday"), the first hour of which is governed by Mars. According to the above scheme for matching successive diurnal hours with the planets, the third and eighth on this tournament Tuesday acquire greater symbolic resonance because Venus governs the former and Mars returns to rule the latter.[31]

Our narrator may also be pointing numerically to Mars as he registers the size of the amphitheater, which has "più di cinquecento giri" ("more than 500 tiers") rising from the ring in circular steps (VII.110). This possibility is strengthened by the fact that his commentator, too, has a predilection for the number 5 and its multiples by 10, an interest evident much earlier in the *Teseida*. It happens, for example, that the glosses on Book I cite the number 50 just five times. In I.7 the author compares the Amazons' mad slaughter of their menfolk with the ferocity of "the granddaughters of Belus," and the glossator then explains,

> Belo fu re in una parte di Grecia, e ebbe due figliuoli; l'uno ebbe nome Danao, il quale fu re dopo la morte del padre e ebbe *cinquanta* figliuole; l'altro ebbe nome Egisto e ebbe *cinquanta* figliuoli maschi; e di pari concordia diedono le *cinquanta* figliuole di Danao per mogli alli *cinquanta* figliuoli d'Egisto.

> (*Tes.* I.7.gl.: Belus was king in a part of Greece, and he had two little boys; one was named Danaus, who was king after his father's death, and he had fifty daughters; the other was named Aegystus [sic], and he had fifty male children; and by mutual agreement they gave the fifty daughters of Danaus as wives to the fifty sons of Aegystus).

Seven stanzas later, he tells how a magnificent deed of valor accomplished by a man called Tydeus inspired Teseo to attack so courageously the Amazons. The heroism of Tydeus, which he knew, of course from Statius,[32]

> fu in questa forma: Etiocle e Polinice figliuoli d'Edippo, re di Tebe, composero insieme di regnare ciascuno il suo anno, e mentre l'uno regnasse, l'altro stesse come sbandito fuori del regno. . . . E essendo finito l'anno che Etiocle dovea avere regnato, venne a Tebe Tideo, a richiedere il regno per Polinice; il quale non solamente non gli fu

renduto, ma fu di notte in uno bosco assalito da *cinquanta* cavalieri,
li quali Etiocle avea mandati a stare in guato, perchè l'uccidessero;
li quali Tideo, fieramente combattendo, tutti uccise, e poi consacrò
a Marte, iddio delle battaglie, il suo scudo.

(*Tes.* 1.14.gl.: took this form: Eteocles and Polynices, sons of King
Oedipus of Thebes, arranged together to reign each for his year,
and while one was reigning, the other would be as if banished from
the kingdom. . . . And when the year that Eteocles was to have
reigned ended, Tydeus came to Thebes to request the kingdom for
Polynices; but not only was it not rendered unto him, but he was
assailed at night in a grove by fifty knights whom Eteocles had sent
to wait in ambush so as to kill him; Tydeus, fighting fiercely, killed
them all, and then he consecrated his shield to Mars, god of battles.)

If the marginalia of *Teseida* I yield a 50 five times, three further pentavalent
referents appear in its preliminary companion piece, Book II. So the rubric
introducing II. 10 with the author's "Transgressione dalla propria materia,
per mostrare qual fosse la cagione per la quale Teseo andasse contra Creonte"
("Transgression from his matter proper to show the reason why Teseo
went against Creon") prompts a longer annotated account of the war between Eteocles and Polynices, which again requires mention of the fifty
slain by Tydeus and lexically calls our attention to the ensuing march of
five against Thebes, as opposed to the more predictable seven:

fu, tornandosi egli [Tideo] ad Argo, assalito una notte da *cinquanta*
cavalieri d'Etiocle, gli quali egli tutti uccise; e, tornato ad Argo, com-
mosse ad andare a vendicare la ingiuria fatta a Pollinice, e quella che
stata era fatta a lui, Capaneo re, Anfiorao re, Ippomedone re,
Partenopeo re, e Adrasto suo suocero; e con grandissimo esercito
di gente a piè e a cavallo, e egli e Pollinice co' predetti altri *cinque*
re andarono ad assediare Tebe.

(*Tes.* II.10.gl.: While returning to Argus, he was assailed one night
by fifty of Eteocles' knights, all of whom he killed, and having returned to Argus he incited King Capaneus, King Amphiaraus, King
Hippomedon, King Parthenopeus and Adrastus his brother-in-law
to go and avenge the injury done to Polynices and the one that had

been done to him; and with a very great army of people on foot
and on horseback both he and Polynices, with the aforesaid other
five kings, went to besiege Thebes.)

Finally, at II.70, as Boccaccio's Teseo advances victorious into the fallen
city, his glossator proffers a last reminder—the third in the epic—of the
fifty who had ambushed Tydeus, "Que' *cinquanta* de' quali è detto di sopra"
("those fifty who are discussed above"). In other words, the Italian epic's
commentary thrice alludes to these fifty in a broader pattern proceeding
from the Danaids and containing 5 + 3 occurrences of 5 and 50 that extend from I.7 to II.70.

Our glossator, privy to his author's prime numerological plan, col-
laborates with him in another tripartite scheme matching Diana and her
twin, Apollo, with the number 7 doubled. During Teseo's preparations
for Arcita's splendid funeral, the author borrows a formula from Dante
to report that the Athenians' grief was surely greater than that of the
Thebans "quando li sette e sette d'Anfione / figli fur morti en la trista
stagione" (XI.16: "when Amphion's seven and seven children were killed
in the season of sorrow".)[33] Here the glossator notes, "Detto è di sopra
come per la superbia di Niobè fossero uccisi i suoi xiiij figliuoli" ("It is
told above how Niobe's 14 children were killed because of her pride").
Turning back to X.8, we find that the number of those killed in the tournament equalled that of the funeral urns Niobe carried after Latona's
vengeance. Again the commentary refers us to an earlier passage.

> Mostrato è di sopra come i figliuoli e le figliuole di Niobè per la
> sua superbia fossero uccisi da Apollo e Diana, figliuoli di Latona.
> Li quali furono xiiij, e ciascuno fu dalla madre, cioè da Niobè, messo
> per sé in una urna. . . . E così mostra [l'autore] che xiiij fossero col-
> oro che in quella battaglia morirono.

> (*Tes.* x.8.gl.: It is shown above how the sons and daughters of Niobe
> were killed because of her pride by Apollo and Diana, children of
> Latona. There were 14 of them and each one was put by the mother,
> that is by Niobe, in a separate urn. . . . And thus [the Author] shows
> there were 14 who died in that battle.)

For a full account of Niobe's pride and punishment, we must retrogress to Arcita's synopsis of his city's history, that is, the grim recital starting in v.55. Explaining the verses, "Latona uccise i figliuoi d'Anfione / intorno a Niobè, madre dolente" ("Latona killed Amphion's children around Niobe, sorrowing mother"), the glossator writes that Amphion was a king of Thebes married to Niobe, "della quale aveva xiiii figliuoli, vii maschi e vii femine" ("by whom he had 14 children, 7 boys and 7 girls"). He goes on to narrate the familiar Ovidian myth,[34] concluding that, as Niobe was disporting in a meadow "con tutti questi suoi xiiii figliuoli, in poca d'ora, saettando, Apollo uccise li vii maschi, e Diana le vii femine" ("with all these 14 children of hers, in a matter of moments, with bows and arrows, Apollo killed the 7 boys and Diana the 7 girls"). Understood as 7 + 7, this triplicity of 14's in the marginalia on v.58; x.8; and xi.16 reiterates the numerical structure tying Diana to the heptad at the seventh book's center.

Another line of textual exploration reveals figurative patterns of kinship linking Mars, Venus, and Diana with their earthly fictional counterparts, Arcita, Palemone, and Emilia. Arcita, who will pray to Mars for victory the night before the tournament, decides to conceal his identity after embarking on the bitter path of exile, and changes his name to Penteo. The pseudonym, which then accompanies him through the duel in Book v, is derived from the Greek word for 5, "pentē." This poetic cipher would probably have been suggested to Boccaccio by Latin treatises on the Pythagorean decad, which often used the Hellenic forms to designate each digit, "monas," "dyas," "trias," and so forth.[35] Palemone is apprised that Arcita has returned secretly to Athens, "E ch'e' servia Teseo / e faceasi per nome dir Penteo" ("And that he was serving Teseo and giving his name as Penteo") in v.5. The rubric entitled "La forma e l'esser d'Arcita" ("The appearance and nature of Arcita") introduces the fifth chapter and fiftieth stanza of Book iii. In Book iv Arcita will lament the destruction of Thebes for five stanzas (13–17) and raise a plea of five stanzas for help from Amore (67–71). His rehearsal of Theban history beginning with v.55 also occupies five stanzas, as does the "Orazione d'Arcita a Marte" ("Arcita's orison to Mars") in Book vii (24–28).

We have already seen the cluster of 7's surrounding Diana in conjunction with her temple and vengeance on Niobe. So Emilia's arrival on the scene of the duel in v.77 may have been calculated by Boccaccio to coincide with this number, especially since she comes as a huntress, "sopra d'un bel pallafreno / co' can dintorno, e un corno dallato / avea e . . .

/ dietro alle spalle, un arco avea legato / e un turcasso di saette pieno" ("on a fine palfrey in the midst of her dogs, and she had a horn at her side, and strapped to her shoulders she had a bow and a quiver full of arrows"). These verses recall Boccaccio's gloss on Emilia's prayer to the goddess of chastity at VII.80: "on earth she is called Diana, goddess of chastity, and then she is depicted with a bow and quiver in the guise of a huntress." The poet will withhold his description of Emilia's "forma e bellezza" ("appearance and beauty") until the twelfth chapter of Book XII. It begins, as does the epic itself, with an invocation to the Muses, this time in the name of "Anfione," whom they had helped build the city walls for Thebes. The stanza's number (XII.52) suggests a 7 (52 = 5 + 2 = 7), a sum implicitly related to the three preceding cross-referenced allusions to Amphion's 7 + 7 children.

"La forma e l'esser di Palemone" ("The appearance and nature of Palemone"), who entrusts himself to Venus before the tournament, is the title of the central chapter in Book III. It consists of a single stanza, the forty-ninth. Again, the sum of these digits (4 + 9 = 13) could count symbolically since Boccaccio elsewhere uses 13 as a number of love, most obviously for the thirteen "questioni d'amore" debated in the *Filocolo*. We are told how Palemone's confidant, appropriately called Panfilo ("all love"), engineers his escape from prison in a chapter of three stanzas, the third of Book v. Palemone, who invokes "Latona's silvery offspring" for three *ottave* beginning with v.30, will then reach Arcita sleeping in the wood at v.33, that is, at the start of the fifth chapter of Book v.

Finally, the 3 of love fulfills Palemone's good fortune in marrying Emilia because she had twice before been a bride-to-be. Several times vague mention is made of Acate, a man to whom Teseo would have given her hand had cruel fortune not caused his untimely death (v.94). Next she is wed to Arcita, who had emerged victorious, but gravely injured, from the tournament, "Arcita Emilia graziosamente / quivi sposò, e furon prolungati / li dì delle lor nozze veramente, / infin ch'el fosse forte e ben guarito" (IX.83: "Arcita then gracefully wed Emilia, and the days of their nuptials were truly postponed until he should be strong and well-recovered"). Arcita, of course, never recovers and dies but ten days later. Thus it must be thanks to the protection of Venus that Palemone, third in line, becomes her spouse in a true marriage, sealed by consummation and a formal nuptial celebration ("nozze").[36]

The above-sketched ties between mythological and mortal participants in the *Teseida* invite three working conclusions. First, the poem's governing numbers signal important thematic content, such as planetary dispositions (III.5), prayers to the gods (v.30, VII.70), and crucial shifts in narrative development hinging on character action or intersection: Palemone comes armed to Arcita at midnight (v.33) for a duel preordained by the curse on Thebes (v.55) that will be halted by the morntide arrival of Emilia (v.77) with Teseo. Second, what seemed at first a simple relationship between Venus and 3, Mars and 5, Diana and 7, now becomes an interlocking system involving these numbers collectively because they tend to keep occurring in conjunction with one another. Third, the glosses seem to share in the numerical plan governing disposition of material into books, chapters, and stanzas. Scattered traces intimate that both *what* the commentator says and *where* may be significant on this count. He thrice recalls the death of Amphion and Niobe's 7 + 7 children beginning with a gloss (v.58) in which the sums 7 and 14 are named seven times. All told, he finds occasion to use the number 50 seven times, first in I.7 (the Danaides) and last in II.70 (the Theban fifty who ambushed Tydeus). These curious coincidences bring us now to a closer consideration of Boccaccio's marginalia.

Almost all the "chiose" on the *Teseida* exemplify the first kind of commentary Boccaccio will later apply to his readings of Dante's *Commedia*, "esposizione litterale" ("literal exposition"). Only a handful go deeper, disclosing some of the moral truth the author means to convey "poeticamente fingendo" ("poetically pretending"). Early in the epic, as Mars returns from Tideo's bloody triumph and musters "magnanimous Teseo" to sail with an army against the Amazons, the poet gives us a first glimpse of his work's allegorical possibilities by establishing a connection between the god of war and the emotion of anger (I.14–15.gl.). But he chooses not to exploit them more fully until the night preceding the tournament, when Arcita and Palemone pray for assistance in the Athenian temples of Mars and Venus. Their "Orazioni," which fly personified to these deities' abodes and view them in virtually every detail, occasion the two longest, most rigorously constructed, moralistic glosses in the entire poem. They are attached through a striking numerical chiasmus to the thirtieth stanza (for Mars) and the fiftieth stanza (for Venus) of Book VII.

The resulting conjunction of the numbers 3, 5, and 7 should not at this point be surprising. After all, it is precisely in this pair of dense, didactic expositions at VII.30 and VII.50 that Boccaccio finally extends a key opening the way to the *Teseida*'s underlying allegory. In the former, which resumes the note on Mars's Thracian home accompanying 1.15, he states that all men have two principal appetites, "de' quali l'uno si chiama appetito concupiscibile . . . l'altro si chiama appetito irascibile" (VII.30: "of which one is called the concupiscible appetite, . . .the other is called the irascible appetite"). Each in turn may be laudable or reprehensible depending on whether it is subject to the higher power of reason. The god Mars can therefore represent righteous anger as well as blind wrath:

> due maniere d'ira sono, e ciascuna fa arrossare l'adirato: l'uno si è l'adirarsi senza ragione, e questa è viziosa e è quella di che qui si parla; l'altra può essere ragionevole, sì come il turbarsi d'alcuna cosa non giustamente fatta, e questa riceve il consiglio della ragione in riprendere e in fare ammendare quella cotale cosa mal fatta.
>
> (*Tes.* VII.30.gl.: There are two kinds of ire, and each one makes the angered person turn red; one is when a person becomes angered without reason, and it is evil and is the one that is spoken of here; the other can be reasonable, as when a person becomes upset over something done unjustly, and this receives the counsel of reason in reproving and correcting that particular wrongly done thing.)

Venus is similarly twofold, either a goddess of matrimony and generation or an incitement to wanton concupiscence:

> La quale Venere è doppia, perciò che l'una si può e dee intendere per ciascuno onesto e licito disiderio, sì come è disiderare d'avere moglie per avere figliuoli, e simili a questo: e di questa Venere non si parla qui. La seconda Venere è quella per la quale ogni lascivia è disiderata, e che volgarmente è chiamata dea d'amore; e di questa disegna qui l'autore il tempio e l'altre cose circustanti ad esso.
>
> (*Tes.* VII.50.gl.: This Venus is double because one of them can and must be understood by every honest and legitimate desire, such as desiring to have a wife in order to have children and things similar to this, and this is not the Venus spoken of here. The second Venus is the one through whom all lasciviousness is desired and who is

commonly called goddess of love, and she is the one whose temple and the other things belonging to it the author here describes.)

Applying these distinctions to the narrative in the *Teseida*, we can say that the "good" Mars and Venus assist "good Teseo" in his just warfare against the Amazons' proudly truculent, unnatural, antimatrimonial society (Book I). Announcing imminent surrender, Ipolita informs her subjects,

> Se di ciascuna qui fosse il marito,
> fratel, figliuolo o padre che fu morto
> da tutte noi, non saria stato ardito
> Teseo mai d'appressarsi al nostro porto;
> ma perché non ci son, ci ha assaltate,
> come vedete, e ancora assediate.
> Venere, giustamente a noi crucciata,
> col suo amico Marte il favoreggia.

(*Tes.* 1.116–17: If each of our husbands, brothers, sons, or fathers whom we all killed were here now, Teseo would never have been so audacious as to approach our port; but since they are not here, he has attacked us, as you see, and further besieged us. Venus, justly vexed with us, together with her friend Mars, is favoring him.)

The same Mars moves Teseo to end the tyranny of King Creon (Book II), whose hubris had also led him to violate social custom, more particularly, another aspect of the marriage bond, by denying aggrieved widows the time-honored privilege of granting their husbands ritual burial. Scythia and Thebes stand in moral juxtaposition to Athens, recognized by the commentator as the city of Minerva and wisdom, "Minerva tenevano gli antichi che fosse dea della sapienzia, e questa oltre a ogni altro iddio era onorata in Attene, sì come i Fiorentini più che alcuno altro santo onorano San Giovanni Batista" (*Tes.* 1.60.gl.: "the ancients held that Minerva was goddess of wisdom and that she was honored above every other god in Athens, just as the Florentines honor Saint John the Baptist more than any other saint"). Having conquered Ipolita's kingdom, Teseo's first act on returning to Athens is to enter the temple of Pallas-Minerva, "diritto andò al tempio di Pallade / a reverir di lei la deitade. / Quivi con reverenza offerse molto, / e le sue armi e l'altre conquistate" (II.23–24: "he went straight to the temple of Pallas to revere her divinity. There with reverence he made a great offering with both his arms and the others he had conquered"). Minerva's is, moreover, the first of the several religious sanctuaries visited in the poem by the wise Duke of Athens. An embodiment of moral enlightenment, he will end toward high noon the duel begun in a dark wood at midnight between Arcita and Palemone, whose rivalry had been caused by the irrational Mars and his adulterous, concupiscent consort, the 'wrong' Venus. To these gods they pray, again at night, before the civilized, rationally planned tournament, through which, as Apollo shines for five hours, reason personified by Teseo dominates the knights' destructive appetites. Its outcome will permit the poet to end the twelfth book of his matrimonial epic as he had the first, with a nuptial ceremony celebrated in the temple of the 'good' Venus who fosters the legitimate desire to marry and bear children.[37]

But there is more to be said about the marginalia surrounding Arcita and Palemone's prayers to Mars (VII.30) and Venus (VII.50). The stanzas to which these conceptually central glosses are attached stand exactly at the poem's structural center. Again, as we saw for Book VII, there are two, one based on a verse count and the other on the sum of the chapters demarcated by rubrics. The *Teseida* has 1238 *ottave*, making a total of 9904 verses, which puts the central stanza (the 619th) at VII.30. The central verse (4952) coincides with VII.30.1, where the solemn description of Mars' tenebrous castle begins, "ne' campi trazii, sotto i cieli iberni" ("in Thracian fields, beneath the Hybernian skies").[38] The rubrics distributed among the twelve books of the epic create 176 chapters. The central chapter (the eighty-eighth), "Come l'orazione [di Palemone] pervenne a Venere, e come fatto e dove sia il tempio suo" ("How the orison [of Palemone] reached Venus, and how her temple is made and where it is"), is the sixth in the seventh book. It opens with VII.50, and recalls explicitly the corresponding description of Mars's dwelling that had begun in VII.30: "Come d'Arcita Marte l'orazione / cercò, così a Venere pietosa, / se n'andò sopra 'l monte Citerone / quella di Palemone" ("As Arcita's orison had sought Mars, so Palemone's went off to merciful Venus on Mount Citheron") The author's main theme, announced in the proem, is love. It is therefore appropriate that the gloss on this stanza, running to nearly five thousand words, should be by far the longest in his poem. The second longest is its pendant on Mars, the god of whom Boccaccio first sang in the noble

vernacular of Latium. These glosses, together with the conspicuous absence
of any analogous text following Emilia's prayer to Diana, allow us to see
Venus and Mars, who rule for better or worse successive portions of the
Teseida, as a couple presiding allegoricaly at its numerologically determined
structural centers.

Now we must recall that if the author declares love and battle as his
"matters," Fiammetta's title marks marriage as the poem's theme. Could
she have seen in the pairing of Mars and Venus a symbol of matrimonial
union? Through survival of the Homeric account, medieval mythographers
had condemned them as archetypical adulterers, and some found in Venus'
seduction of Mars a pagan counterpart to Eve's temptation of Adam.[39]
There was, however, a second way of interpreting the influence of the
goddess on her warrior lover, *in bono*. She could have the beneficent capacity
of tempering his ferocity. Statius sees such a potentially tender relationship between them in the *Thebaid*, when Mars affectionately consoles her,

> O mihi bellorum requies et sacra voluptas
> unaque pax animo! soli cui tanta potestas
> divorumque hominumque meis occurrere telis
> impune et media quamvis in caede frementes
> hos adsistere equos, hunc ensem avellere dextrae!

(O thou who art my repose from battle, my sacred joy and all the
peace my heart doth know: thou who alone of gods and men canst
face my arms unpunished, and check even in mid-slaughter my
neighing steeds, and tear this sword from my right hand!)[40]

This more favorable view was reinforced by a parallel astrological tradition in which, since Mars "follows" Venus through their planetary revolu-
tions, she becomes his gentle, subduing mistress. Chaucer so presents the
two in his *Complaint of Mars*:

> For she forbad him jelosye et al,
> And cruelte, and bost, and tyrannye;
> She made him at her lust so humble and tal,
> That when her deyned to cast on hym her ye,
> He tok in pacience to lyve or dye.
> And thus she brydeleth him in her manere,

With nothing but with scourging of her chere
(lines 36–42).[41]

By the end of the next century in Italy, Mars and Venus will evolve to
legitimate status as figures typifying man and wife. A subject for paintings on marriage *cassoni* ("chests") by Botticelli and Piero di Cosimo,[42]
they also appear in nuptial portraits, symbolic as well as real, by Mantegna,
Titian, and Paris Bordone. Panofsky reports a Roman custom, dating from
the Antonine period, of sculpting distinguished married couples in the
guise of Mars and Venus.[43] The Lehmanns find literary precedent for the
motif in Ovid's *Fasti*,[44] a work that Boccaccio already knew when he glossed
the *Teseida*.[45] There, Mars and Venus, whom Romulus considered his
"parents," are mated in the calendar as god and goddess of the first two
months: "Martis erat primus mensis, Venerisque secundus: / haec generis
princeps, ipsius ille pater" ("the month of Mars was the first, and that
of Venus the second; she was the author of the race, and he its sire").
Venus can rightly claim April because all growing things, for whose creation and continuation she is responsible, then return to life,

nec Veneri tempus quam ver erat aptius ullum:
vere nitent terrae, vere remissus ager,
nunc herbae rupta tellure cacumina tollunt,
nunc tumido gemmas cortice palmes agit.
et formosa Venus formoso tempore digna est,
utque solet, Marti continuata suo est.

(And no season was more fitting for Venus than spring. In spring
the landscape glistens; soft is the soil in spring; now the corn pushes
its blades through the cleft ground; now the vineshoot protrudes
its buds in the swelling bark. Lovely Venus deserves the lovely season
and is attached, as usual, to her dear Mars.)[46]

Whether Boccaccio intended Mars and Venus as a marriage couple in
the *Teseida* is problematic. He does report the myth of their adultery
(VII.25.gl.).[47] At the center of this poem he asserts that *there* he is talking
about the god of senseless wrath (VII.30.gl.) and the goddess of unbridled
sensuality (VII.50.gl.). Conjunction of these two deities as planets portended

adultery and fornication for many medieval astrologers, including those whom Boccaccio cites on Mars in his *Genealogie*.[48] This evidence combines to shape a strongly negative image of the couple. On the other hand, we have from antiquity the tradition of a matrimonial Mars and Venus that has firmly reasserted itself in the visual arts by the end of the Quattrocento and rests partly on literary texts familiar to Boccaccio. His glossator distinctly says that Venus and Mars are not always "bad"; each can also be a morally and socially positive force. If this holds for the two separately, it must be true of their coupling as well. The title given the *Teseida* by Fiammetta (but chosen by Boccaccio) clearly marks it as a marriage piece. Mars and Venus, who rule the poem by turn, are present at its center. Its protagonist, Teseo ("*Teseida*"), vigorously combats the powers, both human (Ipolita, Creon) and abstract (ire, concupiscence), that threaten lawful union between husband and wife. He himself will marry at the close of Book I, and he arranges the marriage promised by the title that is realized in Book XII. Both marriages take place after Martian conflicts have been met and overcome. It is, as Robert Hollander has argued, the matrimonial Venus who then triumphs at the beginning and the end of the *Teseida*.[49] I am therefore inclined to think that Boccaccio's Mars and Venus are ambivalent. Their menacing presence at the poem's center stands in explicit, admonitory contrast to the implicitly constructive influence they are capable of exercising ideally. Baneful as appetites, they are amicably beneficent when serving the rational goals of order in the soul and the state. Their "friendship," furthermore, seems to symbolize a prototypical union between male ($\male$) and female ($\female$) in the *Teseida*, because union of the sexes is signified in its numerological plan.

The number 5 that accompanies Mars and then crosses over to Venus at the center of the *Teseida* is a Pythagorean marriage number. According to the Pythagorean theory, numbers have gender. Odd ones, being superior to even, are masculine, the latter feminine. The monad, origin of number, does not count in the sequence leading to 10, which therefore proceeds from 2:

> Consequently, since two makes the first of the even numbers and three the first of the odd, and five is produced by the union of these numbers, very naturally five has come to be honoured as being the first number created out of the first numbers; and it has received the name of 'marriage' because of the resemblance of the even num-

bers to the female and of the odd number to the male . . . let it suffice to say that the Pythagoreans called Five a 'Marriage' on the ground that it was produced by the association of the first male number and the first female number.[50]

Here I cite Plutarch's explanation, a convenient synthesis of Greek reasoning on this marriage number. Although Plutarch himself was not known to Boccaccio, the tradition he describes was. Boccaccio could have learned it from the respected allegorical encyclopedia on the seven liberal arts by Martianus Capella, who refers to the pentad as a natural coupling of male and female, "pentas . . . qui quidem permixtione naturali copulatur; nam constat ex utriusque sexus numero; trias quippe virilis est, dyas femineus aestimatur" ("the pentad . . . represents natural union, for it is the sum of numbers of each sex, for three is considered a male number, and two a female number").[51] He had apparently read Martianus by the summer of 1339, and he also certainly understood by then the "virtues" of odd and even numbers. We find mention of them in his *Sacre famis*, one of four rhetorical epistles dating from that summer.[52] The accomplishments attributed to the letter's unnamed, and probably fictitious, recipient include mastery of the seven liberal arts, divided into Trivium and Quadrivium. First among the latter is Arithmetic, "et quia in fortiorem etatem evaseras, viso iam per arismetricam parium dispariumque numerorum virtutes, voluptuosam musicam sequebaris. . . ." ("and because you had reached a fuller age, having seen through arithmetic the virtues of even and odd numbers, you took up delightful music . . .").[53]

The number 5 associated with marriage, present in authors as distant as Philo Judaeus[54] and Ben Jonson,[55] surfaces elsewhere in Boccaccio's own works. The fifth day of the *Decameron* (excluding Dioneo's usual exception) is given to love stories that turn out happily, and their endings always coincide with a marriage. This is not true for any other day in the *Decameron*. Boccaccio seems similarly to use the pentad in his *Filocolo*, another tale of two lovers who marry. It begins as *Quintus* Lelius Africanus and his wife, Giulia Topazia, after *five* years of marriage are blessed by conceiving a child under the sign of the Virgin. She is Biancofiore, born like Florio on *Pente*cost, the same feast day that brings a blissful end to Florio/Filocolo's quest, when he will be reunited with her in the Alexandrian tower. They wed twice for good measure, once privately before consummating their love, and then in a public ceremony arranged by the

Admiral. The felicitous outcome of this nuptial romance, written in five books, depends, as it happens, in large part on Mars and Venus, who generously help the protagonists master all the plotted obstacles to their well-deserved marriage.

In the *Teseida* Boccaccio construes both 5 and its numerological variant, 15, as marriage numbers. Teseo promises that one of the two knights shall take Emilia "per moglie" ("as wife") at the end of Book v, stanza 96 (9 + 6 = 15). Emilia's marriage will be celebrated at the temple of Venus in a chapter of three stanzas, the thirteenth of Book XII. It culminates with the exchange of vows at XII.69 (6 + 9 = 15):

> E poi in presenza di quella santa ara
> il teban Palemon gioiosamente
> prese e giurò per sua sposa cara
> Emilia bella, a tutti i re presente;
> e essa, come donna non già gnara,
> simil promessa fece immantanente;
> poi la basciò sì come si convenne
> e ella vergognosa sel sostenne.

(*Tes.* XII.69: And then before that holy altar the Theban Palemon joyously pledged to take beautiful Emilia as his dear wife in the presence of all the kings; and being a woman who was hardly ignorant, she immediately made a similar promise; then he kissed her, as it was fitting, and she forebore it blushingly.)

The next chapter, "Come, tornati al palagio, si celebrarono le nozze" ("How, on returning to the palace, they celebrated the nuptials"), has five stanzas, and in the first we learn when the wedding banquet began, "e l'ora *quinta* già venia del giorno, / quando, venuti nel palagio, messe / trovar le mense, e assisersi ad esse" (XII.70: "and the fifth hour of the day was already starting when, having come into the palace, they found the tables laid and sat down at them"). The fifteenth chapter playfully accounts for their wedding night, "Venere, anzi che 'l dì fosse chiaro, / sette volte raccesa e tante spenta [era] nel fonte amoroso" (XII.77: "Venus, before the day was bright, had been kindled seven times and spent as many in the amorous font"). It reports as well how long the ensuing celebration lasted, "Durò la festa degli alti baroni / più giorni . . . / ma dopo il dì *quindecimo* si pose / fine alle feste liete e graziose" ("The celebration of the great barons lasted some days . . . but after the fifteenth day, they put an end to the joyful and delightful celebrations").

This latter chapter recalls the marriage of Chrétien's Erec and Enide, "Ensi les noces et la corz / durerent plus de quinze jorz / a tel joie e a tel hautesce; / par seignorie et par leesce / et por Erec plus enorer, / fist li rois Artus demorer / toz barons une quinzaine" ("Thus the nuptial feast and courtly gathering lasted more than fifteen days with such joy and such grandeur; through lordship and happiness and to honor Erec the more, King Arthur had all the barons stay on for two weeks").[56] For the French poet "quinzaine" may mean simply a two-week period, but Boccaccio's "quindici dì" are more than a calendrical quantity. Before the wedding, "Disegna l'autore la forma e la bellezza di Emilia" (p. 651: "The author portrays the appearance and beauty of Emilia") in a chapter of fifteen stanzas XII.XII), where he reveals her age: "Né era ancor, dopo 'l suo nascimento, / tre volte cinque Apollo ritornato / nel loco donde allor fé partimento" (XII.64: "Nor had Apollo yet, after her birth, returned to the place where he then was rising three times five times"). Our conscientious glossator kindly solves this problem in multiplication. Equating "three times five" with "fifteen" and "Apollo" with "the sun," he then pithily rephrases the author's solar circumlocution, "aveva xv anni" ("she was 15 years old"). Emilia has reached the proper age for a woman to enter wedlock.[57] The number 15, here explicitly divided into 3 and 5, is especially suited to Boccaccio's epic bride, for it is another product of union between Venus and Mars, the two gods secretly at work as nuptial forces in the tale.

Appropriately, this product also regulates the number of sonnets framing the *Teseida*'s twelve books. There are fifteen: a general proem; an individual sonnet preceding each book and summarizing its contents; and after the close of Book XII, another pair of sonnets in which the author speaks to the Muses and they reply. Since these last two are missing in many manuscripts,[58] Boccaccio may have added them, as he apparently did the glosses, after writing the rest of the poem in order both to enhance and better articulate its internal numerological design.[59] Fifteen sonnets so disposed would have had the further advantage of generating a center (the eighth sonnet) standing before the epic's central seventh book. A diagram better illustrates the relationship:

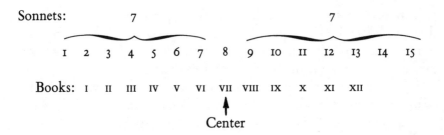

Sonnets: 7   7

Books: I   II   III   IV   V   VI   VII   VIII   IX   X   XI   XII

Center

Now in an epic of twelve books, the symmetrical halfway point would obviously be the end of the sixth. As we have discovered, however, each of the *Teseida's* formal components marks the number 7 as the center: the central verse, the central chapter, the central glosses, and the central sonnet all gravitate within the seventh book. If 3 is for Venus and love, 5 for Mars, battle, and marriage, what might 7 stand for beyond Diana? Singularly honored as the arithmetic sign at the *Teseida's* center, the number 7 has manifold potential meanings in medieval numerology, more than for any other integer. The problem of isolating solutions is therefore a difficult one, and I can only speculate on those that seem most plausible to me.

Venus, Mars, and Diana's numbers derive immediately from their positions in the ranks of the seven wandering stars. For this reason it would be logical to take the 7 marking center in the *Teseida* as a sum embracing the planets collectively. Book VII might then have special astrological implications pertaining to the plan of the poem more generally, and I shall here tentatively present one of them. When casting horoscopes, the astrologers divide the zodiac according to a mobile scheme starting from the ascendent into twelve houses that describe twelve aspects of the life or event under examination. A traditional pair of mnemonic verses lists them, "Vita lucrum fratres genitor nati valetudo / Uxor mors pietas regnum benefactaque carcer" ("Life wealth brothers parents children health / Wife death piety power benefactions prison"). Based on slightly variant terminology, the houses and what each concerns can be given as follows: I, *Vita* (Life); II, *Lucrum* (Wealth); III, *Fratres* (Brothers); IV, *Parentes* (Parents); V, *Filii* (Sons); VI, *Valetudo* (Health); VII, *Nuptiae* (Nuptials); VIII, *Mors* (Death); IX, *Peregrinationes* (Travels); X, *Honores* (Honors); XI, *Amici* (Friends); XII, *Inimici* (Enemies).[60] Interestingly, in the seventh place we find the marriage house. There could thus be a correspondence between this astrological marriage house and Book VII in Boccaccio's nuptial epic, at the center of which we find Diana-Luna following a paired poetic conjunction of Mars and Venus. In the seventh book of the *Teseida* might the combination of these three pagan gods, who had survived from antiquity as planets, be a heavenly configuration relevant and auspicious to marriage in a 14th-century Italian horoscope? The question is one I am not yet able to answer, but, meanwhile, for those with more specialized knowledge of medieval astrology, it may open a line of investigation that would permit developing certain "closed" but decipherable relationships between the twelve houses in a horoscope and the twelve books in Boccaccio's epic.

Turning from astrology to literature, we can see other possibilities for 7 at the center. Charles S. Singleton has found that at the center of the *Divine Comedy* Dante concealed the number 7 as a symbol of Christian conversion.[61] The number expresses a "turning" from this world, created in six days, to the next and God, represented by 7 because it was on the seventh day that He rested. Whether or not Boccaccio noticed the pattern in the *Commedia*, he would have understood Dante's iconographic intent. Explaining in the *Genealogie* how the seven-day week originated, he writes,

Insuper cum humana solertia respectu habito ad septenarium numerum, quem quibusdam ex causis veteres voluere perfectum, disposuerit omne tempus per septimanas dierum efflui, et dies illas septimane nominibus variis nuncupare, consuevere nonnulli nominum talium exquirere causas; quas ego has puto, cum a planetis apud nos quinque denominentur, sexta sabbatum ab Hebreis dicta, a christianis postea immutata non est, eo quod requiem dicant significare latine, ut appareat cum creavisset omnia Deus in sex diebus, eum septima ab omnibus operibus suis quievisse. Dominica autem dies, que nobis christianis est septima, sic eo dicta est, quia ea die Christus Dei filius, non solum ab omnibus laboribus suis quievit, verum victor surrexit a mortuis et sic illam a domino nostro patres incliti vocavere dominicam.

(*Genealogie* I.34: Moreover, since out of respect for the number seven, which for various reasons the ancients held to be perfect, human ingenuity disposed that all time proceed by weeks of days, and to those days of the week they gave various names; some people were

wont to seek out the reasons for those names which I retain to be
as follows. Since in our times five are named after the planets, the
sixth, which was called sabbath by the Hebrews, was not changed
afterwards by the Christians because they say it means "rest" in Latin
as can be seen from the fact that God created all things in six days
and on the seventh He rested from all His labors. The day Sunday,
however, which for us Christians is the seventh, is so named because
on that day Christ the son of God not only rested from all His labors
but arose truly a victor from the dead, and thus the learned fathers
named it after our Lord "the day of the Lord.")[62]

Conversion could underlie the "perfect" 7 at the center of the *Teseida* because
the seventh is preeminently a book of prayer. Each of the protagonists
respectfully enters a place of worship and turns to a power above, gentile
gods dwelling in the sevenfold planetary hierarchy. Mars receives Arcita's
winged prayer (VII.30), Palemone's reaches Venus (VII.50), and Emilia
sacrifices to Diana (VII.70). After these pious vigils and orisons, on the
tournament morning Teseo himself escorts the two Thebans into the temple
of Mars (VII.96). Their devotions last through nocturnal quiet and the
peaceful dawn of a new day, marked contrasts to the violent battle clash
that begins with Book VIII. The number of conversion might also apply
to the *Teseida*'s overall allegorical thrust, which moves in a morally cor-
rective direction toward triumph in the soul over sinful, irrational appetites. Two spiritual forces that counter the appetites, virtue and wisdom,
may be signified as well by the number 7.

Denoting Diana-Luna, 7 implies both virginity and virtue. For the
Pythagoreans it is "virgin" because it is the first prime that has no multiple within the first decad, "nam virgo creditur, quia nullum ex se parit
numerum duplicatus qui intra denarium coartetur, quem primum limitem
constat esse numerorum" ("indeed, it is regarded as a virgin because, when
doubled, it produces no number under ten, the latter being truly the first
limit of numbers").[63] This Pythagorean virgin may well serve in the *Teseida*
as an emblem of chastity, a maidenly quality and wifely attribute appropriate
to the symbolism of a marriage piece. When transferred to a Christian
frame of reference, the virgin heptad evolves to define more broadly the
seven virtues, women in their personified forms. Diana's numerological
consorts as early as Boccaccio's *Caccia di Diana*,[64] they return to accompany her for a time in the *Commedia delle ninfe fiorentine* as seven ladies

who had been her chaste nymphs before becoming followers of Venus. After each Florentine lady has told her tale, seven swans and seven storks fly across the sky. The birds begin to fight each other fiercely, "in sette e sette divisi" ("divided in seven and seven"), and the swans drive away the storks. Trinitarian Venus descends, to whom Ameto prays, thanking her for the "sette fiamme" ("seven flames") now entwining his soul.[65] Seven ladies, seven swans, seven flames—all are the Virtues in the *Commedia delle ninfe*. The seven virtues also appear in the *Filocolo*. Filocolo initially encounters them in a miraculous vision, "sette donne di maravigliosa bellezza piena" ("seven ladies filled with marvelous beauty"), who come unnamed but identified by their traditional iconographic attributes as four preceding three. At the end of the romance, the dying King Felice exhorts his son, Florio, to flee the vices, of which he names seven; next he preaches on each of the virtues: prudence, justice, fortitude, temperance, charity, faith and hope.[66] For Boccaccio then, the number 7 is a figure of virtue, tied specifically with Diana in the *Caccia* and the *Commedia*. This suggests that in the *Teseida* the number of the planets, among whom Diana is the virgin seventh, may allusively encompass the Virtues. Since Diana is Emilia's patron and they participate together in the poem as 7's, its chaste heroine Emilia herself would then become a numerological representative of virtue.

Diana appears to share this number in the epic with her mythological twin, Apollo. We have already seen brother and sister joined through a double 7 (14) in the glossator's accounts of the Niobe myth. After returning incognito to Athens and just before entering Teseo's household, Penteo worships in the temple of Apollo, a deity whom love had also once driven into servitude. The prayer is in the seventh chapter of Book IV, which has seven stanzas, and on Apollo the commentary reports, "Fu Febo innamorato d'una figliuola d'Ameto, re di Tesaglia, la quale non potendo altrimenti avere, si transformò in pastore, e posesi col detto re, e stette con lui guardandogli il bestiame suo, in così fatta forma, *sette anni*" (*Tes.* IV.46.gl.: "Phoebus was in love with a daughter of Admetus, king of Thessaly, and since he could not have her any other way, he transformed himself into a shepherd and joined the aforesaid king and stayed with him guarding his livestock in this guise for seven years"). During the duel, Penteo calls on Phoebus as his witness in a stanza (v.70) that is at the center of the seventh chapter of Book v. Among the heroes who march into Athens from all Greece (Book VI) to match arms in the tournament is King Ameto of Thessaly, who carries a silver shield with a golden image of Apollo on it. He comes in the seventeenth chapter, and the marginalia remind us, "Di sopra è detto come Febo, innamorato d'una figliuola d'Ameto, transformato in pastore, guardò *sette* anni gli armenti d'Ameto" (vi.55.gl.: "It is told above how Phoebus, in love with a daughter of Admetus, transformed into a shepherd, guarded the herds of Admetus seven years").

As Boccaccio notes in the gloss on iv.77, "Febo è iddio della sapienza" ("Phoebus is god of wisdom"). In this capacity Apollo could logically attract the number 7 because it is a well-established symbol of wisdom. In addition to the seven pillars of Biblical wisdom,[67] there existed seven branches of secular knowledge. Thus the lady holding book and scepter who personifies "Sapienza" in the first triumph of the *Amorosa visione* is surrounded by seven women, "dal sinistro e dal suo destro lato / sette donne vid'io, dissimiglianti / l'una dall'altra in atto ed in parato" ("on her left and right side I saw seven ladies, each one unlike the others in deed and dress"). They have been interpreted as the seven Liberal Arts, the Trivium on her left, and the more noble Quadrivium in the place of honor at her right.[68] These disciplines and their figuration as women had been fixed by Martianus Capella in his enormously influential *De nuptiis Philologiae et Mercurii*. Accompanying Philology as she marries Mercury are seven maidens-of-honor, none other than the seven sciences, each of whom offers in turn a treatise on the category of learning she represents. Although Boccaccio would have been familiar with this famed group of seven from other sources as well,[69] Martianus provides a precedent for placing it in a marriage allegory.

The Seven Liberal Arts, a trio and a quartet like the Virtues, also parallel the planets. Dante, we may remember, had correlated arts and planets. Telling what he means by "third heaven" in the *canzone* to its moving intelligences, he says, "Dico che per cielo io intendo la scienza e per cieli le scienze, e per tre similitudini che li cieli hanno con le scienze massimamente; e per l'ordine e numero in che paiono convenire" ("I say that by heaven I mean science and by heavens the sciences chiefly because of the three similarities that the heavens have with the sciences, and because of the order and number in which they seem to correspond"). On the last two similarities, his discussion begins,

Sì come adunque di sopra è narrato, li setti cieli primi a noi sono quelli de li pianeti; poi sono due cieli sopra questi, mobili, e uno sopra tutti, quieto. A li sette primi rispondono le sette scienze del Trivio e del Quadrivio, cioè Gramatica, Dialettica, Rettorica, Arismetrica, Musica, Geometria, e Astrologia.

(So then, as discussed above, the first seven heavens for us are the planets; then there are two mobile heavens above these and one quiet one above them all. To the first seven correspond the seven sciences of the Trivium and the Quadrivium, that is, Grammar, Dialectic, Rhetoric, Arithmetic, Music, Geometry, and Astrology.)[70]

Although Boccaccio does not systematically correlate arts and planets, he does sequentially couple them in the epistle, Sacre famis. The sender's dear friend joins the Chorus of the Muses to study grammar, dialectic, and rhetoric. After a distraction involving activity as a merchant, he returns to take up the remaining four, starting with arithmetic, as we have seen:

et quia in fortiorem etatem evaseras, viso iam per arismetricam parium dispariumque numerorum virtutes, voluptuosam musicam sequebaris . . . geometrie figuras aspiciebas, diversas suas mensuras studio celebri perquirendo. Hinc igitur ad astra transfereris, et circulationem vagorum luminum rimaris et sydera; hic Cynthie motus varios tuo intellectui reserantur, et qualiter ipsa depositis cornuis formam capiat circularem, non ipsius defectus nec virtutes multiplices ignorando; hic vides Stilbonis regiones intrantibus quibus cunque concordes hinc ferventis amoris radios rutilantes, Cythereie domus ascendis; et per consequens intras regnum lucidum magni Yperionis filii, et ipsius stellarum principis notas effectus. Sed tibi non istud sufficiens, aggrederis castra Mavortis belligeri, et rubicondi coloris causam perscruptaris; et argentee etatis tecta regis subintrans, sua moderata iudicia laudas intuendo. Hinc a antro patris expulsi perquirens, inertia sua dismissa, tendis ad nidum Lede.

(And because you had reached a fuller age, having seen through arithmetic the virtues of even and odd numbers, you took up delightful music . . . [next] you viewed the figures of geometry, carefully exploring its different measures with outstanding eagerness. Thence you proceed to the stars, and you examine the circling of the wandering lights and the constellations; here the various move-

ments of Cynthia are opened to your intellect, and how, when she
has laid down her horns, she takes on a circular form, and you are
not ignorant of either her recurring waxings or wanings; here you
see the regions of Stilbon, harmonious for whomsoever enters hence;
thence you ascend to the dwelling of Cytharea, glowing with golden
rays of fervent love; and next you enter the bright kingdom of the
great son of Hyperion, and you note the effects of this prince of
the stars. But as this much is not sufficient for you, you will approach the camps of warlike Mars, and you will scrutinize the reason
for his rubicund color; and entering into the palace of the king of
the silver age, you praise his moderate judgments as you contemplate
them. Thence exploring from the cave of the banished father, whose
inertia has sent you away, you reach out for Leda's nest.)[71]

Next, in a literary motif foreshadowing the *Teseida*, the friend will
abruptly become a warrior, and just as suddenly give up warfare for marriage. This rhetorical exercise, a "dictamen dictaminum," actually ends
with the writer's request for a glossed copy of Statius' *Thebaid*. Billanovich
speculates that what prompted the rhetorical loan request was Boccaccio's own recent discovery of the commentary by Lactantius Placidus, adduced as a model for the glosses on his *Teseida*.[72] The *Sacre famis* letter,
thus an important pre-text for the Italian epic, gives us the Liberal Arts
as 3 + 4 listed in traditional order ascending to astronomy, the highest,
from which there naturally develops a similarly ranked catalogue of the
seven planets.

The venerable number 7 at the center of the *Teseida* is a richly allusive
figure. On one level it is planetary and may have ties with the seventh
house in a horoscope, "Nuptiae." As it calls our attention to the heavens
and characterizes a book of prayer, the figure could also be a godly heb-
domad, expressing the spiritual concept of conversion. A "virgin" accompanying Diana and Emilia, it can symbolize both chastity and virtue. A
"perfect" number, it is bound as well to the sun, sevenfold wisdom and
the heavenly sign of the moral illumination motivating the deeds of Teseo,
duke of Minerva's city. Further research on late medieval literature and
Trecento painting would reveal many other such groupings of 7's with
diverse registers of meaning mutually related through numerical analogy.[73]

We have now, I think, gained grounds for better reconciling the author's
themes ("amore," "Marte") and principal characters (Arcita, Palemone)

with Fiammetta's title, "Teseida di nozze d'Emilia." His perspective on the poem is accurate, but hers is more penetrating, guiding us beyond the letter to deeper truth conveyed through "chiuso parlare" ("closed speech"). Venus (3) and Mars (5), coupled in the seventh book (VII.30 and VII.50), are emblematic of the marriage celebrated in the poem's numerological plan (5 x 3 = 15). That book, which is the longest in the poem and its center, carries a number pointing upward to the planetary gods (7). It belongs especially to Luna and Emilia but also appears with Apollo, who always shines for Teseo. If we take the *Teseida* as a love story, Arcita and Palemone are indeed its fictional heroes. Allegorically, however, they manifest wrath and lust, and so stand in a secondary, antagonistic relationship to Teseo and Emilia. It is these latter, solar and lunar sources of enlightenment, that conquer the appetites and are the moral protagonists in Boccaccio's book of Theseus and the epic of Emilia's marriage.[74]

Notes

1. *Teseida delle nozze d'Emilia*, ed. Alberto Limentani, *Tutte le opere di Giovanni Boccaccio,* II (Milan: Mondadori, 1964), p. 246. This is the text cited throughout. Translations are my own.

2. The "naked" muses are those who have doffed their traditional Latin garb. Boccaccio here recalls, of course, the passage in the *De vulgari eloquentia* (II.2) where Dante states that Italian, which has so far produced poetry of love and moral rectitude, still awaits an epic voice whose song will turn to "righteous feats of arms" ("armorum probitas").

3. "Risposta delle Muse," *Tes.*, p. 664.

4. Boccaccio defines "fabula" (lit. "fable"), of which he distinguishes four types, in the *Genealogie deorum gentilium libri*, ed. Vincenzo Romano (Bari: Laterza, 1951), XIV.9: "Fabula est exemplaris seu demonstrativa sub figmento locutio, cuius amoto cortice, patet intentio fabulantis" ("Fiction is a form of discourse, which, under guise of invention, illustrates or proves an idea; and, as its superficial aspect is removed, the meaning of the author is clear"). The first kind of "fiction" is the fable strictly speaking (e.g., Aesop's). Myths ending in metamorphoses exemplify the second, which has been used from earliest times by the most ancient poets, "quibus cure fuit divina et humana pariter palliare figmentis" ("whose object it has been to clothe in fiction divine and human matters alike"). The third, "potius hystorie quam fabule

similis" ("more like history than fiction"), is represented by the epic writings of Virgil and Homer, "longe tamen aliud sub velamine sentiunt quam monstretur" ("yet their hidden meaning is far other than appears on the suface"). The last are old wives' tales ("delirantium vetularum inventio"). Applying this scheme to the *Teseida*, "storia" would correspond with the author's epic narration proper with its 'historical' ties to Statius' *Thebaid*; and "favola" could describe many of the myths related in the commentary as short stories by his glossator. English translations of the *Genealogie* are mine, except for Books XIV–XV, for which see Charles G. Osgood, *Boccaccio on Poetry* (1930; rpt. Indianapolis and New York: Library of Liberal Arts, 1956).

5. For an introductory excursus on "Numerical Composition" see Ernst Robert Curtius, *European Literature and the Latin Middle Ages*, tr. Willard R. Trask, Bollingen Series, XXXVI (New York: Pantheon, 1953), pp. 501–9.

6. MS. Florence, Mediceo-Laurenziana, Doni e Acquisti 325, on which see G. Vandelli, "Un autografo della *Teseida*," *Studi di filologia italiana*, II (1929), 1–76; and *Teseida*, ed. Salvatore Battaglia (Florence: G. C. Sansoni, 1938), pp. XI–XV; CXI–CLVIII.

7. A more complete analysis is given by Antonio Enzo Quaglio, *Scienza e mito nel Boccaccio* (Padua: Liviana, 1967), pp. 101–6; 177–82. The programmatic literary function of the planetary allusions in the epic is lucidly unveiled by Janet Levarie Smarr in "Boccaccio and the Stars: Astrology in the *Teseida*," *Traditio*, XXXV (1979), 303–32. Discussing the horoscope at III.5, Smarr points out that Venus, powerful to begin with since she is ascendent, gains influence by being in Taurus, her day house, and becomes stronger still through proximity with the sun.

8. *Purgatorio* I.19, from Dante Alighieri, *The Divine Comedy*, trans. with a commentary by Charles S. Singleton, Bollingen Series, LXXX (Princeton: Princeton University Press, 1973).

9. See Dante's catalogue of the spheres in *Convivio*, ed. G. Busnelli and G. Vandelli (Florence: Le Monnier, 1954), II.3.7 and n. 3, p. 113, for precedents, e.g., Alfraganus:

> Minor vero earum est illa quae est propinquior terrae et est sphaera Lunae, et secunda est Mercurii, et tertia Veneris est, et quarta est Solis, et quinta est Martis, et sexta est Iovis, et septima est Saturni, et octava est stellarum fixarum.

> (The smallest of them is the one that is nearest to the earth, and it is the sphere of the Moon; and the second is Mercury's, the third is Venus's, and the fourth is the Sun's, and the fifth is Mars', and the sixth is Jove's, and the seventh is Saturn's, and the eighth is [the sphere of] the fixed stars.)

Typical also is the list in Isidore of Seville's *De natura rerum* (P. L. LXXXIII.995–96):

> In ambitu quippe septem coelestium orbium, primum in inferioris sphaerae circulo luna est constituta. Inde proxima terris posita, ut nocte nobis facilius lumen exhibeat. Dehinc secundo circulo Mercurii stella collocata, soli celeritate

par, sed vi quidam, ut philosophi dicunt, contraria. Tertio circulo Luciferi circumvectio est, inde a gentilibus Venus ita dicta. . . .

(In the revolution of the seven celestial circles, first in the ring of the lower sphere the moon was placed. It was set next to the earth so that at night it could display its light for us more easily. Next in the second circle the star of Mercury was located, equal to the sun in speed, but contrary to it, as the philosophers say, in influence. The revolution of Lucifer is in the third circle, thence called Venus by the gentiles. . . .)

10. Ed. and tr. Kenelm Foster and Patrick Boyde in *Dante's Lyric Poetry*, 2 vols. (Oxford: Oxford University Press, 1967). This *canzone* is the first of the allegorically explicated poems in Dante's *Convivio*.

11. *Amorosa visione* A, II.1, 1–5, ed. Vittore Branca, *Tutte le opere di Giovanni Boccaccio,* III (Milan: Mondadori, 1974).

12. *Filostrato* III.74, ed. Vittore Branca, *Tutte le opere,* II.

13. *Filocolo* IV.43.1, ed. Antonio Enzo Quaglio, *Tutte le opere,* I (1967).

14. "Dietro al pastor d'Ameto alle materne," lines 7–8; and "Dante, se tu nell'amorosa spera," lines 9–11. The sonnets are in *Le Rime, L'Amorosa visione, La Caccia di Diana,* ed. Vittore Branca (Padua: Liviana, 1958).

15. *Esposizioni* v, litt., 160, ed. Giorgio Padoan, *Tutte le opere,* VI (1965), "Piace ad Aristotile esser tre spezie d'amore, cioè amore onesto, amore dilettevole e amore utile: e quell'amore, del quale qui si fa menzione, è dilettevole" ("According to Aristotle there are three kinds of love, that is, honest love, pleasurable love, and useful love: and the love of which mention is made here is pleasurable love").

16. *Filoc.* IV.44.3–7 and n. 5, p. 872.

17. *Am. vis.* A, XXXVIII.79–88 and note, p. 710.

18. *De vulgari eloquentia* II.2.10, ed. Aristide Marigo (Florence: Le Monnier, 1938); tr. A. G. Ferrers Howell, *Dante's Treatise 'De Vulgari Eloquentia'* (London: Temple Classics, 1890): "I do not find, however, that any Italian has as yet written poetry on the subject of Arms."

19. See, e.g., *Thebaid* I.680, where Polynices identifies himself, "Cadmus origo patrum, tellus Mavortia Thebe" ("Cadmus was the ancestor of my sires; my land Mavortian Thebes"); and III.269–70, as Venus pleads with Mars for peace, "bella etiam in Thebas, socer o pulcherrime, bella / ipse paras ferroque tuos abolere nepotes?" ("War even against Thebes, O noble father, war dost thou thyself prepare, and the sword's destruction for all thy race?"). *Statius,* tr. J. H. Mozley, 2 vols., Loeb Series (London: Heinemann, 1928).

20. *Thebaid* II.265 ff. and III.269 ff.

21. *Conv.* II.13.20: "And the heaven of Mars can be compared to Music because of its most beautiful relationship, for when numbering the mobile heavens, from whichever one begins, whether the lowest or the highest, this heaven of Mars is the fifth; it is the middle of them all, that is, of the first ones, the second ones, the third ones, and the fourth ones."

22. *The Works of Geoffrey Chaucer*, ed. F. N. Robinson, 2nd ed. (Cambridge, Mass.: Riverside Press, 1957). For a recent study on number symbolism in Chaucer see Russell A. Peck, "Numerology and Chaucer's *Troilus and Criseyde*," *Mosaic* v (Summer 1972), 1–29.

23. *De natura deorum* II.27.68, ed. G. F. Schoemann (Berlin: Weidmann, 1876): "Diana is called Omnivaga (far-wandering), not from her hunting, but because she is numbered seven just as the wandering stars." For a recent translation see *Cicero. The Nature of the Gods*, tr. C. P. McGregore (Penguin Books, 1972).

24. *Scipio's Dream* III.7–v.1, in *Macrobius' Commentary on the Dream of Scipio*, tr. William Harris Stahl, Columbia Records of Civilization, No. 48 (New York: Columbia University Press, 1952).

25. Ibid., p. 10. The inventory of Boccaccio's books that passed into the "parva libraria" at Santo Spirito includes a "Macrobius de sopno Scipionis conpletus," the incipit of which coincides with the beginning of Cicero's *Somnium*. See Antonia Mazza, "L'inventario della 'parva libraria' di Santo Spirito e la biblioteca del Boccaccio," in *Italia medioevale e umanistica*, IX (1966), 1–71.

26. Macrobius, *Commentarii in somnium Scipionis*, ed. Jacob Willis (Leipzig: Teubner, 1970), I.5.2: "nam cum aetas tua septenos octies solis anfractus reditusque converterit."

27. Recall Philo's reverential encomium, "I doubt whether anyone could adequately celebrate the properties of the number 7, for they are beyond all words. Yet the fact that it is more wondrous than all that is said about it is no reason for maintaining silence regarding it. Nay, we must make a brave attempt to bring out at least all that is within the compass of our understanding, even if it be impossible to bring out all or even the most essential points." *De opificio mundi*, in *Philo*, tr. F. H. Colson and G. H. Whitaker, Loeb Series (London: Macmillan, 1929), I, p. 73. Cf. Macrobius, *Commentarii in somnium Scipionis*, 1.6.45–47:

> hic numerus 'ept5aw nunc vocatur, antiquato usu primae litterae, apud veteres enim sept5aw vocitabatur, quod Graeco nomine testabatur venerationem debitam numero. nam primo omnium hoc numero anima mundana generata est, sicut Timaeus Platonis edocuit . . . non parva ergo hinc potentia numeri huius ostenditur quia mundanae animae origo septem finibus continetur, septem quoque vagantium sphaerarum ordinem illi stelliferae et omnes continenti subiecit artifex fabricatoris providentia, quae et superioris rapidis motibus obviarent et inferiora omnia gubernarent.

Tr. Stahl VI.45–47:

> (This number is now called [h]eptas, the first letter no longer being in use; but the ancients used to call it *septas*, the Greek word testifying to the veneration owing to the number. It was by this number first of all, indeed, that the World-Soul was begotten, as Plato's *Timaeus* has shown . . . The fact that the origin of the World-Soul hinges upon seven steps is proof that this number has no mean ability; but in addition the Creator, in his constructive

foresight, arranged seven errant spheres beneath the star-bearing celestial sphere, which embraces the universe, so that they might counteract the swift motions of the sphere above and govern everything beneath.)

Note also Martianus Capella's awe before the number in *De nuptiis Philologiae et Mercuriae*, ed. A. Dick (Leipzig: Teubner, 1925), p. 372, "quid autem te, heptas, venerandam commemorem?" ("What reasons should I recount for your veneration, O Heptad?"). The translation, by William Harris Stahl and Richard Johnson with E. L. Burge, is in *The Marriage of Philology and Mercury*, vol. II of *Martianus Capella and the Seven Liberal Arts* (New York: Columbia University Press, 1977), p. 281. For further references see Vincent Hopper, *Medieval Number Symbolism* (1938; rpt. New York: Cooper Square Publishers, 1969), esp. pp. 43–44.

28. *Comm. in somnium*, ed. Willis, 1.6.48–54; tr. Stahl VI.48–54.

29. *De nuptiis*, pp. 373–74: "ex tribus et quattuor septem fiunt, qui numerus formas lunae complectitur . . . hic numerus lunae cursum significat" ("seven consists of three and four. It is the number that marks the phases of the moon . . . This number also marks the orbit of the moon"). Isidore echoes the tradition in his *Liber numerorum*, P. L., LXXXIII.188, "Idem quoque septenarius numerus formam lunae complectitur; tot enim habet luna figuras . . . hic etiam numerus et nomina lunae significat. Nam unum, duo, tria, quatuor, quinque, et sex, et septem viginti octo faciunt" ("this number seven marks the phases of the moon, for the moon has seven phases . . . this number also defines the moon, for one, two, three, four, five, and six, and seven make twenty-eight").

30. Boccaccio is guilty of an oversight in these calculations. He glosses "terzo" ("third") in VII.104 as "Cioè era già sesta o presso, perciò che in quella stagione, cioè verso l'uscita di maggio, il dì è di xviii ore o presso, il terzo delle quali è presso a sei" ("That is, it was already about the sixth hour because in that season, that is, toward the end of May, the day is about eighteen hours long, and one third of them is about the sixth"). But in IX.29 he clearly says that the battle, which ended with the "*ora ottava*" ("eighth *hour*"), had begun in "[l'*ora*] terza" ("the third [*hour*]"). The inconsistency indicates confusion between solar and symbolic time.

31. Smarr (see above, n. 7) presents these discoveries in her study on astrology in the *Teseida*, referring to Boccaccio's *Genealogie* 1.34:

Sed cum longe alius sit ordo planetarum quam in nominibus dierum habeatur, est sciendum secundum planetarum ordinem successive unicuique diei hore dari dominium, et ab eo cui contingit prime hore diei dominium habere, ab eo dies illa denominata est, ut puta si diei dominice Veneri secundam horam tribues, que Soli immediate subiacet, et Mercurio terciam, qui subiacet Veneri, et Lune quartam, que subiacet Mercurio, quintam autem Saturno, ad quem convertendus est ordo cum in Luna defecerit, sextam Iovi, et sic de singulis XXIIII[or] horis diei dominice, sub nomine vel dominio Mercurii invenietur hora XXIIII[a], et XXV[a] que prima est diei sequentis sub nomine vel dominio Lune.

(But since the order of the planets is quite different from that of the names of the days, it must be understood that the planets, according to their order, are given dominion successively over the hours of each day, and the one that has dominion over the first hour of the day is the one from which that day takes its name. So, for example, if you attribute the second hour of the day Sunday to Venus, which lies immediately below the Sun, and the third to Mercury, which lies below Venus, and the fourth to the Moon, which lies below Mercury; and the fifth to Saturn (to whom the order must revert because it stops at the Moon), the sixth to Jove, and so on for each of the 24 hours of the day; the 24th hour of Sunday will appear under the name or dominion of Mercury, and the 25th, which is the first of the following day, will be under the dominion of the Moon.)

See also Quaglio, *Scienza e mito*, pp. 200–201.

32. *Thebaid* II.1, 482 ff.

33. Cf. *Purgatorio* XII.37–39, "O Nïobè, con che occhi dolenti / vedea io te segnata in su la strada, / tra sette e sette tuoi figliuoli spenti!" ("O Niobe, with what grieving eyes did I see you traced on the roadway between seven and seven children slain!").

34. *Metamorphoses* VI.165 ff.

35. Characteristic is the section on Arithmetic in Martianus Capella's *De nuptiis*, "pentas, qui numerus mundo est attributus; nam si ex quattuor elementis ipse sub alia forma est quintus, pentade est rationalibiter insignitus," pp. 369–70; ("The pentad comes next, the number assigned to the universe. This identification is reasonable, for after the four elements, the universe is a fifth body of a different nature"), Stahl, p. 279.

36. Henry Ansgar Kelly discusses the terms "sponsalizie" (the act of marrying) and "nozze" (the feast that follows it) as used by Boccaccio in *Love and Marriage in the Age of Chaucer* (Ithaca: Cornell University Press, 1975), esp. pp. 180–85, 194–95.

37. My line of argument here owes much to Robert Hollander's interpretation of the *Teseida*, initially shared with me in collegial discussions and later published in *Boccaccio's Two Venuses* (New York: Columbia University Press, 1977), pp. 53–64. Hollander gives special and rightly deserved attention to the prayers and their glosses in Book VII, where "the crucial moral action of the *Teseida* occurs." I have also drawn informing suggestions from Janet Levarie Smarr's "The *Teseida*, Boccaccio's Allegorical Epic," in *NEMLA Italian Studies*, I (1977), an essay that identifies Teseo as Reason, the power that combats the appetites, epitomized by Arcita and Palemone.

No one has yet, to my knowledge, published any note on Boccaccio's probable source line for his information on man's "two principal appetites," which suggests to me Thomistic and Augustinian antecedents. Thus Thomas Aquinas, *Summa contra gentiles*, Ch. 25, in *Basic Writings of Saint Thomas Aquinas*, ed. Anton C. Pegis, (New York: Random House, 1945), II, p. 45: "Now of all the parts of man, the intellect is the highest mover, for it moves the appetite, by proposing its object to it; and the intellective appetite, or will, moves the sensitive appetites, namely the irascible and concupiscible." Cf. also *Summa Theologica*, Book I (*ibid.*, vol. 1), Q. 59, Art. 4: "The Philosopher says that the irascible and concupiscible are in the sensitive part;" Q. 81, Art. 2: "the sensitive appetite is one generic power, and is called sensuality; but it is divided into two powers, which are species of the sensitive appetite—the irascible and the concupiscible;" Q. 82, Art. 5: "the Philosopher says that will is in the reason, while in the irrational part of the soul are concupiscence and anger." Thomas draws here on Aristotle's *De anima* III.9–11. If Boccaccio's glossulary nomenclature is scholastic, he seems also to be recalling Augustine when affirming that the Venereal and Martial appetites may operate either for good or evil. So in the *City of God* XIV.19 we read that the rational mind commands as from a citadel the defective divisions of the inferior soul, anger and lust ("ira," "amor"), so that justice may be preserved among all the soul's parts. "It is for this reason that the mind by repression and restraint curbs and recalls them [anger and lust] from things that they are wrongly moved to do but allows them to follow any course that the law of wisdom has sanctioned. Anger, for example, is permitted for the display of a just compulsion, and lust for the duty of propagating offspring." The text quoted is *The City of God Against the Pagans*, tr. Philip Levine, Loeb Series (Cambridge, Mass.: Harvard University Press, 1966), IV, p. 365.

38. Robert Hollander also discovered independently that VII.30.1 is the central verse in the poem, noting that it is "precisely the numerical center of the work that Boccaccio chooses for the first of his two *chiose 'singolarissime.'* " His detailed discussion of the glosses, which he suggests were written to give the epic "the status of 'instant classic,' " appears in "The Validity of Boccaccio's Self-Exegesis in his *Teseida*," *Medievalia et Humanistica* (1977), 163–83. Susan Noakes, who dedicates a chapter of her forthcoming book on *The Historicity of Reading* (II.3) to the *Teseida*'s glosses, reaches conclusions that dovetail with Hollander's findings and my own: artistically conceived, the commentary goes far beyond simple explication to enhance poetically the text through such devices as thematic repetition, which enrich our perspectives on the characters and foreshadow events in the plot.

39. Fulgentius interprets Mars caught with Venus in Vulcan's net as manly valor fettered by ardor, *Mitologiae* II.7, in *Fabii Planciadis Fulgentii u.c. Opera*, ed. R. Helm (Leipzig: Teubner, 1898). Similarly, the Third Vatican Mythographer, known to Boccaccio as "Albericus," in *Scriptores rerum mythicarum latini tres Romae nuper reperti*, ed. G. H. Bode (1834; rpt. Hildesheim: G. Olms, 1968), pp. 231–32: "Mars igitur complexu Veneris pollutus, id est, virtus libidinis illecebris corrupta, sole teste apparet, id est, tandem veritatis iudicio rea esse cognoscitur. Quae quidem virtus prava consuetudine illecta vinclis constrictioribus, ostenditur catenata" ("When Mars had thus been stained by the embrace of Venus, that is, virtue corrupted by illicit passion, the sun appeared as a witness; that is, in the judgment of truth his virtue was seen to be corrupted. This virtue, seduced through depraved habits with constricting bonds is shown enchained"). On these as well as Arnulf of Orleans' treatments of the myth see Thomas D. Hill, "La Vieille's Digression on Free Love: A Note on Rhetorical Structure in the *Romance of the Rose*," *Romance Notes*, VIII (1966), 113–15. Robert P. Miller discusses the Venus-Mars story as illustrating "the essential conflict of Christian life—the tempting allurements of the flesh against the rational 'manliness' of the spirit," and "a mythological reenactment of man's fall to

sin" in "The Myth of Mars' Hot Minion in *Venus and Adonis*," *Journal of English Literary History*, XXVI (1959), 470–81.

40. *Thebaid* III.295–99.

41. *The Works of Geoffrey Chaucer*, ed. Robinson, p. 530.

42. Paul Schubring, *Cassoni. Truhen und Truhenbilder der italienischen Frührenaissance*, 2 vols. (Leipzig: K. W. Hiersemann, 1923), plates 313, 410. See also Paul F. Watson, *The Garden of Love in Tuscan Art of the Early Renaissance* (Philadelphia: Art Alliance Press, 1978), p. 115.

43. Erwin Panofsky, *Studies in Iconology* (New York: Harper and Row, 1962),p. 164; *Problems in Titian. Mostly Iconographic* (New York: New York University Press, 1969), p. 127. See also E. H. Gombrich, "Botticelli's Mythologies," in *Journal of the Warburg and Courtauld Institutes*, VIII (1945), 7–60, esp. pp. 46–49; Egon Verheyen, *The Paintings in the "Studiolo" of Isabella d'Este at Mantua* (New York: New York University Press, 1971), pp. 35–38. I wish to thank Peter Porçal for bibliographical guidance and generously sharing helpful information from his research on the Renaissance iconography of marriage.

44. Phyllis Williams Lehmann and Karl Lehmann, *Samothracian Reflections. Aspects of the Revival of the Antique*, Bollingen Series, XCII (Princeton: Princeton University Press, 1973), pp. 157–66.

45. Quaglio, *Scienza e mito*, p. 178.

46. *Ovid's Fasti*, tr. Sir James George Frazer, Loeb Series (London: G. P. Putnam's Sons, 1931), I.39–40 and IV.125–30.

47. In the *Genealogie* he condemns it in much the same terms as the Third Vatican Mythographer (IX.3).

48. Albumasar, Andalò, and Aly, *Genealogie*, IX.3; IX.4. Smarr, who also adduces Firmicus Maternus, strongly affirms the dire consequences of Mars in astrological combination with Venus ("Boccaccio and the Stars," above, n. 7).

49. *Boccaccio's Two Venuses*, pp. 64–65.

50. Plutarch, *De E apud Delphos*, in *Plutarch's Moralia*, v, tr. Frank Cole Babbitt, Loeb Series (Cambridge: Harvard University Press, 1936), pp. 217–19.

51. *The Marriage of Philology and Mercury*, p. 279.

52. On these epistles and Martianus see Giuseppe Billanovich, *Restauri boccacceschi* (Rome: Storia e Letteratura, 1947), pp. 68, 72; Giovanni Boccaccio, *Opere in versi, Corbaccio, Trattatello in laude di Dante, Prose latine, Epistole*, ed. Pier Giorgio Ricci (Milan: Ricciardi, 1965), p. 1064, n. 2. The *Teseida*, which has important affinities with the letter *Sacre famis*, is tentatively assigned to 1339–41 by Limentani (Intro. to *Teseida*, p. 231) and Vittore Branca, *Giovanni Boccaccio. Profilo biografico* (Florence: Sansoni, 1977), p. 49.

53. *Sacre famis*, in Giovanni Boccaccio, *Opere latine minori*, ed. Aldo Francesco Massèra, Scrittori d'Italia, IX (Bari: Laterza, 1928), pp. 118–19.

54. After remarking that the fifth of the seven stages in men's growth brings "ripeness for marriage," he refers to a sequence of couplets on the seven ages of man by Solon, who writes of the fifth, "Let him in his fifth week of years a bride bespeak, / Offspring to bear his name hereafter let him seek." *Philo*, tr. Colson

and Whitaker, I, pp.83–85.

55. I am indebted to Carol Kaske for calling to my attention the marriage number in Jonson's *Hymenaei*. Among the symbols in the masque are five waxen tapers whose meaning Reason reveals:

> And lastly, these five waxen lights,
> Imply perfection in the rites:
> For five the special number is,
> Whence hallow'd Union claims her bliss.
> As being all the sum that grows
> From the united strength of those
> Which male and female numbers we
> Do style, and are first two and three.
> Which joined thus, you cannot sever
> In equal parts but one will ever
> Remain as common; so we see
> The binding force of Unity;
> For which alone the peaceful gods
> In number always love the odds,
> And even parts as much despise,
> Since out of them all discords rise.

Hymenaei, lines 196–211 in *Works of Ben Jonson*, ed. Charles H. Hereford et al., x (Oxford: Oxford University Press, 1950).

56. *Erec et Enide*, vv. 2065–71 in *Les Romans de Chrétien de Troyes*, ed. Mario Roques (Paris: Champion, 1953). We also find a fifteen-day marriage celebration in the thirteenth-century Provençal *Flamenca*, whose author had read Chrétien and may have taken the number from him. See Alberto Limentani, "Dalle nozze di Erec et Enide alle nozze di Archimbaut e Flamenca," *Miscellanea di studi offerti a Armando Balduino e Bianca Bianchi per le loro nozze* (Padua: Presso il Seminario di Filologia Moderna dell' Università, 1962), pp. 9–14. Limentani also points to Chrétien's *Erec* as a model for Boccaccio, Intro. to *Teseida*, esp. p. 244.

57. It is often fifteen for Boccaccio, as Branca notes, *Decameron, Tutte le opere di G. B.*, IV (Milan: Mondadori, 1976), Intro. 49 and n. 13, p. 991; II.6.35 and n. 8, p. 1088.

58. Of the twenty-eight mss. described by Battaglia in the Intro. (pp. xi–xxiii) to his edition for the Accademia della Crusca (1938), excluding two that are fragmentary and three others that are incomplete at the end, thirteen lack the last two sonnets. Of these thirteen, however, allowance being made for missing initial folios and occasional internal lacunae, all but one ms. contain the general proemial sonnet and those preceding each book.

59. There has been general agreement that the commentary postdates the text: Vandelli, "Un autografo," *Studi di filologia italiana*, p. 70; Battaglia, Intro., p. cccxv, n. 2; *Amorosa visione*, ed. Branca (Florence: Sansoni, 1944), pp. cxlviii-cxlix;

Billanovich, *Restauri*, p. 85 and note; Alberto Limentani, "Tendenze della prosa del Boccaccio ai margini del *Teseida*," *Giornale Storico della Letteratura Italiana*, CXXV (1958), 524–55, esp. p. 529.

60. F. Boll, C. Bezold, W. Gundel, *Storia dell'astrologia*, intro. Eugenio Garin, Biblioteca di Cultura Moderna, DCCCI (Bari: Laterza, 1977), pp. 87–89.

61. Charles S. Singleton, "The Poet's Number at the Center," *MLN*, LXXX (Jan. 1965), 1–10.

62. See also Victoria Kirkham, "Reckoning with Boccaccio's *Questioni d'amore*," *MLN*, LXXXIX (Jan. 1974), 47–59.

63. Macrobius, *Comm. in somnium* I.6.11.

64. Victoria Kirkham, "Numerology and Allegory in Boccaccio's *Caccia di Diana*," *Traditio*, XXXIV (1978), 303–29.

65. *Comedia delle ninfe* XL.4 and XLIV.7.

66. *Filoc.* IV.74.2–8; V.92.17–21.

67. Prov. 9.1: "Sapientia aedificavit sibi domum, / excidit columnas septem" ("Wisdom hath builded her house, she hath hewn out her seven pillars").

68. *Am. vis.* (1974) A, IV,34–36 and n., p. 571.

69. Cf. Isidore's *Etymologie*, ed. W. M. Lindsay (1911; rpt. Oxford: Oxford University Press, 1962), I.2, "De septem liberalibus disciplinis."

70. *Conv.* II.13.2–8.

71. *Opere latine minori*, ed. Massèra, pp. 118–19.

72. *Restauri boccacceschi*, pp. 75–76 and note. Limentani, "Tendenze della prosa," compares B.'s glosses with those of Lactantius Placidus, for the text of which see *Commentarios in Statii Thebaide et commentarium in Achilleida*, ed. R. Jahnke (Leipzig: Teubner, 1898). Hollander, on the other hand ("The Validity of Boccaccio's Self-Exegesis"), finds the Lactantian glosses substantially different in character from Boccaccio's, arguing that even if he was familiar with them, he chose not to imitate them.

73. For example, a fascinating pictorial composition based on the number 7 is the Florentine fresco of St. Thomas enthroned in the Spanish Chapel at Santa Maria Novella by Andrea di Buonaiuto (1366–68). Above the great Dominican, who displays a book open to the text of Wisdom 7:7, there circle seven winged women, the Virtues. Below him on the right are the seven Liberal Arts, each above a corresponding, representative historical personage; on the left are seven Theological Sciences similarly paired with seven theologians. Over the Theological Sciences preside the seven gifts of the Holy Spirit, over the Liberal Arts, the planets. In connection with my search for simultaneous sequences of 7's, I thank Salvatore I. Camporeale, O.P., for discussing this fresco with me and citing his interpretation of it, published in "Lorenzo Valla tra Medioevo e Rinascimento. *Encomion s. Thomae* - 1457," *Memorie domenicani*, NS 7 (1976), 11–194, esp. pp. 22–24. See also Millard Meiss, *Painting in Florence and Siena after the Black Death. The Arts, Religion and Society in the Mid-Fourteenth Century* (1951; rpt. New York: Harper and Row, 1964), pp. 99–100.

74. Earlier, considerably different and shorter versions of this paper were read in 1975 for the Midwest Modern Language Association meetings at Chicago and

the Renaissance Society of the University of Pennsylvania. But the greater part of the research preparatory to the present article was carried out in Florence during 1977–78, when I was on academic leave with a Fellowship awarded by the Harvard University Center for Italian Renaissance Studies and funded by the National Endowment for the Humanities, a grant generously supplemented by the University of Pennsylvania. For help with this study, which became the subject of a talk on "Boccaccio's Numerology" given at I Tatti in April, 1978, I am deeply indebted to the Fellows, Research Associates, and Director of I Tatti, Craig Hugh Smyth, who were generous with suggestions and encouragement. I express thanks as well to Richard Seagraves for assistance with some thorny medieval Latin and special appreciation to Robert M. Durling for his comments on the manuscript as a whole.

Metodi di lettura
degli scritti ascetici trecenteschi

GIORGIO PETROCCHI

DOPO UN PERIODO, ANCHE ABBASTANZA LUNGO, di stasi o di quasi letargo, in parte determinato dai differenti interessi perseguiti dalla storiografia idealistica, lo studio della letteratura religiosa del Trecento ha ripreso a fiorire in Italia nell'ultimo trentennio, con una richezza e varietà d'istanze che testimoniano anzitutto lo iato col metodo di lettura meramente estetico del crocianesimo. Il punto centrale è proprio nel saggio, "Letteratura del Trecento. Letteratura di devozione", di Benedetto Croce,[1] in cui non era assente la voce degli scrittori religiosi, ma mescolata ad altre voci e in una prospettiva oggi superata, e tra l'altro relegata nelle poche pagine,[2] insomma una *reductio* del grande movimento religioso del secolo di S. Caterina da Siena e, ovviamente, di Dante e del Petrarca, ad elemento meramente accessorio, quand'anche, negli epigoni del Croce, subalterno.

Lo svincolo dall'estetica storicista, un neo-storicismo di marca non più idealistica ma legato ad un'intensa ricerca negli archivi e nelle biblioteche, una quasi totalmente nuova rielaborazione delle condizioni storico-sociali nelle quali operarono i movimenti francescani, domenicani, degli Agostiniani, dei Celestiniani, dei Gesuati, hanno cambiato il volto al panorama complessivo del Trecento, contribuendo a porre gli scrittori mistici e ascetici al centro dello spirito del secolo, e non nei margini.

Onesto è riconoscere che qualche sforzo in tal senso era stato compiuto anche nel periodo precedente, parlo sempre in Italia; ad esempio nel *Trecento* di Sapegno[3] il contributo recato dai prosatori sacri era allargato a dimensioni maggiori, e s'era avuta la bella antologia d'Arrigo Levasti, *I Mistici*[4] (di cui s'è poi avuta un'importante silloge dal titolo *Mistici del Duecento e del Trecento*[5]). La ripresa d'interesse per la religiosità trecentesca è dovuta a due personalità diverse, e operanti in ambiti culturali profondamente differenti: Giovanni Getto, presso l'Università Cattolica di Milano, col suo *Saggio letterario su S. Caterina da Siena*,[6] col suo libro sul Passavanti,[7] e con varie ricerche, culminanti nella silloge *Letteratura religiosa del Trecento*;[8] e Giuseppe De Luca, viva e splendida figura di ricercatore e di scrittore, autore dei *Prosatori minori del Trecento*, tomo sugli *Scrittori di religione*,[9] animatore di studi sulla spiritualità che hanno sollecitato i contributi centrali di Arsenio Frugoni, *Celestiniana*;[10] di Raoul Manselli sul Clareno, l'Olivi e gli Spirituali,[11] di Massimo Petrocchi, nella recentissima *Storia della spiritualità italiana*,[12] e di una serie di prodotti filologici, l'edizione del *Quaresimale* di Giordano da Pisa,[13] quella delle *Laudi* di Jacopone, a cura di Franco Mancini;[14] e poi del *Dialogo* di S. Caterina, a cura di G. Cavallini,[15] del Torini, del Pagliaresi, del Panziera, del Marsili. Eccelle per richezza di testi e d'informazione la lunga ricerca di Ignazio Baldelli, *Medioevo volgare da Montecassino all'Umbria*.[16]

Ma non è nostro intendimento tracciare una rassegna bibliografica (a tal fine rinviamo alle copiose note bibliografiche di Massimo Petrocchi), quanto un panorama delle linee maestre della ricerca sul Trecento ascetico, considerando nel complesso dei reperti scientifici l'impostazione metodica data dagli studiosi italiani al problema della conciliabilità tra poesia e misticismo. Infatti la incomunicabilità dell'esperienza mistica è vera in quanto gli stadi dell'estasi non possono avere una giustificazione razionale tra momento e momento della vita dell'anima, ma per quanto inafferrabile e superiore "alla possibilità espressiva del mistico", essa può essere riferita in tutta la sua estensione e profondità, senza che nessuno stato mistico venga dimenticato. Si vedano la *Vita* e i *Pensieri sull'amore di Dio* di Santa Teresa. Si guardino le *Lettere* di S. Caterina da Siena, anche testo magistrale dell'aureo Trecento, anche terreno di vibrazioni poetiche, ma, soprattutto, documento di una esperienza religiosa che è tramandata in un'opera letteraria, e che, partecipando di tutti gli attributi elaborativi del sentimento, entra limpidamente nel concetto di "letteratura religiosa", inteso nella finalità moralistica e insegnativa, ma non già "sterilizzatrice" (per usare il termine crociano di espulsione dal terreno della poesia), sterilizzatrice d'ogni esigenza di libera ricreazione dello stato mistico personale, anche nelle più accese forme di esaltazione interiore o di esterna costruzione oratoria.

Non è possibile restare nell'aratura idealistica, fra il solco della poesia e la maggese della letteratura oratoria o didascalica, giacché la posizione di S. Caterina[17] è perfettamente risolvibile in libera fantasia lirica, quando c'è svincolo dal fine insegnativo e cronachistico delle sue epistole, allorché l'esperienza mistica illumina in pagine di poesia il "semplice dramma umano" di chi si snatura nell'estasi e canta il suo rapporto immediato con Dio fuori d'ogni finalità d'ordine pratico e pedagogico, e quindi al di là della "letteratura", in un campo dove l'esperienza mistica, per essere tramandata in pagine di scrittura, può coincidere con la natura della poesia: proprio là dove non è ragionamento dell'intelletto che indaga i suoi rapporti con la Divinità, né costruzione volontaristica a scopo d'edificazione o di racconto autobiografico. Nell'impostazione crociana del concetto di "letteratura di devozione" l'esperienza mistica riferita ad un rapporto extra-filosofico ed extra-pedagogico apre una falla, creando un artificioso e schematico rapporto tra mistica e poesia che non può ricadere sul terreno coatto della letteratura. Se concorrono i due elementi, di esperienza mistica e di prodotto poetico, evidentemente la poesia non deve sorpassare lo stato mistico quasi si trattasse di un fine pratico o di un ragionamento filosofico, ma deve coincidervi, giacché né la poesia ha vita fuori della precisa elaborazione di immagini e fatti dettati dall'estasi, né l'esperienza mistica può esimersi o sfuggire dal tormento poetico che essa stessa ha creato e alimentato per aver vita al di là della trasfigurazione religiosa dell'anima. D'altronde l'ipotesi della incomunicabilità dello stato mistico, quale elemento risolvente di un'assenza totale della poesia, riceve una limpida smentita dalle pagine del Beato Giovanni Colombini, dove l'esperienza mistica non è documentata dal racconto delle fasi estatiche, sì piuttosto da quei momenti di espressività dell'ineffabile, quando il mistico comunica quel solo ricordo del rapimento che può essere aperto e definito agli altri, e descritto o cantato, nella linea di quella esperienza descrittiva dell'estasi che ha trovato la maggiore celebrazione poetica nell'ultimo canto del *Paradiso* dantesco.

Si pone ora il problema se possa essere condotto un discorso critico organico sulla lauda del Colombini rispetto alle sue *Lettere*, le quali appartengono a quella memoria dell'esperienza mistica che non è di sprone all'autore, né d'incitamento alle persone cui sono dirette le *Lettere*: istanti di sospensione nella predominante finalità pratica e didattica del suo epistolario, dove l'esperienza trascorsa è spoglia di attributi contingenti ed è cantata nella sua assolutezza esprimibile ed espressa:

E per la carità e grande dolcezza unitasi l'anima con Cristo, e a lui perfettamente isposata, si è più che per la grande ebrezza e per lo smisurato caldo del fervore, unitasi col suo dolce Cristo e in lui tutta trasformata, e per accendimento e fuoco diventata l'anima quasi esso Cristo. Unde l'anima, quando è in questo stato ed in questa fornace ardente accesa e inebriata, grida coll'Apostolo e dice: chi mi separrà o partirà dalla carità di Dio? non fame, non sete, non ingiurie, non fuoco, non ferro, non demoni, non angeli, non cosa che sia, né che possa essere non mi partirà dalla carità di Dio, sì m'à inebriato il mio Cristo Jesù, per lo cui amore io voglio ed eleggo povertà santa, senza la quale vivere gli sarebbe grande pena. Elegge allora la santa anima ingiurie, villanie, pene e ismisurate infirmità; elegge il martirio; non può l'anima santa trovare il martirio che a lei sia sufficiente, ama tutti i suoi perseguitatori, abbraccia allora tutti e nemici, tutta la terra, tutte le bestie, tutte le cose, che Dio à create per lo suo amore. Grida quell'anima inebriata di Cristo: pazzia, mortificazioni, vergogne; in breve desidera in tutte le cose patire per Cristo, quello che Cristo patì per lei. Torna quest'anima ripiena di tutte le virtù, odiatrice di tutti i vizi, va quest'anima usata a trasformarsi et unirsi; così quando all'umanità di Cristo, quando alla passione si trasforma, quando alle santissime piaghe, quando cerca vita eterna, quando colla donna nostra, quando cogli altri santi e in molte altre e variate cose; quando si trasforma nelle criature; quando in cose che essa desidera. E così, secondo che l'è dato e che essa desidera, s'unisce e si trasforma con giubili e canti meravigliosi l'anima santa, trasformata in Cristo o per Cristo.[18]

I contenuti espliciti della spiritualità del Colombini, come in genere tutte le forme di cristocentrismo del movimento dei Gesuati sino a Feo Belcari, non appaiono chiara eredità francescana, e nemmeno evidente eco delle posizioni caratteristiche degli Spirituali. Si avverte nel complesso nella letteratura gesuata, tanto nei testi poetici quanto nei trattati e nelle missive, non un riferimento pratico e pedagogico ad una concreta esperienza subita, dunque, e nemmeno lo sforzo di esprimere una trasfigurazione mistica incomunicabile al prossimo, ma una successione di stati mistici esprimibili in termini di poesia, col medesimo dettato lirico di tante esperienze extramistiche che il Colombini racconta in alcune delle sue lettere più affascinanti.[19] Insomma il rapporto poesia-mistica entra in gioco nei momenti in cui il Colombini si libera sia dalla finalità insegnativa delle sue *Lettere*, sia dal racconto materiale o spirituale di una giornata terrena in cammino per l'apostolato o per la predicazione. L'importanza massima, tuttavia, delle *Lettere* colombiniane risiede fuori degli istanti di conciliazione tra poesia e stato mistico e quindi nella formazione e maturazione dell'esperienza mistica attraverso il documento letterario. In tal senso il problema critico che offrono le *Lettere* del Gesuato è ben diverso da quello poetico-linguistico che aspetta all'opera del Passavanti o (per nominare una valutazione particolarmente riuscita al Croce nel suo studio sulla letteratura religiosa trecentesca) all'opera del Cavalca, avvertendo che sul primo esiste una probante esegesi critica che dal Getto giunge all'Aurigemma, mentre il Cavalca solo in questi ultimi anni ha trovato uno studioso che abbia la capacità di affrontarlo globalmente, il Del Corno, del quale gioverà segnalare la bellissima voce sul *Dizionario biografico degli Italiani* (1978).[20]

Il problema critico della letteratura religiosa non può ovviamente contenersi nella sola storia della sua esperienza letteraria, ché una storia del linguaggio (sia pure nell'eccezione molto estesa del termine) rischierebbe, da per sé sola, di non poter risolvere tutto il processo religioso e storico dello scrittore, i suoi rapporti col pensiero e la cultura del tempo in quanto non si riflettono direttamente sulla qualità e struttura della sua espressione letteraria, ma determinano una crisi spirituale non documentabile nell'estensione e sede della "interna logica espressiva", e nemmeno documentabile con i dati biografici in possesso. Né si dica che quella parte di esperienza religiosa che non si traduce in espressione, sia perciò decisamente fuori del terreno della letteratura religiosa, e comporti piuttosto a storici della teologia o della filosofia o della agiografia. Anzi l'interno processo spirituale e religioso di uno scrittore (ad esempio del Passavanti nello *Specchio della vera penitenza* o del Cavalca nella *Mondizia del cuore*), oltre chiarire il linguaggio personale diversamente dal puro contributo dell'espressione, e rientrando negli essenziali elementi costituitivi della letteratura, determina un giudizio più esatto sul particolare carattere di una lauda o di una prosa mistica, sulla sua struttura letteraria, sulla scelta dell'argomento come decisa apertura sull'intimità religiosa. Dunque non è più uno strumento di studio, è un incentramento più sicuro del problema critico sulla base della ricerca di nuovi documenti o sul riesame dei cogniti, come si è avuto di recente nella preziosa raccolta di *Laude duecentesche* curata da G. Varanini,[21] come pure nell'edizione delle *Rime sacre* di Neri Pagliaresi,[22] nelle indagini sui codici del Cavalca da parte di C. Del Corno, nell'importante iniziativa filologica di F. Mancini e G. Varanini per una raccolta dei laudari dei secoli XIII–IV.

L'esperienza mistica del Colombini non è empirica e istintiva ma si muove lungo una direttrice spirituale ben precisa come non farebbe supporre una prima lettura del suo epistolario così semplice e candido. Bisogna aggiungere che la vita religiosa del Colombini non sorge da una fortissima prova mistica che travolge e risana tutte le scorie della vita giovanile passata in attività pubbliche e commerciali. Il *raptus* nasce successivamente, dopo infinite esperienze umane e sociali seguite alla rapida conversione: prima il rimorso per le colpe commesse in gioventù, poi il ripudio della carne, poi privazioni e penitenze (ma sempre nell'ambito di una mortificazione privata), abbandono della attività civica e commerciale, e infine la confessione con Francesco Vincenti, la prima vita in comune, le prime opere in favore del prossimo. E' un lento processo spirituale, dove non arde improvvisa la vita mistica, ma l'uomo faticosamente conquista uno strenuo senso attivistico e sociale, cessa di chiudere in sé le tappe del proprio pentimento e comunica tutto sé agli altri, ai primi seguaci e compagni.

Le prime esperienze mistiche si realizzano nel ritrovamento della potenza e bontà divina in tutte le cose, nell'armonia del creato verso cui sospinge il fervore dell'anima. Ma l'anima per stringere a sé la perfetta semplicità delle cose, deve essersi trasformata in Cristo. Egli esorta:

> Lassando tutte le altre sollecitudini e tutti gli altri esercizi, datevi a trovare e a inebriare e a innamorare di Cristo, e a trasformarvi in lui, ove l'anima santa, ripiena e inebriata di lui, griderà: diletto mio, ora di te godo, ora inebrio, ora ti posseggo; tutta l'abbraccerà, tutta si struggerà, ed essa griderà con l'Apostolo, e dirà: che mi partirà dalla fonte viva di vita eterna? E dessa aprirà le braccia dell'anima sua andando, abbracciando tutte le criature per amore del suo diletto sposo. Ella abbraccerà tutte le bestie, tutte le mura, istruggendo sé medesima di dolcitudine d'amore santo di Cristo. O anima così trasformata in Jesù Cristo, quanto con ogni verità gridi povertà, quanto gridi umiltà, e chiedi ogni vergogna, quanto desideri d'essere tenuta pazza e rea, quanto di ogni infamia rea, o pessima ti godi! Quanto più ti vedi dilongare dall'onore, tanto più ti vedi accostare a Cristo tuo sposo, tua corona, tuo bene, e vero diletto.[23]

L'indirizzo mistico della scuola francescana non è solo in questo fraterno abbraccio del creato, ma anche nella rivoluzione realistica e sentimentale che il misticismo di S. Francesco ha portata sopra la dialettica scolastica nel suo operato oltre i confini terreni della vita dell'Assistente. In tutti i mistici del Trecento la prevalenza dell'ontologia sulla logica è appunto sentimentale, in uno slancio speculativo anche il processo spirituale del Beato Giovanni Colombini. Però c'è qualcosa di molto diverso in lui, rispetto all'itinerario mistico dello spirito francescano: qualcosa che riporta molto indietro la qualità di esperienza mistica colombiniana, quasi nell'area dell'ispirazione immaginosa delle Benedettine tedesche del XII e XIII secolo.

La mistica francescana, infatti, risiede nella comunicabilità dell'uomo con le cose, in quanto è la vita del divino che è scesa nell'uomo e nelle cose. La trascendenza delle cose è invece, nel beato Colombini, conseguenza della completa trasformazione dell'uomo in Dio. Concetto che egli ripete in numerosi passi, sempre con la stessa intensità di evento vissuto: "Arda l'anima nostra nel fuoco de cieli, arda e con Cristo si trasformi l'anima nostra nel divino amore, inebri Jesù,"[24] o altrove: "E sempre [la carità] ci faccia essere trasformati in lui".[25]

Tale diversità dalla mistica francescana spiega l'assenza, nella ispirazione e nella pratica di vita del Colombini, del concetto di "perfetta letizia". Egli parla d'umiltà, di carità, di povertà, di totale comunione con Dio, di verità e d'amore verso le creature con un pathos severo e quasi affannoso, come di chi sappia d'aver poco tempo in questa vita per compiere tutte le opere assegnate dalla Provvidenza, "portando ferma fede e diritta con isperanza e perfetta carità e continuo e ardente desiderio di fare grandi cose per lo suo amore (di Cristo)".[26]

Iddio non è l'espressione interiore della lirica felicità dell'universo che offre all'uomo la grazia di una letizia spirituale che lo purifica e guida. Egli è il sollecitatore continuo per operare e contemplare, l'incalzante maestro d'apostolato, e il Colombini non si stanca di seguirlo: "Ricordivi che 'l tempo nostro è molto breve, e 'l dì perduto mai non si ricovara. Oimé tanti n'ò perduti! Ogni tempo che non si spende a onore di Dio è male speso".[27] Questo è nelle opere. Pur nella contemplazione di Dio e del creato una visione pessimistica, della propria miseria d'uomini, incombe nell'istante in cui l'anima si unisce a Dio direttamente o nella molteplicità delle vite nell'universo.

L'apertura prospettica della mistica di S. Caterina postula interrogativi e problemi che non possono avere simiglianze con quelli d'altri scrittori di religione. Anche il loro timbro realistico ha una coloritura peculiare, che non si può confondere col realismo, non meno potente, ma quasi di scorcio e fugace, che vibra nella prosa latina della beata Angela da Foligno, il *Liber sororis Lellae de Fulgineo*.[28]

E' da ricordare una pagina di Angela sulla lavanda del Giovedì Santo.

Il giovedì santo dissi alla mia compagna che cercassimo il Cristo, e proposi di andare all'ospedale per trovarlo tra quei poveri, penati e dolenti. Recammo con noi tutti i veli da testa che erano in casa, e che rappresentavano pure la nostra unica possessione. Incaricammo Gigliola, che prestava servizio presso gli infermi, che li vendesse e comperasse del cibo per i malati.

Quantunque in un primo tempo essa rifiutasse, pensando che la insultassimo, tuttavia cedette alla nostra insistenza, e col ricavato della vendita acquistò dei pesci; da parte nostra vi aggiungemmo tutti i pani che ci erano stati donati per il nostro sostentamento.

Fatta l'offerta, lavammo i piedi delle donne e le mani degli uomini, specialmente di un certo lebbroso, che le aveva putride, marciose e perdute; poi bevemmo di quel lavaggio. Sentimmo tanta dolcezza, che lungo la strada provammo quella soavità, come se ci fossimo comunicate. Mi sembrava infatti di essermi comunicata perché sentivo quella massima soavità, quasi avessi ricevuto il Signore. E poiché un brano di quelle piaghe era restato attraverso la mia gola, e invano mi sforzavo di inghiottirlo, la coscienza non mi permetteva di fare alcuno sforzo per emetterlo, come se mi fossi comunicata, benché volessi solo staccarlo dalla gola e non rigettarlo . . . .[29]

Al problema critico della letteratura religiosa s'aggiunge qui un problema di tecnica e uno di struttura. Infatti l'architettura dottrinaria del *Liber*, cui non sottrae coerenza la vastità eterogenea delle apparizioni e delle estasi, rivela nella beata Angela una qual disposizione a superare gli aspetti affettivi e psicologici di un misticismo meramente contemplativo, a favore di una faticosa conquista della personale mistica speculativa.

Cioè, a differenza dei mistici italiani del Trecento, tutti contemplativi ed "affettivi", Angela ci richiama piuttosto alle grandi figure della mistica speculativa del Duecento, massime al "correligionario" Bonaventura. La sua visione teologica, che accentra la vita e la trasformazione spirituale in Cristo e attraverso il possesso di Cristo attua l'unione dell'anima con i divini attributi della Volontà, della Sapienza, e della Potenza, mostra eccezionali capacità di approfondimento dottrinario.

Ma, inoltre, la sua tecnica espositiva, il potere letterario di esprimere lo stato estatico e, direi quindi, il suo senso tutto sciolto ed esplicito di "raccontare", ne fanno una scrittrice tipica del Trecento. La sua posizione, e spirituale e letteraria, è veramente di cerniera tra la speculazione duecentesca e il fervore trecentesco. Non si comprendono Ubertino e Caterina, Passavanti e il volgarizzatore degli *Actus* senza percorrere lo sterminato campo visionario della Beata Angela.

Accanto a questa posizione storica, che è poi quella più facilmente comprensibile, c'è un complesso di atteggiamenti extra-umani, di distacco persino sdegnoso della vita, che è tutto di Angela, e che non troveremo nella stessa misura davvero spietata in nessun altro mistico (non si dica di Santa Caterina, la quale ha così profondi agganci con la vita pubblica e privata, politica e familiare, del suo tempo). Il *Liber* di Angela mostra una totale disumanizzazione dell'esperienza mistica; disumanizzazione che non muove dalla inenarrabilità delle cose viste e contemplate, ma da un personale distacco verso tutto ciò che è umano nel senso comune del termine.

Nelle *Lettere* di santa Caterina da Siena s'attinge il vertice della prosa mistica e ascetica del Trecento. Tutto in Caterina diviene forma d'esperienza religiosa: lo stile, la struttura epistolare, il racconto autobiografico, l'invettiva politica, il ragionamento concettuale. L'epistolario cateriniano è stracolmo di sperimentazioni formali e di assimilazioni culturali, di cui è sovente impossibile stabilire la genesi se non si tenga conto della vivace partecipazione della Santa senese alla vita religiosa italiana, oltre che della propria città, e alla pubblicistica politico-spirituale. Vari appaiono i toni delle *Lettere* e subordinatamente quelli dell'altra opera cateriniana, il *Dialogo della Divina Provvidenza*: s'alternano pagine d'infuocata energia spirituale a pagine intese a rappresentare in modo serenamente affettuoso le piccole cose della vita quotidiana. La trattazione trascorre da momenti d'ardore a momenti di quiete, da un ricorso tumultuoso a similitudini e metafore ardite, tipiche del linguaggio biblico a un pacato intercalare di termini del parlare domestico, sostenuto da frequenti e brevissime proposizioni interiettive, da locuzioni di grande tenerezza umana, talvolta anche dal guizzo d'un sorriso trepido d'affettuosa sororale umanità.

La battaglia cateriniana contro il secolo, incentrata in tre direzioni particolari (il ritorno della sede papale da Avignone a Roma, la riforma delle strutture della Chiesa, l'indizione di una nuova Crociata) è espressa nelle

Lettere in tutta l'amplissima gamma della tematica politico-sociale, mostrando l'eccezionale vitalità della Santa in ogni momento della sua breve vita, l'impressionante forza con cui essa sa rivolgere la parola a re, papi, cardinali, come anche a umili personaggi, ai peccatori, ai dubbiosi, ai poveri, alle amate consorelle. Ma i temi sono presupposti da una profonda e originale visione mistica che scaturisce dalla conoscenza di Dio connaturata al sentimento del rapporto che l'uomo istituisce con Dio, al sentimento dell'abisso che separa la perfezione di Dio dall'infinita imperfezione dell'uomo, il quale avverte la necessità di chiudersi tutto nella cellula spirituale della conoscenza e di nutrirsi dell'ardore della carità divina. La conoscenza dell'essenza della Divinità (conoscenza tanto metafisica che morale) sollecita e alimenta la contrizione, unita all'umiltà. Soltanto nel processo conoscitivo di Dio è possibile attuare quella totale comprensione dei propri peccati che non è umano rammarico, ma sublime consapevolezza della carità divina, la quale opera sugli uomini coi mezzi del disgusto delle colpe e del pentimento. La presenza della carità è visibile nella fiamma inestinguibile che riscalda il cuore: "Debbe essere [il cuore] siccome la lampana, ch'è stretta da piedi e larga da capo; cioé che 'l desiderio e affetto suo sia ristretto al mondo e largo di sopra; cioé dilargare il cuore e l'affetto suo in Cristo crocifisso, amandolo e temendolo con vera e santa sollecitudine. E allora empirai questa lampana al costato di Cristo crocifisso. Il costato ti mostra il segreto del cuore".[30]

Capovolgendo le posizioni della teologia tomistica, Caterina afferma che Iddio, colui che è, è presente entro l'uomo, il quale "non è" fuori di questo rapporto amoroso. Quel che Iddio fa esistere, non è l'uomo in generale, ma quel certo particolare uomo che Dio ha veduto in se stesso e della cui bellezza Egli s'è innamorato: "Tu, Dio eterno, vedesti e cognoscesti me in Te, e perché Tu me vedesti nel lume tuo, però innamorato de la tua creatura, la traesti da Te, creandola alla immagine e similitudine tua".[31] Le rivelazioni mistiche e le riflessioni ascetiche s'originano sempre dal concetto centrale della presenza, in tutti gli uomini, del Dio amore e aprono la strada a una serie di immagini di timbro affettuoso e di significato caritativo, le quali a loro volta pervengono alla dottrina del corpo mistico di Cristo. Da questa impostazione dottrinaria è agevole il passaggio a un vero e proprio programma di riforma del governo della Chiesa. A tal fine Caterina rimprovera aspramente Gregorio XI e Urbano VI, ponendoli di fronte alle loro gravi responsabilità e censura il clero per il troppo amore ch'esso rivela per le cose temporali. Ai pontefici rivolge la forte esortazione a "lavare il ventre" della Chiesa, cioé a togliere ogni macchia dal corpo mistico di Cristo.

La scrittura immaginosa di santa Caterina tradisce due ascendenze fondamentali: da un lato la tradizione biblica, innografica e apologetica degli scritti sacri ch'ella era solita farsi leggere, e d'altro canto il linguaggio del popolo in mezzo al quale era cresciuta e viveva; non si può dire quale influsso predomini (forse quello scritturale e ecclesiale nel *Dialogo* e nelle epistole rivelatorie d'un *raptus* mistico; lo stile demotico nella corrispondenza ai familiari e alle consorelle), ma nel complesso si può affermare che il linguaggio cateriniano risulti ben omogeneo, in virtù anche della compattezza dell'ispirazione interiore, e per merito anche della precisa struttura quadripartita dell'epistola, fornita d'un protocollo iniziale cui tengono dietro una parte relativa al racconto personale d'un'esperienza e un'altra zona in cui si dà motivo dell'occasione che ha dettato il testo, per finire con un protocollo finale. Questo equilibrio espressivo contribuisce a donare agli scritti cateriniani una singolare importanza nella storia letteraria del Trecento, così come Caterina, nella storia civile e religiosa del secolo, fu tra i personaggi più alti ed emblematici dell'epoca.

Da quanto s'è detto, si può intendere l'esigenza teoretica che deve sovraintendere a qualsivoglia impostazione del problema critico della letteratura religiosa come molto più e molto meglio di un tentativo d'elaborare una "concreta storia del linguaggio", sia pure estendendo il termine linguaggio alla massima dilatazione definitoria possibile. Direi piuttosto che lo storico della letteratura deve porsi fondamentalmente l'istanza critica di definire il punto di soluzione tra l'esperienza religiosa e l'esperienza letteraria del singolo mistico o asceta o apologeta o agiografo.

Senza un totale fondersi, nell'atto creativo della memoria mistica o della meditazione ascetica, delle due esperienze, entrambe fondamentali, non può nascere letteratura religiosa, ma invece due distanti contenuti: il mero resoconto dell'esperienza religiosa spoglio di qualsiasi impegno tecnico e linguistico o la pura esercitazione accademica, dove l'afflato spirituale dello scrivente non è diventato ricreazione poetica o letteraria del ricordo o del ripensamento. E, precisiamo, non è affatto necessario perché sgorghi letteratura religiosa che lo scrittore sia posseduto da un impegno letterario estrinseco e velleitario, nascendo nella maggior parte dei casi (San Francesco, Santa Caterina, San Bernardino, ecc.) da un clima di civiltà spirituale che è già all'atto stesso della creazione poetica o letteraria insita nell'animo dello scrittore, anche se questi s'affanni a dichiarare a se stesso o ai suoi discepoli, o a noi, tardi ascoltatori, il totale ripudio d'ogni accorgimento retorico, il disdegno per la letteratura intesa come artificio squisito e profano. Noi sappiamo che in quel momento lo scrittore religioso rifugge dalla letteratura in quanto la intende come vacuo esercizio delle armi della retorica, ma non ripudia la letteratura intesa come forma d'espressione e di comunicazione tra sé e gli altri, come unico tramite tra un fondo di cogitazioni e d'impulsi spirituali e il devoto cristiano che ascolta e deve comprendere, deve restare colpito e persuaso, deve completare la propria conoscenza. E la parola non è tale se non ha un destinatario: il grido dell'anima di Caterina o di Teresa o di Giovanni della Croce non è totale se non può essere trasmesso a tutti.

La *traditio* tra lo spirito estatico e noi, tra lo spirito mortificante e noi, s'opera soltanto con la poesia o con la sua ancella di civiltà, per ripetere una nota immagine del Croce, e cioé la letteratura. Studiare la letteratura religiosa deve significare per i ricercatori d'oggi approfondire il rapporto che lega l'esperienza con la sua espressione, il moto dell'anima col suo linguaggio. Così noi riusciremo a respingere le interpretazioni della nostra storia letteraria religiosa che considerino il dato offerto dal singolo scrittore cristiano come puro elemento documentario di una crisi spirituale o di un'illuminazione, e d'altro canto a respingere la lettura estetica, delibante e raffinata quanto si vuole, della bella pagina francescana o cateriniana, quasi che i classici del nostro Trecento o Cinquecento o Ottocento fossero stati soltanto degli accoliti di una squisitissima setta segreta di letterari, e non formidabili interpreti della fede cristiana, i quali hanno scritto in quanto hanno vissuto spiritualmente, e sono vivi nella nostra ammirazione anche perché hanno scritto, anche perché sono stati scrittori.[32]

Note

1. In *Poesia popolare e poesia d'arte* (Bari: Laterza, 1933).
2. Croce, pp. 163–87.
3. Natalino Sapegno, *Il Trecento* (Milano: Vallardi, 1933, seconda edizione, 1960).
4. Arrigo Levasti, *I Mistici*, 2 v. (Firenze: Bemporad, 1925).
5. Arrigo Levasti, *Mistici del Duecento e del Trecento* (Milano: Rizzoli, 1935, seconda edizione, 1960).

6. Giovanni Getto, *Saggio letterario su S. Caterina da Siena* (Firenze: Sansoni, 1939).

7. Giovanni Getto, *Umanità e stile di Jacopo Passavanti* (Milano: Casa Editrice Leonardo, 1943).

8. Giovanni Getto, *Letteratura religiosa del Trecento* (Firenze: Sansoni, 1967).

9. Giuseppe De Luca, *Scrittori di religione* (Milano-Napoli: Ricciardi, 1964).

10. Arsenio Frugoni, *Celestiniana* (Roma: Istituto Storico Italiano per il Medio Evo, 1954).

11. *La "Lectura super Apocalipsim" di Pietro di Giovanni Olivi. Ricerche sull'escatologismo medioevale* (Roma: Istituto Storico Italiano per il Medio Evo, 1955).

12. Massimo Petrocchi, *Storia della spiritualità italiana*, 3 v. (Roma: Edizioni di Storia e Letteratura, 1978).

13. Giordano da Pisa, *Quaresimale*, a cura di C. Del Corno (Firenze: Sansoni, 1974).

14. Jacopone, *Laudi*, a cura di Franco Mancini (Bari: Laterza, 1974).

15. S. Caterina, *Dialogo*, a cura di G. Cavallini (Roma: Centro di Studi Cateriniani, 1966).

16. Ignazio Baldelli, *Medioevo volgare da Montecassino all'Umbria* (Bari: Adriatica, 1977).

17. Vedi S. Caterina da Siena, *Le Lettere*, a cura di Misciatelli (Siena: Giuntini e Bentivoglio, 1913–21); ad es. nella lettera 152 (II, pp. 432–33): "La prima dolce Verità . . . elesse per nostro esempio e regola nella natività sua la povertà tanto strema che non ebbe pannicello a sé condecente, dove si potesse involvere; in tanto che, essendo tempo di freddo, l'animale alitava sopra il corpo del fanciullo"; oppure nella lettera 353 (v, pp. 260–61): ". . . e pregovi che vi ritroviate in questo dolce avvento e nella santa pasqua, nel Presepio con questo dolce e umile Agnello, dove troverete Maria con tanta riverenzia a quel figliuolo, e peregrina in tanta povertà, avendo la ricchezza del Figliuolo di Dio, che non ha panno condecente di poterlo involvere, né fuoco da scaldare esso fuoco, Agnello immacolato; ma gli animali eziandio, sopra il corpo del fanciullo, il riscaldavano col fiato loro . . . . Adunque visitate questo prezioso luogo . . . ."

18. Vedi *Lettere del b. Gio. Colombini da Siena*, a cura di A. Bartoli (Lucca: Tipografia Balatresi, 1856), pp. 48–49.

19. Ibid.

20. *Dizionario biografico degli Italiani* (Roma: Istituto della Enciclopedia Italiana, 1960–). Vedi XXII, pp. 577–86.

21. *Laude duecentesche*, a cura di G. Varanini (Padova: Antenore, 1972).

22. *Rime sacre*, a cura di Neri Pagliaresi (Firenze: F. Le Monnier, 1970).

23. *Lettere del b. Colombini*, ediz. Bartoli cit., p. 153.

24. Ibid., p. 83.

25. Ibid., p. 9.

26. Ibid., p. 1.

27. Ibid., p. 2.

28. Anche detto *Liber de vera fidelium experientia*, edizione a cura di M. Faloci Pulignani (Città di Castello: Casa Editrice "Il Solco," 1932).

29. Ed. Faloci Pulignani cit., pp. 90–92.

30. *Lettere di S. Caterina da Siena*, I, p. 200.

31. Ibid.

32. Per una rapida conoscenza degli autori di cui al presente saggio si vedano: G. Petrocchi, "La letteratura religiosa" e "Cultura e poesia nel Trecento", nei vol. I e II della *Storia della letteratura italiana*, a cura di E. Cecchi e N. Sapegno (Milano: Garzanti, 1965); cfr. inoltre: G. Fallani, *La letteratura religiosa italiana* (Firenze: F. Le Monnier, 1963); A. Tartaro, "Scrittori devoti", in *La letteratura italiana. Storia e testi*, a cura di C. Muscetta, vol. II, tomo II (Bari: Laterza, 1972), pp. 435–515; G. Petrocchi, *Scrittori religiosi del Trecento* (Firenze: Sansoni, 1974).

Dante, Petrarch, Boccaccio is a tribute to Charles S. Singleton, who has been called "the greatest living *dantista*." The editors have gathered together major original essays by some of the foremost scholars of the Trecento, largely exemplifying Singleton's exegetical approach or reflecting other aspects of Singleton's impact on modern critical thought.

Two of the essays deal with earlier exegetes: Vallone on Jacopo della Lana, and Raimondi on Castelvetro. Durling's essay involves the most famous and most devoted of such exegetes, Boccaccio, both as theorist and as interpreter of Dante. The approach of Freccero and Shapiro to formal elements in the prosody of Dante and Petrarch, as well as Ferrante's analysis of "divine" words and images in the *Paradiso*, are reminiscent of Singleton's deep interest in such linguistic and stylistic devices. Cassell turns to another interpretative tool — iconography. The elements of the *Comedy* and of the *Decameron* studied by Kirkham, Chiarenza, and Kaske are in the best Singletonian tradition, while the concern with modes of interpreting medieval texts displayed in the essays by Petrocchi, Hollander, and Sturm-Maddox reflect Singleton's method of close reading of texts in their historical-cultural context. Finally, Bergin's translation of and commentary on a primary *Metrica* of Petrarch brings us close to the moment of historical shift in modes of allegory, not only in Petrarch's use of Virgil but also in his celebration of the supreme value of poetry in both the classical and Christian tradition.

Aldo S. Bernardo is Distinguished Service Professor of Italian and Comparative Literature at the State University of New York at Binghamton. He is an internationally known Petrarch scholar and is Honorary Member of the Accademia Arcadia of Rome.

Anthony L. Pellegrini is Professor and Chairman of Romance Languages at the State University of New York at Binghamton and is Editor of *Dante Studies*, the journal of the Dante Society of America.

mRts

medieval & Renaissance texts & studies
is the publishing program of the
Center for Medieval & Early Renaissance Studies
at the State University of New York at Binghamton.

mRts emphasizes books that are needed —
texts, translations, and major research tools.

mRts aims to publish the highest quality scholarship
in attractive and durable format at modest cost.

DATE DUE

9-5-88			

GAYLORD   PRINTED IN U.S.A.